9

The Politics of Lying

Other books by David Wise
(with Thomas B. Ross)

The U-2 Affair
The Invisible Government
The Espionage Establishment

David Wise

The POLITICS OF LYING

Government Deception, Secrecy, and Power

Random House • New York

Library of Congress Cataloging in Publication Data
Wise, David.
The politics of lying.
1. Government information—United States.
2. Government and the press—United States. I. Title.
JK468.S4W57 323.44'5'0973 72–13911
ISBN 0–394–47932–7

Portions of this book have appeared
in *Esquire* and *The Atlantic Monthly*.

Manufactured in the United States of America

First Edition

For Joan, Christopher, and Jonathan

Contents

Part I Deception

Part II Secrecy

Part III Misinformation

Part IV The Press

Part V A Conclusion

Part I

DECEPTION

" . . . there has been this feeling that perhaps the government is lying . . ."

*—Herbert G. Klein, Director of Communications
for the Executive Branch, November 11, 1969*

1

The Politics
of Lying

Thanksgiving dinner with the President. Roast stuffed turkey with all the trimmings, cranberry sauce, candied sweet potatoes, giblet gravy, and Richard Nixon. For the 106 wounded veterans of the Vietnam war, the invitation to dinner at the White House on Thanksgiving Day, 1970, was a special occasion. From Bethesda Naval Hospital, from Walter Reed Army Hospital, from Malcolm Grow Hospital at Andrews Air Force Base, they came by military bus. Not all of them would see the President; some were blind. Many were in wheelchairs, for a number had lost legs or arms.

For President Nixon, the Thanksgiving dinner was, on one level, a humane gesture to a group of servicemen. On a public relations level, however, it was an occasion certain to generate national television coverage, which meant that millions of people would see it. Because of its warm, human interest content, and because it was an event particularly suited to the medium of film, the dinner was sure to make the network news shows.* The morning newspapers, too,

---

*Like all modern Presidents, Nixon was concerned about his image. Within the Nixon White House, the problem was handled by the Image Committee, then comprised of Communications Director Herb Klein, Special Counsel Charles W. Colson and Deputy Assistant Dwight Chapin. The existence of the committee was little known and its title was wholly secret. The committee frequently encouraged Nixon to participate in news events that would counter the belief that he was "cold."

could be expected to carry stories and photographs of the Commander in Chief surrounded by disabled and wounded G.I.'s. In addition, the event might serve as a reminder of Nixon's continuing public concern over a group of servicemen who were *not* there—the American prisoners held by North Vietnam.

The prisoner issue was, in fact, uppermost in Richard Nixon's mind on this Thanksgiving Day. Just five days earlier, on November 21, a special team of airborne American commandos had landed in the night at Son Tay, the site of a suspected North Vietnamese prisoner-of-war camp only twenty-three miles west of Hanoi. It was a dramatic but futile rescue attempt. The camp was empty; the team brought back no prisoners.

There was more than a flicker of suspicion among some members of the White House press corps that another group of men might have joined the wounded veterans for Thanksgiving dinner with the President—had the raid been successful. It was not hard to imagine the scenario: the gaunt American prisoners quickly debriefed and given medical treatment, then, those who were able, flown halfway across the world to the White House in time for turkey with the President.

As it was, the President talked a great deal about Son Tay. He told Army Sergeant Corris Sworn, who sat on his left, and who had been wounded in both legs and the mouth, that there would "definitely" be future attempts to rescue American POW's. "The possibility of more raids should not be overlooked," the President said; he would "use any means possible" to get the men out.

George "Steve" Lowry, a young Marine sergeant, sat on the President's right. Turning to Lowry, Nixon was the Old Coach: "Sometimes you have to take them by surprise. It's like football. You run a play and it fails. Then you turn around and call the same play again because they aren't expecting it."

Chance and the war had brought Steve Lowry to the White House and made him a dinner partner of the President of the United States; but his story was otherwise not unlike that of a lot of other young Americans who went to Vietnam. Lowry came from Sophia, West Virginia, in the heart of the soft-coal country; he was the son of a coal miner and had spent some time in the mines himself. But he was cool and bright, and he broke away from Appalachia. He finished college in West Virginia, then joined the Marines in August, 1968. Parris Island, Camp LeJeune, then out to Camp Pendleton, near San Diego. Danang, early in 1969, and at age twenty-one, a private with the 9th Marine Regiment. Lowry's unit saw heavy combat in the Ashau Valley that winter; by June he was fighting in the Northern I Corps area. "We were on patrol on a ridge top; I had the point. We were looking for an enemy headquarters that was supposed to be dug in just on the other side of the ridge." He had just reached for his compass to take a reading when the North Vietnamese AK-47 opened up. The bullets shattered his left hand and severed an artery in his left leg. Evacuated by helicopter to a base hospital at Quang Tri. Danang. Tokyo. And finally, Andrews Air Force Base and Bethesda Naval Hospital. He was able to walk again after the leg healed, but it was a long stay at Bethesda, a year and a half all told, while doctors performed plastic surgery on his hand. There were nine operations in all, plastic surgery is slow, and in June, 1970, while still in the hospital, he made sergeant.

About a month before Thanksgiving, notices were posted around the hospital inviting those patients who were interested to have dinner at the White House. Lowry signed up.

He had not expected he would sit next to the President. There were a number of small tables, each seating eight or ten persons, in the dining room. "Nixon, Mrs. Nixon, Mamie Eisenhower and Tricia Nixon each headed a table," Lowry recounted. "I was looking for a seat when one of the escort officers tapped me on the shoulder and said 'Would you like to sit at the President's table?' I said sure, and he took me over and the only chair empty was next to the President."

Before the meal Nixon stood up and spoke briefly to the servicemen about his own lonely Thanksgivings during World War II. "Being away from home is the hardest thing of all," he said.*

As Lowry recalled, "Then the President said we had to give two

---

*In fact, the White House apparently had some difficulty in finding *enough* lonely, disabled veterans in the Washington area to fill the hall. According to Steve Lowry, "The way this deal worked, when the notices are posted at the hospital, you're supposed to sign up if you're interested. But the population of the hospital was down—there weren't as many wounded men coming in by then. We all got two-or three-day leaves to go home to our families for Thanksgiving, and a lot of guys wouldn't give up their leaves to stay for dinner with the President. I signed up because I thought it was quite an opportunity. But most of the people who went from Bethesda were Navy corpsmen stationed at the hospital, because they couldn't get enough patients to go."

It did not matter. Ritual news events of this sort fall into reporting patterns and clichés that are almost unvarying; the television viewer or newspaper reader, in turn, unconsciously sorts them into mental bins that require no thinking. This was a "President-has-Thanksgiving-turkey-with-lonely-wounded-G.I.'s"-type story and that is how it came through to the public.

minutes to the press. So they opened up the doors and this big bunch of reporters and photographers came in. There were television cameras—some of the people back home told me they saw it—and flashbulbs." Then the press left.

At dinner, Nixon was kept busy autographing White House matchbooks for the servicemen. And he began talking about Son Tay. "He said how they had planned it," Lowry recalls, "how they built a scale model of the prison, and they crashed a chopper right in the middle of the compound. Then two larger choppers landed on each side. The commandos killed all the enemy they could find."

But the President added something else. "Of course there were bombing raids going on to distract attention," Nixon said. During the rescue mission, there had been "an air attack on a nearby military base." The purpose was to keep the enemy pinned down while the rescue helicopters landed in the compound. "It was," the President concluded proudly, "one of the best raids ever pulled."

Perhaps Nixon was carried away by the setting—the Commander in Chief of the Armed Forces explaining military tactics to the men who had fought in Vietnam. Or perhaps it was the football similes: Nixon has always been stirred by both the gridiron and the military (he is said to have seen the film *Patton* twice in the White House screening room before ordering U.S. troops into Cambodia) and the combination of the two may have proved overpowering. Whatever the reasons, in describing the air attack near Son Tay, Nixon had let a very large cat out of the bag.

For six days the United States government and Secretary of Defense Melvin Laird had flatly, unequivocally, and in glorious detail denied that any such attack had taken place in the Hanoi area or in connection with the rescue mission. Now the President was saying there *had* been an air attack, after all.

Nixon knew there had been an air attack because he had closely followed the details of the secret mission, which took place only with his personal approval. And to a large extent, he had himself generated the circumstances in which the mission was conceived and organized. Nixon had focused national and world attention on the plight of the prisoners; this, in turn, strengthened the political voice of the prisoners' wives and familes, who were understandably militant in their demands for action. And the growing power of the prisoners-of-war lobby put the administration under pressure to "do something" about the problem.

One of those who wanted to do something was Brigadier General Donald D. Blackburn, a World War II jungle fighter who headed a special counterinsurgency office created under President Kennedy. As head of this office, known as SACSA (Special Assistant for Counterinsurgency and Special Activities), Blackburn operated from behind a door marked 1E962 on the ninth corridor of the first floor of the Pentagon.

Late in May, 1970, Blackburn won permission from the Joint Chiefs to study the possibility of rescuing some of American prisoners. The CIA, working from reconnaissance photographs, built Blackburn a scale model of the half-acre compound at Son Tay. Why Son Tay? Oddly enough, the topography of the camp—perhaps more than the degree of likelihood of finding any U.S. prisoners there—dictated the choice. "We looked over all of the suspected POW areas," Laird told the Senate Foreign Relations Committee after the rescue attempt, "and we found that of all of the areas in North Vietnam, this was the only camp in which there were areas surrounding the camp that made it possible for us to make a landing with our special mission ground forces outside the site." In other words, the helicopters could land at Son Tay.

Laird approved the plan in July. To head the mission, he picked an Air Force counterinsurgency expert, Brigadier General Leroy J. Manor, and an Army colonel, Arthur D. (Bull) Simons, a tough battle-decorated officer who had led a Ranger unit in the Pacific in World War II. In August a volunteer commando force began training in secret in the rough terrain of Eglin Air Force Base on Florida's Gulf Coast.

After the rescue mission had failed, Laird refused to say when aerial reconnaissance had last indicated the camp to be occupied. Nor would he discuss the nature of the alleged "very good" intelligence information that the camp had American prisoners in it. Under questioning by Senator J. William Fulbright, chairman of the Senate Foreign Relations Committee, Laird admitted, some three weeks after the commando mission, that there had been only "a fifty-fifty chance" of finding and bringing back any prisoners.

But the project, like a mini-Bay of Pigs, had acquired something of a life of its own. Within the government it is almost impossible to call off something once it is begun. The commandos at Eglin were ready to go; if the project had been canceled, there might have been grumbling among the men, leaks to the press, and political embarrassment. What official, from the President on down, would care to cancel a daring raid to rescue American prisoners of war? Laird almost conceded as much in testimony to the Senate: "I concluded that there was no other acceptable alternative than to recommend that the volunteer force, now highly trained and well rehearsed for its humanitarian mission, should be authorized to make a valiant attempt to save their fellow Americans." Obviously there were public relations dividends as well; even if the rescue attempt failed, it would, as Laird later put it, "demonstrate to all of our citizens and to all the world that we have not forgotten our prisoners of war."

The President approved the mission, and discussed final details with Laird and Secretary of State William P. Rogers on November 18. Simons led his men in at 2:18 A.M. Vietnam time on Saturday, November 21; at the rescue group's command headquarters, General Manor monitored the mission by radio and broadcast a play-by-play account of what was happening at Son Tay over a 12,000-mile direct line to the National Military Command Center in the basement of the Pentagon. There, Laird, General Blackburn, Admiral Thomas H. Moorer, the chairman of the Joint Chiefs of Staff, and other high officials were gathered around a loudspeaker. The news that came over the speaker was gloomy, however; Son Tay, it was quickly learned, was empty of prisoners.

Within minutes of the rescue mission, Radio Hanoi interrupted its regular broadcast to announce that U.S. planes had bombed near the North Vietnamese capital and had also struck a prisoner-of-war camp. Early that Saturday, Laird issued a statement in Washington. American warplanes had indeed bombed North Vietnam in a "protective reaction" to protect the pilots of unarmed American reconnaissance planes; but these raids had taken place south of the 19th parallel, in the southern part of North Vietnam, more than a hundred miles south of Hanoi. Later in the day Laird took note of "erroneous" reports from Hanoi that U.S. planes had struck a prisoner-of-war camp. "Such reports," said the Secretary of Defense, "are false."

On Monday, November 23, at 3:30 P.M. Laird held a news conference at the Pentagon, and with Simons and Manor at his side, revealed the Son Tay rescue mission for the first time. ("Ladies and gentlemen, I want to give you now the details of the only operation that took place north of the 19th parallel this past weekend.") Regrettably, said Laird, the helicopter rescue team discovered that "the camp had recently been vacated."*

At the press conference, Laird stated that U.S. Navy planes had dropped flares along the coast in "diversionary actions" to draw attention away from the rescue effort at Son Tay. "There were diversionary operations of a very small nature . . . but there was no ord-

---

*But not as recently as Laird may have sought to imply. Later in the news conference, this exchange occurred:

QUESTION: Any indication how long that camp had been abandoned?
GENERAL MANOR: Several weeks . . .

nance involved as far as North Vietnam was concerned above the 19th parallel, involved in those diversionary missions which were flown by the United States Navy."

For the second time in three days Laird had denied that any U.S. air raid had taken place north of the 19th parallel or in connection with Son Tay. There was "no ordnance involved." The Navy had dropped flares. That's all.*

On Tuesday afternoon the Defense Secretary appeared before the Senate Foreign Relations Committee to discuss the rescue attempt at a televised hearing. Laughter broke out in the hearing room when Laird, despite the fact that no prisoners were found, insisted "we have made tremendous progress as far as intelligence is concerned." But in testifying to the senators the Defense Secretary made no reference to any U.S. attack in the Hanoi area during the prisoner rescue mission. He repeated that as "diversionary action . . . we had some flares dropped by Navy planes" operating from a carrier off the east coast of Vietnam.

On Wednesday, Laird implied to the House Foreign Affairs Committee that he had not, originally, intended to announce the rescue attempt. "It was not my plan to bring this [Son Tay] to the attention of the public necessarily." He had disclosed the mission to prevent a "credibility problem" with the public.

Laird reiterated that Navy planes had dropped flares, but now he suggested a new theory: he noted that North Vietnam had fired SAM antiaircraft missiles which "exploded within population center areas"; the clear implication was that Hanoi had mistaken its own SAM missiles for U.S. bombs.

Then on Thursday, Nixon, in his unguarded remarks to Steve Lowry and the other servicemen, completely contradicted Laird. Even so, the cat scampering around the East Room might quickly have been stuffed back in the bag but for Aaron Latham.

A twenty-six-year-old reporter on the city staff of the *Washington Post*, Latham was junior enough so that he was stuck with working on Thanksgiving. It was Latham's first newspaper job, and normally he covered local news. Since it was a holiday, however, and there was only a small staff working, Latham was sent over to the White House. It was the first time Latham had ever been assigned to cover the President, and because he lacked a plastic White House

---

*Only one newspaper reported otherwise. In the *Los Angeles Times* of November 24, 1970, correspondent Stuart H. Loory wrote that "a reliable Pentagon source" said American planes had attacked radar sites over a wide area above the 20th parallel.

identification card, it took twenty minutes before guards cleared him through the northwest gate.

As a result, Latham missed the opening glimpse of the dinner afforded other reporters and cameramen; by the time he got through the gate, they were back in the White House press room, watching a football game on television. Boredom is endemic among correspondents who must cover the White House beat day in and day out, but to Latham, it was all new and therefore interesting. On his own initiative, he asked that a list be made up of the servicemen sitting at the President's table; Latham thought it might be worthwhile to try to talk with them.

When the dinner ended, the press was allowed back into the main lobby of the White House. With the servicemen, they gathered in the East Room to hear the after-dinner entertainment provided by The Spurrlows, a twenty-two-member singing group. "The Spurrlows sang part of the Declaration of Independence," Latham said, while slides of Washington memorials and monuments were flashed on a large screen.

In the milling crowd, Latham was unable to locate any of the men on his list. But later, by telephone from his office, he reached several of them, including Sergeant Sworn and Sergeant Lowry, back at their hospitals. They related Nixon's dinner-table conversation. All of the servicemen agreed on one point: Nixon had said that there had been an American air raid on a military base near Son Tay.

Latham consulted with the acting national editor; he thought he had a pretty good exclusive about Son Tay, but it was decided, nevertheless, that he should write his story mainly as a Thanksgiving Day feature about the President and the wounded veterans. On Friday morning the story was played on page one of the *Post*. Latham had followed instructions; the story led with the Thanksgiving dinner, but it also contained the damaging Nixon disclosure.

Friday must have been exceedingly painful for the Secretary of Defense. He had lied repeatedly in public statements and in testimony to the Congress. Why he had denied the U.S. air attack at Son Tay all week in such explicit detail is uncertain. One obvious reason, and possible explanation, is that the raid clearly violated the bombing halt that President Lyndon Johnson had announced on October 31, 1968, and which the Nixon administration had not publicly repudiated. And, possibly, Laird felt that disclosure of the fact that American warplanes were clobbering the area around the compound did not fit well with the image of the raid that he preferred to present to the public: that of a group of daring commandos slipping in alone under cover of darkness and striking the foe swiftly and silently.

In any event, something clearly had to be done, and Assistant

Secretary of Defense Daniel Z. Henkin was nominated. As the Pentagon's chief spokesman, Henkin for the first time announced to newsmen on Friday that American planes had used "appropriate ordnance" against North Vietnamese antiaircraft, missile, and artillery positions "immediately adjacent" to the Son Tay camp. He declined to explain this "ordnance," but declared, "I would not say flatly that no bombs were dropped in the area."

It was a very bad scene. Later in the day the Pentagon added that "about a dozen" Shrike missiles had been launched near Son Tay during the rescue attempt. Shrikes are air-to-ground missiles that ride down the radar beams of Soviet-built SAM antiaircraft missiles. The Defense Department may have mentioned the Shrikes specifically because North Vietnam was claiming that parts of Shrike rockets had been found near Hanoi. In addition, the Pentagon said that dummy ammunition such as that used in mock battles—so-called "noisemaker" bombs—had been dropped at Son Tay to sow confusion.

"U.S. Admits It Hit Bases Near Son Tay," the *Washington Post* headlined on Saturday. "Pentagon Concedes Attack After Days of Denials," said the *The New York Times.*

On Sunday, Senator Fulbright went on *Face the Nation.* Asked about Laird's testimony to the Foreign Relations Committee, Fulbright said Laird had misrepresented the facts: "Now I wouldn't ever call anybody a liar in public except by inadvertence; they misrepresent the facts."

Monday morning Laird met with newsmen at the Pentagon. When a reporter asked him why he had not mentioned the U.S. air raid at Son Tay when he testified before the Senate Foreign Relations Committee, Laird replied: "I was never asked the question . . . If you'll read over the record, you'll find that the question was not asked . . . that is not my responsibility . . . Now I answer questions, but I only answer the questions that are asked.

"I think," added the Secretary of Defense, "you'll find that I've been as forthright as one could possibly be . . ."

In August, 1970, *Life* magazine charged that Senator Joseph D. Tydings, Maryland Democrat, had used his influence and official position to promote a Florida-based company of which he was a major stockholder. Specifically, the article said that Tydings, as a senator-elect in 1964, had visited Paul Bridston, an official of the Agency for International Development, in an attempt to influence him to help the Charter Company, which was seeking a $7 million AID loan guarantee for a housing project in Nicaragua. Tydings was accompanied on this visit by Raymond K. Mason, president of the Charter Company, in which Tydings later held stock valued at nearly $2 million, *Life* said. The article had a stunning impact. It seriously damaged the reputation of Senator Tydings and very likely contributed to his defeat that November by Republican J. Glenn Beall, Jr.

The *Life* piece was written by the magazine's able senior investigative reporter, Pulitzer Prize winner William Lambert. In January, 1972, Lambert told the author of this book a fact about the Tydings story that had not been revealed before. Lambert said it was from the White House office of Charles W. Colson, Special Counsel to President Nixon, that he first spoke to Bridston, the AID official who provided the key information about Tydings. This was in June, 1970. Moreover, Colson had placed the telephone call to Bridston at Lambert's request. "You call him and tell him I'm here," Lambert said he told Colson. "I wanted some muscle. He [Colson] called him and I took the phone in Chuck's office." The Special Counsel to the President reached Bridston at New Haven, where he was attending his Yale twentieth class reunion. Lambert arranged to meet Bridston for a drink at the St. Moritz Hotel in New York on Monday, June 15. Bridston, who had been instructed by the President's assistant to tell all to the *Life* reporter, confirmed the crucial fact of the Tydings visit.

After the *Life* exposé appeared, Tydings charged that the magazine was being used by "the Republican administration" to smear him in an effort to cause his defeat in the coming election. "Persons in the White House itself " had worked with *Life*, Tydings said.

Ronald L. Ziegler, Nixon's press secretary, indignantly denied these charges. On August 22, for example, he was asked whether White House officials had indeed assisted *Life* in getting its story on Tydings. He replied: "Any suggestion that the White House would have been involved . . . with *Life* regarding the publishing of this story would be incorrect."

On February 8, 1971, it was announced in Washington that South Vietnamese troops backed by American air power had crossed over into Laos, in a major operation designed to cut the Ho Chi Minh trail and "choke off the flow of supplies and men during the dry season." The so-called Laos "incursion," code-named Lamson 719, was under way, with American helicopter gunships, B-52's, and fighter-bombers pounding the area in support of the South Vietnamese troops on the ground. How long would the invasion last? In Saigon, Vice-President Nguyen Cao Ky said in an interview on February 10 that South Vietnamese forces would probably remain in Laos until the dry season ended in May. The same day, in the war room of the Pentagon, Lieutenant General John W. Vogt, director of the Joint Staff of the Joint Chiefs of Staff, held a background briefing for reporters, arranged by Jerry W. Friedheim, Deputy Assistant Secretary of Defense for public affairs. General Vogt used a silver-tipped pointer as he crisply explained the operation with the aid of military maps and charts. Reporters were not permitted to identify General Vogt; his words were attributable to "senior defense officials."

General Vogt explained that when the rainy season began in May, it would be impossible to operate half-tracks and other vehicles in the muck. "So this puts natural time limits on the extent of our involvement. You can't run heavily armored units—track vehicles or otherwise—in that environment when the heavy rains come in."

Then this exchange occurred:

Q: Excluding any other factors, when would the rain drive you out?

A (by General Vogt): It's variable each year, but I think you can assume that when May comes, the rains will be there heavily.

Reporters accordingly came away from the briefing with the clear impression that the Laos invasion was to last until the beginning of May. Vogt had left the identical impression with members of the Senate Foreign Relations Committee, to whom he gave essentially the same briefing at a closed session the day before. The press duly reported that South Vietnam's forces would remain in Laos until May.

By the end of March, long before the rains of May, the South Vietnamese army was in precipitate retreat in Laos. South Vietnamese soldiers were clinging to the landing skids of American helicopters in their effort to get out. In some cases, the troops reportedly fell to their death from the skids. "We just have to kick some of them off," an American pilot said. "We have to think about ourselves, too. You just cannot lift this bird with fifteen guys clinging to it."

The Nixon administration saw victory, not defeat in the Laos operation, however. Although South Vietnam's forces were in retreat six weeks before May 1 and the rainy season, officials in Washington denied there had been a rout. Friedheim, for example, said the South Vietnamese troops were engaged in "mobile maneuvering" and were proceeding "according to plan."

•   •   •

These and other such episodes led Richard Nixon to ask an unprecedented question. On April 7, 1971, Nixon addressed the nation on television to defend his Vietnam policy. The recent South Vietnamese move in Laos, with American air support, had, he said, been a great success. More American troops would be coming home; the administration's policy of "Vietnamization" had succeeded. "I can assure you tonight with confidence," the President said, "that American involvement in this war is coming to an end."

Then Nixon paused, looked directly into the camera, and adopting an earnest expression, asked: "But can you believe this?"

Even a decade ago it would have seemed an unthinkable question for the President of the United States to ask the American people. That Richard Nixon felt it necessary to ask it reflected a central fact about the American political system today: large numbers of people no longer believe the government or the President. They no longer believe the government because they have come to understand that the government does not always tell the truth.

This erosion of confidence between people and government is perhaps the single most significant political development in America in the past decade. Because of it, an American President today operates within a new political framework. He can no longer assume that a majority of the people will believe him.

During the decade of the sixties lack of confidence by the public in government information came to be called the "credibility gap." The phrase has been overworked, but the phenomenon it describes is real. The credibility gap helped to drive one President, Lyndon B. Johnson, out of office. Although the term came into use during his administration, the problem it described did not begin with Johnson.

In a sense, the problem is as old as the republic. But in a modern context, 1960 was a watershed. That was the year of the U-2 affair; the spy-plane episode took place under President Dwight D. Eisenhower and it marked the first time that many Americans realized that their government lied.

President Kennedy had his Bay of Pigs, which required Adlai Stevenson to read an official lie into the record of the United Nations. And it was under Kennedy that an Assistant Secretary of Defense proclaimed "the right to lie."

But it was official deception over the war in Vietnam that caused a major erosion of confidence of the American people in their government. During the 1964 campaign President Johnson seemed to promise that he would not send American boys to fight for Asian boys, but after his election he sent more than half a million American troops to fight in Vietnam. He won the support of Congress with the

Tonkin Gulf resolution, based, as it only later became clear, on official misrepresentation of staggering proportions.

By the election of 1968 the crisis in confidence, the lack of belief, had become an issue in the Presidential campaign. In a nationwide radio and television address during that campaign, Nixon asked how, if elected, "would I avoid the credibility gap?" His answer was that he would "tell the American people the hard truth." And he pledged "an open administration."

At the Hotel Pierre in New York, on November 25, 1968, Ronald Ziegler, press secretary to the President-elect, announced the appointment of Herbert G. Klein as Communications Director for the Executive Branch. "Thank you very much, Ron," Klein responded. "I'm confident we will—truth will become the hallmark of the Nixon administration . . . We feel that we will be able to eliminate any possibility of a credibility gap in this administration."

But the Nixon administration was soon awash in credibility problems. By 1972 the question of belief in the word of the government had once again become the subject of debate in a Presidential campaign, and it was much more than that.

Since the issue of government lying has been with us, in more or less recognizable form, since 1960, under four Presidents—two Democratic and two Republican—plainly it is not confined to any one party or administration. Rather it has emerged as a continuing condition, with serious implications for the democratic system.

Government deception, and the resultant loss of public trust, is supported by a system of official secrecy. The publication of the Pentagon Papers in 1971 caused a sensation because the papers revealed in voluminous detail how much the people had *not* been told about the Vietnam war. Moreover, these papers demonstrated that the nation's policy makers, from the President on down, had often practiced conscious deception.

In January, 1972, columnist Jack Anderson published secret documents that gave the public a glimpse of how the Nixon administration and the President's national security adviser, Henry A. Kissinger, sought to "tilt" American policy in favor of Pakistan during the 1971 India-Pakistan war.

The Pentagon Papers and the Anderson documents focused public attention on government secrets and on the system of security classification that is designed to protect them. This system is complicated, and in fact, the public knows very little about its arcane workings. Even Congress, on the whole, has only limited knowledge of its dimensions.

The disclosures of the Pentagon Papers did demonstrate, however, how easy it is for government officials to use the security classification system to keep from public view policies, decisions, and actions that are precisely the opposite of what the public is told. In other words, through official secrecy, we now have a system of institutionalized lying.

Policy makers who consider it desirable to mask their decisions or their objectives, or who wish to mislead the public or withhold information, can do so as easily as reaching for the nearest rubber stamp. In short, lying and secrecy are two sides of the same coin.

The government can lie, withhold information, or classify it. But equally important is what the government *does* choose to communicate. And the Executive Branch has at its disposal today a large and powerful government public relations and information machine. It uses this machine to sell those policies and distribute those official truths that it wishes the public to receive. Centered in the White House, but with branches in every department and agency, the size, scope, and operations of the information establishment are largely hidden from public view. Nobody knows how big it is, how many people it employs, or the size of its annual budget. Even at the top, its outlines are somewhat shadowy. In the first Nixon administration, for example, Herb Klein had the title of Communications Director, but the power to make key PR decisions, especially politically sensitive ones, rested not with Klein or Ronald Ziegler but with Special Counsel Charles Colson. If anyone could be said to be pushing the buttons of the administration's sprawling PR and propaganda machine it was Colson, a political gut-fighter and—for a time—unchallenged king of the President's image makers.*

Government misinformation, then, is buttressed by the classification system and distributed by the government information machine. But like a tree falling unheard in the forest, the message would have little meaning if there were no medium to transmit it to the public. The press is the medium.

There are 915 television stations in the United States, 7,227 radio stations, 1,700 daily newspapers, three major news weeklies, and

---

*Sooner or later Colson's back-room political operations were bound to get him into trouble. It finally happened in 1972, when it developed that Everette Howard Hunt, Jr., a former CIA agent and one of seven men indicted by a federal grand jury for conspiracy to bug the Watergate headquarters of the Democratic National Committee, had been hired as a White House "consultant" by Colson some months earlier. Three weeks after Nixon's reelection, it was announced that Colson was departing the White House. The President, Ronald Ziegler said, "regrets Chuck is leaving the administration . . . "

dozens of other periodicals that report or interpret current affairs. But only a portion of the American media—the Washington press corps—is directly involved in reporting national news and foreign policy. The nightly network news shows are produced in and broadcast from New York City, but most of the correspondents who report on national affairs for NBC, CBS, and ABC television are based in the nation's capital. The two major wire services, the Associated Press and United Press International, and newspapers published in major cities maintain bureaus in Washington. It is the Washington correspondent who deals with the federal government day in and day out, and it is the Washington correspondent, and the syndicated columnists based in Washington, with whom the men in power must deal.

Under the Nixon administration, there has been an unprecedented effort—unprecedented in modern times, at least—to downgrade and discredit the American press. Nixon made his own feelings toward its members perfectly clear in 1962, at the famous news conference he held following his defeat for Governor of California. ("You won't have Nixon to kick around any more, because, gentlemen, this is my last press conference . . .") Under Nixon, Vice-President Agnew took the lead in denouncing the press—the national television networks in particular, but Eastern newspapers and the "seaboard media" in general. Under Nixon, government pressure and attempted pressure on the news media reached new levels of intensity. For fifteen days in 1971, until the Supreme Court acted, *The New York Times* was prevented by a federal court order from publishing the Pentagon Papers. The *Washington Post* and two other newspapers were similarly restrained. It was the first time in the nation's history that newspapers had been barred in advance from printing information that the government found objectionable. And under the Nixon administration, the public was openly encouraged to distrust and to criticize the news media.

To the extent that the public could be persuaded, through such attacks, to doubt the credibility, accuracy, and impartiality of the American press, attention would, of course, be diverted from the question of the administration's own credibility. If the viewer can be goaded to kick the tube when Walter Cronkite appears, he may be less likely to vent his anger at Richard Nixon. This, at any rate, was the administration's theory, and it had a remarkable degree of short-range success. Doubt *was* cast on the credibility of the press, and latent hostility toward the television networks and the news media in general was crystallized and exploited. Over the long pull, however, it was a terribly dangerous policy, since the press is at least as important as the government and utterly essential to the democratic system, a fact which the Founding Fathers implicitly recognized when, with some prodding, they added the First Amendment to the Constitution.

The American press is often called "the Fourth Branch of government," a term that at once reflects its quintessential importance and a major weakness. For the press is *not* a branch of government, and to the extent that singly, or collectively, its members forget this fact, or confuse themselves with the government, the public is not served.

The press can indeed validly be criticized, not for analyzing the actions and decisions of government too much—which was the theme of Agnew's laments—but for analyzing too little. The press's failure to question government information more vigorously, the willingness to accept official "handouts" as fact, the tendency toward passive reporting—what Tom Wicker has called "the press box mentality"—has made it that much easier for government to mislead the public.

The American system is based not only upon formal checks and balances among the three branches of government, it depends also, and perhaps more importantly, on a delicate balance of confidence between the people and the government. That balance of trust has been altered.

By 1972 the politics of lying had changed the politics of America. In place of trust, there was widespread mistrust; in place of confidence, there was disbelief and doubt in the system and its leaders.

The consent of the governed is basic to American democracy. If the governed are misled, if they are not told the truth, or if through official secrecy and deception they lack information on which to base intelligent decisions, the system may go on—but not as a democracy. After nearly two hundred years, this may be the price America pays for the politics of lying.

Why has it happened? Why has the government of the most powerful democracy in the world found it necessary to mislead its own people? What are the circumstances that have led to the deceit of the governed?

2

Remember the
Alamo

On Halloween, 1966, the crowds lining the streets cheered President Lyndon B. Johnson as he arrived in Seoul, South Korea, near the end of a seventeen-day, 30,000-mile trip through Asia.

The next morning Johnson reviewed troops of the United Nations Command near the Demilitarized Zone and flew by helicopter to Camp Stanley, a U.S. Army base. There he inspected an honor guard as the Eighth Army band played "Stout Hearted Men." Then he lunched cafeteria-style with the troops. The engineers' mess hall was packed with soldiers when the President arose to speak.

It was pure Johnson, at his oratorical best, and worst. He started off slowly, in low gear. "The average fellow in the world doesn't ask for much . . . He wants . . . a roof over his head, a chance for his kids to go to school . . . a little recreation for his family, a movie now and then, or to be able to load them all in the old jalopy and take them to see Grandma on Sunday.

"But except for you," Johnson assured his audience, "people couldn't do that." We had tried to stay out of wars, "to avoid getting involved in all these things." But when there was trouble in the world, "pretty soon it gets on our doorstep." Warming to his theme, Johnson invoked the Kaiser, the *Lusitania,* Hitler marching through Poland, and Pearl Harbor.

"Some people have said: 'Why don't we let the old men go fight?' . . . Well, I think it would be a pretty good idea if the old men could get the job done. But they can't do it. They are a little broader around the middle . . . They can't stand the pace you can."

Then he said it: "My great-great-grandfather died at the Alamo."*

The President went on to a stirring finish. "You weren't born into this world . . . to liquidate the freedom and liberty that your grandfathers fought for with bows and arrows or old muskets. You have a heritage, a tradition to carry on."

General Westmoreland, who landed in Korea "with his paratrooper boots on," had told him only the other day that no President "in the history of all glorious America" ever commanded a more courageous army. So forget the draft-card burners, the President told the men. "Keep your chin in and your chest out and do your duty as you see it."

He added: "Your parents and your dependents may not see some of you again, but they will always be mighty proud that you came this way, and so am I."

It was a classic patriotic stump speech, and the men cheered and applauded when he was through.

Then Johnson flew south to Suwon, where he stood atop a hillside renamed in his honor. He was greeted by Choi Si Jong, a dignified sixty-five-year-old village elder with a wispy oriental beard, Choi, handsome in his flowing green and white formal robes and a traditional Korean black hat, presented a Korean robe to Johnson. In turn, LBJ gave an appropriate symbol of western culture to Choi— a television set.

"They couldn't get a picture on the TV set," one newsman who witnessed the scene recalled, "so both LBJ and the village elder were hunkered down fiddling with the controls. It was no use." Possibly to offset this failure of American technology, Johnson was suddenly inspired to invite Choi for a ride in the Presidential helicopter. The old man accepted, and soon they were aloft, swirling over the green cabbage fields and the brown rice paddies.

After they landed, Choi was asked how he enjoyed his first plane ride. "It was just like going to heaven," he said, calmly waving a hand skyward. Had he been frightened? "Not a bit."

---

*I have listened to a tape recording of this speech. To both the author and an experienced audio engineer who also heard the tape it sounded very much as though LBJ actually said "great-great-grandfathers," plural. But it is hard to be sure, and in the official transcript it appears in the singular. See Johnson, Lyndon B., *Public Papers of the Presidents of the United States,* 1966 (Washington: U.S. Government Printing Office, 1967), Book II, p. 1287.

At this point Johnson, possibly forgetting his disastrous experience in 1961 with a Pakistani camel driver, Bashir Ahmed, asked Choi if he would like to visit America.*

"Sorry," the village elder replied politely, "but I do not have the time today."

Correspondents who heard this zany exchange duly reported it, along with the other colorful events of the crowded day. But only one or two newsmen from Texas reported the President's revelation that his great-great-grandfather had perished before Santa Anna's onslaught.

It seemed a most dubious possibility, since Johnson had not, to anyone's knowledge, mentioned it before, and having a great-great-grandfather who died at the Alamo is not something that any Texan, especially one who had entered politics, would normally be expected to conceal.

Moreover, a genealogical study of the President's family, written by his mother, Rebekah Baines Johnson, and published only a year before, did not support the claim. It showed that one of LBJ's great-great-grandfathers, John Johnson, was born in 1828 and would have been eight years old when the Mexicans captured the Alamo in 1836 and killed all 188 defenders, including Davy Crockett. Another paternal great-great-grandfather, Joseph Robert Bunton, died peacefully in Tennessee some years after the fall of the Alamo, and there is no indication that two others, John William McIntosh and Leonard Barnett, passed away from other than natural causes. On the President's mother's side, the great-great-grandfather picture was equally dismal, Alamo-wise. One maternal great-great-grandfather, Thomas Baines, did die in 1836, but in Mississippi, which is a considerable distance from San Antonio. Another, John Smith Huffman, an energetic breeder of Shorthorn cattle, rode a horse until at the age of eighty-five he died in Texas in the year 1880. Two others, Nealy

---

*"My camel is getting old," Ahmed told Johnson when the then Vice-President stopped to talk to him in Karachi. Deeply moved, Johnson assured Ahmed "our President wants to see your camel." He then invited him to come to the United States. In due course Bashir Ahmed flew to New York, visited the LBJ ranch, and was presented with a blue Ford truck. Back in Karachi, Ahmed, now an international celebrity, abandoned his camel for the truck. It was a mistake. Unlike a camel, which requires little maintenance, the truck, in time, wore out. Ahmed, lacking money to repair or replace it, or even to buy another camel, cursed the day he had encountered the smooth-talking American Vice-President.

Butler and William Perrin, were alive and well for some decades after the fall of the Alamo.

By the time the President wound up his Asian journey and got back to the White House, his remark at Camp Stanley had become an embarrassment, and reporters were citing it as another example of Lyndon Johnson's "credibility gap."

George Christian, the fourth and last press secretary to serve Johnson in the White House, valiantly attempted to explain LBJ's remark in his book, *The President Steps Down*. In the sentence immediately following Johnson's controversial remark, Christian notes, he had referred to the battle of San Jacinto. The President, Christian conceded, had "no relative" at the Alamo, but his great-great-uncle John W. Bunton was at the battle of San Jacinto and was one of seven men who captured Santa Anna. So it was Uncle Bunton whom LBJ undoubtedly had in mind, Christian went on, but he "got his tongue twisted in the emotion of the moment." But Uncle Bunton lived to the age of seventy-two, and did not die until 1879, forty-three years too late, so it is a measure of Christian's loyalty, but rather difficult to understand, how he might be confused with an ancestor who expired at the Alamo.

Now, it would be wrong, and unkind, to read too much into Johnson's Alamo fiasco. He is said to have admitted privately to reporters that he had no great-great-grandfather at the Alamo, and had gotten carried away when he made the speech. But the remark *was* symptomatic of Johnson's larger credibility problem. As it demonstrated, he was at times capable of saying things that were not necessarily so.

There was a certain inevitability that the term "credibility gap" should have been born during the Johnson administration.* It was a

---

*The phrase "credibility gap," which soon came to haunt the Johnson Presidency, is a direct descendant, etymologically speaking, of the alleged "missile gap" of the late 1950's. In his book *The Tragedy of Lyndon Johnson*, Eric F. Goldman, the Princeton historian, credits the headline that the copy desk placed over a news story I wrote in the *New York Herald Tribune* of May 23, 1965, as probably the first use of the phrase "credibility gap" in print. The story used both the words "credibility" and "gap" and the headline writer put them together in quotes (Dilemma in 'Credibility Gap'). The article dealt with President Johnson's varying explanations for his intervention in the Dominican Republic, and it began: "For the past two days the Johnson administration has been grappling with what might best be described as a credibility problem of its own making . . . The administration is discovering . . . as other administrations have in the past, that when the gap between a case where the man and the times fused. By nature, Johnson was complex and immensely secretive—there were occasions when he did not appoint an official or change a policy simply because it had leaked to the press before he was ready to announce it. To the public, Johnson projected a devious, "wheeler-dealer" image, and he could not overcome it. But in his televised speeches he felt it necessary to adopt a kind of benign, pious expression, and a patently false geniality, which were magnificently captured by the mimic David Frye. People sensed, however, that the sunny, avuncular personality on the tube was not the real Lyndon.

Beyond all this, it was the frequent gulf between his words and reality that created a credibility problem for Johnson. To take only one small example, when Bobby Baker, the former Senate pageboy from Pickens, South Carolina, got into all sorts of trouble in 1964, everyone in Washington knew that he had been Lyndon Johnson's protégé and his key assistant when Johnson was Senate Majority Leader. A Senate investigation had disclosed that Baker had used his position to make a great deal of money, and had once caused a $584 stereo set to be given to Johnson. Now that Johnson was President, Baker was, to say the least, an embarrassment. At a press conference on January 23, 1964, Johnson dismissed the stereo set as a gift from "an employee of mine." When a television interviewer questioned the President on March 15 about the Senate investigation of Baker, "your protégé and your friend," Johnson replied that the Senate was investigating "an employee of theirs—no protégé of anyone; he was there before I came to the Senate for ten years, doing a job . . . He was elected by all the senators . . . appointed by no one . . ." This sort of comment was very damaging, because it was well known that Johnson, in the Senate, had regarded Baker virtually as a son.

In 1965, even as Johnson dispatched the Marines to Santo Domingo, he was escalating the war in Vietnam. His actions and words in both cases contributed to the growing "credibility gap," and before the end of the year, the phrase had entered the language. These developments, combined with Johnson's character and per-

---

government's actions and its words becomes discernible, it is in trouble."

I do not know if Goldman is correct, although I have been unable to find any earlier use of the phrase. On December 5, 1965, the *Washington Post* ran an article by reporter Murrey Marder, which also took note of public skepticism about official statements. "The problem could be called a credibility gap," the article said, adding that it applied to Vietnam, the Dominican Republic, and other subjects. The *Washington Post* article further helped to popularize the phrase.

sonality, probably help to explain why the phrase flowered during his administration. But the roots of the problem went much deeper; Lyndon Johnson made a lasting contribution to the credibility gap but he did not create it.

In a sense, of course, the credibility problem is as old as government. Once man moved out of a primitive state, entered into forms of social organization, and chose or accepted leaders, the problem was inevitable. If politics is the pursuit and exercise of power over other human beings, truth is always likely to take a secondary role to that primary objective.

It can be argued, too, that lying and secrecy are basic to any government; that it is only human nature for political leaders to tend to conceal the truth, hide their mistakes or wrongdoing, and mislead the public. That easy rationale is not acceptable, however, in a democracy, which depends upon an informed public.

The case may also be made that placed in historical perspective, the "credibility gap" of the 1960's and 1970's is not a new phenomenon. As the revisionist historians have been making clear, much of the lore and legend surrounding the Founding Fathers, the American Revolution, and many later political leaders and events bear no more relation to the truth than "Parson" Weems' fictionalized account of George Washington and his cherry tree.* American history does not lack instances where Presidents shaved the truth or simply lied.

When in 1830 President Andrew Jackson approved a brutal policy to remove all Indians to lands west of the Mississippi, he announced that the Indians were not happy living among whites, anyway. Once we "open the eyes of those children of the forest to their true condition," Jackson said, the Indians would realize "the policy of the general government toward the red man is not only liberal, but generous." The statement sounded as if it had been scripted by W.C. Fields. The Black Hawk War and the long struggle to subdue the Seminoles indicated that for the Indians at least, Jackson's credibility was low.

---

*An itinerant book salesman and writer, Mason Locke Weems invented most of the stories that have become part of the Washington myth. ("I can't tell a lie, Pa; you know I can't tell a lie. I did cut it with my hatchet.") Weems correctly realized that there was a quick dollar to be turned from the public's worship of our first President. A few weeks after Washington's death in 1799, he wrote to his publisher: "I've something to whisper in your lug. Washington, you know is gone! Millions are gaping to read something about him. . . . 6 months ago I set myself to collect anecdotes of him. . . . We may sell it with great rapidity for 25 or 37 Cents and it [would] not cost 10."

In 1846 James K. Polk asked Congress to declare war against Mexico, which it did, because Mexico had crossed "the boundary of the United States, has invaded our territory and shed American blood on the American soil." In fact, the clash had taken place in a disputed area between the Rio Grande and the Nueces River. The battle had its modern parallel in the Tonkin Gulf incident of 1964; it provided the excuse to go to war. The Kentucky Whig Garrett Davis declared during the debate over Polk's war message: "It is our own President who began this war."

Lincoln, who once conceded that his own impulse for dealing with the slavery problem was to "send them to Liberia," is secure in American history as the Great Emancipator. Yet the Emancipation Proclamation, which, as Richard Hofstadter has pointed out, "had all the moral grandeur of a bill of lading," freed no slaves. It exempted Southern states and areas held by Union troops and applied only to the states that were in rebellion. Those states, of course, had no intention of complying with a proclamation issued by Lincoln.

McKinley, who once assailed annexation of the Philippines as "criminal agression," thought differently when the Spanish-American war brought the islands within reach of America's manifest destiny. It was, McKinley decided, America's duty "to educate the Filipinos, and uplift and civilize and Christianize them."

Wilson's 1916 campaign slogan "He Kept Us Out of War" proved true for five months, anyway. During the campaign Wilson warned that a Republican victory would guarantee "that we will be drawn . . . into the embroilments of the European war." And, said Wilson, "some young men ought to be interested in that."

Wilson's promises found their echo in Franklin D. Roosevelt's famous pledge in Boston, six days before the election of 1940: "I have said this before, but I shall say it again and again and again: Your boys are not going to be sent into any foreign wars."

And so on. But to dwell on historical examples of misleading government pronouncements, or to dismiss government lying in the 1970's as simply an old problem, is to miss the point entirely.

First of all, it is only in the past decade that government deception has been *perceived* by large numbers of people. That fact alone immediately puts a new dimension on the problem, because, just as between individuals, the relationship between government and people is instantly altered the moment the question of mistrust arises. Unlike some problems, which are the same whether seen or not, government duplicity creates a new political environment once it is detected by the public at large.

The history of the decade of the sixties, beginning with the U-2 episode and the emergence of the term "credibility gap" at almost precisely the midpoint of that decade suggest that these years corresponded with the public's perception of government lying as a major political issue.

But the curve of public disenchantment has been more precisely charted by poll data. In May of 1971, for example, after Nixon had been in office for twenty-eight months, the Gallup Poll reported that 69 percent of the public believed the administration was not telling the public enough about the war in Vietnam. Nixon's credibility rating in this respect was actually worse than that of President Johnson; in a Gallup Poll taken at a comparable point during the Johnson administration the figure was 65 percent.

In November, 1971, a team of University of Michigan social scientists reported that surveys taken over a six-year period, starting in 1964, showed that the American people had steadily lost confidence in the federal government.

The Center for Political Studies of the university's Institute for Social Research found that in 1964, 62 percent of a national sample of adults expressed a "high" degree of trust in the federal government. By 1970 the proportion had plunged to 35 percent.

Polls taken by the Michigan researchers prior to 1964 showed that the level of public trust in government was consistently high. The researchers said that evidence from the 1964–70 surveys and other polls suggested that the decline in public confidence was related to the war in Vietnam.

"What we are witnessing," said the respected Dr. Warren Miller, director of the center, "is a massive erosion of the trust the American people have in their government."

Yet Americans born before World War II know instinctively, without poll data, that public trust in government has diminished in recent years. Many Americans can remember growing up in a time when people assumed that if the government said something, it was true. That era is gone, and faith in government belongs to the nostalgia for a vanished American past.

Distrust of government is, of course, deeply rooted in much broader social, political, and cultural forces at work in postwar America. The civil rights movement, radical protest, the youth revolt, the antiwar movement, Black Power, and Women's Lib are only a few of the phrases that have symbolized an age of alienation and protest. It is hardly surprising, for example, that many American youths should distrust a government that sent many thousands of them to die in an unpopular war in Vietnam. Or that some black Americans should distrust the government of a society that denies social justice and full equality to more than 22,000,000 citizens.

Against such a background of turbulence and political and personal alienation, the loss of public confidence in government cannot, obviously, be attributed solely to government lying and secrecy. Yet these are terribly important factors, meriting separate attention, for they threaten the democratic process.

It is not only that government misinformation has been perceived relatively recently as a political danger, and credibility recognized as a political issue. Quantitatively as well, the amount of government misinformation today is far greater than it was prior to World War II.

The United States emerged from that war a major world power. In its new global role, America developed a powerful national security establishment, including a secret intelligence bureaucracy that spends more than $5 billion annually and a defense establishment that spends $78 billion a year. With this expansion of American power, the opportunities and temptations for information distortion by the federal government increased proportionately. To put it simply, government had more chances to lie.

Moreover, in the national security and foreign policy area, in intelligence, military, and diplomatic activities, *government controls the channels of information.* No AP reporter, for example, was permitted to accompany the helicopter rescue attempt at Son Tay; the American people were wholly reliant on the word of Melvin Laird for news of that episode. And Laird lied. There was simply no way for the news media, or the public, to obtain independent information about what had happened at Son Tay, because the channels of information were entirely under government control. The truth emerged only because something went wrong—President Nixon talked out of turn over the Thanksgiving turkey; one or two servicemen at his table listened carefully—and because of the enterprise of a single newspaperman.

Similarly, no *New York Times* correspondent sat in the cockpit of Francis Gary Powers' U-2 as it flew over the Soviet Union; John Chancellor did not splash ashore at the Bay of Pigs; nor were any newsmen aboard American destroyers in the Tonkin Gulf in August, 1964.

Often, in the foreign policy and national security area, what the government says *is* the news. The Tonkin Gulf episode was a classic illustration of this. The public was told that on August 4 two American warships on "routine patrol" had, in Defense Secretary Robert McNamara's words, been under "continuous torpedo attack" by North Vietnamese PT boats; in response, Lyndon Johnson ordered the first bombing attack on North Vietnam and pushed the Tonkin Gulf resolution through Congress, thereby acquiring a blank check to escalate the war. Later it became clear that there had been much confusion and considerable doubt within the government as to whether any PT-boat attack had taken place at all. The public, however, had to rely entirely on Lyndon Johnson and Robert McNamara for their news of the incident. If the details seem unimportant in the larger tapestry of the war, we need only recall that at the time 163 Americans had died in Vietnam.

In short, in the crucial field of national security, the government controls almost all the important channels of information. And where government controls the channels of information, there is a greater possibility that information will be distorted. In the foreign policy area, therefore, the potential for government lying is high.

In places such as the Tonkin Gulf or the Bay of Pigs, the military, in the case of the former, and the Central Intelligence Agency, in the case of the latter, physically controlled access to the event, so that it could not be witnessed by the news media and independently reported. But in other instances, such as the Pentagon Papers, the government has used the classification system to prevent access to documents. Not until Daniel Ellsberg released to the press most of the Pentagon's secret study of the Vietnam war did Americans realize how little they had been told about Vietnam decision-making during a period that spanned several administrations.

Because classified documents are so familiar a part of the contemporary political scene, it is difficult to realize that a classification system has existed for civilian agencies only since 1951. With its control over information supported by an official system of secrecy and classification, the government has almost unlimited power to misinform the public. It does so for various reasons. The government lies to manipulate public opinion, to generate public support for its policies, and to silence its critics. Ultimately, it lies to stay in power.

In the past, policies were generally formed by government officials to respond to events, or to anticipated events and crises. Today we have reached the point where *events* are shaped to fit policies.

The Tonkin Gulf incident is a superb example of the shaping of an event, through government power, to conform to government policy. The policy was to punish North Vietnam—thus demonstrating Johnson's "toughness" in the midst of a Presidential campaign against Barry Goldwater—and to whip up public and Congressional support behind the President. (Two years later Assistant Secretary of State William P. Bundy told the Senate that "prior to August, 1964" the administration had ready "contingent drafts" of what became the Tonkin Gulf resolution.)

During the Tonkin Gulf episode, the men in power found it much easier to mold the news of the event (and therefore the event itself) to meet the administration's goals than to change the policy.

Thus the credibility gap is related to a larger problem: the shaping of events by the President and his advisers, through their control over information about these events, to conform to predetermined government policies.

Even when the facts about an event are reported accurately by the government, the event may only be used as a justification for actions already decided upon. Lyndon Johnson ordered the sustained bombing of North Vietnam after the enemy had attacked a U.S. barracks at Pleiku in February, 1965, killing nine men and wounding seventy-six. But as McGeorge Bundy, who was in Vietnam at the time, noted, "Pleikus are streetcars," that is, if you wait long enough, one is sure to come along.

Where government controls access to both events and documents, information becomes a commodity, a tool of policy. It is shaped and packaged by the government, and sold to the public through the media. In such a chain, information is reduced to something like processed cheese; there is no longer a concern for the truth, only for process.

Technology has facilitated government deception. Television has not only increased the impact of news and the speed of communication, it has also increased the ease and effectiveness of information distortion by the government. A president uses television to get elected and he can usually preempt prime network time to talk directly to the people on government-licensed stations. Presidential requests for network time are rarely refused.

A President can go on television, as Nixon did in 1972 to announce the mining of Haiphong harbor and other North Vietnamese ports, and rally substantial public support for military actions that may lead to war. In many such cases, the President completely controls the version of events that he chooses to tell his audience. In the nuclear age, when mankind lives less than thirty minutes away from destruction, this is a truly frightening power.

Few Americans are emotionally resistant to a dramatic, sudden appearance by the President on television in the midst of a foreign policy crisis. There is a special tension in the pit of the viewer's stomach, and the adrenalin flows a bit more, as the announcer intones: "From the White House, in Washington, D.C., we bring you a special address by the President of the United States." The familiar face comes on screen, and begins: "My fellow Americans . . ."

What is it? Are Soviet missiles on the way? Has World War III begun? It *must* be important if the President has cut into the networks in prime time. When Kennedy went on TV during the Cuban missile crisis, remember how relieved his listeners felt, relatively speaking, when he announced it was the quarantine of Cuba and not the end of the world?

Presidents use television as a magnet for public attention and as a filter to enhance their political images. President Nixon's trip to Communist China in February, 1972, was a television spectacular, beamed back home via a special satellite stationed over the Pacific. The White House selected the news organizations whose reporters accompanied the President; of the eighty-seven members of the press chosen to travel to China, forty-three were from the electronic media; only twenty-four were newspaper reporters and columnists.* This allocation reflected the considerable public interest in watching the President's trip, but it also reflected the fact that TV is the medium used by government to reach the mass public.

Along with technology, the rise of policy-making elites, particularly in the national security area, has exacerbated the credibility problem. The policy makers and crisis managers, drawn largely from the universities and the upper echelons of the bureaucracy, typically and arrogantly believe that only they possess the necessary intellect and skills to manage the nation's foreign policy. Moreover, they routinely receive secret intelligence information and other classified data on a daily basis, and such information is heady knowledge. As a result, it is easy for such officials to assume that the ordinary citizen is not equipped to understand complex issues of war and peace. From such an attitude, it is but a short step to justify misleading the public.

The last three Presidential assistants for national security— McGeorge Bundy, former Harvard dean, later president of the Ford Foundation; economic historian and Vietnam hawk Walt W. Rostow; and Henry A. Kissinger, Harvard government professor and nuclear strategist—have symbolized the new breed of elite policy makers. From their offices in the White House basement, they have wielded enormous personal power.

During the Cold War years American policy was designed to "contain" Communist expansion. Operating in what they saw as an essentially hostile world, the men in power in Washington came to feel that the interests of the United States required that more and more decisions be made in secret. These decisions, they argued, had

---

*The precise breakdown was as follows: twenty-one newspaper reporters and three columnists; six magazine correspondents; six wire-service reporters; eighteen radio and television correspondents; seventeen broadcast technicians and executives; eight television cameramen and eight still photographers.

to be kept secret from America's adversaries; but in the process, inevitably, the information was also denied to the American public. Nevertheless, that outlook remains deeply ingrained in the official mind; and fear of other countries is used to justify closed decision-making at home.

One could choose almost at random, but a Deputy Under Secretary of State, William B. Macomber, Jr., personified many of the elitist attitudes in almost classic form. Tall, square-jawed, Ivy League and super-WASP, Macomber went to Phillips Andover Academy, Yale, and Harvard Law School. At Georgetown dinner parties his friends call him by his middle name, "Butts." Macomber was a CIA official for two years; he was a popular figure on Capitol Hill as the State Department's liaison man with Congress during the Eisenhower administration, and later he became ambassador to Jordan. Under Nixon, Macomber was the official who spoke for the State Department during the Pentagon Papers controversy.

Appearing on a television panel in June, 1971, at the height of the furor, Macomber presented the government's case for suppressing the publication of the papers in *The New York Times.* "Perhaps if we could talk only to the American people," he said, "we could tell a lot of secrets, but there is no way you can talk only to the American people. Other people listen in." It was an almost perfect statement of the elitist view. Appearing a week later before a House government information subcommittee, Macomber said he favored "something along the lines of the British Official Secrets Act" for America. He added: ". . . we have made this government work for a long time by having the most frank exchanges at the very senior levels of the Congress with the very senior levels of the Executive Branch. What often happens is that in those situations they take off their constitutional responsibilities momentarily and as Americans sit down and worry about a problem . . . and I think that is the way you can get an awful lot done but I think you have to deal with small groups."

Government lying has also resulted from the growth of a huge intelligence establishment since 1947. This invisible government, with the CIA at its center, has frequently engaged in secret operations that have led the United States to tell official lies. In the language of intelligence, these are "cover stories." As already noted, the U-2 affair was one dramatic example, and it abruptly educated Americans to the fact that their government may deceive them. The intelligence practitioners are apparently unconcerned with the long-range effect on American democracy of government lying; their concern is much narrower and pragmatic; they speak of confining intelligence operations to those that are "plausibly deniable." Thus the standard is not truth, but fashioning lies that will be believed.

To sum up, America's vastly expanded international role, the growth of a powerful national security bureaucracy, government control of information channels, the establishment of a system of official secrecy, the communications explosion, elitism in national security policy-making, and secret intelligence operations have all contributed to government lying and the erosion of public trust. These are the major institutional factors, more important than Lyndon Johnson's Alamo syndrome, that have brought us to Credibility Gap.

This is where we are; and we have only to glance backward to see how we got here. To attempt to describe in detail all of the untruths told by the government over the past four administrations would require more than one volume; Vietnam alone could run to several. But the growth of government deception can be traced, at least in general outline, by recalling some of the more disastrous examples of the period. As a people, we have already become partially inured to government lying. Even so, sifted, winnowed, and pulled together in one place, these episodes comprise a sorry, and ultimately shocking, record of official duplicity. It is a dismal history, one that begins, as much as anywhere, with a President who told a lie.

3

The Anatomy
of Deception

It is ironic that the United States first publicly acknowledged a lie during the Eisenhower Presidency. Although to many Americans, Eisenhower, as frequently noted, was a "father figure," his face never lost the ingenuous, open quality of a Kansas farm boy. His public personality was that of a Huckleberry Finn reluctantly and unexpectedly occupying the White House.*

Eisenhower often liked to emphasize that America's "moral" and "spiritual" power was the true source of its strength. Yet this man, who projected such a persuasive image of personal honesty, was hopelessly impaled on a lie and finally forced to admit it publicly to the nation and the world.

On May 1, 1960, high over Sverdlovsk, 1,200 miles inside the

---

*Eisenhower's congenial public image did not always conform to his private personality. He had a sharp temper that flared easily, and his conversation, reflecting his Army career, tended to be punctuated by barracks-room language. One observer who has noted the gulf between the public and private Eisenhower is Richard Nixon, who served under him, although not always happily, as Vice-President. In an interview with reporters on March 13, 1971, President Nixon declared: ". . . you know, he was a great, gregarious, outgoing person, at least as far as his public image is concerned. As a matter of fact, individually, he was quite a man of dignity and reserve . . . I never called him Ike."

Soviet Union, a U-2 plane flown by CIA pilot Francis Gary Powers was downed by a SAM missile. Eisenhower had personally approved the secret development of the spy plane to gather photographic intelligence about Soviet strategic missiles, and U-2's had been overflying Russia for four years. Eisenhower knew this was risky, but he was not too worried when the May 1 flight failed to reach its destination in Norway; the U-2 carried a destructor unit containing enough cyclonite explosive to blow up the plane. In the event of trouble, the pilots were instructed to activate a timing device and bail out, after which, they were told, the explosion would occur. Some of the pilots, as CIA chief Allen Dulles knew, were concerned about the workings of this intriguing and delicate mechanism; they wondered just how much time they would have to bail out.* But as Eisenhower later wrote in his memoirs, the U-2 was extremely "fragile," and in the event of a "mishap," he had been assured, "the plane would virtually disintegrate." It would be impossible, the President had been told, for the Soviets to come into possession "of the equipment intact—or, unfortunately, of a live pilot."

On May 5 Soviet Premier Nikita S. Khrushchev disclosed that an American plane had been shot down inside Soviet territory. Washington announced that a NASA "weather research plane" on a flight inside Turkey had been missing since May 1 when the pilot reported oxygen trouble; perhaps it had drifted across the Soviet border by accident. The pilot was identified as Francis Gary Powers, a civilian employed by Lockheed Aircraft. In truth, of course, the plane belonged not to the space agency, but to CIA, and Powers was employed not by Lockheed, but by the intelligence agency, at a salary of $30,000 a year. On May 6 State Department Spokesman Lincoln White declared: "Now, our assumption is the man blacked out. There was absolutely no—N-O-no—deliberate attempt to violate Soviet air space. There never has been."

The next day Khrushchev triumphantly disclosed to the Supreme Soviet a fact he had carefully omitted mentioning two days earlier: the Russians had captured both the CIA pilot and the

---

*In a book published in 1970, Powers wrote that the destruct mechanism was arranged to allow the pilot "a small but supposedly sufficient margin of time to bail out before the explosion occurred." Powers denied that pilots were worried that the timer was rigged by CIA to explode prematurely, thus destroying the pilot as well as the plane; he maintained that the cause of their concern was the fact that the timers were temperamental, sometimes as much as five seconds off. Ground crews always tested the timers before each flight, Powers noted, because "a few seconds could mean life or death."

plane.* Powers did not blow up his U-2—he testified later to the U.S. Senate that he had been unable to reach the destruct switches—and he had parachuted to safety. At that, the State Department admitted the flight but said it had not been authorized in Washington. This was another lie, since Eisenhower had not only initiated the U-2 program, he had approved flight schedules for the missions. Furthermore, it had the disadvantage of sounding as though the United States had dispatched spy planes over Russia without the President's knowledge. So on May 9, by means of a State Department announcement, Eisenhower reversed himself, admitted the spy flights, took personal responsibility for them, and implied they would continue. Later that week he flew to Paris for a scheduled summit meeting with Khrushchev, President Charles de Gaulle of France, and Prime Minister Harold Macmillan of Great Britain. In Paris, Khrushchev stormed over the U-2 affair and demanded an apology from Eisenhower. At the opening session Eisenhower announced he had suspended the spy flights for good, but it was too late; the summit meeting collapsed.

After he left office Eisenhower bitterly regretted his handling of the U-2 episode. In a filmed interview with CBS in 1961 he conceded that the initial U.S. denial of the spy flight had been a mistake. At the insistence of his son, Lieutenant Colonel John Eisenhower, this comment was snipped out of the film and not shown on the November 23, 1961, program *CBS Reports* in which Eisenhower discussed the U-2. Four years later, however, Eisenhower wrote in his memoirs: "The big error we made was, of course, in the issuance of a premature and erroneous cover story." Eisenhower put it even more candidly in 1962 when reporter David Kraslow interviewed him for the Knight newspapers at his Gettysburg farm. As Kraslow has recalled the scene, at the end of the interview he asked Eisenhower his "greatest regret" as President. "And he floored me when he said, 'The lie we told about the U-2. I didn't realize how high a price we were going to have to pay for that lie. And if I had to do it all over again, we would have kept our mouths shut.'"

Yet the U-2 episode was by no means the first time that the American public had been deliberately deceived by the Eisenhower administration. At least two other major intelligence operations led to high-level official lying; in both instances the CIA was seeking to overthrow another government. The difference was that in these

---

*Khrushchev, Eisenhower reported cryptically in his memoirs, had announced "what to me was unbelievable."

earlier cases, unlike the U-2 affair, the public remained unaware that they were being lied to.

The first episode occurred in 1954, when the CIA financed, organized, and ran a coup in Guatemala against the leftist regime of President Jacobo Arbenz Guzman. As a small CIA air force of P-47 Thunderbolts bombed Guatemala City, Henry Cabot Lodge, Eisenhower's ambassador to the United Nations, categorically denied any U.S. involvement in the coup. Lodge, who could lie convincingly, with the cool self-assurance of a Boston Brahmin, added that the world was witnessing "a revolt of Guatemalans against Guatemalans." Secretary of State John Foster Dulles also announced that "the situation is being cured by the Guatemalans themselves." Since the entire operation was being run by Frank G. Wisner, the CIA's tough deputy director for plans (secret operations), neither Lodge nor Dulles was being, well, candid.

In 1957 the CIA supported a revolt against President Sukarno of Indonesia by rebels based in Sumatra. The CIA recruited pilots to ferry B-26 bombers from Clark Field, near Manila, to a rebel airstrip in the Celebes, and to fly the planes in combat missions against Sukarno's forces. In March, 1958, Secretary of State Dulles, testifying on Indonesia, assured Congress that "we are not intervening in the internal affairs of this country . . ." In April, Dulles repeated that the United States was strictly neutral in Indonesia. That same month President Eisenhower told a press conference: "Our policy is one of careful neutrality and proper deportment all the way through so as not to be taking sides where it is none of our business. Now on the other hand, every rebellion that I have ever heard of has its soldiers of fortune. You can start even back to reading your Richard Harding Davis. People were going out looking for a good fight and getting into it, sometimes in the hope of pay, and sometimes just for the heck of the thing. That is probably going to happen every time you have a rebellion."

The following month the Indonesians shot down and captured one of the CIA pilots, Allen Lawrence Pope, a tall 195-pound Korean War ace from Perrine, Florida. Apparently taking his cue from Eisenhower, the U.S. ambassador to Jakarta, Howard P. Jones, termed Pope "a private American citizen involved as a paid soldier of fortune."*

---

*Pope was sentenced to death, but freed in July, 1962, after President Kennedy established friendlier relations with Sukarno. Five months earlier another CIA pilot, Francis Gary Powers, had been exchanged for Soviet spy Rudolf Abel on a bridge in Berlin.

Less than a year after the U-2 incident and the summit collapse, President Kennedy met disaster at the Bay of Pigs, the CIA-backed invasion of Cuba by exiles who hoped to overthrow Fidel Castro. The invasion began with an air strike from Nicaragua. One of the pilots, flying a B-26 into which the CIA had fired bullets for dramatic effect, landed in Miami by prearrangement as part of the cover story; the United States Immigration and Naturalization Service issued a statement in which the pilot claimed, falsely, that the air raid on Cuba had been carried out by defecting members of Castro's air force.

At the United Nations in New York, it was an agonizingly difficult moment for Adlai E. Stevenson, the U.S. ambassador to the UN. Twice Stevenson had run for President, in 1952 and 1956, only to see Kennedy win the prize in 1960. Kennedy, and more particularly the "Irish Mafia" around him, would never completely forgive Stevenson for flirting with the Democratic nomination in 1960. Yet Kennedy valued Stevenson as a man of great decency. "The integrity and credibility of Adlai Stevenson," Kennedy is said to have remarked during the Cuban invasion, "constitute one of our great national assets. I don't want anything to happen to that."

Stevenson, however, had been put in an impossible position; it is extremely difficult to preserve integrity and credibility while telling an official lie to protect an intelligence operation. In the UN, Stevenson arose to respond to Cuban charges. No United States "personnel" or "government airplanes" had participated, he said; the pilots, he added, had "apparently defected from Castro's tyranny"; and "to the best of our knowledge," the planes were from Castro's air force.

It was widely reported later that when Stevenson said this, he knew nothing of the Bay of Pigs operation; the myth persists even today. But a few days before the invasion Tracy Barnes, a high-level CIA official, had gone to New York to brief Stevenson. His account of Cuban-exile activities was rather ambiguous, but Stevenson was thoroughly alarmed by what he heard.

In October, 1963, while researching the Bay of Pigs invasion for a book, Thomas B. Ross and I lunched privately with Stevenson in his apartment at the Waldorf Towers, his official residence as UN ambassador. Stevenson's distress over his role was evident, even two and a half years later. He confirmed he had been briefed by Tracy Barnes; he said Barnes seemed to be trying to persuade him either that the United States was not involved in the forthcoming invasion of Cuba or that the CIA's role was marginal. But the more he listened to Barnes, Stevenson said, "with all this talk about abandoned airfields," the more alarmed he became, and the more convinced that the United States was, in fact, deeply involved. Stevenson implied that he did not, perhaps, immediately connect the CIA man's briefing with the bombing of Cuba a few days later on April 15; but in any case, Stevenson said, he had his mission to perform, the official statement to read into the record, and the photograph to display of the B-26 that had landed at Miami. Afterward, he said sorrowfully, he had a very difficult task of what he called "recovery," that is, recovering his prestige and credibility at the UN, because he had never done anything like this before.

Words do not convey all in an interview. I had the distinct impression, from his manner and expression as well as the nuances of his language, that Stevenson would have liked to have gone even further in conceding the extent of his awareness of the U.S. role at the time he issued his denials, but to have said more would have additionally damaged his reputation and his position as U.S. ambassador to the UN, a post which he still held. But clearly, Stevenson was struggling to convey the truth to us, as painful as it was for him.

Near the end of the interview, I pointed out that in denying U.S. involvement, he had used qualifying words such as "apparently" and "according to the pilots." Stevenson smiled and replied: "I'm an old trial lawyer."

The Cuban missile crisis of 1962 led to further credibility problems for President Kennedy. A U-2 flight over Cuba brought back the first photographs of Soviet missiles; Kennedy received the news on October 16. To maintain normal appearances, he went ahead with a planned political campaign trip that week. Former Presidential press secretary Pierre Salinger has reported, in his book *With Kennedy,* that in Chicago on October 19, Kennedy's assistant, Kenneth O'Donnell, warned him: "The President may have to develop a cold somewhere along the line tomorrow." The next day Kennedy instructed Salinger to tell the press he had a cold and was cutting short the trip to fly back to Washington. Later, officials argued that this stratagem was necessary to preserve secrecy until Kennedy could reveal both the crisis and the U.S. response on October 22. If there is a Richter scale of official misinformation, a Presidential sneeze must rank fairly low on it, in comparison, for example, with the denial that the United States had sent a spy plane over the Soviet Union. But here again, the justification for misleading the American press and public was the necessity to mislead the enemy. It is a justification that permits almost limitless deception in the name of "national security."

In fact, the announcement about the President's "cold" failed to prevent and may even have stimulated press speculation that a major crisis, possibly in Cuba, was at hand. As Salinger reports in his book, as soon as the President had landed in Washington, the press secretary faced a barrage of questions from newsmen. By Sunday, James Reston, the chief of *The New York Times* Washington bureau, was questioning McGeorge Bundy on the subject of Soviet missiles in Cuba. Kennedy telephoned Reston and Orvil Dryfoos, the publisher of the *Times;* he confirmed the presence of Russian missiles and asked the newspaper not to publish the story until the government could complete its strategic preparations and the President had reported to the nation the next day. The *Times* honored Kennedy's request.

Ironically, the story of the Presidential "cold" triggered what was undoubtedly the most damaging credibility incident of the Kennedy administration. The central figure was Arthur Sylvester, the Assistant Secretary of Defense for Public Affairs, a silver-haired Princeton graduate and former city editor and Washington bureau chief of the *Newark News.* An acerbic man with a low boiling point, Sylvester surprised his old newspaper friends with the zeal he brought to his new role as a government public relations man. During the missile crisis, on October 19, Sylvester had authorized a statement that "the Pentagon has no information indicating the presence of offensive weapons in Cuba."

Sylvester was criticized for this statement, which he later conceded he knew at the time to be untrue. Ten days later Sylvester declared that "news generated by actions of the government . . . are part of the arsenal of weaponry that a President has . . . The results, in my opinion, justify the methods we used."

Then, on December 6, 1962, at a meeting of the New York chapter of Sigma Delta Chi, a national journalism fraternity, a UPI reporter asked Sylvester about President Kennedy's "cold" during the missile crisis. He replied: ". . . it's inherent in [the] government's right, if necessary, to lie to save itself when it's going up into a nuclear war. That seems to me basic—basic." On various occasions Sylvester disputed the transcript which showed this remark; at other times he agreed he had indeed expressed these thoughts, but accused the news media of distorting his words.

Sylvester's error, which could not be repaired by any amount of later explanation, was to articulate publicly a view that was privately shared by many government officials. Sylvester was arguing the "right to lie" in extreme cases where national survival was presumed to be at stake. To the press and public, however, it sounded too much like a blanket rationale for government misinformation.

Government does have an alternative to lying. It can tell the truth, or it can say nothing. As the U-2 affair had demonstrated, it is wiser and more appropriate in a democracy for the government to remain silent in difficult situations.

The Kennedy administration's handling of the Bay of Pigs and the Cuban missile crisis gave rise to charges of "news management." Although it was not widely realized during those years, in retrospect the Kennedy administration's policies in Vietnam also raise major, disturbing questions of credibility.

The whole thrust of Kennedy's Vietnam policy was to move as covertly and as quietly as possible, with a minimum of public disclosure. During 1961 and 1962 the White House began sending U.S. troops into South Vietnam without public announcement. In July, 1962, the Pentagon confirmed for the first time that "several thousand" American military men were in Vietnam; not until January 30, 1963, was an actual figure disclosed; on that date Robert McNamara testified to Congress that 11,000 U.S. troops were in Vietnam. Padding softly into Vietnam may have had some short-run advantages for Kennedy, but the long-run results were predictable. In a democracy, no military action can be waged for very long without public support; later, when Johnson escalated the war and put half a million ·men into combat, Americans had a sense of bewilderment; like a man coming in at the middle of a movie, they had an unsettled feeling that they had missed something important in the beginning. They had; the size of the commitment of U.S. forces to Vietnam during 1962 had been masked as a matter of highest national policy. As a result, the public was asked by Johnson to support a military operation about which it had never been informed when the initial, albeit much more modest, troop commitments were made under Kennedy.

In May of 1961, also without public announcement, Kennedy ordered the CIA to undertake a program of covert action against Hanoi, including the infiltration of agents into North Vietnam for sabotage and intelligence gathering. While announcing publicly that the U.S. goal in Vietnam was to assist South Vietnam "to obtain its independence," Kennedy issued National Security Action Memorandum (NSAM) 52, privately stating the real U.S. objective: "To prevent Communist domination of South Vietnam." Details of the program of covert action are described in the Pentagon Papers, published a decade later in 1971.

As the Pentagon Papers also confirm, the United States supported and encouraged the coup against South Vietnam's President, Ngo Dinh Diem, and the CIA worked secretly with the generals who carried it out on November 1, 1963. For example, a CIA cable to Lodge on October 6 warned the ambassador and the CIA station chief to "preserve security and deniability" in all contacts with the plotters. A week before the coup the generals assured the top CIA agent involved that the plan of operation, marked "Eyes Only for Lodge," would be turned over to the CIA two days before the coup *"for Lodge's review."* (Emphasis added.) McGeorge Bundy cabled Lodge two days before the coup that "once a coup under responsible leadership has begun . . . it is in the interest of the U.S. government that it should succeed."

Yet when Diem was overthrown, the Kennedy administration denied that the United States had supported the coup. On June 30, 1964, when Lodge returned to the United States with hopes of securing the Republican Presidential nomination, he gave a long interview to *The New York Times* in which he said: "Now, the overthow . . . of the Diem regime was a purely Vietnamese affair. We never participated in the planning. We never gave any advice. We had nothing whatever to do with it . . . We had nothing to do with overthrowing the government, and it's— I shall always be loyal to President Kennedy's memory on this, because I carried out his policy . . ."*

Vietnam was to remain central to Lyndon Johnson's monumental credibility problems, but as already noted, the Dominican intervention also played an important role. On the night of April 28, 1965, at 8:40 P.M., Johnson went on national television to announce he had sent the Marines ashore in the Dominican Republic "in order to protect American lives." He made no mention, however, of his political motivation in sending in the Marines. Johnson feared the rebel

---

*However, Lodge's successor, Ambassador Maxwell D. Taylor, had a somewhat different view. "One of the most serious wrongs, in my judgment, was our connivance at the overthrow of President Diem," he said in a television interview in 1971. "Because regardless of what you thought of President Diem, we had absolutely nothing but chaos which followed. And it was that chaos that I inherited—perhaps Homeric justice—in the year I was ambassador." Asked who in Washington had decided to encourage the plotters against Diem, Taylor replied: "Well, obviously, it has to be approved by the President . . . I would be sure that no American ever wanted Diem assassinated, you understand. And it was certainly a terrible shock to President Kennedy when that—when that developed. But the organization of coups and the execution of a coup is not like organizing a tea party; it's a very dangerous business. So I didn't think we had any right to be surprised when —when Diem and his brother were murdered."

At a news conference in the Oval Office on September 16, 1971, President Nixon declared: "I would remind all concerned that the way we got into Vietnam was through overthrowing Diem and the complicity in the murder of Diem . . ."

movement was Communist-led; he saw "another Cuba" in the making. In a meeting with his advisers that had begun at 5 P.M., Johnson debated whether to say this on television, but it was decided to justify the intervention solely on the basis of the danger to American lives. Johnson expressed his concern over the Communist aspect when he briefed Congressional leaders of both parties at 7:30 P.M., before his television broadcast. Not until Sunday, May 2, four nights later, did Johnson publicly mention "Communist conspirators" as the basis for American intervention. Could it be that the "Communists" had appeared only after April 28, and were therefore unknown to Johnson when he announced that saving lives was the basis for his decision to send in the Marines? Not so; Johnson, in talking with members of Congress on May 4, said that intelligence reports coming in "every few minutes" from 3 P.M. until 7 P.M. on the afternoon of April 28 indicated that the rebels were led by "men with a long history of Communist association and insurrections."

At a press conference on June 17 Johnson declared that before the U.S. intervention "some 1,500 innocent people were murdered and shot, and their heads cut off . . . As we talked to our ambassador to confirm the horror and tragedy and the unbelievable fact that they were firing on Americans and the American Embassy, he was talking to us from under a desk while bullets were going through his windows . . ." No one else had located the 1,500 headless Dominicans that Johnson had discovered, however.* As it turned out, the business about the American ambassador and the bullets whizzing in his window was also pure fiction; at six foot two, career Ambassador W. Tapley Bennett, Jr., would have had some difficulty getting under his

---

*Even after leaving the Presidency, Johnson still smarted over criticism of this remark. In his memoir, *The Vantage Point,* Johnson said that he had reports that two police officers had been beheaded, an OAS study "mentioned a headless corpse," and Dominicans reported seeing "many bodies" in the river, "some" lacking heads. Ambassador Bennett had a photograph of another "headless" victim. "I was later criticized in press comments for referring to beheadings," Johnson blandly wrote. "There is no doubt in my mind that these incidents took place." It was characteristic of Johnson that even in his memoir, he found it necessary to mislead his audience. He cited a grand total of four specific reports of beheadings to justify a statement that "some 1,500 innocent people were murdered and shot, and their heads cut off." But in the book he did not quote his original statement; the reader is told Johnson had been criticized merely "for referring to beheadings." This is representative of the disingenuous tone of the Johnson memoir, a perhaps unavoidable hazard in rewriting history.

desk, and in any event, hiding under the furniture is not in the tradition of the foreign service.*

But it was the Tonkin Gulf incident that emerged as the most crucial and disgraceful episode in the modern history of government lying. For Johnson used it to rally public support and to obtain the Congressional resolution that gave him a free hand to escalate the war in Vietnam, a war that had claimed more that 45,000 American lives by January, 1973, when the peace agreement was signed.

The incident began on August 2, 1964, when three North Vietnamese PT boats attacked two American destroyers, the *Maddox* and the *Turner Joy.* In fact, the *Maddox* fired the first shots, but claimed the boats were already closing toward her at high speed. There were no U. S. casualties in this daylight engagement. One machine-gun bullet fired by a PT boat struck the *Maddox.*

On the dark, overcast night of August 4, patrolling in the middle of the gulf, the two destroyers, as previously noted, reported they were under "continuous torpedo attack." All of the twenty-one torpedo reports came from David E. Mallow, a twenty-three-year-old sonarman on the *Maddox* who had enlisted in the Navy two years earlier. The *Turner Joy* fired away in the darkness for four hours, but the *Maddox,* strangely, could find nothing on its fire-control radar to shoot at. And the *Turner Joy* sonar heard no torpedoes. In retrospect, both the captain of the *Maddox* and the commander in charge of

---

*Johnson's Munchausen-like tendency to embellish the truth arose to embarrass Bennett a year later, when he testified before the Senate Foreign Relations Committee at a hearing on his nomination as ambassador to Portugal. Chairman Fulbright drawled that he was "purely curious" about a report "that you were under the desk while the firing was coming through the window. Was that an accurate report?" The question, as Fulbright knew, put Bennett in an excruciatingly awkward situation, since he would either have to agree he was under his desk or disavow a tale told by the President who had nominated him for the Lisbon ambassadorship. This exchange took place:

MR. BENNETT: I would say there has been some exaggeration that has crept into repeated descriptions of various events.

THE CHAIRMAN: You weren't really under the desk, were you?

MR. BENNETT: Well, I hit the deck once when a plane came overhead but it was not that particular time.

What about the bullets flying through the office, Fulbright persisted. Squirming, Bennett said hopefully that there had been "a number of bullets in the garden," but no, none zipping through his windows. The committee, and the Senate, confirmed his nomination.

both destroyers concluded that virtually all of the "torpedoes" reported by the *Maddox* were actually the sound of her own propellers.

In Washington, Johnson convened the National Security Council. But at 1:30 P.M. a cable reached the Pentagon from Commodore John J. Herrick, the task force commander on the bridge of the *Maddox:*

REVIEW OF ACTION MAKES MANY RECORDED CONTACTS AND TORPEDOES FIRED APPEAR DOUBTFUL. FREAK WEATHER EFFECTS AND OVEREAGER SONARMAN MAY HAVE ACCOUNTED FOR MANY REPORTS. NO ACTUAL VISUAL SIGHTINGS BY *MADDOX.* SUGGEST COMPLETE EVALUATION BEFORE ANY FURTHER ACTION.

This cable, which was unearthed by Senate investigators four years later, was, of course, unknown to the public in August of 1964. Although he was there on the scene, and in command of both ships, Commodore Herrick clearly was not in the spirit of things; his warning did not conform to the view of events in the Tonkin Gulf that Johnson and Robert McNamara wished to present to the American public.

There is no doubt that this cable was seen at the highest levels of the government; McNamara testified to the Senate Foreign Relations Committee four years later, on February 20, 1968, that *he* had seen it, and "Well, obviously, we were concerned . . ." So McNamara telephoned Admiral Ulysses S. Grant Sharp, Jr., Commander in Chief, United States forces in the Pacific. Their conversation was taped, and McNamara offered a snippet, but only a snippet, of the transcript of that tape to the senators; he quoted himself as having told Admiral Sharp: "We obviously don't want to carry out the retaliatory strike unless we are damned sure what happened."*

---

*The business of the tape recording led to a curious, or perhaps not so curious, sequence of testimony during the hearing. The first time around, McNamara said: "I then called Admiral Sharp, and I have a transcript of that telephone conversation in which the specific words were 'We obviously don't want to carry out the retaliatory strike unless we are damned sure what happened.'" Tape recordings! This was the first mention of the existence of such transcripts, and Chairman Fulbright began asking McNamara whether the committee had received copies of these conversations. McNamara replied he would be "happy" to see that the chairman received them; but the more he thought about it, the less sure he was of how much was available "on such matters." As a matter of fact, McNamara added a few moments later, only conversations that were through "a very special channel, which is the channel of operational command" are recorded; he did not know "how

But that night, even as planes began taking off from the aircraft carrier *Ticonderoga* to bomb North Vietnam, and as President Johnson waited in his Oval Office to speak to the nation on television, the Pentagon was still sending urgent messages to its Pacific commanders asking them to verify the attack.

For example, shortly after 11 P.M., when the bombers were already on their way, and the President was about to go on television, Vice-Admiral Roy L. Johnson sent an urgent cable to the *Turner Joy:* WHO WERE WITNESSES, WHAT IS WITNESS RELIABILITY? MOST IMPORTANT THAT PRESENT EVIDENCE SUBSTANTIATING TYPE AND NUMBER OF ATTACKING FORCES BE GATHERED AND DISSEMINATED.

In his 1968 testimony, McNamara leaned heavily, as proof of the attack, on classified intercepts by U.S. intelligence of alleged North Vietnamese radio traffic. He did not release the text of these messages, so there was no way for the Senate or the public really to judge. But he talked about and paraphrased them, and from what is known of their contents, the messages are far from conclusive proof of anything.

The controversy over the Tonkin Gulf incident has tended to focus on whether, or to what extent, American destroyers were in fact attacked on the night of August 4. Regardless of whether any attack took place, the messages between Washington and the Pacific that day demonstrate that *at the time* neither the President nor McNamara was certain that an attack had occurred.

There was an unseemly scramble for "evidence" to support the actions the President had determined to take. That evidence was still frantically being sought at 11:37 P.M., when Johnson stood before the cameras in the Fish Room and began: "My fellow Americans . . ."

Three days later Congress passed the Tonkin Gulf resolution, authorizing the President to take "all necessary steps" in Southeast Asia.* And so America moved down the path to war, on the strength

---

much" of his conversation with Sharp had been recorded, he would have to see.

Fulbright then returned to the portion McNamara *had* quoted from the tape:

THE CHAIRMAN: What is the source of your statement there?

SECRETARY MCNAMARA: The source of my statement is my memory of what I myself said and did, since I am reporting on my own conversations.

THE CHAIRMAN: I see.

*Congress did not declare war; it simply expressed its overwhelming support for Johnson and wrote what amounted to a blanket endorsement of his

of "doubtful" torpedo reports by a twenty-three-year-old sonarman and a single bullet hole in a destroyer. Much later Senator Albert Gore, then a member of the Foreign Relations Committee, noted that McNamara and Pentagon official John McNaughton had retrieved the bullet that struck the *Maddox* and had displayed it to the committee. "Every time they came up here they waved that bullet around," Gore said. "One bullet and you went to war—Helen's face is insignificant by comparison."

But during the 1964 campaign, in the weeks after Tonkin Gulf, Lyndon Johnson appeared to promise the voters that there would be no war. Dedicating a dam at Eufaula, Oklahoma, on September 25, he declared: "There are those that say you ought to go north and drop bombs, to try to wipe out the supply lines . . . We don't want our American boys to do the fighting for Asian boys. We don't want to get involved in a nation with seven hundred million people and get tied down in a land war in Asia."

At Akron, Ohio, on October 21, Johnson said: "But we are not about to send American boys nine or ten thousand miles away from home to do what Asian boys ought to be doing for themselves."

Eventually, of course, he sent 536,000 American boys to help the Asian boys in Vietnam, and a good many American voters later felt they had been misled.* Barry Goldwater, who left the impression that he favored using nuclear weapons in Vietnam, had sounded much too risky to most voters; they had overwhelmingly elected Johnson. Johnson's 1964 statements, however, were not unlike those of Wilson in 1916 or Roosevelt in 1940. His remarks could charitably be dismissed as campaign oratory, for which candidates are seldom held too closely to account. But taken together with all the other credibility incidents of the Johnson administration, there is no doubt that the 1964 campaign promises were highly damaging. A President whose reputation for veracity was otherwise impeccable might have been forgiven his campaign promises; Johnson was not.

Moveover, the Pentagon Papers revealed that even as Johnson was indicating in his campaign speeches that he would not "go north

---

future actions. Later the administration contended that the President could constitutionally wage war in Vietnam without the resolution. Quite aside from the legal aspect, however, there is no question that the Tonkin Gulf resolution mobilized public and Congressional support to a significant degree in 1964 and thereby paved the way for later escalation.

*In *The Vantage Point,* Johnson, seeking to explain his 1964 campaign statements, wrote: "I did not mean that we were not going to do any fighting, for we had already lost many good men in Vietnam."

and drop bombs," he was secretly moving in that direction. On August 18, 1964, Ambassador Maxwell D. Taylor cabled from Saigon to propose "a carefully orchestrated bombing attack" on North Vietnam with "January 1, 1965, as a target D-Day." The Joint Chiefs were also pressing for air strikes against the North.

On September 9 Johnson approved NSAM 314, which authorized U.S. retaliation against the North in the event of any "special" attacks against American units by Hanoi or the Viet Cong. Left fuzzy was the degree to which the United States should, in the words of a memo by William P. Bundy, Assistant Secretary of State for the Far East, "deliberately . . . provoke" a reaction by Hanoi "and consequent retaliation by us." Bundy added: "Examples of actions to be considered would be running U.S. naval patrols increasingly close to the North Vietnamese coast and/or associating them with 34A operations.* We believe such deliberately provocative elements should not be added in the immediate future while the GVN [South Vietnam] is still struggling to its feet. By early October, however, we may recommend such actions . . ."

A high-level committee headed by William Bundy, and appointed by Johnson to consider new moves against North Vietnam, held its first meeting on November 3, the day Johnson was reelected in a landslide. The group recommended bombing the North, and a month later Johnson, according to the Pentagon study, approved both this concept in "general outline" and the first part of a two-phase plan to bomb North Vietnam.

---

*President Johnson approved Operation Plan 34A on February 1, 1964. The plan, drawn up by CIA, was a broad program of covert warfare against North Vietnam. It included naval raids by South Vietnam against North Vietnam, one of which took place on August 3, 1964, between the two Tonkin Gulf incidents. McNamara, testifying to the Senate Foreign Relations Committee about Tonkin Gulf on August 6, 1964, said that the U.S. Navy "played absolutely no part in, was not associated with, was not aware of, any South Vietnamese actions, if there were any." He specifically added that the *Maddox* "was not aware" of the South Vietnamese raid. Four years later the committee confronted McNamara with a cable of instructions to the *Maddox*, telling the destroyer it would "possibly draw" North Vietnamese patrol boats "to northward away from the area of 34A operations."

"It is unusual," Senator Fulbright commented dryly, "that having received that cable . . . the *Maddox* did not know what 34A was."

McNamara, without batting an eyelash, replied: "They were not aware of the details is what I said . . ." which of course is not what McNamara had said.

Britain's Prime Minister Harold Wilson, in Washington for a state visit December 7–9, was briefed on the President's plans.* After the enemy struck Pleiku on February 6, 1965, Johnson ordered U.S. bombers to attack, and on February 13 the sustained bombing of the north began.

But the bombing did not defeat North Vietnam, and on April 1, 1965, President Johnson secretly decided to commit American ground troops in South Vietnam. He specifically ordered that the decision be kept secret, and that it be disguised to look as though there had been no change in U.S. policy. Johnson's orders were contained in NSAM 328 of April 6, which must surely be one of the most shameful official documents of a shameful time in American history.

The memorandum was signed by McGeorge Bundy and addressed to Secretary of State Dean Rusk, Robert McNamara, and CIA director John A. McCone. It approved an eighteen-to-twenty-thousand man increase in U.S. troops in Vietnam, the deployment of two more Marine battalions and an air squadron, and "a change of mission" for the Marines to permit their "more active use" —a euphemism for combat. With respect to these decisions, the NSC memo said, "the President desires that . . . premature publicity be avoided by all possible precautions. The actions themselves should be taken as rapidly as practicable, but in ways that should minimize any appearance of sudden changes in policy . . . The President's desire is that these movements and changes should be understood as being gradual and wholly consistent with existing policy."

Did the President of the United States really believe that large numbers of American troops could be sent to fight a war halfway

---

*On February 25, 1965, with a few other Washington correspondents, I attended a lunch for Lord Harlech, the departing British ambassador to the United States. Harlech said that the basic American policy decision to retaliate against Hanoi by bombing North Vietnam had been conveyed and explained to the British as far back as November, 1964, and that, therefore, the raids that began after Pleiku "came as no surprise."

While the record does not show that President Johnson had *decided* to bomb the North even while denying such intentions in his campaign speeches, a reasonable interpretation of the Pentagon Papers leads to the conclusion that both the President and the administration were moving steadily down that path during and after the 1964 campaign. Although the Pentagon Papers are somewhat ambiguous on the chronology of the development of the bombing policy, Harlech's comments would appear to shed interesting further light on the question.

around the world, and that this could be kept secret, or falsified so that it did not seem to be happening? Apparently so, for that is what he ordered, and in writing. And it did remain secret for a time—until June 8, when State Department press spokesman Robert McCloskey let it be known that American forces in Vietnam would be available for "combat support" if needed. As might be imagined, his disclosure caused a tremendous storm, and the next day the White House issued a statement which began: "There has been no change in the mission of United States ground combat units in Vietnam in recent days or weeks."

Connoisseurs of government deception will note the artful insertion of the word "combat" in this sentence. The White House was attempting to admit almost incidentally the crucial fact that the United States had committed combat troops to a ground war, a fact that had been concealed for two months at the specific direction of the President. The words, technically accurate and totally misleading, proved to be symbolic of the Johnson administration's policy. By the time the President left office, in January, 1969, more than 30,000 Americans had died fighting in Vietnam.

President Nixon failed to bridge the credibility gap that had opened to such canyonlike proportions under Johnson. The prisoner raid at Son Tay, the Tydings affair, the Laos invasion have already been described; there were many similar episodes. In May of 1970, for example, Nixon dispatched American troops into Cambodia for the purpose, he said, of cleaning out Communist sanctuaries and protecting American troops in Vietnam. Less than four months later Vice-President Agnew assured newsmen that "we're going to do everything we can to help the Lon Nol government" in Cambodia. As a result, the nature of the American commitment to Cambodia raised questions of candor.

Furthermore, on June 30, as American troops left Cambodia, Nixon himself told the nation in a televised address that while South Vietnam might continue operations inside Cambodia as necessary, "there will be no U.S. air or logistics support." As the United States expanded the air war in Cambodia to include air support for South Vietnamese forces, newsmen thought it appropriate to ask Defense Secretary Laird, in January, 1971, whether this did not contradict the President's promise. The President, Laird replied, had said only that "air support would not be used . . . during the *termination* of those sanctuary operations . " [Emphasis added.] This was a novel and imaginative interpretation of the President's pledge, since Nixon had not said any such thing, and rather clearly was discussing "future policy," not the end of the Cambodia action, but Laird added quickly that he did not wish to get into "semantics."

Laird's celebrated fuel-pipe fiasco during the Laos invasion, while unimportant in itself, was symbolic of the larger problem. On February 24, 1971, Laird and General Vogt unveiled a three-foot section of pipe to Pentagon reporters. This, said Laird, was a segment of the gasoline pipeline running all the way down the Ho Chi Minh trail from North Vietnam, and used by the enemy to refuel his vehicles.

"It is four inches in diameter," said Laird. "It has a very clever, simple disconnect system with a gasket and a simple device to secure or unsecure, if you must, in a hurry." (Very clever, these North Vietnamese.) The United States had been bombing the pipelines, Laird said, but the disconnect feature "has made it possible for the North Vietnamese to take a ruptured section of the pipe out in a few minutes and insert a new section in, and the flow continues."

But, chimed in General Vogt, "in the last two days, ground forces have gotten to the pipeline at this point [indicates map] and they have torn up some three hundred meters of the pipeline. In other words, we have now severed the pipeline . . ."

A few days later, under pressure from newsmen, the Pentagon conceded that the pipe section displayed by Laird had been captured not during the current invasion, but in an earlier, clandestine raid into Laos on a date that the Pentagon would not reveal. Ironically, the pipeline gaffe had forced the Defense Department to confirm for the first time that South Vietnamese forces *had* been crossing the border into Laos.

And it was under Nixon that the disingenuous phrase "protective reaction" was coined by Secretary Laird to describe the resumption of U.S. bombing in North Vietnam.* As Nixon pulled the ground troops out of South Vietnam, he came to rely more and more heavily

---

*Laird introduced the phrase at a news conference at the Pentagon on October 9, 1969. Euphemisms like "protective reaction," the tightening of information policies concerning the air war, and the administration's schedule of gradual troop withdrawals tended to divert public attention not only from the air war but from the overall casualty figures in Vietnam. During the Johnson administration more than 30,000 Americans died in combat in Vietnam and 192,000 were wounded. During the first four years of the Nixon administration more than 15,000 Americans died in combat in Vietnam and more than 111,000 were wounded. As a result, by the time of the peace agreement of January, 1973, combat deaths in Vietnam approached 46,000, and the number of wounded totaled more than 303,000.

on U.S. air power over North Vietnam, Laos, and Cambodia. In the spring of 1972, after North Vietnam launched its massive ground offensive in the South, Nixon openly resumed intensive bombing of the North and mined Haiphong harbor and other North Vietnamese ports. Until then, for more than three years, the public, with its gaze riveted on the troop withdrawals and "Vietnamization," paid relatively little attention to the expanded air war. And it was hard for the news media to cover the air war during these years, since the Pentagon made news about it difficult to obtain.

The Pentagon's own figures on bombing tonnage indicated, however, that more bombs—almost 3,000,000 tons—were dropped in Indochina during Nixon's first three years as President than were dropped during the last three years of the Johnson Presidency. A Cornell University study published in 1971 concluded that by the end of that year, the U.S. had dropped 6,000,000 tons of bombs and other munitions in Indochina, three times the total tonnage used in World War II.

One of the most publicized credibility episodes of the Nixon administration began on December 7, 1971, when Henry Kissinger briefed reporters on the government's position in the India-Pakistan war. "You can attribute it to White House officials, but no direct quotations," said Ronald Ziegler, the President's press secretary. Senator Goldwater somehow obtained a copy of the transcript, however, and put it in the *Congressional Record* two days later, so Kissinger was identified as the source.

"First of all," Kissinger told the newsmen, "let's get a number of things straight. There have been some comments that the administration is anti-Indian. This is totally inaccurate." A position paper distributed to reporters at the briefing began: "The policy of this administration toward South Asia must be understood. It is neither anti-Indian nor pro-Pakistani."

On January 4, 1972, columnist Jack Anderson released the transcript of a meeting attended by Kissinger in the Situation Room of the White House on December 3, four days before he briefed the press. The document, stamped Secret Sensitive, contained verbatim dialogue of the high-level participants at a session of the Washington Special Action Group, an NSC subcommittee.

It contained this now-famous comment:

KISSINGER: I am getting hell every half-hour from the President that we are not being tough enough on India. He has just called me again. He does not believe we are carrying out his wishes. He wants to tilt in favor of Pakistan.

The leak was highly embarrassing to the Nixon administration. Some commentators defended Kissinger on the grounds that he had said little more in the secret meeting in the White House basement than was already publicly known. Nevertheless, in his briefing for the newsmen, Kissinger had seemingly sought to leave the impression that Washington was even-handed in its attitude toward both India and Pakistan, which it was not.

Then in the 1972 Presidential campaign came the burglary and bugging of the Democrats' Watergate headquarters, and the indictment of seven men in the case, of whom three were either officials of the Committee to Re-elect the President or had served in the White House. The arrests were followed by the disclosure that Republican campaign funds, some "laundered" in Mexico City, had turned up in the bank account of one of the defendants, Bernard L. Barker. Later came widespread published reports of Republican political sabotage directed at the Democrats and financed from a huge secret fund. With each new disclosure, White House denials became more preposterous; it was as though the administration no longer even cared whether its explanations were remotely plausible; what was important was to deny everything.

Well before the Watergate controversy, however, Nixon was obliged to comment publicly on the credibility issue. In March of 1971 Howard K. Smith interviewed the President on ABC television. The broadcast took place as South Vietnamese forces were retreating in haste from Laos. Television, Nixon explained, had shown only the South Vietnamese troops "that were in trouble" and not the many other battalions that were doing fine. In covering the U.S. invasion of Cambodia, Nixon added, television had again failed to look at the bright side, but "I do not claim that this was deliberate or distorted or anything."

Smith also asked why American air power had been used to support South Vietnamese forces in Cambodia, although Nixon had explicitly said this would not be done. Well, the President replied, the "primary purpose" was to protect American forces, not to assist South Vietnamese forces.

Other Presidents, Nixon said, had been afflicted with a credibility gap, but the war was a key element, and once Americans were convinced that he was ending the war, "I think the credibility gap will rapidly disappear. It is events that cause the credibility gap," Nixon added, "not the fact that a President deliberately lies or misleads the people. That is my opinion."

Part II

SECRECY

Q. Well, what do you make, General, of the principle of the people's right to know . . . ?
A. I don't believe in that as a general principle.

—*Ambassador Maxwell D. Taylor,*
interviewed on the CBS morning news, June 17, 1971

4

Top Secret

There was nothing about his appearance that set him apart in the crowd of bureaucrats streaming into the State Department each morning. This suited him, for Brewer J. Merriam valued his anonymity. He was a quiet, precise man whose name and face were unknown except at the more rarified echelons of the intelligence establishment in Washington. A bit on the short side, of medium build, with thinning brown hair, Merriam wore half-glasses, because he was farsighted and needed them only for reading.

His reading material, however, was unlike that of almost anyone else in Washington, except for the director of Central Intelligence and a few other key officials. In 1972 Merriam was director of the State Department's Office of Current Intelligence, and the documents he read were stamped with esoteric, strange-sounding classification markings, the very names of which were highly secret.

Merriam's office was a windowless room on the sixth floor of the main building—windowless because this eliminated the possibility of anyone, even another State Department official, reading or photographing the secret classifications, or the contents of the documents, from across a courtyard or from the roof. It also diminished the risk of electronic eavesdropping.

The door to this office, Room 6510A, was kept locked. Few officials were permitted inside. Those who wished to gain entrance could identify themselves over a beige telephone hanging on the wall of the corridor outside. A discreet sign instructed callers: "For

Access During Normal Working Hours Please Use Buzzer."

During the day the buzzer sounded frequently as couriers delivered documents by hand from the CIA, across the Potomac River in Langley, Virginia; from the National Security Agency at Fort Meade, Maryland; and from the Defense Intelligence Agency in the Pentagon. For Merriam's office was the State Department's point of input for secret information produced by the various intelligence agencies of the government.

Much of the information flowing into Room 6510A is Special Intelligence, known in the trade as SI, and it bears the exotic classification markings that are themselves classified. The public, and even most members of Congress, are generally unaware of the existence of a whole spectrum of super-secret classifications, which are, in effect, above and beyond Top Secret.

Special Intelligence is the term usually applied to information acquired by electronic intercept: code breaking, intelligence plucked from the airwaves by radio, and by sophisticated listening equipment located at various stations around the globe.

But secret classifications are also given to other special categories of information—which also flow into Room 6510A—where the source, or the method of obtaining the intelligence, is particularly sensitive. For example, beginning in the 1960's, TK was the special classification for information acquired by intelligence satellites. Data acquired through especially sensitive collection systems were classified BYE-MAN; and very few persons in the government were cleared to read such information. In the Pentagon, under a regulation that is in itself classified, these special categories are termed SPECATS; in the State Department and other agencies they are known, to those few officials cleared to know about them, by their specific names.

These secret classifications are created and controlled by the director of Central Intelligence (DCI), who coordinates the government-wide intelligence machinery.* They are provided for in secret directives issued by him; for example, in Director of Central Intelligence Directive No. 1/7 of October 5, 1970, signed by Richard Helms.†

---

*Under the 1947 law that established the CIA, the director of Central Intelligence wears two hats; in one role he oversees the nine agencies that comprise the U.S. intelligence community. In his other hat, he is director of the most powerful of those agencies, the CIA.

†On December 21, 1972, Nixon named Helms ambassador to Iran and appointed James R. Schlesinger, chairman of the Atomic Energy Commission, to replace him as DCI.

The secrecy surrounding these classifications has been breached, although rarely. One of the most intense behind-the-scenes security flaps of the past decade was touched off on March 28, 1965, when *The New York Times Magazine* ran a profile of McGeorge Bundy, then President Johnson's assistant for national security. The story, written by Max Frankel, was accompanied by a large photograph of Bundy conferring with a somber-looking Lyndon Johnson on the White House lawn. Clearly visible in Bundy's left hand was a spiral-bound document stamped TOP SECRET DINAR. Underneath this appeared the words NATIONAL INTELLIGENCE BULLETIN and beneath that, DAILY BRIEF. Below this were two paragraphs of typewritten matter, illegible in the photograph and mostly covered by Bundy's thumb; and about half of another paragraph obscured in part by the cuff of his suit jacket.

The document in the photograph was a CIA summary of the Tonkin Gulf crisis, and although its substance was relatively undramatic, the word DINAR was one of the most highly guarded special intelligence classifications of the United States government. The photograph had rested in the files of *The New York Times* since August, 1964.

At 9 A.M. on Monday morning, March 29, a CIA agent was at the *Times'* offices in Manhattan, asking for the negative. He got it, and expressed relief that he had arrived there "before another agency," by which, it was clear, he meant the FBI, with whom the CIA has often found itself in competition. Apparently CIA analysts concluded that the text of the DINAR could be read if someone got the negative and blew it up. They were less concerned about the reproduction in the newspaper, since the text was illegible, and enlarging it would only result in a bigger blur.

Although the *Times* cooperated with the CIA, the DINAR classification had to be retired. To replace it with a new classification, according to one knowledgeable official, cost $250,000.*

Special Intelligence marked DINAR was always classified Top Secret as well. After the Bundy episode, the DINAR designation was changed to TRINE, and later to UMBRA. Special Intelligence material at the next level down, requiring less protec-

---

*Why the process was so costly was not disclosed; one possibility is that every document stamped DINAR anywhere in the world had to be found, retrieved, restamped, retyped, or reproduced, and the old documents burned, with all of this activity carried out in secrecy and under secure conditions.

tion, was classified SECRET SPOKE; and so on.*

The classification system was created not by Congress but by Presidential directive, issued first by Truman in 1951 and continued with some modification by every President since then. Beginning in 1953, with the directive issued by Eisenhower, these Executive Orders have designated *only* three classification stamps: Top Secret, Secret and Confidential.

Members of the Senate Foreign Relations Committee were, therefore, understandably bewildered when, during their investigation of the Tonkin Gulf incident in February, 1968, they stumbled on the fact that there existed secret intelligence classifications beyond Top Secret.† As the prestigious, senior body of senators concerned with overseeing the nation's foreign policy, the Foreign Relations Committee might have been expected to know this; yet it is clear from the transcript that its members were completely unaware of, and totally astonished to discover, the existence of a complex, elusive web of secret classifications.

The tip of the classification iceberg surfaced briefly at the hearing when Chairman Fulbright inquired into the source of a report that North Vietnamese patrol boats were about to attack the *Turner Joy* on the night of August 4, 1964. Defense Secretary Robert McNamara, Fulbright, and Senators Frank Lausche and Albert Gore then engaged in the following colloquy:

SECRETARY McNAMARA: We have some problems, because the [committee] staff has not been cleared for certain intelligence . . .

---

*The system is so complex, that within Special Intelligence categories, the secret classification markings are designed to mesh with conventional levels of classification; thus SPOKE material is always SECRET SPOKE, never TOP SECRET. The secret classifications themselves are five-letter combinations chosen at random. Although occasionally the words have meaning, as in SPOKE, or UMBRA (which means shadow), generally, as in DINAR, TRINE or HARUM, they stand for nothing.

†The Executive Order then in force specified that protected information "shall be limited to three categories of classification . . . Top Secret, Secret, or Confidential. No other designation shall be used . . ." Since this language is clear, the senators, like most other persons, naturally assumed that there existed only these three levels of classification. Buried in the fine print of the order, however, was a sentence stating: "Nothing in this order shall prohibit any special requirements" for "communications intelligence, cryptography, and matters related thereto." Secret classifications are apparently based on this "special requirements" clause.

SENATOR LAUSCHE *(incredulously):* I do not understand that. The members of our staff are not cleared?

THE CHAIRMAN: All of those who have worked on this matter, but he is talking of a special classification of intelligence communications . . .*

SENATOR GORE: Mr. Chairman, could we know what particular classification that is? I had not heard of this particular super classification.

SECRETARY McNAMARA: . . . Clearance is *above Top Secret* for the particular information involved in this situation [emphasis added].†

The senators then wandered off into desultory discussion of whether Hanoi claimed a twelve-mile or a three-mile territorial limit, but the committee soon returned to the intriguing problem of secret classifications:

SENATOR GORE: Mr. Chairman, would you please clear up the exact identity of this clearance status that is something superior to Top Secret . . . ? I would like to be informed. I never heard of this kind. I thought Top Secret was Top Secret.

THE CHAIRMAN: I am not sure that I can do it justice. I never heard of this clearance before. But at the meeting I attended . . . with Mr. [Under Secretary of Defense Paul] Nitze, he said that this particular message was beyond Top Secret, and it has to do with intelligence communications, and that was the reason he could not give me that particular communication. He allowed me to look at it . . . He said this was beyond Top Secret, and only

---

*In December, 1967, Fulbright had been shown the Special Intelligence radio intercepts upon which McNamara relied so heavily as proof of the North Vietnamese attack. The Pentagon permitted Fulbright alone to see the material, on an "eyes only" basis, so the other members of the committee did not know what McNamara was talking about.

†Virtually all of the officials in the national security field who were interviewed for this book insisted that the secret classifications were not *above* Top Secret, and in fact, were not really classifications but were "categories" or "administrative control designations." The officials apparently preferred this language because they shared the commonly held belief that the President's Executive Order forbids all but the three standard security classifications. McNamara, however, is on record here in using the words "above Top Secret."

a few people are allowed to see it. I was given to understand it relates to what is called an intercept . . .

SENATOR GORE: Excuse me, what is the classification, what is the name of it?

Gore never did receive an answer to his plaintive inquiry, but the exchange continued:

SECRETARY McNAMARA: . . . Mr. Chairman, may I try to answer it? . . . There are a host of different clearances.* I would guess I have perhaps twenty-five. There are certain clearances to which only a handful of people in the government are exposed. There are others with broader coverage, and overlapping coverage, and it is not really a question of degree of clearance. It is a question of need to know, and need to know clearances apply to certain forms of data.

Now, there is a Top Secret clearance that covers certain kinds of information, and is a rather broad clearance and is related to a level of clearances starting for official use only, rising through Confidential and Secret and Top Secret, and generally speaking, that is a pyramidal clearance. There is another clearance, Q clearance, that relates to certain categories of information.†

There is another clearance which is the Special Intelligence clearance we are talking about, that relates to intercept information, and it is this latter clearance in particular that is at issue here, and the staff members of this committee have not been cleared for that kind of information . . . I do not want to get into a further discussion until the room is cleared of those not authorized to handle it.

Although there was a certain double-talking, frammis-on-the-portisan quality to McNamara's short course in classification for the

---

*Although McNamara referred to "clearances" rather than "classifications," the two terms are usually complementary. Officials speak of having a "clearance for Top Secret information"; or, more commonly, a "TS [Top Secret] clearance." Or an official may say he is "cleared to Top Secret." In every case the meaning is the same: the official has "clearance," i.e., permission, to read classified information up to and including a designated level; in the example given, Top Secret. Thus, generally speaking, clearances and classifications mesh.
†A Q clearance, although McNamara did not explain it, is a clearance required by the Atomic Energy Commission for access to atomic information.

senators, in the process he did reveal an interesting statistic. If the Defense Secretary did indeed have twenty-five clearances, this would seem to suggest that aside from the three standard classifications, and the Q clearance, there existed some twenty additional classifications the names of which were themselves classified.

Material stamped with secret intelligence classifications is so closely held, that when it becomes necessary, for example, for a State Department official to have access to it, he must first go to Brewer Merriam's windowless office for a special briefing that rather resembles an initiation rite. Merriam, a veteran of more than twenty-five years as a State Department intelligence official, took over this task in April, 1970, when he became director of the Office of Current Intelligence.

An official who had been inducted into the world of secret intelligence classifications by Merriam's predecessor, William M. Marvel, who ran the office for seven years, described the procedure:

"It was a little creepy. You would go into this room with no windows, it's really like a large bank vault or a safe, and Marvel would brief you in sepulchral voice. He would have a little pamphlet for each type of classification and he would read from it. Each category of Special Intelligence had its own slug, or name, and you had to have a separate briefing for each. You were told not to talk about the information. You had to sign several pledges, one for each type of intelligence, saying you would never initiate or reply to a conversation about that classification, or the information contained under it, unless you were *certain* that the other person was cleared, too. If the material dealt with something happening in Zambia, and somebody came in and said 'Hey, Frank, did you see the material about Zambia?' then you're supposed to answer 'What material?' unless you are sure the other person is cleared."

Special precautions are taken when material classified beyond Top Secret leaves the double-locked vault of the director of the Office of Current Intelligence. "The director," one official explained, "puts the document in a locked briefcase that is chained to his wrist. He comes to your office and gives it to you. You read it and hand it back to him. He records the fact that you have read it. The stuff is never left with anybody."

Windowless vaults in Foggy Bottom, briefcases chained to wrists, arcane terms like DINAR and TRINE, pledges of silence, State Department officials playing verbal games with one another—all are aspects of a system of official secrecy so complicated that even its practitioners often do not fully understand its workings. The spectacle of a distinguished committee of the United States Senate discovering, more or less accidentally, the existence of classifications that are themselves secret, McNamara's slippery, marvelously imprecise explanation, delivered as if to a group of under-achieving schoolboys —all of this would be comic if the subject were less serious, the results less damaging.

But the same system of official secrecy can be used by a President to hide incriminating cables during a Tonkin Gulf crisis, to mask the truth from Congress so that it will overwhelmingly pass a resolution supporting the President, or to conceal the commitment of American troops to combat in Vietnam. In sum, the classification system is the institutional machinery that makes it possible for officials not only to proclaim, but to practice, the "right to lie." It is a system that permits the government to tell the people selective truth, and, as previously noted, to shape events to fit policy.

Governments have always had secrets; the *Journal* of the United States Senate for August 4, 1790, shows that President Washington submitted for Senate approval a secret proviso to be included in a treaty with the Creek Indians. And as far back as the Revolutionary War, military officers or other officials used designations such as Secret or Confidential.

The Army was the first to classify on an organized basis; it did so during World War I and kept the system after the war. In March, 1940, President Roosevelt issued an Executive Order recognizing the military classification system and permitting the Secretaries of War and Navy to stamp documents Secret, Confidential, or Restricted. This order provided the basis for the wartime system of classification.

"There really was no classification system prior to World War II," according to William M. Franklin, director of the historical office of the State Department. "I came to the department in 1941; the assumption then was that *everything* was regarded as confidential. In those days a paper might have a hand scrawl at the top, 'Confidential,' and if it was a really important document, it might say 'Strictly Confidential.' If it were more important than *that*, it would say 'For the Secretary.' If it said 'For the Secretary,' my God, you didn't breathe a word.

"We got the classification system during the war. We caught it by contagion from the British. We had to have a system equal to theirs, since we shared papers with the British. They had 'Most Secret,' which we translated into 'Top Secret.'* They had 'Secret' and

---

*Although the term was unofficial until Truman issued a directive formalizing it in 1950, some of Roosevelt's own papers were stamped Top Secret during World War II. For example, on April 6, 1945, six days before his

'Confidential' as well, which we also used. The military had pretty well organized the system during the war, and from there it later spread to the civilian agencies."

On September 24, 1951, Truman issued the first Executive Order extending the secrecy system to civilian departments. It allowed *any* agency of the Executive Branch to classify what is called "official information the safeguarding of which is necessary in the interest of national security."

In November, 1953, Eisenhower replaced Truman's order with a new Executive Order that provided the basic framework for the classification system in effect since then.* Some amendments were added by Presidents Kennedy and Johnson. In March, 1972, in the wake of the furor over the Pentagon Papers, and amid increasing public and Congressional pressure for reforms in the secrecy system, President Nixon issued a new Executive Order.† While it provided for a number of major changes, and an equal number of new loopholes, the Nixon order preserved much of the basic framework laid down by Eisenhower in 1953.

The significant point in all this is that the classification system was not established by law through an act of Congress. It was created by the President, and applies only to employees of the federal government. The classification system, in other words, is a set of rules and regulations for government officials, generally equivalent to any other Presidential order—for example, one specifying which holidays may be taken by federal workers.

When a State Department or Pentagon official takes out a rubber stamp and marks a document Top Secret, he is not acting under any law, he is performing a ministerial act. He is deciding, rightly or wrongly, whether a particular document fits the definition of information that must be protected from disclosure under the President's order.

The system of official secrecy that has grown up since World War

---

death, FDR sent a cable marked Top Secret to British Prime Minister Winston Churchill. The message agreed on the need for taking a "tougher" stand in dealing with Stalin.

*Executive Order 10501, *Safeguarding Official Information,* November 9, 1953.

†Executive Order 11652, *Classification and Declassification of National Security Information and Material,* March 8, 1972, effective June 1, 1972. Like its predecessors, the Nixon order contains a proviso permitting secret classifications for intelligence data. The language appears under Section 9, "Special Departmental Arrangements."

II, therefore, is a *Presidential* system. It has played a significant role in the general expansion of Presidential power during the same period, and in the emergence of the Presidency as the most powerful of the three branches of the federal government.

In addition to the formal classification system, which denies information to the public, Presidents also withhold information from Congress—classified or otherwise—under the traditional, but dubious, doctrine of "executive privilege." The doctrine rests on the constitutional separation of powers of the three branches of the federal government. Under the doctrine, Presidents have claimed inherent power to hold back information from Congress, even though the Legislative Branch has extensive power to investigate the operations of the government. Boiled down, "executive privilege," for all of its constitutional trappings, simply means that if a President does not wish to provide information, he can tell Congress: "You can't have it." There is not much Congress can do about it.

Although the heads of cabinet departments are generally willing to testify when invited by Congressional committees, Presidential advisers and members of the White House staff seldom do so; the President usually invokes "executive privilege" to prevent their appearance. The rationale is that if Presidential advisers can be questioned about what they tell the President, he will be deprived of their full and frank advice. But the tradition becomes ludicrous when a White House adviser takes over a cabinet function; during President Nixon's first term, for example, Congress could question Secretary of State William Rogers, but it was frustrated in its efforts to question Henry Kissinger, the real architect of the President's foreign policies.

Secrecy is one of the President's most important tools of power, for it permits him to control information about crucial foreign policy decisions and events, and to filter the truth before it reaches Congress and the voters. Because the secrecy system facilitates official lying, it has helped to erode the confidence of Americans in their government.

Neither President Truman nor any of his successors have claimed that their Executive Orders were based upon, or authorized by, any specific statute. The Nixon order made public in March, 1972, like its predecessors, was issued "by virtue of the authority vested in me by the Constitution and statutes" of the United States. Since no specific statute is cited, however, the entire system of official secrecy presumably rests on the general powers of the President, expressed or implied, contained in Article II of the Constitution.

In the abstract, most Americans probably support the right of the President, and the government, to keep certain vital information secret. Whether they support secrecy by Presidential directive on the grand scale that has developed since 1953 is another question entirely; the polls show that insofar as Vietnam is concerned, in 1971 more than two-thirds of the public did not; they believed there was too much secrecy.

The great difficulty, of course, is in deciding how much information need be protected, and in setting standards to define what may be kept secret and for how long. For there is an ultimate absurdity inherent in overclassification. ". . . When everything is classified," Justice Potter Stewart noted in the Pentagon Papers case, "then nothing is classified."

The problem is one of degree; to accept the premise that *some* things must be kept secret is not to accept the conclusion that all things may be kept secret. Yet starting from the rationale that some secrecy is necessary, the government has succeeded in imposing upon the American people, for the first time in history, a formal, peacetime system of official secrecy under which enormous quantities of information have been hidden from public view. And this has been done by Presidential fiat alone, in just two decades, with little or no challenge from Congress.

Because the classification system is complex, there are widely held misconceptions about its workings. For example, contrary to popular opinion, there is no general prohibition in the law against possessing or disclosing classified information as such. Since the President's order applies to government employees, an official who violates the order can be reprimanded, or perhaps even dismissed. But no law bars a member of the public, or a newspaper reporter, from possessing, reading, disclosing, or publishing a "classified" document, unless it concerns the narrow, special area of codes or communications intelligence.

The Espionage Act of 1917, still the basic law relied upon in national security cases, generally bars disclosure not of "classified information" but of "information relating to the national defense." When it seeks to use this law to enforce the classification system, the government must prove that a particular classified document, one marked Top Secret, for example, correctly fits this statutory definition.

There is, in other words, a gap between the espionage laws and the classification system.* If the arrangement were otherwise, if as a

---

*Only two narrow legislative bridges have spanned this gap. Section 798 of Title 18 of the United States Code, added to the espionage law in 1951, does bar the publication or unauthorized use of "classified information" about codes or communications intelligence, i.e., electronic intercepts. And the

general rule possession or publication of classified information was illegal per se, the law would be an invitation and a license for government to classify anything and everything it pleased. Under such a system, the government's control over information would be total, and the First Amendment reduced to nothing.

The three standard security classifications, Top Secret, Secret, and Confidential, are usually referred to in the national security bureaucracy as TS, S, and C. The definitions are vague. Top Secret is information which, if disclosed, "could reasonably be expected to cause exceptionally grave damage to the national security." For Secret, the phrase is "serious damage." The standard for Confidential is that disclosure could reasonably be expected to "cause damage" to the national security.*

Truman's order had been criticized because it permitted every agency to classify, whether or not it handled defense information. The Eisenhower order deprived twenty-eight agencies of the power to classify, but left hundreds of others—the precise number was never calculated—with full authority to stamp documents Top Secret, including such agencies as the Migratory Bird Conservation Commission and the Indian Arts and Crafts Board. Not until January 9, 1961, as he was leaving office, did Eisenhower restrict the power to classify to thirty-two agencies listed by name; in thirteen others, with only partial defense responsibilities, the power to classify was limited to the agency head.†

This change was largely the result of pressure from Congressman John E. Moss, the California Democrat, who kept chopping

---

Internal Security Act of 1950 makes it a crime for a government official to hand over "classified" information to a foreign agent or a member of a "Communist organization." But these are the only two statutes that acknowledge the existence of "classified" information as such.

*These definitions, from the Nixon secrecy order, are essentially the same as the standards in the previous Executive Orders; the Nixon order substituted the phrase "could reasonably be expected" for the vaguer "could result," the words used in earlier orders. The language of the Nixon order still leaves enormous discretion to the individual bureaucrat.

†Among the agencies that lost the right to classify was the Migratory Bird Conservation Commission. When the House subcommittee on government information discovered that the bird commission had defied the Presidential order, and was continuing to stamp certain documents Confidential, Secretary of the Interior Stewart Udall wrote to assure the subcommittee that in the future these documents would be labeled Restricted rather than Confidential.

away at the secrecy order, using the dual weapons of ridicule and the investigatory power of his House government information subcommittee.

In a 1958 hearing before the Moss subcommittee, for example, a witness revealed that the Army had actually classified the bow and arrow. "One of the nation's outstanding physicists has a hobby of archery," Dr. Wallace R. Brode, a State Department official, told the congressmen. During the war, the witness explained, the physicist had done some experimental work "on more efficient and effective bows and arrows. This work was, of course, classified, and after the war he tried to get it declassified but without success. So far as I know it is still classified."

The subcommittee investigated further and found that the physicist in question was Dr. Paul E. Klopstag, who had done the work for the Office of Strategic Services, the wartime predecessor of the CIA. The report ended up in Army Ordnance, which classified it Confidential. When Moss wrote to the Secretary of Defense to verify this, he received a reply from the Army confirming the story. "An examination of available records," Major General J.H. Michaelis replied with dignity, "discloses that a report on silent flashless weapons was prepared . . ."

Moss' subcommittee also discovered that the Navy had classified as Secret a report about what a witness termed "the state of the art of shark repellents." The Navy said the report had been classified because it dealt with shark attacks on survivors of Navy ships torpedoed in World War II; but when the subcommittee obtained the document it turned out that the great bulk of the reports described attacks between 1907 and 1940; the secret document included a treatise published by the Brooklyn Museum in 1916, entitled "The Shark Situation in the Waters About New York."

John Moss' onslaughts were bound to bring a counterattack, and on April 10, 1959, Representative Clare Hoffman, the Michigan Republican, arose on the floor to denounce Moss for asking the Pentagon to explain why it had classified the fact that it was sending monkeys into outer space. Moss, Hoffman charged, was demanding that "we make available to our enemies, the Communists," invaluable "technical information." He added: "We might just as well install a Communist in every executive department."

The same day, Robert Dechert, the general counsel of the Defense Department, dispatched an incredible letter to Moss, charging that the subcommittee's actions "not only have served to encourage disrespect for the security system, but . . . the only real beneficiaries can be the Communist propagandists who want to stir up trouble between us and other nations." Dechert then demanded that Moss identify the Pentagon employee who had disclosed the classified monkey data to the subcommittee; with this kind of unauthorized disclosure going on, Dechert warned, America would soon be on the "road to anarchy."

As the debate escalated, the *Washington Post* reported that sources close to the Moss subcommittee suggested that the Pentagon secrecy had really been imposed to avoid offending persons in India who "worship monkeys." Hoffman then accused Moss of trying "to inject the religious issue." Moss responded that it was a matter of record that during a period in 1958, a ban had been imposed on shipments of monkeys from India, "where there is a cult of monkey worshippers." As for the source of his original tip, Moss said, it was not a Pentagon employee but an Air Force press release. Despite the fact that the Pentagon had classified information about the use of monkeys in outer space, Moss noted, "out at the Washington Zoo is a cage containing a Macaque monkey, and . . . a plaque which reports that this is one of two monkeys sent up in 1952 in an Air Force Aerobee rocket to a height of 200,000 feet into the upper atmosphere from New Mexico." He was, Moss added, "subject to fifteen G's pressure on takeoff."

Although Eisenhower had created the basic system for keeping government secrets, his order did not provide any machinery for opening up papers when it was no longer necessary to keep them secret. To meet this problem, Kennedy grafted onto the order a system for downgrading and declassification. It sounded fine, but wasn't.

What Kennedy did was to require that when documents were classified, they also be placed in one of four groups. Groups 1 and 2 were for especially sensitive material, and were excluded indefinitely from automatic downgrading; Group 3 documents were to be downgraded at twelve-year intervals, but not automatically declassified, which meant that after thirty-six years a document could still be classified. Only Group 4 documents were to be automatically downgraded at three-year intervals and declassified after twelve years. Needless to say, most bureaucrats would put nothing of interest in Group 4.

Moreover, even those officials who tried to comply with the system were hard put to remember which group was which. George MacClain, the director of classification for the Defense Department, tried to explain the workings of the secrecy system in an affidavit filed in federal court in June, 1971, during the government's effort to stop the *Washington Post* from publishing the Pentagon Papers. An excerpt will suffice to give the flavor of both the classification system and the special vocabulary of the officials who administer it:

. . .the time-phased system of automatic downgrading and declassification established by EO 10501 [the Eisenhower order] as amended by EO 10964 [the Kennedy order] and as implemented in DOD [Department of Defense] by DOD directive 5200.10, provides for four categories or groups numbered from one through four. For groups 1, 3 and 4, there is no necessary relationship between a level of classification, TS, S or C, and the particular group. Thus, Top Secret, as well as Secret or Confidential information can be placed in either group 1, 3, or 4. Group 2 information, however, is used for only very sensitive information, and may be applied only on a unit basis, such as, document by document. The classification level of group 2 information must always be either TS or S.

Even if this paragraph is reread several times, it remains fairly mind-boggling. Nixon's 1972 order mercifully abolished the formal group numbers but substituted a new and equally complicated system for downgrading and declassifying. Under it, documents remain classified for six, eight, ten, thirty years, or forever, depending on their category. How long a secret *remains* secret, in other words, may be more significant than how it is classified. *

The classification stamp on a government document is only one of several components that control its degree of secrecy. The classification level may even be the least important control. To understand the system, one must take into account various other secrecy restrictions and markings, some of which are outside of, and unrelated to, the President's order.

Seen as a whole, the classification system is really a five-layer grid, all or part of which may be imposed on a particular document. The parts are these:

1. The level of classification—TS, S, C, or one of the esoteric secret intelligence classifications.

2. The length of time the document is to remain secret—from six years to infinity.

3. Special access controls, such as NODIS, EXDIS, LIMDIS and NOFORN, which limit who may see a given classified document.

---

*In 1972 the House government information subcommittee asked the Defense Department to identify its "oldest classified document." The Pentagon replied: "It appears that the oldest classified document is . . . a 1912 contingency plan, currently classified Confidential, on the ground that its contents could be exploited for purposes prejudicial to current national security interests."

4. Code names applied to a series of documents dealing with one subject, such as MARIGOLD, the slug assigned to a secret Vietnam peace initiative in 1966.

5. Priority, if the document is a cable or other communication. For example, a message marked CRITIC would indicate that a grave crisis, perhaps even war, was at hand; it would, hopefully, be transmitted ahead of less urgent traffic.

Nixon's 1972 Executive Order revising the classification system was the result of a year-long study by an interagency panel known inside the government as "the NSSM 113 Committee." The committee was so named because it owed its creation to National Security Study Memorandum 113, issued by Nixon on January 15, 1971. Ironically, there was no initial announcement of the classified NSSM or the formation of the secret committee on secrecy.* Six months later, in June, when the publication of the Pentagon Papers stirred public anger at government secrecy, the fact that the secret study was under way was revealed by the White House "in view of the widespread public interest in this subject."

Meeting privately with the group in his small office in the Executive Office Building on July 1, Nixon cited a number of examples of what he considered excessive secrecy; he complained that even the menus of official dinners for visiting heads of state came over to the White House stamped Top Secret.

Under Nixon's order, classified documents are now placed on a "General Declassification Schedule," or are exempted from it. For example, a Top Secret document placed on the general schedule moves down to Secret in two to three years, to Confidential in four to five years, and is declassified in ten to eleven years.†

There is an important and often overlooked distinction, how-

---

*During most of the period that it conducted the study, the NSSM 113 Committee was headed by Assistant Attorney General William H. Rehnquist; he resigned after President Nixon appointed him to the Supreme Court. The names of the other members of the committee were not announced; they were Thomas Latimer of the National Security Council, William D. Blair, Jr., of the State Department, Joseph J. Liebling of the Defense Department, Howard Brown of the AEC, and Ermal Geiss of the CIA.

†The time span for declassification varies by as much as a year, because, under Nixon's order, declassification can occur only at the end of a full calendar year; and the clock does not start to run until the beginning of the calendar year after a document is classified. Thus a document stamped Top Secret on December 31 would be declassified ten years later, but one stamped January 1 would not be declassified for eleven years.

ever, between a document that is declassified and one that is made public. A secret document may be "declassified" after the specified number of years, but remain in government files, inaccessible to newsmen or other citizens. A formal request under the 1967 Freedom of Information Act requires that one know of the existence of the document and be able to describe it, no mean feat in the case of a document that was stamped Secret in the first place. The request may be refused, in any event, on any one of several grounds. In short, a Top Secret document may remain just as secret ten to eleven years later when the classification stamp is crossed out.

If a document is exempted from the general schedule, it never gets put on the "conveyor belt" for automatic declassification.* Moreover, the Nixon order allows officials to exempt *any* classified document from the general schedule (thereby removing it from automatic declassification) if it falls into one of four categories. The first of these is information furnished in confidence by foreign governments or international organizations. The second is material about codes or intelligence. The fourth is information which, if disclosed, "would place a person in immediate jeopardy."

The third category is information "the continuing protection of which is essential to the national security." This category, which might well be called Catch 3, permits officials to continue to lock up secrets at will. The quantity of information that officials will decide requires such "continuing protection" is not difficult to imagine.

The provision that any classified document can be exempted from automatic declassification when essential to the national security insures continuing secrecy on a massive scale. It is true that exempt material may be reviewed after ten years, but only if a department or a citizen requests a review and describes the document "with sufficient particularity to enable the Department to identify it" and to find it "with only a reasonable amount of effort."

One does not have to wait ten years to know that if the government wishes to keep a document hidden, a citizen requesting it will be told he has failed the "particularity" and "reasonable amount of effort" tests. Even if, through clairvoyance, he is able to describe a secret document in sufficient detail so that it can be retrieved without unnecessary exertion, the fine print promises only that the docu-

---

*Classifiers have a tendency to invent new secrecy labels at every opportunity. Although the Nixon order does not provide for it, under departmental rules, documents exempted from the General Declassification Schedule are now stamped XGDS, in addition to TOP SECRET, or whatever other labels they bear.

ment shall be subject to "review." There is no guarantee that it will be declassified, and no assurance that if declassified, it will be made available. The entire secrecy system, in short, is Kafkaesque.

Finally, the Nixon order provides that "all" secret documents are to be declassified after thirty years, except—except for information "which the head of the originating Department personally determines in writing at that time to require continued protection" because it is "essential to the national security" or because disclosure would endanger lives.

In rather broad paraphrase, the Nixon order provides that secrets must be declassified after a set period of time unless it is decided that they need not be because secrecy is "essential," in which case they may be reviewed, but not necessarily released, after ten years, provided they can be described and found; but they will be declassified after thirty years, unless, of course, continuing secrecy is essential, in which case they may continue secret indefinitely.

Under such a system, the government clearly has sufficient means to block public access to a classified document. Within the government itself, the problem is somewhat different. Since tens of thousands of officials are cleared to read classified documents, stamping a piece of paper Top Secret does not make it very secret, at least within the bureaucracy. In the State Department, for example, virtually all employees are cleared to read Top Secret material. And it was in the State Department that access controls, the third major component of the classification grid, originated in 1964. Since that date incoming cables and other documents considered especially sensitive have been marked in a way that automatically limits their distribution to a set number of people. This system, and its terms, NODIS, EXDIS and LIMDIS, were created by Benjamin H. Read, executive secretary of the State Department in the Johnson administration.

Under Nixon, the system was run by Theodore L. Eliot, Jr., a tall, affable Harvard man and career foreign service officer who succeeded Read as executive secretary. Eliot, dark-haired and partial to bow ties, wielded considerable power within the department, although he was virtually unknown outside of it. As the top staff assistant to Secretary of State William P. Rogers, it was Eliot who controlled the distribution lists.

The access controls worked this way: On the fifth-floor Communications Center at State, a battery of analysts sit in front of a console on which there are fifteen television screens. Decoded cables from U.S. missions overseas are continuously flashed on the screens at high speed. The analysts watch for symbols indicating which officials will receive the cables. When an analyst finishes scanning a cable, he punches the indicated distribution data into a machine. The message is then reproduced and as many copies as necessary are distributed by pneumatic tube. When the analyst sees the slug NODIS, however, he does not handle it in the usual manner; instead, the cable is relayed by teletype directly to Eliot's office two floors above. NODIS means No Distribution, except to the Secretary of State, and anything so marked remains in Eliot's custody, in Room 7224, under a yellow cover sheet. There are times when even the CIA director must personally come to the State Department to read a NODIS. For example, Richard Helms sometimes did so. Normally, however, copies are shown to six to eight top officials, and sometimes to more.

When a message marked EXDIS flashes on the cathode ray tubes in the Comm Center, it is relayed directly to the department's Operations Center for distribution according to a list made up by Eliot. EXDIS stands for Exclusive Distribution; under green cover sheets, about twelve to sixteen copies are disseminated. A cable slugged LIMDIS, for Limited Distribution, has no cover sheet, and Eliot's senior watch officer decides who shall see it; often as many as forty or fifty copies are distributed.*

"The decision to label a series NODIS is made in Washington as a rule," an official familiar with the system explained. "It might be used for a sensitive negotiation. For example, when Nixon arranged to meet Pompidou in the Azores, all the cables about it were NODIS. The NODIS channel being the most discreet, that is what was used. In 1970, when we launched Lamson 719, the Laos incursion, we did not want a leak in advance. So it was also NODIS."

Before the formal system of access controls was created under President Johnson, ambassadors usually stamped a message Eyes Only if it was particularly sensitive.† When he served as ambassador in Saigon, Henry Cabot Lodge caused unintended hilarity back in Washington by marking his cables to the President: "Literally Eyes Only." As one official recalled, "Lodge was naïve to think that only the President would see it; a dozen people in the State Department and the White House would see it as well."

---

*In addition to the NODIS, EXDIS, and LIMDIS access controls, the State Department has eight code-named communications channels for cables and documents too sensitive for general distribution within the department; for example, ROGER CHANNEL is the slug for communications to or from the director of Intelligence and Research; SY CHANNEL goes to the head of State Department security, and DIRGEN CHANNEL to the director general of the Foreign Service.

†The Eyes Only stamp is still used by the United States Information Agency and the U.S. Arms Control and Disarmament Agency.

Jack Rosenthal, a Washington correspondent of *The New York Times* who served in the State Department during the Johnson administration, has noted that the yellow cover sheet on a NODIS document and the green cover on an EXDIS document are designed to help preserve secrecy, but often have the opposite effect. "Officials are swamped with papers," he said. "When somebody sees yellow or green, he figures it must be important, so he turns to that first and fishes it out of the pile. A system designed to limit distribution becomes a flag for attention."

In addition to the standard access controls, special projects are sometimes given code names. For example, during the Johnson administration one series of behind-the-scenes contacts aimed at ending the Vietnam war—centering on talks in London in 1967 between British Prime Minister Harold Wilson and Soviet Premier Alexei N. Kosygin—was given the secret code name SUNFLOWER. The contacts were part of a so-called "flower series" that included the previously mentioned MARIGOLD.* In 1968 the Paris peace talks on Vietnam were code-named HARVAN, an acronym that stood for Averell Harriman and Cyrus Vance, the U.S. negotiators. For each code-named project, there is a separate list of officials cleared to read the material.

In the Pentagon, where secrecy is a way of life, an official who wishes to assign a code name to an operation cannot use any designation that may strike his fancy. He must select one from something called JANAP 299, or its successor volumes, the official Pentagon book of code names.† As a Defense Department directive notes: "A code name shall always be classified."

When an operation is over, the Pentagon does not allow a code name simply to be thrown away. Unless the term has been compro-

---

*MARIGOLD was the code name given to secret peace negotiations involving Janusz Lewandowski, the Polish ambassador to the International Control Commission, and the Italian ambassador to Saigon. MAYFLOWER was the code name for a bombing halt ordered by President Johnson in May, 1965. Later, there was a switch to place names: ASPEN was the code name assigned to efforts by the Swedish government to settle the Vietnam war during the 1966–68 period; OHIO was the designation for similar peace contacts by the Norwegian ambassador to Peking, Ole Algard; PENNSYLVANIA was the code name for a peace channel activated in 1967 by Henry Kissinger and two French intermediaries, Herbert Marcovich and Raymond Aubrac.

†JANAP is not a classified word. It stands for Joint Army, Navy, Air Force Publication.

mised, or is suspected to have been compromised, it is, after two years, frugally returned to an "available inventory" of code names, where it can be used over again.* Presumably, however, used code names are not as popular as brand-new ones.

Priority slugs, the final component of the classification grid, control cable traffic but are closely related to secrecy, since high-priority messages are often classified. "CRITIC," said one official "could mean 'hardware moving toward you,' and is used only in dire emergencies."† In descending order, the other priorities are FLASH, IMMEDIATE, and PRIORITY. Routine messages have no priority stamp.

Aside from the classifications, access controls, and code names already discussed, there are various miscellaneous secrecy labels that

---

*The Defense Department is much more relaxed about "nicknames." Under the directive in effect in 1972, "nicknames may be assigned to actual real world events, projects, movement of forces" or other activities, whether classified or not, but the nickname itself must be unclassified. The directive warns, however: "Nicknames, improperly selected, can be counterproductive. A nickname must be chosen with sufficient care to insure that it does not:

(a) Express a degree of bellicosity inconsistent with traditional American ideals or current foreign policy;

(b) Convey connotations offensive to good taste or derogatory to a particular group, sect, or creed; or,

(c) Convey connotations offensive to our allies or other Free World Nations."

The directive also forbids the use of combinations that include the words "project," "exercise," or "operation," and it bans the use of "exotic words, trite expressions, or well-known commercial trademarks."

†In the nuclear age, the CRITIC stamp on a cable is a potentially scary business; it may mean anything from a false alarm to imminent war. During the Johnson administration an urgent secret cable reached Washington from the Far East at three o'clock one morning. Its approximate wording: "Large force of Chinese planes heading for main fleet units; have ordered full alert." The ominous message galvanized into action the sleepy duty officer at the State Department; President Johnson was alerted at the LBJ ranch in Texas, and McNamara and Rusk were immediately awakened at their homes. By the time top officials reached the Pentagon and the State Department, it was discovered that the alarm had resulted from a Chinese test message picked up by NSA. "It was the sort of cable that sent your adrenal zooming," one official recalled. "It turned out that the Chicoms were testing their own communications and radar, and we thought it was real." The incident went unpublicized.

crop up from time to time. For example, some national security agencies stamp certain documents NOFORN, which is short of "Special Handling Required, Not Releasable to Foreign Nationals." "As a practical matter," said an official familiar with the term, "NOFORN means it can't go to the British, Canadians, or Australians—since those are the only foreign governments shown anything by the United States anyway."

The multi-volume Pentagon Papers were classified Top Secret-Sensitive, a designation nowhere provided for in the President's Executive Order. In testimony before the House government information subcommittee in June, 1971, Pentagon witnesses tied themselves up in knots trying to explain how this could happen. Congressman William S. Moorhead, a Democrat from Pittsburgh who succeeded Moss as chairman of the House panel, and Congressman Ogden R. Reid of New York were questioning Pentagon official David O. Cooke and George MacClain, the Defense Department's top classifier:

MR. MOORHEAD: What are the categories of classification used by the Defense Department?

MR. COOKE: . . . Mr. Chairman, there are only three categories of classification: Top Secret, Secret and Confidential.

MR. MOORHEAD: But you do use the category Top Secret-Sensitive, do you not?

MR. COOKE: I would like to turn to Mr. MacClain on that . . .

MR. REID: Would the chairman yield on that point? Am I not correct that anything that has "sensitive" triggers certain degrees of access or nonaccess, and, therefore, becomes an extra legal classification which is expressly forbidden by the Executive Order? . . .

MR. MacCLAIN: Mr. Chairman, I should like to comment very briefly on that. The word "sensitive," which is used in various situations, has no published meanings that I am aware of . . . The word . . . would have only such meaning as the person applying it would intend . . . I do not know of any particular authority to use it.

MR. COOKE: . . . I think the use of the term "sensitive" which was not drawn up in our regulations . . . was merely to highlight or make sure that whoever you are giving this information to really has a need to know it. It is not a definite classification . . .

Definite or not, it is used, just as the State Department often stamps documents Limited Official Use, another phrase not to be found in the Presidential order. Still other classifications are ATO-

MAL, a NATO secrecy stamp indicating that the document contains U.S. atomic information, and COSMIC, the NATO designation for Top Secret material. Documents that relate to the strategic plan of the Joint Chiefs of Staff, the plan that would be used in the event of a nuclear war, are stamped SIOP (Single Integrated Operational Plan) and some Atomic Energy Commission papers are marked Restricted Data or Formerly Restricted Data. The secrecy designation CRYPTO is used by, of all places, the Department of Transportation.*

Paradoxically, despite all these layers of classification, if a President *really* wants to do something secretly he must take special, extraordinary precautions to prevent leaks within his own bureaucracy. In July, 1963, President Kennedy was anxious that there be no leak from the negotiations with the Soviet Union over a nuclear test ban treaty. Before sending Averell Harriman to Moscow, Kennedy asked him to set up an ironclad secrecy system. Only five officials in Washington besides the President were to be shown the cables from Moscow: McGeorge Bundy, Dean Rusk, Robert McNamara, Under Secretary of State George Ball, and William C. Foster, director of the Arms Control and Disarmament Agency. In the end, the list included John A. McCone, director of the CIA. But Kennedy resisted any broader dissemination within either the Defense Department or the CIA. As one official recalled Kennedy's view, "he felt that once it was in the Pentagon, once it was in the Agency, it was gone."†

Carl Kaysen, a senior deputy to Bundy on the staff of the National Security Council, supervised the creation of the special secrecy channel that Kennedy had demanded. The cables were given the code name BAN. Whenever a message from Moscow bearing the secret slug arrived in Washington, it was quickly pulled out of the normal system. "For the first few days, only two copies were made," the official recounted, "one for the President, which was delivered

---

*The term CRYPTO is used by the Coast Guard, which is part of the Department of Transportation, to mark code and cryptographic material. The label is also used by the State Department for the same purpose. In 1972 there were no less than sixty-three miscellaneous secrecy labels used by the government, in addition to the standard Top Secret, Secret, and Confidential labels and the various secret ingelligence classifications.

†Officials in Washington almost never refer to the Central Intelligence Agency by name, or as "CIA." The usual euphemism is "the Agency," or, sometimes, "the people out in the woods." Some employees refer to CIA as "the Pickle Factory." CIA director Richard Helms privately referred to his agents as "the fellas."

by hand to Bundy, and one to be shown to Rusk, Ball, and Foster. After a day or two we made a third copy for McNamara." There were no leaks from the BAN channel during the ten days of negotiations, and on July 25, 1963, the test ban treaty was initialed in Moscow by the United States, Britain, and the Soviet Union. Strict secrecy was preserved, but only because Kennedy ignored the official system of classification and reached outside to set up his *own* system.

Nicholas deB. Katzenbach, who served as Under Secretary of State for President Johnson, maintains that in normal circumstances, the government is simply unable to restrict secrets to a tight circle of officials. "I always thought the whole business was kind of silly," he said. "The classifications didn't mean anything. NODIS went to ten people. You can't run the government that securely. The tightest thing we had, the negotiations leading up to the Paris peace talks in 1968, had a flower code name. I never dared to tell the President how many people knew. He had said that under no circumstances could it go over ten people. In fact, over fifty people knew. At State, along with Rusk, me and our assistants, there were three people in the Secretariat, Bill Bundy, *his* assistants, another ten people in the Agency, ten more at DOD [the Department of Defense], and so on."*

Katzenbach himself figured in a classification misadventure that led to an angry confrontation between President Johnson and Robert F. Kennedy. On a trip to Europe early in 1967, Kennedy called at the French Foreign Ministry. There an official relayed a message that he claimed came from Mai Van Bo, Hanoi's representative in Paris. In essence, the message was that peace talks could begin if the United States stopped the bombing of North Vietnam. John Gunther Dean, an official of the American embassy in Paris, who was with Kennedy at the meeting, immediately cabled a report to Washington.

Kennedy returned to the United States on Saturday, February 4. The next day *Newsweek* magazine carried a story saying that Kennedy had received one of two recent "peace signals" from North Vietnam. Within minutes of the time *Newsweek* reached the White House, an irritated Lyndon Johnson was on the phone to Katzenbach. "What is this?" Johnson demanded. "Why didn't I know about this?"

---

*In addition, of course, numerous code clerks, teletype operators, and communications personnel also handle classified cables. And technicians at this level, because of their access to almost unlimited amounts of secret information, are often the target of espionage and intelligence operations among the major powers.

Katzenbach, recalling the telephone conversation, said he assured the President that "I didn't know anything about it. He asked me to see Bobby." Johnson, of course, had immediately assumed that Kennedy had given the story to *Newsweek* to embarrass him.

The President's phone call put Katzenbach in an awkward position, since he was a friend of Robert Kennedy, and had served under him in the Justice Department, but was now working for Johnson. To guard against just such a leak, Katzenbach had asked that all cables from U.S. embassies abroad relating to the Kennedy visit be given a special slug and distributed only to the State Department bureau responsible for Vietnam and the Far East. On Monday, Katzenbach instructed his assistant, Jack Rosenthal, to start searching the cables under the special Kennedy slug to see whether anything matched the *Newsweek* story.

Then he telephoned Robert Kennedy and arranged to have lunch in Kennedy's Senate office. "He said he was not responsible for the leak," Katzenbach recalled. Kennedy also noted that John Dean had considered the French message significant and had undoubtedly cabled Washington; very likely this cable was the source of the story.

While they lunched, Marvin Watson, the President's appointments secretary, called to summon both men to a 4 P.M. meeting at the White House. Only four persons were present, the President, Walt W. Rostow, his national security assistant, Kennedy, and Katzenbach.

Johnson was furious. "It was," said Katzenbach, "an unpleasant meeting. The President was confident that Bobby had leaked the story. Bobby, who had not done it, could not understand what he was being accused of. They were both bristling, really bristling."

When Kennedy suggested the leak might have come "from your State Department," Johnson retorted: "It's not my State Department. It's *your* State Department." The barb reflected the fact that not only Katzenbach, but dozens of other Kennedy men, still occupied key foreign policy positions under Johnson. The conversation in the Oval Office deteriorated into further nasty exchanges before it ended.

Meanwhile, back at the State Department, Rosenthal learned that the *Newsweek* story had been written by Edward Weintal, the magazine's diplomatic correspondent, who regularly covered the department. This suggested that a cable received in Washington was the source of the story, but Rosenthal could find nothing in the message file that remotely resembled the Weintal article.

Much later, leafing through routine cables, Rosenthal by pure chance found a long message from John Dean misaddressed to EUR (the Bureau of European Affairs), and stamped Secret. "It was an ordinary Secret cable," Rosenthal said, "swallowed up in thousands of cables that come in. There was no green EXDIS cover sheet, which there should have been, and the message did not bear the special Kennedy slug. It was routine Secret. But Secret doesn't mean anything. Instead of maybe twenty copies, which should have been the case, there were 550 copies, or whatever the number was. This meant two things: first, the people who should have seen the cable never did and, second, a lot of people who should *not* have seen it did see it. It then became clear the story had been leaked not in Paris but in Washington. Nick [Katzenbach] had reported to Johnson that we could find no leak in Washington—that was before I found the cable—and Nick's call must have confirmed LBJ's suspicion that Bobby had done it." *

According to a former aide to Robert Kennedy, the unhappy episode "ended in a complete rupture; it was the final break between Bobby and LBJ. If there had been any chance for reconciliation between the two men, there was certainly no chance after that."

Classifying documents, in a sense, is only the beginning of the secrecy process. Once classified, there are elaborate rules and regulations for their physical protection. Top Secret material must, by regulation, be stored in safes or steel file cabinets that have "a three-way dial combination lock." Combinations must be changed "at least once every year." And records of lock combinations must be classified as high as the material protected by the lock.† "Top Secret Control Officers" are designated in each department and agency that handle such material. Classified documents must be transmitted in double "opaque" envelopes; the inner envelope is marked with the

---

*Weintal confirmed that he got the story in Washington. "I just picked it up at State," he said. "I went round to several people and said, 'What's new on peace feelers?' One of them said 'Bobby Kennedy's got something,' and with this information I went around and found out more. Johnson thought Kennedy leaked it to torpedo Johnson's own peace initiative; Johnson at that time had written a letter to Ho Chi Minh."

†The combinations are written down in only one place, on a Safe Card, which must be kept under secure conditions. For officials using the locks, "Combination numbers must be committed to memory. When closing a combination lock, the dial must be turned at least four complete revolutions in the same direction after closing. It is not sufficient to manipulate the dial in a to-and-fro motion to clear the combination."

secrecy stamp but the sealed outer envelope must bear no indication that it contains a classified document.

Top Secret documents may be transmitted only by courier or in code; a document classified Secret may be sent by registered mail provided it "does not pass through a foreign postal system." Documents stamped Confidential can be sent by certified or ordinary first-class mail. Shorthand notes, carbon paper, and rough drafts used in preparing classified documents must be burned, or destroyed in some other approved manner.

In addition to the Presidential order, the State Department, Pentagon, CIA, and NSA have their own elaborate rules on classification and secrecy. Some of these regulations go into the most astonishing minutiae. For example, one Pentagon directive declares: "A document shall be considered to be permanently bound when the pages cannot be removed without damage or mutilation. It must be sewed, and have the glued binding common to the bookbinding craft."

Not only documents, but all sorts of other objects can be classified. Since typewriter ribbons, particularly carbon ribbons, can be read, the Pentagon directive specifies that "typewriter ribbons, carbons, etc., developed in connection with . . . classified information shall be classified . . ." Indeed the Defense Department's official definition of the word "document" includes "any recorded information regardless of its physical form," including "data processing cards and tapes; maps; charts; photographs, negatives; moving or still films; film strips; paintings; drawings; engravings; sketches; reproductions of such things by any means or process; and sound, voice, or electronic recordings in any form."

There are presumably limits to what can be classified, but the limits are by no means clear, and official opinion differs on the question. "You cannot lock up a man's mind," former Supreme Court Justice Arthur J. Goldberg has declared. "You cannot classify my mind." Then again, Robert E. Stein, a young Washington attorney, recalls awakening one morning when he was an official of the Arms Control and Disarmament Agency.

"I had an interesting dream last night," he told his wife, Jane.

"What was it, dear?"

"I can't tell you—it had classified information in it."

Although it may not be possible to classify a dream, the CIA does maintain its own psychiatrists to listen to the troubles of its spies and intelligence officials, lest any secrets fall into the wrong hands. Certain private psychiatrists are also specially cleared to take CIA patients. At CIA headquarters in Langley, there is even a "classified" dining room, restricted to the most covert operatives. "Even people with TS clearance from other agencies aren't allowed in," said one former intelligence agent. "They might recognize someone."

Classified documents and objects cannot be discarded casually; the current Defense Department directive on classification includes this paragraph, which sounds as though it were written by Ian Fleming:

"Methods of Destruction. Classified material shall be destroyed in the presence of an appropriate official by burning, melting, or chemical decomposition, pulping, pulverizing, shredding, or mutilation sufficient to preclude recognition or reconstruction of the classified information . . ."

The directive adds: "Classified information recorded magnetically on a disc or drum may be considered as having been destroyed if completely overwritten at least three times with streams of random characters, using saturating current."

Every State Department office has a Burn Bag, which looks like an ordinary brown paper bag, the kind people use to bring groceries home from the supermarket, except that printed on it are the words BURN in large black capital letters, PAPER ONLY and CLASSIFIED WASTE. During the night security agents move through the building checking offices and desks, and the official who forgets to place classified papers in the Burn Bag, or lock them up, will find a pink slip on his desk: Notice of Security Violation. One former official recalls that he received such a notice one morning after having left out on his desk overnight an utterly innocuous letter from the Treasury Department. He was required to go to the State Department office of security and fill out elaborate forms. When he asked for an explanation of his sins, he was shown that he had failed to notice the typewritten words "For Official Use Only" on the bottom of the letter. The fact that this is not an official security classification under the President's order did not seem to matter.

"It got so that you kept nothing in your desk except Oreo cookies and blank paper," the official said. "You would lock everything up at night. You're supposed to have two wastebaskets, a classified and an unclassified wastebasket. After a while, to be safe, I put everything in the classified wastebasket, including orange peels. That's an abuse of the rules, because you aren't supposed to overload the classified system, but if there is a choice between doing that and having more security violations—for me, I chose to put in the orange peels."

Scattered throughout the building are chutes for the Burn Bags. The chutes lead to Room B527, in the State Department basement, where the bags fall out onto a metal grill. Carbon ribbons are retrieved, to be burned elsewhere. An attendant shoves the bags off a platform and they drop below him into a huge gray vat, twelve feet high and six feet in circumference. The vat is the centerpiece of a machine called a Somat Macerator, and it would not be advisable to fall in. Inside the vat, powerful jets of water press the documents against cutting blades; the shredded, wet paper is pumped into a smaller chamber, then dried and blown out through a pipe into a huge bin in an adjoining room, where it emerges as a heap of soft gray dust. "The paper," a security official explained in a satisfied voice, "cannot be reconstructed."

Twice a week the pulverized secret documents are hauled away by truck. "The General Services Administration tries to sell the stuff to paper companies," the official said. "But clips and staples get in with the paper, and some companies won't use it. So it can't always be sold. What GSA can't sell is used as land fill." Presumably, therefore, some government buildings are constructed on a foundation of classified land fill.

The Somat blades are kept whirring eight hours a day. In 1972 the security office began experimenting with another machine in the basement room, known, ominously, as "a Disintegrator." The machine has a yawning orange funnel into which the documents are fed, there to be chopped up and mashed in a dry pulp process.

Communications security is even stricter than the protection of documents and papers. The bulk of the diplomatic cables that flow between Washington and U.S. posts abroad are transmitted on the State Department's own radio-teletype network. "We assume that all transmissions are monitored," one official said, "so most cables are encrypted to protect them." Although not all information is sent in code the bulk of the traffic is protected by "on-line encryption." Under this system, automatic coding devices are cut into the line, messages are encrypted and then automatically decoded on the other end. "It's easier to encrypt almost everything than to decide whether each cable should be coded," the official explained.

In the State Department, every major bureau must name a COMSEC, or Communications Security officer, and the regulations are precise: "The appointment is to be documented on Form DS-1657, Cryptocustodian and Alternate Cryptocustodian." Special Cryptographic Clearances are required for access to information about codes, and the protection of codes is controlled by the super-secret United States Communications Security Board (USCSB), a virtually unknown government agency that is nowhere listed in the *United States Government Organization Manual.*

Some of what goes on in the field of codes and communications is fairly spooky; for example, for some time now, U.S. security technicians have known that the American embassy in Moscow is the object of a steady electronic beam. But they have been unable to figure out the purpose: whether it is designed to pick up conversations inside the embassy or has some other use. "We don't know why it's there," one security official admitted, "whether it affects the digestion, or what. Who knows? Maybe it's supposed to make our diplomats sterile." There is always the possibility, of course, that the electronic beam has no purpose at all other than to worry U.S. officials.

It was Soviet Premier Nikita S. Khrushchev who succeeded in giving U.S. security its worst scare. The incident, unpublicized up to now, occurred early in 1964. The American ambassador to Moscow was Foy D. Kohler, a short, tough, chain-smoking career diplomat whose voice retained the flat accents of his native northern Ohio. At the time the Russians were engaged in a project of major strategic importance—the construction of a pipeline to Eastern Europe to supply their military forces there with gasoline and oil. The Soviets called it the Friendship Pipe Line.

Although no U.S. companies were supplying steel for the Soviet pipeline, a West German manufacturer was interested and so were several other firms in Western Europe. With Kohler taking an active role, NATO adopted a policy of denying the export of materials that the Russians needed to construct the pipeline.

Khrushchev would occasionally have a drink with Kohler and liked to cross verbal swords with the American ambassador. At a reception in Moscow, Kohler recalled: "Khrushchev jumped me. He said, 'You're the guy behind the embargo on steel piping.' The Russians were trying to import forty-inch-wide diameter steel piping. The question was—how had he fingered me? He talked as though he had some knowledge of embassy telegrams."

Khrushchev's pointed remark to Kohler led to a frantic intensive search for a security breach. "For God's sake," Kohler told his aides, "let's start looking." An American official who recalled the episode declared: "The security people were appalled. They launched a massive, fruitless hunt for the leak. They went over U.S. codes and cable security, they combed the embassy for bugs, and went into a tremendous flap that lasted a long, long while. Khrushchev must have known exactly what he was doing."

From the start Kohler tended to suspect a communications breach rather than KGB eavesdropping on conversations inside the embassy. Kohler believed the eavesdropping problem was under control, since sensitive conversations were supposed to take place in the "tank," a room-within-a-room inside the embassy. The tank rests on a platform raised above the floor, to make bugging more difficult. Curtains are drawn around it to muffle conversations, and a noise-making device emits the steady sound of whirring machinery to foil listeners. As a practical matter, however, officials canot repair to the tank for every important conversation, so the system is not foolproof. And Kohler was aware that in 1952, during Ambassador George Kennan's tenure, a tiny transmitter had been found inside a carved wooden replica of the Great Seal of the United States. The seal, presented by the Russians to Ambassador Harriman in 1945, was hanging over the fireplace in Kennan's study in Spaso House, his official residence, at the time the bug was uncovered during an electronic sweep of the room.*

The source of Khrushchev's information was never determined, however, despite the enormous effort. And there remained the possibility that Khrushchev's remark was a shot in the dark."†

Despite the special security surrounding communications and codes, there have been a number of embarrassing incidents. On May 1, 1965, seven kids slipped through a drainage pipe into an underground manhole in the tiny community of Rosedale, Maryland, and started a fire that knocked out the Hot Line between Washington and Moscow. The Hot Line, known by the code name MOLINK, is a teletype circuit that runs from the White House and the Pentagon to New York, to Nova Scotia, under the sea to England, and then to Copenhagen, Helsinki, Leningrad, and Moscow. The teen-age boys did not realize that it also ran through manhole Number 610, four miles east of Baltimore.‡

---

*The bug and the carved seal were displayed at the United Nations by Ambassador Henry Cabot Lodge on May 26, 1960, to counter Soviet indignation over the U-2 incident, which had occurred earlier that month. Harriman said the seal had been given to him by a Soviet officer in 1945, but he doubted the listening device was in it then. He noted that the bug was of a transistor type: "That's one of the reasons why I don't believe it was bugged at the time I had it. The Russians didn't have that sophisticated type of miniature equipment at that time."

†In March, 1964, some time after the Khrushchev-Kohler conversation, U.S. technicians discovered forty microphones embedded in the walls of the American embassy. Kohler said, however, that the discovery did not result from, and was unconnected with, the security search instituted at the time of Khrushchev's remark about the steel piping. The microphones were found on three upper floors of the ten-story structure of Tchaikovsky Street —including the ninth floor, where Kohler's office was located—and in apartments below. The security people assumed the mikes had been installed when the Soviet government remodeled the embassy for American occupancy in 1952.

‡In addition to cutting the Hot Line, the boys knocked out CBS-TV sound during the entire running of the Kentucky Derby. Millions of Americans

In a somewhat similar incident in February, 1966, Joe Washburn, a twenty-seven-year-old college student fiddling with his shortwave radio in Scottsdale, Arizona, somehow tuned in on Air Force One as the Presidential jet flew across the Pacific from Honolulu with President Johnson and other high officials aboard. Among the conversations he overheard—and taped—was one between General Maxwell D. Taylor and General William C. Westmoreland, then U.S. commander in Vietnam. ("Hello, Westy? Go ahead, Westy, I can hear you . . .") Washburn taped an official in the White House warning Air Force One that "McNamara is headed for real trouble" over Vietnam in the Senate; he also recorded the code name CROWN, the secret designation for the White House communications center.

Despite such occasional lapses, for the most part, the secrecy and classification system effectively prevents the public from gaining knowledge about information that the government wishes to conceal. Obviously this secrecy breeds public distrust. Less understood is that the system also breeds distrust inside the government. In the State Department, for example, some officials have been convinced for years that the military couriers who hand-carry classified documents from State to high-level civilian officials in the Pentagon are slipping Xerox copies to the Joint Chiefs of Staff. Repeatedly, these State Department officials have urged their Pentagon counterparts to use civilian messengers to handle the secret documents—to no avail. The Pentagon officials insist that they have complete trust in their military couriers.

Like the diplomat who puts his orange peels in the Burn Bag, many officials, at least outside of the Pentagon, find the secrecy system burdensome and faintly ludicrous. One former official who shares this general view is NBC's John Chancellor, who served for a time as director of the Voice of America.

After he was appointed by President Johnson, Chancellor realized, with some anticipation, that he was finally on the inside and in a position to look at some of the government secrets he had pursued for so long as a newsman. A few days after he moved into his new office, Chancellor turned to his assistant and commanded: "Let me see your box of secrets." The assistant laughed. "I mean it," said

---

were watching the race when the audio on their television sets suddenly went dead. The network immediately switched to the voice of Win Elliott, who was describing the race on CBS radio. Since Elliott had no TV monitor, the pictures seen by viewers did not always match what he was saying. The network was swamped with telephoned complaints. Lucky Debonair, with Willie Shoemaker up, won by a neck and paid $10.60.

Chancellor. "You must have a box of secrets around here somewhere. I want to see it.

"But," Chancellor recalls mournfully, "they never produced it." Chancellor conceded he had visions of poring over the box, tossing secrets in the air, and chortling to himself: "Here's a good one—Hey! . . . here's another . . . look at this one . . ."

The episode paled, however, by comparison with Chancellor's demand to see the button. In the nuclear age, politicians are forever talking about whose finger is on the button, and Chancellor assumed it must exist *somewhere*. He had become a good friend of George Stevens, Jr., director of motion pictures for the United States Information Agency, "and we decided we wanted to see the button. Stevens and I insisted that we see it. Well, it took three months to fight it through the bureaucracy. We had to cook up a phony reason to explain our interest. We decided that if there were a national disaster, George would have to film the button. And I would have to know where it was in order to be credible."

The two conspirators decided to push their campaign independently, on the theory that two people demanding to see the button were better than one. After months of refusals and delays, Chancellor finally received a cryptic telephone call telling him "it was 'laid on.' " Would he mind if a Mr. Stevens, who had also expressed interest in seeing the button, accompanied him? He would not.

"We were taken to a communications room in the bowels of the Pentagon," Chancellor said. "But it turned out to be an ordinary Gray Line, tourist version of a communications room. Right away we knew we were being jobbed." One of the SAC colonels conducting the briefing asked Chancellor: "Would you like to talk to a B-52 in Greenland, sir?"

"Sure," said Chancellor. He picked up the phone. "Hello, sir," he heard, "this is a B-52 over Greenland."

After a few minutes of this, Chancellor gave up and asked to call his office, which was located in the Department of Health, Education and Welfare, across the Potomac river in Washington about a mile distant. He couldn't get through. "It was very embarrassing," he said. "The three SAC colonels were dialing furiously on separate telephones. But it was no use. The Pentagon Communications Center could not make contact with HEW."

Needless to say, Chancellor never got to see the button. He was thwarted, one more victim of what New York University Law Professor Norman Dorsen has called a "medieval system of secrecy which has been erected by the executive branch." Since the Executive Branch makes all the rules of the classification system, it also feels free, as we shall see, to break them.

5

"The President Is Sort of Outside the Law"

Lafayette Square is a gracious island of green in the middle of Washington, directly across the street from the White House. The western edge of the park is formed by a narrow street called Jackson Place, on which there stands a row of beautifully restored Federal and late nineteenth-century houses. A visitor sitting in the park who let his gaze wander in that direction might, if he was particularly observant and if it was a sunny morning, notice something very odd about the house at Number 716.

In most respects the house, the fourth in from the corner of Pennsylvania Avenue, resembles the others in the row. It is four stories, light beige with dark-brown trim and Federal Revival in style. But at the right hour of the morning, the sun reflects blindingly off the windows of 716 as though they were mirrors.

This is because the windows of the house, but of no other house in the row, are in fact mirrors, although of a very special kind. To be precise, they are bulletproof two-way mirrors. People in the park, or passers-by on the sidewalk, cannot see into the house. Staring at a window, they are greeted only by their own reflections. From inside the house, however, one can see out perfectly well; from that side, the glass looks like ordinary windowpane.

On the first floor of the house at Number 716 are the offices of the Special Assistant to the President for Liaison with Former Presidents. The upper floors are designed as a residence for former Presidents who might be visiting Washington. The trick windows were installed to insure their privacy and safety.

President Nixon created the post of Special Assistant to the President for Liaison with Former Presidents through an Executive Order he issued on February 14, 1969, less than a month after his inauguration. Amid a panorama of grander events, his action received minimal publicity, and few persons, even in Washington, were aware that the office existed. To the new post Nixon named retired Army General Robert L. Schulz, who had served as an aide to General, and then President, Eisenhower for twenty-two years. Since the number of living ex-Presidents was small, and the amount of liaison they required seldom excessive, General Schulz's duties were not burdensome.

To the house at Number 716, however, there came a request late in 1969 from a former President that caused an unaccustomed flurry of activity in the normally placid first-floor offices, and indeed, before it was over, in several departments of the government.

The former President was Lyndon B. Johnson, who was then engaged in writing his memoirs.* The request: that the government declassify as many as possible of the thousands of secret documents in his possession. At the time most of these papers were in the federal building in Austin, Texas, in a vault which had been specially constructed to house the classified documents until the LBJ library could be completed.

Concerned over his place in history, anxious to justify his policies in Vietnam, and to make sure that Americans did not forget his notable achievements in domestic legislation, Johnson had begun planning both his book and the Presidential library long before he left the White House.

In the spring of 1968 Presidential assistant Joseph Califano, Jr., had sent a memo to all agencies of the government directing each to submit a "full written history" of the Johnson era, prepared under "close supervision by a senior official." These narratives were to be deposited in the LBJ library, but *The New York Times* noted they would also be "of the greatest use" to Johnson when he came to write his memoirs. When the White House order was disclosed in the press, Senator John J. Williams, the Delaware Republican, unkindly accused the President of seeking to produce "high-powered propaganda" at public expense and "a Texas version of American history."

Johnson also asked all of his cabinet and subcabinet officials to turn over all their papers to the LBJ library, then under construction

---

*The Vantage Point, Perspectives of the Presidency 1963–1969, published in November, 1971, by Holt, Rinehart and Winston. (With Johnson's death in January, 1973, there were no living former Presidents.)

in Austin on the campus of the University of Texas. Roosevelt, Eisenhower, and Truman had engaged in somewhat parallel efforts to pull together the record of their administrations, but Johnson's interest was personal and intense. On one occasion, aides recall, he used a cabinet meeting to urge members to turn in their papers; as far as anyone knew, no President before Johnson had made such a plea at a cabinet meeting. Some members complied; others, perhaps with their own memoirs in mind, held back part of their material.

While this was going on, during the summer of 1968, Johnson sought to sell his planned memoir to a publisher. Reportedly, he was asking for an advance of at least $1 million. The President got his friend Arthur B. Krim, president of United Artists, the movie company, and top fund raiser for the Democratic party, to approach publishers in New York.

With the help of an assistant, Sam Gelfman, who knew the literary scene, Krim contacted Doubleday, Harper, McGraw-Hill, Random House, and Holt, Rinehart and Winston, seeking the highest bidder. Krim was not unaware that Holt was now owned by CBS, which in turn was headed by Frank Stanton, a close personal friend of the President's. For this reason, Krim from the start considered Holt a logical market. And in the end, the book was published by Holt, although enthusiasm over the purchase was not universally shared by the company's senior editors. In publishing circles the advance was reported to be $1.5 million. Johnson assigned his income from the book to a tax-free foundation that supports the Lyndon B. Johnson School of Public Affairs, which is located next door to the LBJ library on the Austin campus.*

---

*The precise financial arrangements for the Johnson book have never been disclosed. Aaron Asher, vice-president and senior editor at Holt, declined to state the size of the advance. "Although there have been many published reports giving various figures, we have never issued a statement regarding the exact amount," he said in answer to an inquiry by the author.

According to records of the Internal Revenue Service, Johnson assigned his income from, and rights to, the book to the HEC Public Affairs Foundation in Austin, which holds the copyright. Holt's contract is with HEC, which grew out of a merger in April, 1969, with a predecessor foundation, the Lyndon B. Johnson Public Affairs Foundation, which had been incorporated in Washington, D.C., June 14, 1968. In applying for tax-exempt status, HEC said it expected to devote "a substantial part of its activities" to supporting and promoting the LBJ School of Public Affairs. In 1970 HEC's officers included Harry H. Ransom, chancellor of the University of Texas, and Frank

Holt also signed a separate contract with Lady Bird Johnson and published her book, *A White House Diary*, in 1970. In addition, CBS signed up Johnson to do a series of television interviews with Walter Cronkite after he left office. According to news reports, Johnson received $300,000 from CBS.*

By November, 1971, when Johnson's 636-page book was published, Daniel Ellsberg was under indictment for unauthorized possession of the Pentagon Papers. A federal grand jury in Boston was questioning witnesses about Neil Sheehan, *The New York Times* reporter who obtained the Pentagon Papers and wrote the articles based upon them. The government had sought to suppress the articles, and did for a time, but was overruled by the Supreme Court of the United States. Yet Johnson's book, priced at $15 a copy, contained numerous quotes from many of the same classified documents contained in the Pentagon Papers.†

One might jump to the erroneous conclusion that Johnson included classified material in his book only *after,* and because of, the release of the Pentagon Papers in the news media, an event that eliminated the need for further secrecy. But this was not the case. Johnson had completed his book before the Pentagon Papers burst upon the world, and he had quoted classified documents.

When *The New York Times* series began, a number of skeptics in Washington and elsewhere assumed that Johnson would rewrite portions of his book, then awaiting publication, to conform to the disclosures. But Johnson did not change a line; indeed, he would have found it most awkward to do so, even if that had been his intention. The reason was as follows:

C. Erwin, Jr., chairman of the Board of Regents. At the end of 1970 the foundation listed assets of more than $3 million.

*One White House official told me in October, 1968, while Johnson was considering his television interviews: "I know he is curious about what CBS paid Ike for those walks around the farm." Shortly afterward a second White House assistant, unaware of my conversation with the first, asked me casually: "Say, what do you suppose Ike got paid by CBS?" During the 1964 campaign Johnson listed his net worth at $3.4 million. *Life* magazine put the family's assets at $14 million.

†To take just a few random examples, on page 45 of his book Johnson quoted from NSAM 273 issued November 26, 1963, reaffirming U.S. policies in Vietnam. On page 126 he quoted a long report he received from McGeorge Bundy after Pleiku. On page 369 he quoted from a May 19, 1967, memo from McNamara on Vietnam. All of these documents also appear in the Pentagon Papers.

On June 8, 1971, Aaron Asher, chief editor at Holt, had sent letters to newspaper and magazine editors and syndicate representatives inviting them to read the galleys of the Johnson book and to make bids on the serialization rights. In order to preserve the security of the manuscript, the editors were required to come to New York and read the proofs at Holt by appointment. On Sunday, June 13, the first article in the *Times* series on the Pentagon Papers was published. Asher's invitations were already out, editors were arriving in New York, and the next day, June 14, the first readers arrived at Holt to look at the Johnson galleys. For two weeks thereafter, there were news editors at Holt every day reading the galleys. And these editors noted, of course, that Johnson's book quoted from some of the same documents that had appeared in the Pentagon Papers.

Johnson used classified material in a book that sold for a reported $1.5 million. Daniel Ellsberg had used the same classified material and faced prison. The contrast raised obvious questions; and the issue of the use of such documents in a Presidential memoir was discussed in the lead review of *The Vantage Point* that appeared in *The New York Times Book Review* of October 31, 1971.

A few days after publication of this review, a former White House assistant to Johnson wrote to me, saying that LBJ went through an "elaborate State Department drill" to get the material used in his book declassified, something which he claimed the *Times* reviewer could have verified.

As there had been no public mention of such an effort by Johnson, I sought to check this information with a high State Department official. The official, who much preferred not to be identified, confirmed that Johnson had indeed tried to get papers declassified, but had been turned down.

"We really didn't want him to use certain papers," the official said, "and we sent down a special team to Texas to look at certain files he wanted to use, to see if they could be declassified. The people on those teams had to be pretty strong-minded. We told him no." The former President's request, he added, had been forwarded to the State Department by General Schulz; further information should really come from the house on Jackson Place.

Government officials are instinctively cautious about discussing anything that relates to a President, or even, it quickly became apparent, a former President. General Schulz was no exception, but in a telephone interview he reluctantly confirmed the story. "All I did," Schulz said, "was at the request of the President, former President Johnson—he wanted to use certain material out of certain files. He suggested one subject to use as a test case."

From various sources, the details slowly emerged. After Johnson's request was received by General Schulz in the fall of 1969, a panel of five officials from the State Department, the CIA, and the Pentagon had been formed; the team flew to Austin early in January, 1970. The team was headed by William M. Franklin, the State Department's official historian, and Rudolph A. Winnacker, director of the historical staff of the Pentagon. In Texas, the group met with Walt W. Rostow and William J. Jorden; both had served Johnson in the White House and were now helping him write *The Vantage Point.*

Since the team could not possibly plow through all of the former President's classified papers, Johnson and his staff selected "Dominican Republic, 1965–1966" as the test subject. "If it worked there," said one official familiar with the team's assignment, "perhaps LBJ thought it could be done elsewhere." For three weeks the team pored over the Dominican papers and met with Johnson's assistants. In the end, the team concluded that none of the classified documents about the Dominican intervention, and therefore none of Johnson's other papers, could yet be declassified. "The team presented its findings to the President," General Schulz declared, "and he made the final decision; he may have decided to paraphrase certain material."

Up to that point, the story seemed clear-cut; Johnson sought to declassify certain material for use in *The Vantage Point,* and the government said no. After my inquiries, however, the official version of what had happened began to shift subtly. "At the time former President Johnson was preparing materials for his memoirs," General Schulz wrote to me officially in February, 1972, "the question arose as to whether information contained in classified documents in his files could be declassified and released *to the public.*" [Emphasis added.]

There was, of course, a difference between a request by the President to declassify material for his personal use in a memoir, and a request that the documents be declassified for the public. The former might be expected to result in some public outcry; the latter could only bring public approval. The difference might not be as great, however, as it would initially appear, since the first member of the public to benefit from any declassification would presumably have been Lyndon B. Johnson; as a practical matter, one can be certain that the declassified documents would have been published first in *The Vantage Point,* and made available "to the public" only thereafter, at some unspecified later date.* To assume otherwise, one

---

*From this point onward—that is, after General Schulz had sent his letter to me—all of the officials interviewed on the subject unanimously agreed

must be prepared to believe that Johnson wished to scoop himself, which might have seriously impaired the sale of valuable prepublication serialization rights for his book, a degree of altruism that hardly fit LBJ's reputation for business acumen.*

Although the government team declined his request, Johnson made liberal use of classified documents in his book.† In using such material, Johnson followed the custom of other recent Presidents. Truman and Eisenhower both quoted from classified documents in their memoirs. Since this precedent existed, one might ask why Johnson had bothered to seek official declassification of his papers. One explanation is that official approval, had it been obtained, would have headed off any potential criticism directed at Johnson for using classified material in his memoirs. One of Johnson's most powerful White House assistants, once considerably involved in the LBJ library project, said he himself had not heard about any Johnson attempt to get papers declassified for his book, but he added: "LBJ is too smart not to have tried."

Regardless of what Johnson was up to in hauling the declassification experts down to Austin in 1970—and Johnson's motives for anything were seldom uncomplicated—his subsequent use of classified documents in his book once again focused attention on the anomaly of a classification system that can be freely violated by its creator.

---

that Johnson had not asked that papers be declassified for his own use, but for the public weal. In preparing his official reply, Schulz had consulted with Winnacker and others; at least two of the officials whom I interviewed had copies of Schulz's letter to me on their desks.

*The Johnson papers are housed at the Lyndon B. Johnson Library at Austin, which, like all Presidential libraries, is part of the National Archives and Records Service of the federal government. Had the special team declassified any of LBJ's papers, the documents would, in time, have been available at the library. Johnson's book was published in November of 1971. Although the LBJ library was dedicated in May, 1971, it was not until January 25, 1972, that the first papers were made available to scholars and to the public, and those dealt not with national security but with education. So, in actual fact, if any papers *had* been declassified as a result of Johnson's request, the public would not have had access to them until long after the publication of *The Vantage Point.*

†Officials interviewed on the subject said Johnson made no other request for declassification of documents after receiving the negative results of the 1970 survey. Nor did he submit the manuscript of his book to the government for security clearance; but, the officials said, no other President has done so, either.

Even if it were desirable to prevent the use of classified information in memoirs, it would be extremely difficult to devise any system that could be enforced, particularly against a former President. The government moved against *The New York Times*, but it seems scarcely likely that the Justice Department would have sought to enjoin Lyndon Johnson, even if his book had been published before, instead of after, the Pentagon Papers.

Since the classification system is purportedly designed to protect important secrets affecting the national security, do ex-Presidents have a legal right to use classified documents in memoirs sold to the public? The answer is by no means clear. One may argue that since the entire classification system is based upon a Presidential order, a President has the power to "declassify" whatever he wishes. This is probably correct. But no Presidential power follows the Chief Executive out of office; once a President has left the White House, it must be assumed he has no more power to declassify a document than any other citizen.

Accordingly, to have quoted legally from secret papers in their memoirs, Truman, Eisenhower, and Johnson would, in theory at least, have had to declassify the quoted material before leaving office. But there is no evidence that this was the case, and it would be difficult for a President to know in advance just what he wished to quote after he left the White House. He might, therefore, have to resort to blanket declassification of all his papers. This, in turn, conjures up the highly improbable scene of an outgoing President waving his hand over a sea of file cabinets on his last day in office, and pronouncing: "I hereby declassify you." Of course, if he did so, and this fact became known, the awkward possibility would arise that some troublemaking historian or newsman would thereupon demand to see the declassified papers.

In fact, no such declassification ceremonies take place; Presidents generally regard their papers as belonging to them. And at least this tradition is older than the custom of Presidents' quoting from classified documents in their memoirs.

"The President takes all of his documents out of the White House when he leaves," William Franklin, the State Department historian, noted. "That's been tradition since George Washington. FDR was the first President to give them back to the government."

Harry Truman, Franklin said during an interview in 1971, had papers in his office at Independence "that he hasn't let people in to *yet*." The State Department, which prepares and publishes a series of volumes entitled *Foreign Relations of the United States*—the official foreign policy record of the government—was clearly rather exasperated with Truman, "who doesn't want to be bothered, and keeps telling us we are going to get his papers when he is dead.*

"Presidents make their own rules," Franklin added. "The President is sort of outside the law."

This was vividly demonstrated on February 6, 1970, when Walter Cronkite interviewed former President Johnson on CBS-TV, in the second of three interviews for which Johnson had contracted. At one point Cronkite started to ask about Defense Secretary Clark Clifford's role in dealing with a request that the administration send 206,000 more troops to Vietnam in 1968. Johnson interrupted him. The former President held up a document in view of the television audience, flipped through it, and said: ". . . that's totally inaccurate. Now, if you would like to, Walter, if I may have the directions, I'll declassify them now for a moment and show you just how much in error such an assumption can be, regardless of who makes the error . . . if you'll indulge me . . . I can read you a portion of it. The Directive was written on February 28: the *Memorandum to Secretary of State and Secretary of Defense.* '. . . as I indicated at breakfast this morning, I wish you would develop by Monday morning, March 4, recommendations in response to the situation presented to us by General Wheeler and his preliminary proposal. I wish alternatives examined.' " Here was a former President of the United States announcing that he was declassifying a secret document—before the eyes of millions of American television viewers. Yet no one seemed to think it was unusual.

What the viewers could not see on their television screens, moreover, was that Johnson had access to scores of other classified documents as he spoke to Cronkite. During the interview Walt Rostow and Tom Johnson, a bright young former newsman from Macon, Georgia, who had served the President in the White House as assistant press secretary, sat just out of camera range with armloads of files. As Cronkite would turn to a new subject in the interview, Rostow and Tom Johnson would pull out the relevant documents and hand them to the former President.

Although Johnson thus felt free to use classified documents for his own purposes both in his memoirs and on television, he nevertheless reserved the right to edit the CBS interviews for "national security" reasons. All three interviews were filmed at the LBJ ranch in Texas in September and October, 1969. After each filming Johnson was handed an audio tape cassette of the interview; he then had twenty-four to forty-eight hours to make any deletions for security.

When the third Johnson interview was shown on May 2, 1970,

---

*Franklin was interviewed almost a year to the day before Truman's death.

it included this message about thirty seconds into the program: "Certain material has been deleted from this broadcast at President Johnson's request, made on the ground of national security." During the filming of the interview Johnson had expressed some misgivings about the Warren Commission's central finding that Lee Harvey Oswald, acting alone, had killed President Kennedy. Johnson indicated to Cronkite that he still retained some doubts and that, possibly, a conspiracy had been involved.

Later Johnson apparently thought the better of these remarks, but he did not ask to delete them until several weeks had gone by. Cronkite, backed by Richard S. Salant, president of CBS News, opposed the deletion, arguing that the request had come too late. But they were overruled, possibly by CBS president Frank Stanton.

Cronkite, a newsman of great integrity and high professional standards, had been unhappy from the start with Johnson's right to edit the tapes. In this case he felt that Johnson was misusing his right to make deletions, since it was difficult to see how, six years after the assassination, any "national security" was involved.

As the CBS interviews suggested, Presidents or former Presidents can freely ignore the secrecy label when it suits their purposes, or invoke it to suppress embarrassing information. The system exists not so much to protect national security as to provide a flexible tool of power for political leaders.

Although Presidents have the widest latitude in using classified documents in their memoirs—and enjoy the greatest immunity from prosecution or public censure—scores of other White House assistants and government officials have followed the same practice. Many officials are well aware of the immense potential market value of information to which they gain access through their government positions. Often they leave office with voluminous files, Xerox copies of official documents, notes and diaries. And they have seldom hesitated to quote from classified materials or to reveal secret information. In his account of the Kennedy administration, for example, Arthur M. Schlesinger, Jr., who served as an assistant to the President, summarizes and quotes from the conversation between Kennedy and Khrushchev at their summit meeting in Vienna in June, 1961. The record of that conversation is, of course, still highly classified. Robert Kennedy's memoir of the Cuban missile crisis, *Thirteen Days*, published posthumously, contains portions of a still-secret letter sent by Khrushchev to Kennedy at the height of the nuclear confrontation. In *First Hand Report*, Eisenhower's principal assistant, Sherman Adams, used lengthy, verbatim quotes from a high-level meeting held in November, 1956, during the Suez crisis. President Johnson's press secretary, George Christian, in his book *The President Steps Down,* gives details of still-secret 1968 Vietnam peace negotiations in Paris. Numerous other examples could be cited.

Obviously, former Presidents and other officials who leave the government are profiting from the sale of classified information. This same classified information, however, is not contemporaneously shared with the press and public.

To put it simply, the classification system has been used to deprive the American people of vital information, which is then later sold to them by political leaders whom they elected, or by appointees of those elected leaders. But the same information is denied to Americans when it is current, when it might be pertinent to the opinions they hold and the manner in which they express those opinions at the ballot box.

The practice, therefore, is more serious than the sale of government secrets in book form. It means that information has been denied to the public on national security grounds, information that apparently need not have been kept secret, since it is later published by the very officials who withheld it. The argument sometimes offered, that the passage of time has removed the need for secrecy, is not entirely convincing, since the information remains undisclosed up until the very moment it is published in a memoir.

Although officials who leave the government sometimes walk off with classified documents and other papers, they frequently circumvent the rules by claiming that they have removed only their personal notes and diaries. Suppose a Presidential assistant takes notes at an NSC meeting; the official summary of the meeting may be classified Top Secret, but the assistant regards his own notes as personal property.

That raises an interesting question; some legal theorists argue that it is the information that is classified, not the document. Under this theory the official's personal notes would be considered classified material. But this concept breaks down under closer examination; what, then, of the official's *memory* of the meeting? Is that classified too? The purpose of the classification system, it is true, is to protect "information," but as a practical matter, information that is not recorded in physical form cannot be "classified." G. Marvin Gentile, a tall, gray-haired former FBI and CIA man who heads State Department security, believes in the principle that classified information in any form should be protected, "but of course, a document is the only thing you can mark and control."

It is difficult, if not impossible, to prevent officials from making notes. It is equally difficult to determine to what extent the notes reflect information contained elsewhere in classified documents.

During the Kennedy years Roger Hilsman, director of State Department intelligence, assembled what he termed "my Top Secret personal file. I had a small battery-operated tape recorder," Hilsman recalled, "and at the end of the day I would clip the microphone to my tie as I was driven home." In the car Hilsman would "debrief" himself on the days events. "My secretary would type it up the next day and that went into the file." After he left the government Hilsman published *To Move a Nation,* a combination memoir and analysis of foreign policy decision-making. In writing the book, Hilsman was able to draw upon his daily tape-recorded memory bank.

Of course, memoirs by Presidents and other former officials serve history. They help to inform the public, however belatedly and however self-serving. But the public should also understand that officials do profit from the sale of material to which they had access while in the government.* Wider public understanding of this truth might help to cut through some of the hypocrisy surrounding the classification system, and restore a sense of balance to the whole issue of national security and government secrecy.

Some efforts have been made within the government to discourage memoir writers from making off with everything but the kitchen sink when they leave, but these measures have proved largely ineffectual. Theoretically, government officials are not supposed to take classified material or other papers from their offices without official permission.† But at the State Department and the Pentagon, the two major departments handling classified documents, guards do not check briefcases and packages carried by officials leaving the building.

---

*Until Congress passed the Tax Reform Act of 1969, former government officials could donate their papers and letters to the National Archives, or to an educational institution, and take a healthy tax deduction equal to the fair market value of the documents. Then, with continued access to their papers, they could produce a memoir for profit—thus benefiting two ways. Since 1969, however, the tax deduction for such material has, in effect, been limited to its actual cost—so the donor would be restricted to deducting a few cents for paper and paper clips.

†According to Marvin Gentile, the State Department security chief, "Certain senior people can take home documents for overnight storage if they have approved safekeeping facilities." That means a safe wired to an alarm system, an arrangement that very few Washington officials have in their homes. "Dean Rusk would never keep classified material at home," Gentile said. "He never wanted it in the house. If he had to read classified information, it would be picked up by the security people at night and brought back out to him in the morning, if necessary."

Although Foy Kohler rose to become ambassador to Moscow and then Deputy Under Secretary of State, his career was briefly jeopardized in December, 1952, when he was arrested after a traffic accident in Virginia with two classified documents in his car. The Kohlers were coming home from a dinner party at 2 A.M. when their car, with Mrs. Kohler driving, left the road and sheared off a telephone pole. Police charged Kohler with public intoxication and his wife with drunken driving.* Kohler, then a member of the State Department's policy-planning staff, had the presence of mind to hold on to the documents while he and his wife were treated for minor injuries at Arlington Hospital.

When Kohler informed the police that his briefcase contained important papers, they notified the State Department. Security agents from the department came to the police station and retrieved the documents from Kohler. The papers, classified Secret, dealt with the political situation in Morocco and Tunisia. A State Department board, taking note of Kohler's distinguished record in the Foreign Service, suspended him for thirty days without pay, and he was reassigned as counselor of embassy in Ankara.

Because of a strange loophole in the law, it is not even entirely clear that officials who take copies of classified documents with them when they leave the government are acting illegally. Under the Federal Records Act of 1950, government records must not be removed or destroyed without authorization, but the law does not cover "extra copies of documents," such as carbons or other kinds of copies. Since the act was passed before the heyday of the Xerox machine, it is fairly meaningless.†

Nevertheless, when hired, State Department employees sign a form J-4 in which they promise not to disclose classified information to anyone during or after their government employment. When they leave the government, they are required to sign a J-3, stating that they have "surrendered" all classified documents, and adding: "I shall not publish, nor reveal to any person, any classified or administratively controlled information" without official permission.

Sometimes departing employees raise questions about the pledge, one security official said, but "everybody signs." No one has been prosecuted for violating the pledge, but in at least one instance

---

*The *Washington Post*, in a sympathetic editorial, noted that imbibing too much at parties "has happened to a lot of us," and concluded: "Let him who never drank a martini hurl the first olive."

†In 1971 the State Department had 119 Xerox, Apeco, and other copying machines.

the government has taken legal action to enforce such an agreement. In April of 1972 the Central Intelligence Agency blocked a former CIA official, Victor Marchetti, from publishing a book about the intelligence agency. Marchetti had already signed a contract with Alfred A. Knopf for the book when the government went into federal court to enforce the secrecy pledge Marchetti had signed before leaving CIA. His attorneys argued that his right to publish under the First Amendment could not be limited by the secrecy agreement. But in December, the Supreme Court declined to review a lower-court order forbidding Marchetti to publish anything about CIA without the prior approval of the intelligence agency.

Certain members of the foreign policy establishment have long enjoyed special access to classified information in government files, a privilege unavailable to the press or other citizens. Under the State Department's notorious Old Boy rule, senior officials who leave the department are permitted continued access to their own and related papers.

Dean Rusk formalized the rule in 1967. "The special access for Old Boys," William Franklin explained candidly, "was designed so they don't need to squirrel copies away. We have no way of keeping them from doing their memoirs, so at least we want them to be correct." There are two hitches under the rules, however: the Secretary of State can veto access for a former official if he feels it would not "serve the national interest," and the Old Boys must submit their notes for clearance prior to publication of any book based upon their special access.*

Consequently, if the Secretary of State suspects that a former diplomat is planning a hostile or critical book, the official may find that for him, the Old Boy rule does not apply. On the other hand, reliable, trusted members of the foreign policy elite can expect no difficulty in gaining access to the classified documents. Dean Acheson, an Old Boy if there ever was one, had full access to all his papers when he was writing *Present at the Creation,* his memoir of government service. In 1971 former Assistant Secretary of State William P. Bundy spent considerable time at the State Department reading classified material for the preparation of a book. As the new editor of *Foreign Affairs,* the quarterly published by the Council on For-

---

*The rules for Old Boy access to files appear in State Department regulation 6.9 in Title 22 of the Code of Federal Regulations. President Nixon's 1972 Executive Order on classification extended the Old Boy rule to all departments of the government.

eign Relations, Bundy was, by definition, a charter member of the foreign policy establishment.

Although its existence is little known, there is, literally, an Old Boy reading room at the Department of State. It is not formally called that, of course, but officials invariably refer to it by that name within the department. William Bundy or other former officials could go to this room and browse through the documents in the Pentagon Papers long before they were published by *The New York Times*. The Old Boy reading room is located in Room 1239 on the ground floor of the main State Department building. The reading room is a modest glass-enclosed area set aside within the much larger Central Files Room. The file room is located in a secure area which must be entered through a door with special locks. Inside are row upon row of gray file cabinets containing index cards to all State Department documents.

In sharp contrast to the Old Boy reading room, where favored former officials may read secret information denied to ordinary citizens, the State Department also maintains a public reading room, where, in theory, citizens may go to request State Department documents under the Freedom of Information Act. Under the act, government departments must establish such locations; and in June, 1967, the State Department duly issued regulation 6.6, declaring: "A public reading room or area where . . . records . . . shall be made available is located in the Department of State, 2201 C Street NW, Washington, D.C. The receptionist will refer the applicant to the proper room."

To test the regulation, on a visit to the State Department, I asked the receptionist at the north entrance to direct me to the public reading room. She gave me a blank stare and said: "I've never heard of it." When I persisted, she made a call to the State Department library and then telephoned another receptionist. Finally she said that she could not help me; as far as she knew, no public reading room existed.

Undaunted, I went around to C Street, the main diplomatic entrance and the address specified in rule 6.6 as the location of the Department of State. "We don't have a public reading room," the receptionist declared briskly. Did I mean the Foreign Service lounge perhaps, or the library? I did not, and when I insisted that there was, too, a public reading room, she replied: "If you find it, let us know," and from her tone, she seemed to mean that sincerely.

I did find it, but only with the help of Donald J. Simon, a gentle gray-haired man who is chief of the department's Records Services Division, and as such, in charge of all State Department documents, classified or otherwise. I had an appointment to interview Simon, and when I asked to see the public reading room, he escorted me to a small ground-floor room with a counter, rather like a post office. The reception area was bare except for a little glass-covered bookcase, which proved to contain the unclassified portion of the Foreign Affairs Manual—the State Department rule book—and forms to request documents under the Freedom of Information Act.

The room, Simon explained, does get a bit of traffic from people who need to have birth certificates or other papers validated. But he conceded that very few people have come to the room to seek information since it was opened in 1967. "We probably haven't had more than twenty visitors requesting documents under the Freedom of Information Act," he said. It is a mystery how even twenty people could have found their way to the room, since the receptionists do not seem to know about it. And there is no indication on the door that it is the public reading room.

There is a room number on the door, however, and it is 1237; ironically, the elusive public reading room is right next door to the Old Boy reading room. Somehow, the juxtaposition of the two rooms symbolizes all that is wrong with the classification system, perhaps with government itself. In the one room, behind security locks, privileged access for an elite to potentially valuable secret information; in the other, a public reading room which the public cannot find, a barren counter, a tiny bookcase, and a stack of forms.

All of this helps to bring into sharper focus the fact that the classification system is essentially a political mechanism for the control of information. Documents may be stamped in the name of national security, but their continuing secrecy, or their disclosure, is often guided by domestic political considerations.

During Eisenhower's first term, as the 1956 Presidential election year drew near, Sherman Adams conceived the idea of letting a journalist have access to the administration's internal papers, classified and otherwise, to write a book. Originally the White House approached columnist Roscoe Drummond, of the Republican *New York Herald Tribune.* When Drummond was unable to take on the job, Presidential aide Kevin McCann turned to Robert J. Donovan, the paper's White House correspondent. Donovan, a facile and graceful writer and one of Washington's great reporters, turned the project down initially.

"In those days," Donovan said, "it was unusual for a reporter to have done a book. I had written *The Assassins* and I was known as a reporter who had written a book. McCann approached me in the spring of 1955; they wanted the book by 1956. I was afraid it would be a campaign book, and I turned it down. About a week later McCann called and we had lunch again, and he seemed to have answers to all my objections." McCann also raised the possibility that the *Herald Tribune* might be able to syndicate the book, which he knew would make it more difficult for Donovan to say no. After many further discussions, Donovan agreed, but he set his own ground rules: "No one could see anything I wrote until it was in book form, except for classified information, which would be submitted for security check. Adams insisted I have a Q clearance."

After Donovan got his clearance, he took a leave from the newspaper and in the fall of 1955 moved into the White House. He was given an office formerly used by Robert Montgomery, Eisenhower's television adviser. By this time Eisenhower had suffered a heart attack, and it was not at all clear that he would run again, but the book project went ahead anyway. "They brought in documents in wheelbarrows and on dollies. I was inundated in documents. A great many were classified, but the most interesting thing about them was the classification mark, because the contents were well known by then." Reading the supposed innermost secrets of the government, Donovan realized that there was massive overclassification.

In time, since he was dealing with so many classified documents, Donovan began to be somewhat casual about them. He was permitted to take classified papers home to work on them; as it happened, on one occasion, Richard Rovere of *The New Yorker,* visiting Donovan at home in Chevy Chase, came away with an interesting anecdote involving Secretary of State John Foster Dulles. The item got into *The New Yorker,* and perturbed administration officials never did figure out the source of the leak.

One of the most chilling secrets that Donovan learned while researching the book came not from a classified document but in a conversation with Robert Cutler, Eisenhower's assistant for national security affairs. Some of the most tight-lipped men in the White House became babbling fountains of information when Adams told them curtly: "The President wants you to talk to Bob Donovan."

Certainly Cutler was not normally celebrated for talking to newsmen. But over dinner at the Harvard Club in Manhattan, Donovan said, Cutler cryptically disclosed that "there had been discussions of preventive war within the councils of the government." Cutler provided no details, and it was clear that if Donovan pursued the matter further, Cutler would refuse to discuss it. But, as Donovan recalls the meeting, "when he got into preventive war, I nearly fell off my chair."

Leafing through government secrets at the White House one day, Donovan came across a Top Secret document that concisely summarized the administration's philosophy of the military New Look. "It was stated so superbly," said Donovan, "that I paraphrased it closely, so close in fact that the NSC raised holy hell and threatened to blow the whole thing out of the water." Dillon Anderson, a conservative Houston lawyer who had replaced Cutler, wrote a two-page memo to Sherman Adams on why the book should not be published.

The memo led to an angry White House confrontation between Adams and Anderson, with Donovan present. "Adams was white and shaking," Donovan said, but he held fast to his commitment to Donovan and the project continued. Then, according to Donovan, people like Tom Stephens, who had been Eisenhower's appointments secretary, and press secretary James C. Hagerty "became worried that the book would tell too much." Despite all these pressures, Donovan wrote the book in 163 days; it was published in May of 1956, and became the nation's number one best seller.*

Classified information is not only made public in book form by Presidents and their aides; it is leaked to the press virtually every day, printed in newspapers and broadcast on television. From the President on down, officials of the government regularly leak classified data—and sometimes classified documents—to the press when it suits their political and policy goals.

In an affidavit filed with the federal district court in New York during the Pentagon Papers case, Max Frankel, then the chief of the Washington Bureau of *The New York Times,* noted that officials and Washington reporters "regularly make use of so-called classified, secret, and top secret information and documentation . . . without the use of 'secrets' . . . there could be no adequate diplomatic, military, and political reporting of the kind our people take for granted, either abroad or in Washington . . ."

Frankel added: "I know how strange all this must sound. We have been taught, particularly in the past generation of spy scares and Cold War, to think of secrets as *secrets*—varying in their 'sensitivity' but uniformly essential to the private conduct of diplomatic and military affairs and somehow detrimental to the national interest if prematurely disclosed. By the standards of official Washington—government and press alike—this is an antiquated, quaint, and romantic view. For practically everything that our government does, plans, thinks, hears, and contemplates in the realms of foreign policy is stamped and treated as secret—and then unraveled by that same

---

*Robert J. Donovan, *Eisenhower, The Inside Story* (New York: Harper and Brothers, 1956). The paraphrased material from the Top Secret document on the New Look stayed in, and forms the basis for the opening of Chapter 4, pp. 51–53.

government, by the Congress and by the press in one continuing round of professional and social contacts and cooperative and competitive exchanges of information."

As Frankel went on to point out, Presidents make "secret" decisions only to reveal them to frighten another nation, gain votes at home, or protect their reputations. The military services leak "secrets" about weaponry to inflate their budgets. (It is a standing joke in Washington that the Navy sees Soviet submarines off the coast at appropriations time.)

The *Times'* Washington bureau chief detailed several specific instances in which he was given secret information. During the Cuban missile crisis, he said, a State Department official "let me take verbatim notes" of the conversation between President Kennedy and Soviet Foreign Minister Andrei Gromyko. By agreement, the *Times* published the conversation without direct quotes; the actual record of the talks remains an official secret.

"I remember President Johnson, standing beside me, waist-deep in his Texas swimming pool, recounting for more than an hour his conversation the day before, in 1967, with Prime Minister Kosygin of the Soviet Union at Glassboro, N.J., for my 'background' information, and subsequent though not immediate use in print . . ."

Frankel, one of the most brilliant and perceptive reporters in the capital, explained to the court: "This is the coin of our business and of the officials with whom we regularly deal . . . Learning always to trust each other to some extent, and never to trust each other fully —for their purposes are often contradictory or downright antagonistic—the reporter and the official trespass regularly, customarily, easily, and unselfconsciously (even unconsciously) through what they both know to be official 'secrets' . . . The government hides what it can . . . and the press pries out what it can . . . Each side in this 'game' regularly 'wins' and 'loses' a round or two."

Presidents and other officials leak such information to the press in various forms and under varying circumstances. The information or document may pass in the course of a private interview by a newsman with an official. Or government secrets may be freely discussed at a "backgrounder" attended by half a dozen or more than a hundred reporters. Customarily the information may be reported, but it is attributed to some generalized source such as "administration officials" or "White House officials." Sometimes it is made available only on "deep background," in which case the newsman must agree to report it on his own authority, giving no source.

During one period President Johnson favored holding backgrounders in peripatetic fashion, which made it difficult for the reporters to take notes, since Johnson's long stride and seemingly boundless energy carried him along faster than most of the newsmen. I accompanied Johnson on one such walking backgrounder that took place on May 3, 1965, at the height of the Dominican crisis. With other reporters, I went around and around the White House lawn between 2:30 P.M. and 4:20 P.M., in unseasonable 91-degree temperature and under a very hot sun, trailed by beagles, photographers, and secret service agents. During the walk Johnson talked about dozens of subjects, his mood varying from cornball to Presidential, his words sometimes cautious and elliptical, sometimes dazzlingly candid.

Midway through the trek, an aide came up and handed Johnson a report stamped Secret in large letters. Without a moment's hesitation Johnson read it to us. It was a CIA teletype report quoting the American Red Cross representative in Santo Domingo as saying that some 1,500 to 2,000 persons were dead in the streets and that shooting had started up again in the capital at 1:30 P.M.

The document itself was not especially sensitive as secrets go, but clearly Johnson had "declassified" it on the spot because it suited his purpose of the moment: convincing the American press, and the public, that his armed intervention in the Dominican Republic was necessary and justified.

During the 1964 campaign Johnson provided a classic example of the use of government secrets for political purposes. The episode began in the American Airlines "Admirals Club" at the Chicago airport on July 20. Edward T. Folliard of the *Washington Post* asked Barry Goldwater whether he would welcome a chance to meet with President Johnson to discuss how to avoid inflaming racial tensions in the Presidential campaign. Goldwater could hardly say no, and when his reply clattered out over the White House news tickers, Presidential news secretary George Reedy could only agree that Johnson would be more than willing, indeed happy, to meet with Goldwater.

By July 24, the day the meeting was scheduled to take place at the White House, Johnson had become inexplicably nervous about the whole thing. Having the Republican Presidential nominee right in his office for a highly publicized chat about racial tensions somehow seemed a bad scenario to Johnson, and he began frantically casting about for some announcement—any announcement—to steal the day's headlines away from Goldwater. White House aides started telephoning key officials around town. At the Pentagon, Johnson found what he needed.

At 3:30 P.M., only two hours before Goldwater was due to arrive at the White House, Johnson held a press conference. He opened it by dramatically announcing the development of the SR-71, the Air

Force's high-altitude strategic reconnaissance plane. The plane, actually a follow-on to the U-2, had been developed under extraordinary secrecy wraps at a cost of a billion dollars.

"The aircraft will fly at more than three times the speed of sound," Johnson revealed. "It will operate at altitudes in excess of eighty thousand feet. It will use the most advanced observation equipment of all kinds in the world . . ."

An hour after Johnson had finished his news conference, Goldwater's car swept in the southwest gate, and the two political opponents met for sixteen minutes in the Oval Office. Their official statement afterward agreed that "racial tension should be avoided."

During the meeting, which was very pleasant, LBJ pulled out the statement that was later made public, and Goldwater read it and said fine. Then Goldwater, who had heard Johnson's announcement about the SR-71, asked a number of questions about the new aircraft. He did not realize, of course, that it had been specifically unveiled that afternoon as an anti-Goldwater weapon system. How many seats did it have, Goldwater wanted to know? Two, said Johnson. Well, said Goldwater, an enthusiastic pilot, he would like to fly in it as soon as possible. When could he do that?

"It's still kind of early," replied Johnson sweetly. "It won't be test-flown until after the first of the year. Why don't we wait until then and see who's Commander in Chief?"

But Johnson was by no means the only President to release classified information at news conferences. James C. Hagerty, vice-president of the American Broadcasting Company, told the House government information subcommittee in March, 1972, that sometimes documents to be released at Eisenhower's press conferences would arrive "literally covered with classified stamps, including the highest ratings. I would then actually have to take these papers to the President and have him declassify them on the spot. And, believe me, the only thing that was 'Top Secret' about that was what he would say when he had to go through such nonsense."

The Pentagon and CIA periodically leak stories to the press about Soviet missile strength. The stories often go into great detail about the size and configuration of the Soviet missile silos, information that can only have come from highly classified satellite reconnaissance photographs. In March, 1972, Defense Secretary Laird publicly told the Veterans of Foreign Wars that the Russians were deploying multiple warheads on their ICBM's. Although the United States enjoyed a "two-year" lead, he said, it could be lost "if we do not maintain a strong research and development program." The conclusion that the Soviet Union was deploying multiple warheads, if accurate, almost certainly was based upon classified intelligence interpretations of satellite photos. Yet Laird did not hesitate to discuss this information to drum up domestic support for the Pentagon's weapons budget.

Thus the classification system follows the double standard, permitting government officials the appearance of solemn fidelity to official secrecy and national security, with a lot of swinging on the side. It was invented to be violated.

The elaborate regulations to protect the physical security of classified documents—endless rules governing lock combinations, the transmittal of classified documents and their handling and destruction—are all designed to prevent a spy, or a disloyal government employee, from making off with government secrets. Where the system breaks down completely is that there are no similar barriers against the daily political use of classified information by officials, up to and including the President, or by former officials who are writing memoirs. At the highest levels of the government, there is no protection against the system being breached. The situation is rather analogous to an ocean liner, absolutely watertight and safe above the water line but with a gaping hole below decks leading directly to the engine room.

Moreover, the ship has too many captains; one reason for the proliferation of secrecy in government is the fact that in the big national security agencies, almost anyone can classify a document. The Moss subcommittee estimated in 1962 that under Eisenhower's original order, "more than a million government employees" had power to stamp secrecy designations on documents. Testifying before the Moorhead subcomimittee in 1971, William G. Florence, a former Pentagon classifier, estimated that "hundreds of thousands of individuals at all echelons in the Department of Defense practice classification as a way of life." According to a study conducted by the Nixon administration, until mid-1972, 43,586 persons in four major departments and the White House had power to classify documents; 30,542 were in the Pentagon alone. Under Nixon's 1972 Executive Order, the study asserted, the overall total was reduced to 16,238 persons.*

If anything, however, Nixon's 1972 order seemed likely to increase the number of persons entitled to wield a rubber stamp. In the

*The figures covered Defense, State, Justice, the Atomic Energy Commission, and the Executive Office of the President. Since the study did not include the CIA or twenty other agencies of the Executive Branch with power to classify, the statistics did not reflect the total number of government officials with authority to stamp documents secret.

case of thirteen agencies with only marginal national security responsibilities, the Eisenhower order had limited power to classify to the
agency head alone. Under the Nixon order, department heads can
delegate their power to classify, and any official with power to stamp
a document Top Secret can designate any subordinate to use Secret
stamps. In turn, the subordinate can designate his subordinate to
classify documents Confidential. Under this system, officials with
power to classify are bound, in time, to proliferate like rabbits.*

In fact, the numbers game is wholly misleading. One State Department aide put it this way: "Any official of the department can
classify a document that he originates. His secretary takes a rubber
stamp out of a drawer—the rubber stamps themselves are not considered classified materials—and stamps it Top Secret or whatever. It's
as easy as that."

It is true that technically, not every official has *formal,* so-called
"original" authority to classify a document. In practice, however,
almost anyone can stamp a document with a secrecy label, and his
judgment is routinely approved by a superior who wields the formal,
"original" classification power.

The problem is compounded by the fact that—in the jargon of
the classifiers—thousands of officials also possess "derivative classification authority." In the Pentagon, William Florence testified, such
authority is possessed by "any individual who can sign a document
or who is in charge of doing something," a definition that would seem
fairly broad. Derivative classifiers, Florence explained, can classify
documents that are "closely related" to documents already classified.

How much is classified? The answer is that nobody knows. Florence told the House subcommittee in 1971 that there are "at least
twenty million classified documents" in Pentagon files. He said that
under the rules "less than one half of one percent" of the total should
have been classified in the first place. "In other words," he testified,
"the disclosure of information in at least ninety-nine and a half percent of those classified documents could not be prejudicial to the
defense interests of the nation."

---

*Under the Eisenhower order, as amended over the years, by 1972, thirty-
four agencies and the heads of thirteen others had power to classify, making
a total of forty-seven agencies. Under the Nixon order, twelve agencies and
eleven offices directly under the President had authority to classify Top
Secret, and thirteen other agencies had power to classify Secret, for a total
of thirty-six agencies. The Nixon order, therefore, reduced by eleven the
number of agencies with power to classify but liberalized the delegation of
classification authority within the thirty-six remaining agencies.

The State Department estimated in July, 1971, that it had 151,-000,000 documents, of which 25 percent, or 37,750,000, were classified.* The department has also estimated that it is accumulating classified documents at the rate of at least 200,000 a year. Since these figures suggest that there are more than 57,000,000 classified documents in the State Department and Pentagon alone, when the CIA, the NSA, the AEC, and the NSC are taken into account, a conservative estimate of the total number of classified documents in active government files would be well over 100,000,000. The figure is probably much higher. In addition, of course, the National Archives has a vast store of classified documents. In a 1971 report, the Archives estimated that it was holding 458,500,000 pages of classified material created from the start of World War II through 1954. President Nixon asked Congress for funds to begin declassifying the 160,000,-000 pages from World War II, and in 1972 Congress appropriated $1,200,000 for that purpose. The National Archives hired more than a hundred persons to do the work.

Some idea of the extent of overclassification can be gleaned from the fact that in 1966 the Defense Department reviewed 1,000,000 classified documents to see how many it could throw away or declassify. As a result of the survey, 344,300 documents were destroyed—well over one-third. Not surprisingly, only 710 documents were declassified.

During the Moorhead subcommittee hearings, Pentagon witness David Cooke offered yet another measure of classified documents—cubic feet. He estimated that the Pentagon had a total of 6,000,000 cubic feet of documents in its files, of which 17 percent were classified. The staff of the House unit did some rapid calculation that this amount of classified material "equal eighteen stacks of documents 555 feet high, each as high as the Washington Monument."†

A major reason for the tremendous growth of classified paper, in addition to the large number of people empowered to classify, is the

---

*Of this total, State estimated that one-half of 1 percent were classified Top Secret, 5 percent Secret, and 20 percent Confidential. In answer to a query by the author, William D. Blair, Jr., Assistant Secretary of State for Public Affairs, reported in January, 1972, that the State Department handles 218,-000 classified cables a year.

†The House mathematicians were correct about the height of the Washington Monument, but they badly underestimated the size of the Pentagon's classified stack of documents. If 17 percent of 6,000,000 cubic feet of documents are classified, this would be 1,020,000 cubic feet, or 1,275,000 linear feet. That is the equivalent of 2,297 Washington Monuments.

fact that no one has time to declassify anything. Policy-level officials, the only ones competent to decide whether a document can be declassified, are far too busy dealing with new crises and problems to spend time removing the classification stamps from old documents.

The psychology of secrecy also adds to the proliferation of classified documents. Stamping a document Top Secret is an ego-building act for a bureaucrat; and who wants to admit, by declassifying something, that he is no longer dealing with important secrets? "The majority of people with whom I worked in the past few years," William Florence testified, "reflected the belief that information is born classified and that declassification would be permitted only if someone could show that the information would not be of interest to a foreign nation."

Moreover, Nixon's 1972 order, designed to reform the classification system, broadened the definition of what may be classified, making it even easier for officials to use the secrecy label. Under the Eisenhower order, material could be protected in the interest of the "national defense." The Nixon order initially uses the term "national defense or foreign relations of the United States," and then shortens this to "national security." The new definitions cast a wider net.

There is simply no way to estimate the total dollar cost of the classification system. One witness told the House subcommittee that *unnecessary* classification probably cost the taxpayers $50 million annually. A study conducted for the subcommittee in 1972 by the General Accounting Office concluded that four large departments spent $126 million a year in classification and related security costs. According to the study, the Pentagon spends almost $2 million a year on stamping documents; $15.8 million on transmission of classified documents, and $6.8 million on safeguarding classified documents; the State Department spends some $10 million annually for the same purposes. Although the total cost of the secrecy system cannot accurately be calculated, some interesting indicators surface from time to time. For example, according to Defense Department figures, it costs 66¢, on average, to declassify a document. To send an unclassified document from one place to another costs 84¢; to send a classified document the same distance costs $2.14, or almost three times as much.

Secrecy in government is not limited to the classification system. Government departments often keep documents from the public without ever classifying them. Even under the Freedom of Information Act, for example, there are nine "exemptions" that officials may invoke to withhold information from the public. Classification is only one of these; others include "internal" documents, "inter-agency or intra-agency memorandums," and "investigatory files."

And quite aside from the incalculable costs of maintaining the classification system itself, Congress appropriates billions annually in secret funds. The CIA and the various other intelligence agencies of the government spend approximately $5 billion a year. The precise total is classified, as are the details of how the money is spent. Funds for many weapons systems are also classified. In 1971 *Congressional Quarterly*, the Washington-based research service, estimated that secret funds in the fiscal 1972 budget of $229.2 billion amounted to $15-to-$20 billion, or close to 10 percent of the total federal budget.

The Central Intelligence Agency Act of 1949 exempted that agency from all federal laws requiring the disclosure of salaries and personnel totals. It gave the director of CIA power to spend money "without regard to the provisions of law and regulations relating to the expenditure of government funds."

One of the great myths perpetuated by the CIA is that its classified budget and activities are carefully watched by four House and Senate subcommittees. In the Senate, the five-man CIA subcommittee of the Armed Services Committee is headed by Senator John C. Stennis of Mississippi. Stennis, who is also chairman of the parent Armed Services Committee, displays a benign, friendly attitude toward CIA.

"This agency is conducted in a splendid way," he assured the Senate in his courtly Deep South tones during a debate over CIA in November, 1971. "As has been said, spying is spying . . . You have to make up your mind that you are going to have an intelligence agency and protect it as such, and shut your eyes some and take what is coming."

Senator Stuart Symington of Missouri, a member of the CIA subcommittee, did not bother to conceal his irritation. Symington thanked Stennis for his observations and added acidly: "I wish his interest in the subject had developed to the point where he had held just one meeting of the CIA subcommittee this year, just one meeting."

The late Senator Allen J. Ellender of Louisiana arose to defend the Senate's keen scrutiny of CIA activities. Ellender was chairman of the CIA subcommittee of the powerful Senate Appropriations Committee; this is one of the subcommittees that goes over the agency's budget "line by line," as CIA director Richard Helms attested in a speech to editors in April, 1971.

Ellender, thus certified as the chief Senate watchdog over CIA's budget, took the floor end and announced: "This is a rather ticklish subject. It is a subject that I do not care to discuss in the open." Senator J. William Fulbright then suggested that the CIA's funding of a secret army in Laos could be discussed; that, after all, had already been publicized. The full extent of the control exercised over CIA by the appropriations subcommittee then became clear from the following exchange:

> MR. FULBRIGHT: It has been stated that the CIA has 36,000 there [in Laos]. It is no secret. Would the Senator say that before the creation of the army in Laos they came before the committee and the committee knew of it and approved it?
> MR. ELLENDER: Probably so.
> MR. FULBRIGHT: Did the Senator approve it?
> MR. ELLENDER: It was not—I did not know anything about it.

After some further discussion, Ellender explained: "I never asked, to begin with, whether or not there were any funds to carry on the war in this sum the CIA asked for. It never dawned on me to ask about it."

Within the bureaucracy, transfers of money to CIA are handled by the Intelligence Community Branch of the Office of Management and Budget. Since these funds are hidden, largely in the weapons procurement programs of the Defense Department budget, it is very rarely that the public learns how the money is spent. In 1970 the CIA channeled tens of thousands of dollars into Chile through the International Telephone and Telegraph Corporation and other companies in an effort to defeat Marxist candidate Salvador Allende.

During the Senate investigation of ITT in 1972, columnist Jack Anderson published documents indicating that CIA had conspired with ITT to prevent Allende from taking power following his election. The ITT papers showed that the conglomerate was in close touch with William V. Broe, director of the Latin American division of the CIA's Clandestine Services. But CIA's activities against Allende went back much further than 1970. In 1964, CIA informed the budget bureau that it had spent $100,000 to help elect Eduardo Frei, the Christian Democrat candidate, over Allende. In a bizarre touch, the CIA, according to a former high official of the intelligence agency, recruited an election specialist on the staff of Chicago's Mayor Richard J. Daley and sent him to Chile to help Frei. When CIA needed an expert on rigging elections, it apparently knew enough to go to Cook County.

With the dual weapons of secret funds and the classification system to mask its activities, the CIA has almost unlimited power to operate clandestinely, both in this country and abroad. The CIA's ability to protect itself with a classification label is demonstrated by the continuing secrecy surrounding the Galindez file.

On the night of March 12, 1956, Dr. Jesus Maria de Galindez

disappeared on a New York subway after lecturing to a class at Columbia University. A Spanish exile, Galindez was a foe of dictator Rafael L. Trujillo of the Dominican Republic, and suspicion of kidnapping and murder immediately focused on the Generalissmo. On May 29, 1957, the State Department said in a note to the Dominican Republic that "sufficient evidence had now been uncovered to indicate" that a missing American pilot, Gerald Lester Murphy, acting with certain Dominicans and Americans, "may have been connected with the disappearance of Dr. Galindez." There was considerable evidence that Murphy had flown the drugged scholar from Long Island to the Dominican Republic.

In July, 1957, Trujillo, who was known as the Benefactor, hired New York attorney Morris L. Ernst, ex-judge William H. Munson, and publicist Sydney S. Baron to investigate the Galindez disappearance; it was announced the three men would receive $160,000 in fees and expenses from Trujillo. After ten months Ernst reported he was unable to find a "scintilla" of evidence connecting Galindez and Murphy or linking his client, Trujillo, with the vanished professor. Ernst also reported that Galindez had collected more than $1 million as the registered representative in the United States of the Basque government-in-exile. The fiercely nationalistic Basques consider themselves a separate nation within Spain and have never accepted the government of Francisco Franco.

In separate interviews with the author in 1966, both Baron and Ernst said their investigations had convinced them that Galindez was receiving money from the CIA. Both said they believed that the CIA paid Galindez to maintain contact with the anti-Franco underground and to build a non-Communist government-in-exile that could take over in Spain upon Franco's death. Ernst said CIA had admitted to him its relationship with Galindez.

The CIA, Ernst said, had assisted him throughout his investigation, in one instance providing a false passport for a CIA agent who accompanied one of Ernst's lawyers on a trip to Cuba. Ernst said he worked closely during the investigation with "Colonel King," whom he identified as the CIA's Caribbean expert. Ernst also said that CIA told him not to include in his report letters between Galindez and persons in Spain because "three or four hundred people would die if the letters were printed." Ernst said he assumed these were persons identified in the letters who were active in the anti-Franco movement within Spain.

Wherever the truth lies in this tangled story, it is a matter of fact that the CIA has succeeded, through classification, in throwing a twenty-year blanket of secrecy over the case. On December 28, 1964, Ernst and his associate, Alan U. Schwartz, transferred all of their papers and documents connected with the Galindez probe to the National Archives. They asked that the material be reviewed by the CIA for security and restricted from public view for ten years.

In April, 1965, Lawrence R. Houston, CIA's general counsel, wrote to the Archivist of the United States to say that the material had been screened "by Colonel J.C. King of this Agency." Scattered throughout the files, Houston wrote, was material which, if published, "would be detrimental to intelligence sources and methods or to the national interest." CIA believed that the ten-year period suggested by Ernst "is not adequate and that a restriction of twenty years would be more realistic." On April 22 Acting Archivist Walter Robertson, Jr., wrote back to advise that "in accordance with your recommendation, access to the papers will be restricted for twenty years." The Galindez mystery remains unsolved, but whatever answers are available in the files cannot be inspected. The CIA has thrown away the key until 1985.

The secrecy system in America has become so pervasive in the past two decades, and so unpopular, that even those who protect and maintain it find the classification system a useful political target. "The system of classification which has evolved in the United States," President Nixon declared in 1972, "has failed to meet the standards of an open and democratic society, allowing too many papers to be classified for too long a time. The controls . . . have proved unworkable, and classification has frequently served to conceal bureaucratic mistakes or to prevent embarrassment to officials and administrations . . . The many abuses of the security system can no longer be tolerated." Unfortunately, Nixon delivered these ringing remarks on the day he promulgated his Executive Order modifying, but perpetuating and extending, the system of official secrecy.

It is a system that, as we have seen, is freely violated by officials in their daily contacts with the press, and in their memoirs after leaving office. At the same time it gives political leaders almost unlimited power to mislead the public on vital issues affecting war or peace. It mocks the meaning of democracy by restricting the flow of information to the citizenry.

During a debate in Congress in 1971, Senator Fulbright, the chairman of the Senate Foreign Relations Committee, expressed his frustration over the dilemma of secrecy in words that also revealed much about the root cause. "This secrecy and classification has become a god in this country," he said, "and those people who have secrets travel in a kind of fraternity like a college secret society, and they will not speak to anyone else."

6

The President Leaks
a Document

On June 23, 1971, the *Chicago Sun-Times* reported on its front page that President Kennedy and his senior advisers had been "intimately involved" in the events leading to the overthrow and death of South Vietnam's President Ngo Dinh Diem in 1963.

Written in Washington, the story bore the double byline of Morton Kondracke and Thomas B. Ross. Along with it, the newspaper published an extraordinary document—the full text of a memorandum that had been classified Top Secret when it was written for Secretary of State Dean Rusk on August 30, 1963.

The eleven-point memo by Roger Hilsman, Assistant Secretary of State for Far Eastern Affairs, outlined possible United States responses to a whole range of actions that Diem and his brother, Ngo Dinh Nhu, might take to stay in power. In the event of a last-ditch stand in the palace, the memo, under "U.S. Response" No. 10, said: "We should encourage the coup group to fight the battle to the end and to destroy the palace if necessary to gain victory . . . If the family is taken alive, the Nhus should be banished to France or any other European country willing to receive them." Then, in one of the more chilling sentences to emerge from the Vietnam war, it added: "Diem should be treated as the generals wish."

If the document was extraordinary, the story of how it came to be published is even more so. For this Top Secret memorandum of the Kennedy administration, highly damaging to the moral image of Camelot, was initially leaked in February, 1968, at the personal and

explicit direction of President Lyndon B. Johnson—although it failed
to surface publicly at that time.

Because the President himself ordered that a document marked
Top Secret be declassified for the express purpose of transmitting it
—secretly—to the press, the Hilsman affair provides a classic case
study of the deliberate abuse of the classification system for political
purposes.

On January 6, 1961, two weeks before President Kennedy was
inaugurated in the cold and the snow of Washington, Soviet Premier
Nikita S. Khrushchev made his famous speech promising support for
"wars of national liberation." By spring, President Kennedy had
made a series of decisions designed to meet that challenge as—in the
view of the administration—it manifested itself in the jungles of
South Vietnam. Secretly, by decision of the President and the National Security Council, the United States sent 400 Special Forces
troops to South Vietnam, breached the Geneva agreement by increasing the size of the U.S. military mission in South Vietnam,
beefed up the CIA station in Saigon by forty men at an annual cost
of $1.5 million, and initiated a program of covert warfare against
North Vietnam.

Thus Kennedy took the first steps down a path that placed more
than 16,000 American troops in Vietnam at the time of his death in
November, 1963. But over the summer of 1963—despite Defense
Secretary Robert S. McNamara's public and private optimism—it
became apparent that the autocratic Diem regime and, with it, U.S.
policy, were in deep trouble. On June 11 a Buddhist monk, Thich
Quang Duc, burned himself to death with gasoline in protest against
the Diem government. His act of self-immolation shocked the world,
but equally shocking was the reaction of Nhu's vitriolic wife,
Madame Nhu, who dismissed it as a monk "barbecue." In August,
Nhu's secret police and special troops brutally raided the Buddhist
pagodas. Some 1,400 people, mainly monks, were arrested and many
were beaten and shot.

It was at this critical point that Hilsman played a crucial and
controversial role in the swiftly moving political crisis in Vietnam.
His personal background was relevant; during World War II Hilsman
had been a guerrilla leader in Burma for the Office of Strategic
Services. Born in Texas, the son of an Army colonel, Hilsman graduated from West Point in 1943 and left for the Far East, where he
joined Merrill's Marauders, the Army's famed jungle-fighting unit.
He was wounded and rose to the rank of major. Later he commanded
an OSS guerrilla battalion operating behind the Japanese lines in
Burma. In 1945 he led a parachute rescue mission that freed American prisoners being held by the Japanese at Mukden, Manchuria.

Among the prisoners released was his father, Colonel Roger Hilsman, who had been captured in the Philippines three years earlier.

After the war Hilsman earned a doctorate in international politics at Yale. He taught at Princeton, then joined the Legislative Reference Service of the Library of Congress as chief of the foreign affairs division. In that post, he got to know Senator John F. Kennedy, who would occasionally draw on him for research material. When he became President in 1961, Kennedy brought Hilsman into the State Department to head the Bureau of Intelligence and Research. Then in March, 1963, Hilsman was moved up to replace Averell Harriman as Assistant Secretary of State for the Far East. As a scholar proficient in the niceties of how to garrote an enemy on a jungle trail, Hilsman was atypical of the starchy Foreign Service officers who trod the corridors of the State Department. He was outspoken, blunt (abrasive was the word preferred by his detractors), and possessed the brisk self-confidence of a political appointee who enjoyed a personal relationship with the President. And Hilsman, like other New Frontiersmen, was an activist, always eager to move. These were not traits designed to endear a man operating in the cautious Eastern-WASP ambience that once dominated and still permeates the Foreign Service. It is perhaps true that the Foreign Service no longer entirely reflects the values of the Racquet Club, but a certain unruffled demeanor, a kind of cheerful, bland evasiveness are still the qualities best cultivated by the successful career official of the State Department. (The department, President Kennedy once complained, had "all these people over there who are constantly smiling. I think we need to smile less and be tougher.")

Now, late in August, 1963, Hilsman was in a position to exercise strong influence on U.S. policy in Vietnam. On August 23 Henry Cabot Lodge, who had just arrived as ambassador to Saigon, sent a cable to Hilsman, reporting talk of a coup against the government. This message reached Washington on a Saturday morning, August 24. President Kennedy was in Hyannis Port, Massachusetts, for the weekend, Dean Rusk was in New York, and McNamara and CIA Director John A. McCone were both on vacation. Working with Harriman and others, Hilsman drafted a reply to Lodge. Subsequently, this became known as the controversial "August 24 cable."

The cable gave Lodge the green light to support a coup unless Diem "rid himself of Nhu" and Madame Nhu and released the Buddhists arrested in the pagoda raids. If Diem "remains obdurate," Lodge was instructed, the United States would no longer support him. Washington, the cable said, could not give Lodge a detailed plan "as to how this operation should proceed," but assured him that whatever actions he took, "we will back you to the hilt." In his reply,

Lodge saw little point in tipping off Diem, and proposed instead that "we go straight to the generals with our demands, without informing Diem."

In his book *To Move a Nation,* Hilsman asserts that both the President and Rusk received early drafts of the August 24 cable and were consulted by telephone several times about its language.*

Although Kennedy's senior advisers had Monday morning reservations about the strongly worded August 24 cable, it was not rescinded. In Saigon, on August 26, Lodge met with his aides to carry out his instructions and decided, in the words of a CIA cable, that the "American official hand should not show." At the meeting, therefore, Lodge authorized Lieutenant Colonel Lucien Conein, the CIA's key operator in South Vietnam, to begin meeting secretly with, advising, and assisting the generals plotting against the Diem government. Immediately after this meeting, Lodge, in a wondrous bit of scheduling, went off to the palace to present his credentials as ambassador to President Diem.

But four days later Lodge learned that the generals had gotten cold feet; the coup was off. (A little more than two months later, of course, it succeeded. With Conein orchestrating the operation, and

_____

*In an interview and subsequent correspondence with this writer, Rusk confirmed that he had been consulted about the cable, but said he did not recall seeing any early draft. He added: "Everyone was out of town that weekend. My recollection is that I first heard about it when [Under Secretary of State] George Ball called me on the telephone and discussed it in very guarded terms. We were on an unclassified telephone. There was a very general indication of what was in the cable and I was told that the President had cleared it. Later [after everyone returned to Washington] we took some steps to draw back from it. So it was cleared by me on the phone in that sense, in that a general allusion was made to its contents, and it was said the President had cleared it, which of course made a difference."

Hilsman contended in an interview, however, that Rusk revised and strengthened the draft, which he said had been transmitted to Rusk at the UN mission in Manhattan over secure teletype facilities. The unclassified telephone was used only at the end of the clearance process, Hilsman said, when the drafters went to Ball's home; from there, Ball telephoned Rusk in New York for a final check.

The real disagreement, of course, is not over these details but over the question of responsibility; Rusk clearly seeks to take minimal responsibility for a cable that, in effect, approved the overthrow of another government. Hilsman, in turn, argues that he acted only with clear approval of his superiors, including Rusk.

with the full encouragement of the U.S. government, the generals moved on November 1, 1963. At dawn the next morning Diem and Nhu were captured and murdered in the back of an armored personnel carrier.)

On August 30, as the coup attempt was fizzling, Hilsman wrote his eleven-point memo to Rusk. Entitled "Possible Diem-Nhu Moves and U.S. Responses," it began: "The courses of action which Diem and Nhu could take to maintain themselves in power and the United States responses thereto are as follows:" As with the August 24 cable, the memo left no doubt of Hilsman's position. For example, point 8 declared that if the coup began, Diem and Nhu would try to negotiate "to play for time" as they had successfully done once before, in 1960. "Our objective," Hilsman declared, "should, therefore, clearly be to bring the whole Ngo family under the control of the coup group. We should warn the coup group to press any military advantage it gains to its logical conclusion without stopping to negotiate." And "if necessary," he wrote in point 9, "we should bring in U.S. combat forces to assist the coup group to achieve victory." Then came point 10—"destroy the palace if necessary . . . Diem should be treated as the generals wish."

Hilsman's memo ran to six pages, single spaced. Top and bottom, each page was marked Top Secret, meaning, in the language of the Presidential Executive Order establishing the classification system, that disclosure could result "in exceptionally grave damage to the Nation."

In an interview eight years later, Hilsman said the memo was written "at the direct request of Rusk. It was a contingency memo. At the time Rusk was worried; he said things like 'Brother Nhu is on opium. Diem's back is to the wall. There are only 15,000 troops there. What would we do if they arrest the American ambassador? I'd like a memo listing all the possibilities.'"

Hilsman delegated the actual task of writing the draft to Joseph A. Mendenhall, a State Department official working on Vietnam policy. "I signed off on it," Hilsman said "and sent it upstairs." Upstairs meant Rusk's office on the seventh floor, where as far as Hilsman knew, the memo remained behind combination locks in the classified files.

Always strongly identified as a Kennedy man, Hilsman's days were numbered at State after Johnson became President. Within the department, the August 24 cable had added to Hilsman's reputation as a controversial figure. Moreover, there were, in Hilsman's words, increasing "personality and policy differences" with Rusk. Hilsman's free-wheeling style clashed with that of the reserved Rusk, whom Hilsman found "Buddha-like." As Hilsman recalls the policy differ-

ences over Vietnam, "Rusk felt—let the military handle it. It's not a
State Department problem. I wanted a guerrilla war against guerrillas; I wanted to win the people." Circling Sydney airport on a trip
to Australia in January, 1964, Hilsman said, he reached the decision
to resign. Rusk wanted him out and had delegated that task to
George Ball; Hilsman makes no bones about the fact that "if I hadn't
resigned, I would have been fired."*

Hilsman's relations with Rusk and the Johnson administration
became even more frayed when in August, 1964, he published an
inside account of the Cuban missile crisis in *Look* magazine. Besides
reporting on the deliberations that had taken place at the highest
levels of the government during the crisis, Hilsman revealed for the
first time the cloak-and-dagger contacts of ABC-TV newsman John
Scali, who acted for the American government, with a Soviet agent.
(Hilsman referred to the Russian as "Mr. X," but he was subsequently
identified as Alexander Fomin, the chief KGB agent in Washington,
who was attached to the Soviet embassy under diplomatic cover.)
The clandestine meetings, in the coffee shop and a deserted banquet
room of the Statler-Hilton, provided a separate channel of information to Khrushchev, and were credited by Hilsman with helping to
resolve the world's first nuclear confrontation.

Hilsman had shown the manuscript of the article to friends at the

---

*Three years later, in 1967, Rusk's anger at Hilsman boiled over at a private
"background" meeting with editors in New York. Over cocktails and luncheon, the normally impassive Secretary of State said sharply that Hilsman had
not resigned: "I fired him because he talked too much at Georgetown cocktail parties." The story leaked out; the next day Hilsman issued a reply: "I
don't believe Rusk ever said that. In the first place it isn't true. So far as I
know I have never been to a 'Georgetown cocktail party.' I didn't belong to
that set and was never asked. Second, and much more important, Dean Rusk
and I have had our differences, but he is too big a man to do anything like
this." Rusk had said it, however. The Secretary of State was also aware of a
story that had circulated in Washington about a dinner party at which Hilsman allegedly had made some unguarded remarks in the presence of the
then Vice-President Johnson, who, the story went, disapproved of what he
heard. There were various versions of the tale. Columnist William S. White,
a close friend of LBJ, did give a small dinner party in 1963 attended by the
Johnsons and the Hilsmans, but the participants, in *Rashomon* fashion, have
sharply conflicting recollections of whether the conversation centered on
the history of Texas or on Vietnam. Hilsman argues that the cocktail-party
aspect was cited only long afterward as a reason for his departure from the
State Department; he contends it was not a factor at the time.

State Department's Bureau of Intelligence and Research and had asked them to check it over for any security breaches. But the galleys he had promised to Rusk somehow did not arrive in time. Rusk reportedly was furious, suspecting—accurately—that Hilsman had delayed turning in the galleys until it was too late to make any changes in the *Look* piece.

In the fall of 1964 Hilsman went to Columbia to teach and work on a book. In 1965 the Johnson administration began its systematic bombing of North Vietnam. In September, Hilsman testified to a Senate subcommittee that the bombing of the North was "a bad mistake" and the bombing of South Vietnam "a tragic one" because it alienated the people and thus made "the task of true victory, a political victory, even more difficult." Hilsman's choice of a forum was not lost on the White House; it was a subcommittee on refugees and it was headed by Senator Edward M. Kennedy.

After testifying, Hilsman went to the National Archives to do research on his book. He had been there only a few moments when he was summoned to the telephone to take a call from McGeorge Bundy, Johnson's special assistant for national security affairs. Bundy had dug Hilsman out of the archives to express the President's displeasure at his testimony. As Hilsman recalls the conversation, it went like this:

> BUNDY: "The President is on my back because of you. How could you do this?"
> HILSMAN: "Because I'm against the bombing and you're going too strong on the military route."
> BUNDY *(pause):* "Roger, you have no idea of the things we've turned *down*."

Hilsman's book, *To Move a Nation*, combined his general views on foreign policy with a personalized account of the major international crises of the Kennedy years—including the Cuban missile confrontation, the Congo, and Vietnam. The book was critically well received when it was published by Doubleday in June, 1967. But its fans emphatically did not include Rusk and other senior members of the foreign policy establishment—notably William P. Bundy, Hilsman's successor as Assistant Secretary of State for Far Eastern Affairs. These men felt that Hilsman had used information and documents acquired as an official to promote his own views, and to justify his own actions, in a memoir. In part he had, of course, but so had others, and no such avalanche of disapproval greeted the memoirs of George Kennan or Dean Acheson. Hilsman's real sin was that he was not a member of the club.

A month before Hilsman's book was published, President Johnson received a memorandum from one of his White House assistants, John P. Roche. Like Hilsman, Roche was an academic who found himself drawn to power. Roche was a bundle of contrasts: a volatile, tough-talking Brooklyn Irishman who frequently interlarded his conversation with four-letter words, he was also a distinguished constitutional scholar and a practicing Quaker.* Although a professor of politics at Brandeis University, with his ruddy complexion and dark hair flecked with gray, he could easily be taken for your friendly neighborhood bartender. And although he had served as national chairman of the liberal Americans for Democratic Action for three years prior to his service in the Johnson White House, he had become an outspoken supporter of Johnson's Vietnam war policies. Roche had joined the administration in September of 1966 with the title of Special Consultant to the President. Much to his annoyance, he was usually described as the "house intellectual" and replacement for Eric F. Goldman, the Princeton historian who had departed amid thunderbolts of Presidential wrath. In fact, Roche insists, "Bill Moyers brought me in essentially as part of the group working out strategy on Vietnam." Nevertheless, Roche also served as Johnson's tenuous link to the intellectual community. It was an anomalous role, for Roche was a liberal academician who defended a war that was proving increasingly unpopular among academics and liberals.

Despite his general reputation as a hawk, however, Roche insists that he opposed the strategic bombing of North Vietnam from the outset. On May 1, 1967, he said in an interview: "I sent a memo to President Johnson, saying, in effect, that everything in Vietnam is being done wrong." The memo argued that the military had taken over the war but did not know how to run it.

Over the summer, Roche said, it was clear that Johnson realized the war was going badly. For many months, McNamara had been urging the President to cut back the bombing and accept a compromise political settlement. By the middle of May, McNamara's views had placed him in direct opposition to the Joint Chiefs of Staff. Torn by personal doubts over the war, and perhaps by misgivings over his own past role, McNamara seemed to his friends to be under an increasing strain. Apparently Johnson had already lost confidence in

*George Christian, a former press secretary to President Johnson, wrote in his book *The President Steps Down:* "John Roche, an Irish firebrand . . . fascinated Johnson. The President had a genuine affection for him, but tried to restrain his alley-fighter instincts . . ."

McNamara, for Roche asserts that Johnson remarked in his presence: "We can't have another Forrestal."*

During the summer, according to Roche, Johnson instructed him to undertake a study of U.S. involvement in Vietnam. "I want to know what happened. What went wrong?" Roche quotes Johnson as saying to him.

A rather more massive study was already under way about this time. On June 17, 1967, McNamara commissioned the Pentagon's study of the U.S. role in Vietnam, the forty-seven-volume *History of U.S. Decision-Making Process on Vietnam Policy* that surfaced four years later, almost to the day, as the Pentagon Papers. To direct the study, McNamara chose Leslie H. Gelb, head of policy planning for the Pentagon's Office of International Security Affairs. In October, Roche accompanied Vice-President Humphrey to Saigon for the inauguration of South Vietnam's President Nguyen Van Thieu. While in Saigon, Roche said: "I tripped over several of Gelb's workers."

Roche is sure that Johnson did not know of the Pentagon study for several months, because "I told the President about it. He said, 'What the hell are they writing history for? I thought they're supposed to be out winning the war.' "

As Vice-President, Lyndon Johnson had never approved of the U.S. support for the coup against Diem. In one of his more unfortunate oratorical excesses, Johnson, during a trip to Asia in May, 1961, had hailed Diem as "the Winston Churchill of Asia." At the end of August, 1963, after a coup had almost been launched by Hilsman's cable, Johnson presided over a high-level meeting at the State Department in which he opposed any coup, saw no alternative to Diem and, according to the official minutes, suggested the United States "stop playing cops and robbers" in Saigon. If in 1967 Johnson ordered Roche to conduct a study of "what went wrong" in Vietnam, Johnson certainly did not restrict the inquiry to the decisions of his own administration. For, in Saigon, Roche set about investigating the events surrounding the coup against Ngo Dinh Diem four years earlier, during the Kennedy administration.

A major question in Roche's mind, he says, was "Did Kennedy order a coup?" In Saigon, "I talked to Conein and I personally explored the origins of the coup." After questioning the CIA man and

---

*Mentally and physically exhausted from the strain of the job and overwork, James V. Forrestal, the nation's first Secretary of Defense, took his own life by plunging from the window of his sixteenth-floor room at Bethesda Naval Hospital on May 22, 1949.

examining the evidence, Roche concluded no—Kennedy had "half approved" but did not specifically order the coup. The real culprits, he decided, were Roger Hilsman and Michael Forrestal, son of the late Defense Secretary and a senior official of Kennedy's NSC staff, with Harriman "acting as their rabbi." Hilsman, Roche was persuaded, had managed to dispatch the critical August 24 cable only because the President and other senior officials were out of town.

Roche's conclusion was not likely to offend President Johnson. For LBJ, too, regarded Hilsman as an identifiable villain and an architect of the Vietnam troubles that now haunted his own administration and threatened his place in history. In *The Vantage Point*, Johnson later wrote that the "hasty and ill-advised" cable of August 24 stimulated the coup against Diem, "a serious blunder which launched a period of deep political confusion in Saigon that lasted almost two years."

Back in the Johnson White House, Roche began digging into State Department documents from the Kennedy era. "I turned up a whole batch of these cables from Hilsman . . . What was intriguing is that he never discussed these cables and documents in his book at all. I discovered that, without any authority, he declassified every memo that put him in a favorable light and hid every one that didn't. I was annoyed as hell."

How had Roche obtained the Hilsman file? "I had a note from the President—a carte blanche giving me access to any materials. As one of the first steps," he said, "I had a long talk with Rusk," and informed the Secretary of State of the job Johnson had asked him to do. As to the Hilsman file, "I simply asked for materials on the Diem coup. It all came over [to the White House] in a plain brown envelope."

A senior official who served under Rusk during this period recalls that "there were searches for tigerish Hilsman memos" going on at the State Department. "Someone, I don't know who, definitely wanted a search of State Department files to get damaging memos against Hilsman." Since Hilsman had been extremely unpopular with the department's bureaucracy, the search was conducted with considerable enthusiasm.

As he pored over the Hilsman file in the White House, Roche came upon two particularly choice items—the August 30 eleven-point memorandum and a second Hilsman memo to Rusk, this one classified Top Secret-Eyes Only and dated September 16, 1963. The second memo recommended that Washington follow a "Pressures and Persuasion Track" rather than an alternative "Reconciliation Track" in dealing with Diem and Nhu.

Reading these memos, Roche decided they were especially useful; although in his book Hilsman stressed that he had favored a political approach to Vietnam, the memos showed that—at least during the plotting against Diem—Hilsman had supported military force if circumstances in Saigon made it necessary and had taken a generally hard line.

The special consultant to the President also decided that the two classified memos, one marked Top Secret and the other marked Top Secret-Eyes Only, should be publicized. "I went to Johnson with the two Roger Hilsman memos," Roche said, "and I said, 'There is nothing in here affecting national security.' " Roche said he asked Johnson for authority to declassify the documents and leak them to the press. Johnson, Roche said, replied: "Go ahead."*

On the bottom of the top page of each of the two Hilsman memos, Roche typed the words "Declassified by authority of the President, 2/14/68" and scrawled his initials, "JPR," in ink.

Asked why, in the course of a historical study for the President, he had sought and obtained approval to release the Hilsman memos, Roche said he had done so "to shed some light on how an official had used documents for selective, self-serving reasons." He was annoyed at what Hilsman had done; he felt the story should be publicized. "I was outraged," said Roche, "by the abuse of historical method."

As it happened, however, Roche's outrage and President Johnson's decision to approve the declassification and leaking of the Hilsman memos coincided with a period when Senator Robert F. Kennedy was considering whether to challenge Johnson for the Democratic Presidential nomination. And Hilsman was acting as an informal foreign policy adviser to Robert Kennedy, particularly on Vietnam, a fact that was common knowledge in political circles and within the Johnson administration. In the early 1960's President Kennedy had embraced the doctrine of counterinsurgency as the key to the Vietnam problem; he named his brother to oversee that

---

*Roche said that in the course of his two years in the White House, "perhaps twenty-five to thirty documents" were declassified by him in this manner, sometimes with the approval of Walt W. Rostow, the President's assistant for national security affairs. "Often the President would say 'Clear it with Walt' and on occasion he turned down my suggestions." Other documents he declassified and leaked with the President's approval, Roche said, included a CIA study of the use of negotiations as a political weapon by Asian Communist nations, Johnson's own 1961 report to Kennedy on Vietnam and Asia, which had already been quoted by Arthur Schlesinger in his book *A Thousand Days*, and a 1966 State Department study of internal events in Communist China.

effort within the government, and Robert Kennedy worked closely with Hilsman, who championed the strategic hamlet program and other counterinsurgency techniques. They had stayed in touch, and after Robert Kennedy was elected to the Senate, Hilsman from time to time provided material on Vietnam for Kennedy's speeches. In sum, Hilsman was clearly and publicly a Kennedy man.

February 14, 1968—the date the Hilsman memos were marked "declassified by authority of the President"—was just two weeks after the Communist Tet offensive. On January 30–31 the Viet Cong and troops of North Vietnam had launched simultaneous attacks on major cities in South Vietnam and a commando team had even fought its way inside the U.S. embassy compound in Saigon. Tet jolted American public opinion and came as a disastrous blow to President Johnson. By mid-February, Robert Kennedy was under increasing pressure from friends and associates to run for President. On March 2 Jesse Unruh, the California Democratic leader, telephoned Kennedy to say poll results showed he would carry that state if he entered the primary; on March 16 Kennedy announced his Presidential candidacy.

Roche, however, takes the position that Johnson's decision to declassify and leak the August 30 memo "was directed at Hilsman, not at Bobby." If Johnson had Robert Kennedy in mind as a target, Roche said, the President did not mention this to him.* But Roche could not have known what was in Johnson's mind; and Johnson may have had one motive, Roche another. Hilsman is convinced that the

---

*The argument might be advanced that in February, 1968, when the Hilsman memo was declassified, Johnson was not concerned with Robert Kennedy as a possible Presidential rival because he had already privately decided not to run again. LBJ announced his decision to step down on March 31; in stories leaked thereafter by the White House, the claim was elaborately made that the President had reached this decision at various points prior to his announcement—either in 1964, or 1965, or 1967, or earlier in 1968. According to one version leaked with Johnson's approval, LBJ meant to announce his decision in his State of the Union address in January, 1968, but forgot his speech notes on Lady Bird's night table. No comment need be offered on these accounts. In his book *The Vantage Point,* Johnson gives a similar, long chronology of his "intention" or "decision" to retire—the wording is ambiguous—but concedes it was not "irrevocable" until announced. Not all of his listeners believed it even then, of course; and there appears to be some foundation for the thought that as late as August, 1968, Johnson still harbored lingering hopes that he would somehow end up his party's nominee.

leak was aimed at Robert Kennedy, although he does not rule out the possibility that it was also directed at himself. Since Hilsman had served President Kennedy, and was now advising Robert Kennedy, it seems, in retrospect, rather difficult to separate out Hilsman from the Kennedys.

Roche had several copies of the memo Xeroxed and, in his own words, he "passed some copies around town." One of the newsmen to whom Roche passed the memo was Mel Elfin, chief of the Washington Bureau of *Newsweek* magazine. Elfin's excellent sources in the capital included the President's assistant, and he learned of the Hilsman memo during a visit to Roche's house in Northwest Washington. While exercising on a rowing machine in his home at 5111 Watson Street, Roche told Elfin about the memo. He then showed it to Elfin, who took notes as Roche puffed away on his machine.

Elfin retained his notes, but did not write a story. Nor did the other reporters with whom Roche met. "They didn't use it," Roche recalls. "They had no peg at that time." Roche accurately understood the problem of the official leaker in Washington. News has a certain flow and rhythm; often reporters will not write a story unless it has a relationship to other events. This is especially true when the leaked information is clearly designed to embarrass or damage another official; the reporter is often reluctant to write the story unless it has a clear reason for being—otherwise he may feel he is simply performing political hatchet work for the leaker. It is not as easy as the uninitiated might suspect to leak certain kinds of stories, in Washington or elsewhere.

So the effort to leak the Hilsman memo failed in February, 1968. The following month, after the New Hampshire primary and Robert Kennedy's entrance into the race, Johnson announced he would not run again. In July, Roche departed the White House to return to Brandeis. Among the papers he took with him were the two Hilsman memos. Before leaving, he said, he wrote a reassuring memo to Johnson on the results of his Vietnam study. No options, Roche informed the President, had been overlooked in Johnson's Vietnam decisions; on the basis of the information the President had received, his decisions were correct.

The scene shifts to December 30, 1970, the grand ballroom of the Sheraton-Boston hotel. On that date Roche delivered a paper to the annual meeting of the American Historical Association. Its title: "The President and Congress and War: The Perils of 'Instant History.'"

In his speech, Roche lashed out at the "historical validity" of works by three academic colleagues who had served in government: Hilsman, Eric Goldman, Arthur Schlesinger, Jr. The trouble with "instant history," Roche declared, was that no former official had the full picture. He had himself signed up to do a book to be titled *From Camelot to the Alamo,* Roche conceded, but he had decided to put the project on ice until 1980. Then, for the first time, Roche publicly raised the curtain on the Hilsman memo; at least he let his colleagues have a peek by quoting parts of it.

But the story got buried the next day. Only Mel Elfin at *Newsweek,* who knew some of the background, did anything about it. The magazine published a long account of the Roche speech and quoted some snippets from the Hilsman memo.

In the meantime, other events were taking place that moved the contents of the Hilsman memo further into public view. A former student of Roche's, Victor Navasky, a political writer and an editor of *The New York Times Magazine,* had called Roche in December and asked him to do an article. Roche sent along the paper he was delivering to the historical association, and on January 24, 1971, it ran in somewhat adapted form in the *Times* magazine, under the title "The Jigsaw Puzzle of History."* The article assailed "instant historians" and argued that memoir writers had tunnel vision: "Each of us has a set of memos, but only the Presidential archives in Austin contain the whole range." Turning to the Hilsman book, Roche said that its author "declassified a large number of his own Secret and Top Secret memorandums; I am taking the liberty now of declassifying one that he somehow overlooked."

Roche's article then quoted verbatim four of the eleven points of the Hilsman August 30 memo. The "bellicose memo," Roche argued, did not square with Hilsman's claim, set forth in his book, that he had resigned in 1964 because he sensed that Johnson favored a "military solution" in Vietnam. A substantial portion of the document declassified three years earlier was now, finally, in print.

Astonishingly, the news media still did not pick up the published portions of the memo when Roche's article appeared. It was a pretty good story, but even the news sections of *The New York Times* ignored it. Nor did anyone ask in print why a former White House aide had an apparently Top Secret document in his possession or, for that matter, why, by whom, and under what circumstances, the document had been declassified.

Hilsman had had no inkling that his Top Secret memo was floating loose until just after Roche's Boston speech, when a friend who had been in the audience telephoned with the news. In February,

---

*Roche also sent Navasky a copy of the full original Hilsman memo, with the Top Secret markings crossed out, to back up his piece.

after the magazine piece appeared, Hilsman wrote to the *Times.* He defended the memo on the grounds that at the time Rusk had feared that Diem and Nhu "might actually use force against the 15,000 Americans then in Vietnam." And Hilsman sought to draw a distinction between the use of military force in this context and Johnson's later escalation of the war. In a reply printed with the Hilsman letter, Roche now pulled out the second Hilsman memo, dated September 16—the one urging pressure on the Diem regime rather than reconciliation—which he had been holding in reserve. He quoted from it at length and concluded that "by 1963 standards, Hilsman was about the hardest hawk in town."

On the day that the Hilsman-Roche exchange was published in the *Times* magazine, Tran Van Dinh, a professor at the Oyster Bay campus of the State University of New York, wrote to Roche at Brandeis. He had read Roche's article "with great interest," Dinh wrote, and wondered if Roche would be kind enough to make available the two Hilsman memos in full. In 1963, Dinh added, he had served as chargé d'affaires of the embassy of South Vietnam in Washington. Roche replied on March 8 and sent Dinh copies of both memos.

Dinh, a handsome, dark-haired former career diplomat, had served as South Vietnam's ambassador to Burma, then resigned in 1960 to become Minister of Information in the Diem government. Stationed in his country's Washington embassy when Diem was overthrown and murdered, Dinh resigned early in 1964 with a blast at American military intervention in Vietnam. He remained in the United States, teaching; and he became active in the peace movement along with his son, Tran Van Zung, a college student.

On Sunday, June 13, 1971, *The New York Times* ran the first installment of the Pentagon Papers. After three days publication was halted by a federal court restraining order. It was an unprecedented situation, and no one knew whether the government would succeed in permanently stopping the *Times.* While the *Times* was restrained, parts of the Pentagon study and other classified documents began appearing in other newspapers. In this atmosphere, Tran Van Dinh and his son Zung decided to give both memos to the press.*

Among Zung's young friends in the peace movement were Robert B. Johnson, twenty-eight, a writer and West Point graduate, and Jeremy Rifkin, the darkly intense national coordinator of an antiwar group called the Citizens' Commission of Inquiry on U.S. War Crimes

---

*As it later became clear, the Hilsman memos were not among the documents included or mentioned in the Pentagon's history of the Vietnam war.

in Vietnam. Rifkin, twenty-six, had formed the commission in 1969 after author Seymour Hersh had publicized the story of the My Lai massacre. Like other children of the television age, Rifkin had a shrewd, instinctive sense of how to use the news media. The commission began by holding low-key hearings in local communities, in which returning Vietnam veterans told of atrocities they had witnessed; Rifkin knew the hearings would get local press coverage; they built up, and by the time the group held hearings in Washington, the national TV networks were on hand. To Rifkin and Johnson, the commission's Eastern coordinator, the real story of the Hilsman memos was the question of how they came to be pulled out of the bureaucracy. By releasing them, they hoped to focus public attention not only on Vietnam policy under Kennedy, but on the larger issue of secrecy and classification.

At Dinh's home on Morrison Street in Northwest Washington, the former Vietnamese diplomat held a strategy conference with his son, Rifkin, and Johnson. Johnson knew correspondent Mort Kondracke of the *Chicago Sun-Times;* it was decided that Zung and Johnson would bring copies of the memos to the paper's Washington Bureau in the National Press Building; at the same time Rifkin would deliver the documents to the Associated Press, in the hope of getting national wire service coverage. Rifkin gave the memos to AP, along with a copy of Roche's magazine article in the *Times.* But AP, after checking by telephone with both Roche and Hilsman, decided that since the memos had already been published in part, it would not do a story.

The *Sun-Times,* however, decided to give the documents major play; in its June 23 issue, under a banner headline, it ran the story and, for the first time, the full text of the August 30 memo. The paper also published a partial text of the second Hilsman memo.*

In New York, Hilsman called a press conference at Columbia University. Perspiring under the television lights, he defended the two memos and blasted their original use as "a dirty deal" aimed at Robert Kennedy; President Johnson, he charged, through Roche, had been "leaking individual documents to damage critics of the war."

Eight years after Hilsman had written it, the August 30 Top

---

*At the time, not only *The New York Times,* but the *Boston Globe* and the *Washington Post* were under federal court orders not to publish more of the Pentagon Papers. The Justice Department could hardly move against the *Sun-Times,* however, since in this instance, the material had been declassified by a President.

Secret memo was finally out, the result of an odyssey that took it from Dean Rusk's files on the seventh floor of the State Department, to Lyndon Johnson's White House, to John Roche's exercise machine, to the Sheraton-Boston hotel, to the editorial offices of *The New York Times* in Manhattan, back to Washington to Tran Van Dinh's living room on Morrison Street, and finally, to the streets of Chicago. The entire episode stands as a monumental misuse of the classification system at the highest level of the government.

In a larger sense, the story of the Hilsman memo demonstrates that the words Top Secret are meaningless when it suits the convenience of a President, or his assistant, to ignore them. Clearly, a classification system established to protect the national security has at times been put to very different use. Through selective declassification, a President can use the same system to attempt to destroy his political enemies.

7

Secrecy, National Security, and the Press

In 1972 eight men in the United States carried in their wallets a small white identification card with red borders on both sides. The cardholder's height, weight, card number, and a seal of the Department of Defense appeared on one side; on the other, the words "Federal Emergency Assignee, Office of Emergency Planning," the bearer's name, and this sentence: "The person described on this card has been assigned essential emergency duties for the federal government. It is imperative that the bearer be assisted in travel by the fastest means to this emergency assignment."

The eight did not all know each other. Four of the men—the retired vice-president of a television network, a government bureaucrat, an editor of a trade magazine, and a motion picture industry executive—lived in Washington. The other four were scattered in various parts of the country—a retired Army officer with a background in defense communications in Delray Beach, Florida, a corporate executive in Illinois, a former civil defense official in South Carolina, and a college administrator in Maryland.

Only one common bond joined these men from diverse backgrounds: all were members of a very special and little-known government unit. On orders from the President of the United States, they would report to a classified location near Washington to form the core of what was known, until fairly recently, as the United States Office of Censorship.

The censors would report, if instructed, to their secret headquarters, located for the past several years on the campus of Western Maryland College, a small liberal arts institution forty-five miles due north of the White House in the rural town of Westminster, Maryland. There, the men with the little white cards would have the task of interpreting and administering a seven-page, single-spaced Censorship Code.

The code they would supervise from this bucolic setting is designed to prohibit the press from reporting about a wide range of military and diplomatic information. Under the terms of the code, even ordinary weather forecasts could not be published without explicit permission of the federal government.

The eight men would censor all American news media—television, radio, newspapers, and magazines. They would act as arbiters of what the public would be allowed to read, see, and hear. Apparently the censorship would be "voluntary"—although that is not totally clear—but if the experience of World War II is any guide, few publishers or broadcasters would dare to violate the code.

Because of the unpleasant sound of the word "censorship," the Nixon administration quietly changed the name to the Wartime Information Security Program (WISP). Although the name has thus been changed to make it sound more palatable, the unit's function has not.

Officially these censors are members of the federal government's Executive Reserve, an elite group of civilians who would move into various key government positions in the event of a national emergency.*

There is a second part to WISP. Thousands of other Executive Reservists would, if ordered, report to cableheads and to other strategic locations across the country to censor all mail, cables, telephone calls, and other communications entering or leaving the country. There would be nothing voluntary about this part of the program.

The few members of Congress and the press who were aware of

---

*The eight men, as of 1972, were Theodore F. Koop, retired vice-president of CBS and deputy director of censorship during World War II; Edward Cooper, legislative vice-president of the Motion Picture Association of America; Sol J. Taishoff, editor of *Broadcasting* magazine; James P. Taff, chief of personnel for the Bureau of Census, all of Washington; James W. Scully, III, retired Army communications officer, of Delray Beach, Florida; Philip T. Foss, of the Eastman Kodak Company, Oak Brook, Illinois, former chief Army censor; Robert Y. Phillips, retired OEP official, of Beaufort, South Carolina; and Eugene Willis, director of physical plant, Western Maryland College, Westminster, Maryland.

the existence of the censorship office generally assumed that it could never be activated unless Congress declared war. They are wrong. The censors can be ordered into action and the code put into effect any time the President of the United States wishes to do so. He would not necessarily have to declare a national emergency; there would not have to be a declaration of war.

Eight men with special ID cards in their pockets? Official censorship? A secret headquarters on a remote college campus in Maryland? A Censorship Code already prepared that could be invoked by the President? Surely this could not exist in a country with a Constitution and a First Amendment. It all sounds like something out of *Dr. Strangelove* or *Seven Days in May*. But it is not. The men, the code, the headquarters, the machinery are real.

A draft Executive Order already exists to activate the censors. It is not even entirely clear that the President would have to issue an order; it is possible he could act under existing Executive Orders. Or the President could ask Congress to pass standby legislation, also already prepared, to authorize the censors to begin work.

The word "wartime" in the new title of the censorship office implies that the machinery would only be invoked in wartime. But what, precisely, is wartime? The United States became involved in a war in Vietnam beginning in 1961, although Congress never declared war. Testimony by officials of the Office of Emergency Preparedness, which seems to share responsibility for the censorship program with the Pentagon, is fuzzy on the question of what circumstances could trigger press censorship.

For example, on May 12, 1972, Eugene J. Quindlen, assistant director of OEP and the man directly in charge of WISP, told the House subcommittee on government information that "it would be *unlikely* that any element of the Wartime Information Security Program would be implemented in any contingency short of a nuclear attack . . ." [Emphasis added.]

The committee chairman, Congressman William S. Moorhead, was concerned; he asked whether "censorship . . . could be invoked in any situation short of wartime emergency?" Quindlen replied: ". . . *we do not foresee* any situation short of wartime in which it could be invoked . . . the *primary* contingency for which plans should be prepared . . . is the situation of nuclear attack . . . the Wartime Information Security Program should be directed *primarily* at a nuclear attack situation . . ." [Emphasis added.]

The standby Executive Order, it is true, presumes that a nuclear attack has occurred and that the President has declared a national emergency. But the standby legislation merely refers to "the present emergency situation," which could mean just about anything.

Moreover, the "Office of Censorship Basic Plan," which remained in effect under WISP in 1972, lists the "contingencies" that "may require imposition of . . . censorship" as "(a) general war; and (b) limited war, or conflicts of the 'brush fire' type, in which U.S. forces are involved elsewhere in the world on land, sea, or in the air."

Under the proposed standby law, "Whenever the President shall deem that the public safety demands it, he may cause to be intercepted, examined, and controlled . . . communications by mail, cable, radio, television, or other means of transmission crossing the borders of the United States." The same draft legislation authorizes the President to activate WISP and appoint a director. It adds: "The director shall exercise such powers and perform such functions as the President may prescribe." This is so sweeping a grant of power that it would appear to permit mandatory, not voluntary censorship. Anyone violating this law would be guilty of a felony and subject to a fine of $10,000 and ten years in prison.

The existence of WISP and its censorship machinery began to attract some public attention late in 1972, when it developed that James W. McCord, Jr., a defendant in the Watergate bugging case, was a member of a military reserve unit that comprised WISP's Special Analysis Division (SAD). McCord, a former FBI and CIA agent, was coordinator of security for the Committee for the Re-election of the President at the time of his arrest. According to SAD's organizational chart, one of its principal tasks was to prepare a "National Watchlist," which Representative Moorhead charged would apparently contain the names of politically "questionable" American citizens.

The roots of the present shadowy censorship machinery can be traced back to World War II, when Byron Price, a former executive of the Associated Press, served as wartime director of censorship. Price and a staff of fifteen administered a voluntary censorship code; several thousand other persons serving under Price censored mail, cables, and communications. The office issued a Code of Wartime Practices to guide editors. It was not required that news copy be submitted to the director of censorship prior to publication, but editors who had questions, or doubts about whether to publish a particular story, could consult Price and his staff. By and large, editors and broadcasters complied with the code.

In 1945, at the end of the war, Price prepared and sent to President Harry S. Truman a memorandum which, he wrote, "may be helpful in planning and administering censorship in any future war." The memorandum, which was stamped Confidential, urged that Truman appoint a Censorship Planning Commission which "should operate on a strictly confidential basis, and be financed from the President's confidential funds."

The government did plan for censorship. During the Eisenhower administration the Censorship Code was developed, and the President secretly named Theodore F. Koop, the affable, mild-mannered director of CBS News in Washington, as the standby director of censorship. During World War II, Koop had served as Byron Price's deputy. Two dozen other persons, including a few newsmen and former newsmen, were given the little white cards and assigned to serve under Koop in the event the unit office was activated. Occasionally, but rarely, the group would hold meetings. Koop's identity was officially classified.

During the Kennedy administration, just after the Bay of Pigs, Koop and Price were called to the White House. According to Koop, the two men spent the afternoon with Presidential news secretary Pierre Salinger and Theodore Sorensen, the President's Special Counsel, exploring the possibility of instituting some form of voluntary censorship. The President's aides discussed the idea of designating one person to whom editors could refer in deciding whether to publish defense or national security information.

The discussion took place at a moment when Kennedy was distressed over the fact that the press had published stories prior to the CIA-directed Cuban invasion hinting that it was about to take place. Koop said that both he and Price argued against any form of voluntary censorship; in peacetime, they asserted, the country was not mobilized and not ready psychologically to accept such restrictions.

When Kennedy met on May 9, 1961, with seven leading newspaper executives, he proposed essentially the plan that had been outlined to Koop and Price. As later reported by Salinger in *With Kennedy*, the President suggested the publishers appoint a representative who would be fully briefed by the government when a newspaper had doubts about whether to print a story that might involve security. The representative would then advise the newspaper, which could accept or reject his advice. Salinger called the meeting a "total failure." The news executives told the President they would accept no censorship in the absence of a declaration of national emergency.

The present standby Censorship Code was first drafted in 1958, under Eisenhower, and last revised in September, 1963, during the Kennedy administration. Under the terms of the code, the news media would not publish information about "war plans, or diplomatic negotiations," enemy attacks, troop movements, ships, military aircraft, missiles, production data, and travel movements of the President and "other high-ranking civilian or military officials." Weather forecasts would not be published or broadcast unless cleared, and even then, they would be published or broadcast only inside one state and within a 150-mile radius.

"In short," the code states, "it is vital that the enemy should not learn from our press or broadcasters just what the attacking forces have accomplished. On the other hand, there is left considerable scope for news enterprise. It is not intended to place any restrictions on the reporting of local stories of such matters as feats of heroism, incidents of personal courage, or the call of an individual to duty with the military or civil defense organizations."*

In May, 1970, Samuel J. Archibald, director of the Washington office of the Freedom of Information Center of the University of Missouri, wrote to the Office of Emergency Preparedness asking a number of questions about the censorship program, including the identity of the person designated as the director of censorship. OEP director George A. Lincoln wrote back saying the name of the director "currently carries a security classification." Later Archibald wrote to Nixon demanding to know the identity of the chief censor. His request was turned down, but in October, Koop's name was published in the *Washington Star*.

Soon afterward, in an obvious effort to defuse the issue, the administration quietly abolished the position of Director of Censorship. Koop lost only his title, however, since he continued to serve in the Executive Reserve assigned to the censorship unit.† The most experienced censorship official, he would in all likelihood be tapped as director if the unit was activated. Apparently in a further effort to bury any controversy, OEP even said early in 1972, in answer to an inquiry, that the unit had been disbanded, which was not true. The membership was winnowed from twenty-six to eight, and a number of older reservists were dropped, but the unit remained very much in existence.

The eight remaining members are not, individually, a sinister lot. Koop, for example, is a genteel man, a respected and long-established figure in the Washington press corps. Eugene Willis, a poten-

---

*The Censorship Code is not classified, but it has not been generally distributed to newspapers or radio and television stations. If the President activated the censorship unit, the government would ask AP and UPI to move the code on their wires. OEP estimated in Congressional testimony that the code could be in the hands of the news media, and censorship established in the United States, "within forty-five to sixty minutes."
†Koop became a vice-president of CBS and the corporation's Washington representative in 1961. He retired from CBS at the end of 1971.

tial censor of the nation's press by accident of his position as director of buildings and grounds at Western Maryland College—and thus keeper of the secret headquarters—is a hospitable, transplanted Virginia gentleman who enjoys life in the farm country around Westminster and takes pride in its nine-hole golf course.

But that is beside the point. That there should exist in America a shadow group of censors, surrounded by secrecy, that the conditions under which the unit might be activated by the President of the United States—and its mode of operation—are at best imprecisely defined, surely cannot be regarded as a comforting state of affairs in a democracy.

The argument for limiting the right of the press to publish national security information is a familiar one: the First Amendment must be balanced against other parts of the Constitution, the President has a broad responsibility to protect the nation against enemies, foreign and domestic, and this value must be paramount when "national security" is threatened. Those who would place controls on the news media contend that national self-preservation is more important than any other single value, including freedom of the press. If the nation is destroyed, the argument runs, the press is destroyed along with it, so the right to publish must be sacrificed in the interests of security. Essentially, however, this is a better-unread-than-dead argument. It is a rationale for censorship.

It may be that in time of war, the public will accept a degree of censorship. But not only has the definition of "war" become blurred in the last third of the twentieth century, there is a second difficulty. *All* information is of possible value to an adversary, with the result that any attempt to list what kinds of information ought be denied is doomed to be either too narrow or overbroad. It is impossible to arrive at a standard, as the government discovered in the Pentagon Papers case. Moreover, "national security" is a term of political art, which can be defined by a given administration to coincide with its political interests. The men in power tend, sometimes unconsciously, to equate their own personal and partisan interests with the national interest, no matter how noble their motives. There is a third difficulty. Even if general agreement could be reached on the conditions that would warrant restricting the press—and no such consensus exists—and even if a standard could be fashioned to define what kinds of information might be restricted, there would remain the constitutional barrier against abridging freedom of the press. But the Constitution, as Chief Justice Charles Evans Hughes once pointed out, "is what the judges say it is." So there is no assurance that the Supreme Court will at all times prefer First Amendment values to those of national security.

There are two principal ways that government can attempt to restrict the press. It can seek to impose prior restraint, as in the Pentagon Papers case, by asking the courts to enjoin the publication of information allegedly harmful to the United States. Or it can seek to punish the press after the fact, by criminally prosecuting individual members and/or their organizations. As of early 1973 the extent of the government's power to do either was by no means clear.

As already noted, there is no general prohibition in the law against publishing classified information. The President's Executive Order establishing the classification system is simply a set of housekeeping rules within the Executive Branch; it does not apply to the press, since the press, fortunately, is not employed by the President. Only one law, Section 798 of Title 18 of the United States Code, bars the publication of "classified information" as such—in the special area of cryptography or communications intelligence—and its constitutionality has not been tested.

Nor is it clear whether the government can constitutionally apply the espionage laws to the press. The fact that the government has not sought to punish the press for seditious behavior since 1798 does not mean that it could not do so again. The Alien and Sedition Acts were passed by the Federalists in that year in an attempt to suppress Republican newspapers and political opposition. The Sedition Act provided a maximum fine of $2,000 and two years in prison for "malicious writing" or nasty statements against the President or Congress. Congressman Matthew Lyon of Vermont, who had accused President John Adams of "a continual grasp for power," was the first person convicted under the act. There were some twenty-five arrests under the act, and fifteen indictments; the editors of four Republican newspapers were among those prosecuted. The law expired in 1801 and was not passed again, since by then Jefferson was President and the Republicans were in power.

During the Civil War military censorship was imposed on the press. Lincoln reminded war correspondents that they could be court-martialed for espionage if their stories aided the enemy. The Union Army censored the dispatches of correspondents in the field, the Post Office banned antiwar publications from the mails, federal troops seized newspaper offices, and editors were jailed. Several newspapers were shut down or individual issues suppressed.

During World War I, Congress debated what became the Espionage Act of 1917.* As originally proposed, the measure would have

---

*The act became law in June, two months after the United States had entered the war.

given the President sweeping powers to censor the press. But Congress specifically rejected this feature of the bill.

As passed, and as later amended, the whole thrust of the Espionage Act is that of a law designed to catch spies, not reporters and editors. The first section prohibits anyone from collecting information about various types of military installations—there is a long list —"with intent or reason to believe that the information is to be used to the injury of the United States, or to the advantage of any foreign nation." Other parts of this section are designed to prevent the transmittal of government documents or information to unauthorized persons; this was, in part, the language under which the government indicted Daniel Ellsberg. Violators are subject to a fine of up to $10,000 and/or ten years in prison.

A second, and more serious, section of the espionage law prohibits the transmittal of such documents or information to another country, or to an enemy in time of war, and in this section, the penalties include life imprisonment or death. In general, the espionage laws define the kind of data they wish to protect as "information relating to the national defense."

When the law was under consideration, it occurred to a number of congressmen that this was a rather vague phrase, and one of them, Senator Albert B. Cummins, an Iowa Republican, said so during the debate: "Now, I do not know, as I have said a great many times, what does relate to the public defense, and no human being can define it . . . it embraces everything which goes to make up a successful national life in the Republic. It begins with the farm and the forest, and it ends with the Army and the Navy."

Despite the senator's entirely sensible misgivings, the law, as enacted, barred trafficking in "information relating to the national defense." Not until January, 1941, did the Supreme Court pass on the constitutionality of the spy law and come to grips with the definitional problem posed by Senator Cummins. The case reached the court because a Soviet agent made the sort of mistake that might be committed by Woody Allen in an espionage farce. The agent, Mikhail Gorin, had entered the United States in 1936, and two years later was stationed on the West Coast under official cover as the Intourist manager in Los Angeles. Gorin paid a civilian investigator for the Navy, Hafis Salich, to turn over to him the contents of more than fifty reports dealing with Japanese espionage and activities in the United States. The reports were taken from the files of the naval intelligence branch at San Pedro, California. In December, 1938, Gorin sent a suit to the cleaners with some of the papers in the pocket. As a result, he was arrested, convicted, and sentenced to six years. The Supreme Court upheld his conviction in 1941.

In so doing, the court reached three important conclusions. It ruled that the words that saved the espionage statute from being unconstitutionally vague were those requiring "intent or reason to believe" that the information being gathered would be used to injure the United States or aid another power. "This requires those prosecuted to have acted in bad faith," the court said. Secondly, the court defined "national defense" as "a generic concept of broad connotations, referring to the military and naval establishments and the related activities of national preparedness." And finally, it said it was up to a jury in such cases "to decide whether the information secured is of the defined kind. It is not the function of the court, where reasonable men may differ, to determine whether the acts do or do not come within the ambit of the statute."

It is not entirely clear that the court's definition of "national defense" really helped very much—one can almost hear the ghost of Senator Cummins snorting at it—but by passing along the problem to juries, the court did something extremely significant. The decision meant that no bureaucrat could, merely by stamping a document Top Secret, make it so.* A jury would still have to decide whether the document belonged to the farm and forest, or to the Army and Navy.

This ruling was extremely important, because it meant that as a general principle a person could not be convicted under the espionage laws merely for possessing or transmitting a document that someone in the government had classified. To have held otherwise would have created a system of automatic guilt for possession of classified materials. That concept is embodied in the British Official Secrets Act, but not, fortunately, in the basic American law.

Gorin and other espionage cases did nothing to clarify whether the 1917 statute might be applied to the press. Three days before Pearl Harbor the *Chicago Tribune* published a story disclosing a U.S. war plan. The article, based on a "confidential" report, caused a sensation, but the government took no action against the paper. Then on June 7, 1942, the *Tribune* ran a story headlined "Navy Had

---

*This was specifically enunciated by a federal appeals court in a 1965 espionage case, *United States v. Drummond.* The appeals court ruled that marking a document Top Secret was not enough to convict a defendant. The court said the trial judge had properly charged the jury as follows: "Whether any given document relates to the national defense of the United States is a question of fact for you to decide. It is not a question of how they were marked." The Supreme Court let this decision stand by declining to review it.

Word of Jap Plan to Strike at Sea." The story went on to describe in detail the elements of the Japanese fleet at the Battle of Midway. The article, datelined Washington, bore no byline, but the information came from Stanley Johnston, the *Tribune* correspondent in the Pacific. The article did *not* say, as it is sometimes thought, that the United States had broken the Japanese code, but the government feared that Japan would realize this was the case. In the event that the Japanese had not been reading the Chicago papers, the Justice Department seemed determined to bring the story to their attention. On August 7 Attorney General Francis Biddle announced that a federal grand jury in Chicago would investigate whether the newspaper had violated the Espionage Act.* The jury took testimony from the paper's editors, but there was no prosecution.

There was, in fact, only one case where the government had arrested journalists for alleged violation of the espionage laws. This was the celebrated *Amerasia* affair. In June, 1945, FBI agents arrested Philip J. Jaffe, editor, and Kate Louise Mitchell, co-editor, of the left-wing magazine *Amerasia*, along with four other persons: Andrew Roth, a lieutenant in the naval reserve; Mark J. Gayn, a magazine writer; and Emmanuel S. Larsen and John Stewart Service, both officials of the State Department. About 1,700 government documents or copies of documents, many of them classified, were seized in the magazine's office in New York. All six persons were arrested on charges of conspiracy to violate the Espionage Act. But a grand jury returned indictments against only three of the six—Jaffe, Larsen, and Roth—on lesser charges of conspiracy to steal government documents.†

---

*The Japanese did not change their code because of the *Tribune* story or the subsequent federal investigation. In April, 1943, U.S. cryptanalysts intercepted Admiral Isoroku Yamamoto's schedule for a planned inspection trip to Bougainville Island. American P-38 fighter planes were waiting and shot down the bomber in which he was traveling. Even after Yamamoto's death, the Japanese could not believe that their code had been cracked.

†Jaffe pleaded guilty; Larsen pleaded nolo contendere; and they were fined $2,500 and $500 respectively. The charge against Roth was dismissed. John Stewart Service later testified he had passed documents to Jaffe, but maintained that it was the custom for Foreign Service officers to let journalists see such material on "background." Service, a China expert and respected career official, was restored to duty at the State Department but was dismissed in 1951 after he became a prime target of the late Senator Joseph R. McCarthy. In 1957 a federal court in Washington ordered Service reinstated, and he returned to the State Department. In 1964 he took a post in Chinese studies at the Berkeley campus of the University of California.

The issue remained unresolved, and in the years following World War II, government and the press in Washington played a game of cat and mouse. The rules of the game were never articulated, but they went something like this: government officials would leak classified information to reporters when it suited their purposes, and reporters understood that they were free to use this material. But reporters who obtained access to embarrassing government secrets on their own, perhaps from dissident officials within the government, or who delved into the operations of the Central Intelligence Agency, as, for example, the author of this book did, could never be entirely certain what actions the government might take against them. No reporter or writer had ever been prosecuted for publishing material in violation of the espionage laws; and it might be difficult to obtain a conviction, and politically unwise. Still, the *possibility* of such a prosecution was always there, nonetheless real for its not having been tested. This was the framework within which the contest took place, a sort of ongoing Monopoly game in which the government, at any point, might tell the reporter: "Do not pass Go; proceed directly to jail."

That is where matters stood until the case of the Pentagon Papers burst upon the world in June, 1971. The legal battle for the first time brought into sharp focus the question of the right of the press to publish information about national security. Whether the espionage laws could be applied to the press remained an important, but not central, issue in the legal contest that took place over the right of *The New York Times* and the *Washington Post* to publish the Pentagon study.

That is because the case turned on the question of prior restraint. It was fought, therefore, within the confines of this narrow, special area of the law, and the related question of whether the press could be punished after the fact for what it published was not immediately at issue.

The long-established tradition against prior restraint is rooted in English law. When printing developed in England in the fifteenth century, publishers were licensed by the state. After these onerous laws expired in 1695, the right of the press to be free of such censorship became widely recognized. In his *Commentaries on the Laws of England,* the eighteenth-century jurist William Blackstone wrote: "The liberty of the press is indeed essential to the nature of a free state; but this consists in laying no *previous* restraint upon publications, and not in freedom from censure for criminal matter when published."

The purpose of the First Amendment, in part, was to prohibit prior restraint and censorship such as had existed in England. The issue was dealt with at length by the Supreme Court in the 1931 case of *Near v. Minnesota*. A Minneapolis scandal sheet, *The Saturday Press,* had charged that a Jewish gangster controlled gambling, bootlegging, and racketeering in Minneapolis, and that the police were taking graft. Acting under the Minnesota Gag Law, a state court enjoined the newspaper from publishing "scandalous" articles. The Supreme Court reversed the decision.

Chief Justice Hughes, writing the majority opinion, traced the history of the struggle against English censorship. The Minnesota statute, he said, was "the essence of censorship." He quoted Blackstone and concluded that while protection against prior restraint was not "unlimited," the press could be stopped in advance from printing articles only in "exceptional cases."

The decision then named three: "No one would question but that a government might prevent actual obstruction to its recruiting service or the publication of the sailing dates of transports or the number and location of troops."

In seeking to suppress the Pentagon Papers, the government argued that these oft-cited examples were merely illustrative and not inclusive. The contents of the Pentagon study, the government said, should also be regarded as an exception to the general rule against prior restraint.

Never before had the federal government gone into court to try to censor a newspaper. The government charged that the *Times* had willfully published material prohibited by the espionage laws, and that further publication would bring "irreparable injury to the United States." But the government rested its case not on the spy laws, not on the fact that the documents were classified, but on a broad claim of injury to the government and of "grave and immediate danger to the security of the United States."

In argument before the Supreme Court on June 26, Solicitor General Erwin N. Griswold conceded that if the court permitted the Pentagon Papers to be published, the government would find it awkward to prosecute after the fact. "I find it exceedingly difficult to think," Griswold told the court, "that any jury would affirm a conviction of a criminal offense for the publication of materials which this court has said could be published."

The six-to-three Supreme Court decision on June 30 permitted the *Times* and *Post* to resume publication of the Pentagon Papers. The court noted that any government attempt at prior restraint bears "a heavy presumption against its constitutional validity." It added: ". . . the government has not met that burden."

The opinions of the justices reflected widely divergent positions.* As a result, the case settled neither the question of prior restraint nor that of criminal prosecution of the press under the espionage laws. The court decided only that the *Times* and *Post* could publish the Pentagon Papers; it did not rule out government censorship in cases that might arise in the future.

While the question of prior restraint had not been legally resolved, the decision did have a political impact. As a practical matter, the Nixon administration, having lost a case of such spectacular nature, did not seem eager to go into court again very soon to attempt to prohibit a major newspaper from printing military or diplomatic news. Six months later, for example, columnist Jack Anderson printed and made public classified transcripts of secret meetings of a subcommittee of the National Security Council. Although the transcripts were recent, embarrassing, and dealt with a current crisis, the India-Pakistan conflict, the administration took no action against Anderson or the newspapers that printed his material. In 1972 Anderson won the Pulitzer Prize for these stories.

The passage of time, or a change in administration, however, could always bring renewed attempts at government censorship or prosecution. There was another irony, of course; even in losing its case, the government "won," in the sense that the *Times* was prevented from publishing the Pentagon Papers for fifteen days, an event unprecedented in the history of the republic. Judicial consideration of a plea for prior restraint amounts, in itself, to a form of prior restraint.

On the second question, that of possible prosecution of the press, two members of the court virtually encouraged the government to try its luck. Justice White, joined by Stewart, apparently disagreed with the Solicitor General's willingness to throw in the sponge on criminal prosecution. In an unusual opinion, White cited the sections of the espionage laws in great detail, and said the newspapers "were now on full notice of the position of the United States and must face the consequences if they publish." Then, in an extraordinary statement for a Supreme Court justice, he added: "I would have no difficulty in sustaining convictions under these sections . . ." on facts that would not justify prior restraint. White seemed to be

---

*The decision of the court was unsigned, but each of the nine justices wrote a separate opinion. The six justices in the majority were Hugo L. Black, William O. Douglas, William J. Brennan, Jr., Potter Stewart, Byron R. White and Thurgood Marshall. Chief Justice Warren E. Burger and Justices Harry A. Blackmun and John M. Harlan dissented.

inviting the Nixon administration to prosecute the *Times* or its reporters.

In fact, the Justice Department did not need an invitation. For months the federal grand jury in Boston questioned witnesses about the activities of Neil Sheehan and his wife, Susan. Neither the *Times* nor Sheehan regarded an indictment as a remote possibility; Sheehan hired his neighbor on Klingle Street, Mitchell Rogovin, of Arnold & Porter, to help prepare his defense. During the fall of 1971 Rogovin spent a major portion of his time on the case. Washington lawyers of Rogovin's stature are very expensive, as are the *Times'* own attorneys, and the newspaper, one of its editors told me, altogether spent more than $30,000 preparing Sheehan's legal defense. For many months, lawyers involved in the case fully believed that Sheehan would be indicted. No one was certain what was going to happen.

Indeed, one of the long-range effects of the Pentagon Papers controversy may have been to increase government temptation to prosecute reporters under the espionage laws.* If this happens, American democracy will be dangerously transformed.

Even a grand jury investigation, as in the case of the *Times'* Neil Sheehan, has a chilling effect on the news media. An indictment of a reporter or news organization for publishing information in alleged violation of the Espionage Act would virtually be the equivalent of censorship, and for this reason: the moment this happened, the result would be almost indistinguishable from prior restraint. The effect would be to create a system of internalized prior restraints. Reporters, editors, publishers would know that they could not report on military or diplomatic events without risking government prosecution.

And the risk would occur daily. When a news reporter interviews a government official about military, foreign policy, or intelligence matters, he takes notes "relating to national defense." The reporter is often unaware that the official is discussing information contained in classified documents. Even if the reporter knows this, or is actually given a classified document, he cannot be certain in advance that he has violated the law, since the law

---

*In April, 1972, this threat was openly voiced by Kevin T. Maroney, deputy assistant attorney general in the Justice Department's Internal Security Division. In a speech to newspaper editors, he warned that if they published classified information, they would "run the risk of violating a criminal statute . . ."

contains no general prohibition against the release of "classified" information.*

Thus, the threat of prosecution would amount to a system of prior restraint almost as effective as a government censor. Not all legal scholars place equal emphasis on the supposed difference between prior restraint and subsequent punishment. For example, Paul A. Freund has written: "Certain distinctions commonly drawn between prior restraint and subsequent punishment will not bear analysis. It is sometimes said that prior restraint is the greater deterrent. This generality depends on the psychological aspects of the case . . . the judicial sanction takes its bite after the fact in either case, whether the sanction be fine or imprisonment for criminal violation or fine or imprisonment for violation of an injunctive or administrative order."

Since the possibility of prosecution under the espionage laws would be certain to make some reporters and editors avoid reporting about sensitive subjects, the net effect would be seriously to impair the flow of information to the public. If applied to the press, therefore, the Espionage Act becomes a law abridging freedom of the press in violation of the First Amendment.

At the core of all this is the continuing clash between the values of a free press and those of national security. Many constitutional scholars, political leaders, jurists, and others believe those values must be "balanced" and compromised. But a democratic system requires a public informed about the decisions and actions of its political leaders. If democracy is to work, the freedom of the press to report about *the activities of government* cannot be qualified by prior restraint or subsequent punishment.† The press must be free

---

*There is an unresolved question of whether the specific section of the Espionage Act cited by the government in the Pentagon Papers case actually prohibits publication. In federal district court in New York, Judge Murray I. Gurfein noted that the word "publication" did not appear in section 793(e), but that subsequent sections of the law did refer to anyone who "publishes" certain information in wartime or cryptographic and intelligence data. Gurfein concluded that Congress, therefore, did not intend the main section of the spy law to apply to the press. The legislative history of the act supports this view. When the case reached the Supreme Court, Justice White argued that regardless of whether Gurfein was correct, the press could still violate the act through unauthorized possession of documents.

†If a reporter obtained defense information and passed it on to a foreign power, prosecution would not raise insurmountable First Amendment problems. In that case, the government could demonstrate that the reporter was

to publish no matter what the potential harm to an officially defined "national security." The risks of repression are greater. Any legal restrictions imposed upon the press in advance, or by later punishment, that limit what it can report about the government would diminish the First Amendment and change the nature of American democracy. It is always possible to rationalize the case for curbing the press in particular circumstances. But who can say, once it begins, where it will end? Freedom to publish about government is either absolute, or it does not exist. Once qualified, it may be described as something else, but not as freedom of the press.

This does not mean that government can have no secrets. But it does mean that once information escapes from the government's hands, the press should have the right to print it. This argument was brilliantly articulated by Professor Thomas I. Emerson of Yale Law School, a leading First Amendment scholar, in a brief he filed with Congressman Bob Eckhardt of Texas in the Pentagon Papers case.

"The Executive regulations on classification can govern the internal operation of the Executive agencies," the brief noted. "They cannot, under the First Amendment, control communication of information outside the government. To put it colloquially, a cat in the bag cannot be treated the same way as a cat outside the bag. Once the information gets outside the Executive—once the Executive loses its control for any reason—the information becomes part of the public domain."

Emerson expanded on his "cat outside the bag" theory in later testimony to the Senate subcommittee on constitutional rights. "The only way in which our system of freedom of expression can operate effectively is to treat all so-called classified material which escapes from government possession as part of the pool of information available to the whole community in the conduct of its public affairs."

It can be argued, of course, that prosecution of the press for publishing "harmful" security information would not abridge the First Amendment any more than libel and obscenity laws, which already limit what may be published. Obscenity, for example, has been held to be outside the area afforded First Amendment protection.

---

acting as a spy, and that his vocation as a journalist was incidental to his occupation as a spy. Similarly, a reporter who broke into a government office and stole documents might face prosecution for theft, since in this case the sanctions would apply to the manner in which the material was wrongfully acquired and not to its publication.

But sanctions against obscenity and libel of private individuals are scarcely comparable to restrictions that might be imposed upon the press by the government for reporting about the activities of that government. The right of the news media to report freely, and without limitations, on public issues and government policies goes to the heart of the democratic process. In the area of libel, this has been recognized by the Supreme Court; in *The New York Times v. Sullivan* and subsequent cases, the court has ruled that the news media cannot, in the absence of actual malice, successfully be sued for publishing articles—even if erroneous—about government officials, public figures, or persons involved in public events. In articulating what has become known as *The New York Times* rule, the court said that "debate on public issues should be uninhibited, robust, and wide-open, and . . . may well include vehement, caustic, and sometimes unpleasantly sharp attacks on governmental and public officials."

But if the press, under the First Amendment, must be free to publish classified information and government secrets, a corollary legal question arises: Should the government be free to take action against officials who leak the information to the press?

A rational case can be made that to conduct its affairs in an orderly fashion, the government must have the power to reprimand, dismiss, or even prosecute officials who leak defense information to the press. Public servants who follow their private conscience, it can be argued, must be prepared to accept the legal consequences of their moral acts.

The matter, however, is not that simple. Punishment of officials who leak information also has, or may have, a chilling effect. Other officials may then be less inclined to talk to reporters. If so, the flow of information to the press about what the government is doing is bound to be reduced, raising, at least indirectly, a First Amendment consideration.

On June 17, 1971, at a time when the Nixon administration had temporarily succeeded in blocking further publication of the Pentagon Papers, Herb Klein held a background session for newsmen in his office. The administration, Klein said, was more concerned about permitting a precedent that would encourage future leaks than it was with the question of whether the *Times* had endangered the national security. Klein's explanation of the administration's motives in going to court was particularly indiscreet, since government lawyers were at that moment telling federal judges in New York and Washington that the series jeopardized the safety of the United States. In his backgrounder, Klein repeatedly referred to the Pentagon Papers as "stolen goods."

If the government, by prosecution or other sanctions, can frighten enough officials, news sources of this genre will tend to dry up. The public may be deprived of some future Pentagon Papers.

Punishment of officials who privately give information to the press raises another problem. The government is free to leak classified information when it wants to, and it does so all the time. If it acts to penalize *unauthorized* disclosures, the press becomes the captive of the official leak. By applying sanctions to officials who divulge embarrassing news, the government increases its power to shape and distort information, to control the levers of truth. Only sanitized, processed, and approved information reaches the public.

The most celebrated case of government action against an unauthorized leak was, of course, the prosecution of Daniel Ellsberg. He was indicted for conspiracy to impair the government's control over classified documents, to steal government property, and to receive, transmit and retain documents relating to the national defense in violation of the espionage laws.

In preparing Ellsberg's defense, his attorneys quickly focused on the fact that the Espionage Act was so vague and poorly drawn that its language was ambiguous on the key question of intent. Ellsberg's fate, it soon became apparent, might literally hinge on a comma.

Section 793(e) of the Espionage Act outlaws the receiving or transmitting of fourteen specific kinds of documents, "or information relating to the national defense which information the possessor has reason to believe could be used to the injury of the United States or to the advantage of a foreign nation." Since there is no comma after the word "defense," the "reason to believe" requirement could be construed to apply only to "information" and not to the list of documents that precedes it.*

The indictment of Ellsberg accused him of wrongfully using "documents," because by drawing it up this way, the government obviously hoped to avoid the necessity of proving that Ellsberg acted with evil intent or with knowledge that the material he released would injure the United States or help another power. Since Ellsberg had publicly indicated he acted out of conscience and a desire to help the United States, the government was understandably anxious to avoid having to prove harmful intent. But Ellsberg's lawyers argued

---

*The confusing language in question was added in an amendment to the espionage laws contained in the Internal Security Act of 1950. The Senate Judiciary Committee report states that the "reason to believe" requirement was intended to modify only the word "information" and not the list of specific documents.

that the statute as a whole required proof of specific intent to injure the United States or aid a foreign country.* In taking this position, the defense could cite a strong legal precedent; in upholding the conviction of Mikhail Gorin, the court had explicitly ruled that the government must prove bad faith to convict a defendant under the espionage law.

Quite aside from the question of intent, it is difficult to see how punishment or prosecution of government employees, or former employees, who leak secrets to the press can be legally or morally justified so long as Presidents and other former officials are free to publish the same material in their memoirs.

In recent years the government has increased its efforts to preserve and extend official secrecy. And there have even been periodic attempts to dispense with the First Amendment and impose in the United States the equivalent of the British Official Secrets Act. In 1957 the Commission on Government Security, established by Congress to review the entire classification and secrecy system, urged that Congress pass a law, modeled closely on the British act, making it a crime for anyone knowingly to disclose classified information. Reaction in Congress and the press quickly killed the proposal.

But all during the 1960's the CIA quietly pushed for amendments to tighten the espionage laws along the lines of the British Official Secrets Act. The agency argued that the classification system and the Espionage Act did not dovetail, since a classified document did not automatically "relate to the national defense" for purposes of the espionage laws.

In October, 1966, the CIA prepared a lengthy secret study of the espionage laws that included stringent draft legislation to prevent leaks of intelligence information by government officials. The CIA study, which was not, of course, made public, was written by John D. Morrison, Jr., assistant general counsel of the agency.†

"The unauthorized exposure of classified information is a chronic problem for governments and intelligence agencies," the

---

*The question of intent and "reason to believe" would, of course, have to be faced by the government in any similar prosecution of reporters, editors, or newspapers under the espionage law.
†John D. Morrison, Jr., *Protecting Classified Intelligence Information—An Historical Review and Some Recommendations.* Under the title "The Protection of Intelligence Data," a shorter version of the study was published in 1967 in *Studies in Intelligence,* a CIA in-house journal that is not available to the public.

study began. "The problem is particularly acute in a democratic society whose laws and courts must provide broad protection to criminal defendants." If one detects a regretful note in that last sentence, a mild annoyance at those bothersome democratic legal protections, one would be right.

The study goes on to say: "The deterrence provided by the espionage laws and related statutes is weakened by the difficulty of prosecution under them. This is especially true in cases involving disaffected or careless employees of intelligence agencies; the defenses usually include strong equitable pleas which may excite a sympathetic public response." That inconvenient public again.

Moreover, the CIA said, the espionage statutes, "as their name implies, were designed to punish espionage and not to punish simple unauthorized disclosure. Thus, these statutes require that there be an intent to harm the United States or to aid a foreign government. In practice, therefore, prosecutions are successful only where it can be proved that an individual has passed the information to a representative of a foreign government. An individual who simply reveals to the public at large classified data is for all practical purposes immune from prosecution since his defense, of course, would be that he thought the American public had a right to know and the government would not be able to prove intent to aid a foreign government or to harm the United States." Although written in 1966, the CIA interpretation amounted to an unwitting defense brief for Daniel Ellsberg.

The espionage laws provide a "startling lack of protection" for intelligence secrets, the CIA study continued. "No legislation has yet been enacted to cover the new problems arising out of the chronic 'cold war' status of international relations . . ."

Because of what it called this "serious gap" in the espionage laws, the CIA study proposed, in effect, an Official Secrets Act for intelligence information. The draft legislation would create the new category of Intelligence Data. Anything so stamped would be automatically accepted by the courts as secret. Prosecution would take place without any necessity that the government disclose the nature of the information. A jury would not have to decide whether it was properly classified; the government would not have to prove anything more than the fact that the material was stamped Intelligence Data.*

---

*The law would also increase the power of the director of Central Intelligence to seek court injunctions to prevent release or publication of intelligence information.

The study explained: "This would solve a vexatious and recurring problem for which there is no known cure in existing laws. That problem is the immunity enjoyed by an exposer of sensitive information when the information itself cannot for practical reasons be brought into the open for the purpose of prosecution." In short, the CIA would like to convict without proof.

The CIA document added: "It would be a step in the direction of 'crown privilege,' which is the basis of the British Official Secrets Acts." The CIA author was apparently unconcerned that the United States had, at considerable cost, disposed of the British crown and "crown privilege" some two hundred years ago.

Under existing law, the study said, to protect a secret, "the secret must be told." Not only is it undesirable to tell government secrets to a jury, the report continued, there is another great problem, "the capability of the jury to evaluate such data . . ."

With the candor of secrecy—the CIA proposal was not, after all, meant to see the light of day—the document noted that the proposed legislation in effect "would substitute the judgment of the director of Central Intelligence for that of a jury." *That* should take care of those vexatious laws, courts, public opinion, and incompetent juries.

Abandoning traditional democratic legal precepts, the CIA draft bill would reverse the usual requirement that the government prove that someone is guilty: "Instead of the government proving intent, the defendant would have the burden of showing that he had verified the legality of his action in imparting the [intelligence] data."

The report claimed that the law would apply only to CIA employees or former employees, CIA contractors and their employees, and military men detailed to CIA: "It does not address itself to the question of leaks to the press." However, the draft law clearly requires that "Whoever possesses Intelligence Data" guard it from disclosure to unauthorized persons, language that would appear to apply equally as well to a news reporter as to any other unauthorized recipient.

In 1972, in the wake of the publication of the Pentagon Papers, the staff of a Senate subcommittee chaired by Senator John L. McClellan of Arkansas drafted a proposed revision of the federal criminal code that would have made any disclosure of "classified information" a felony. The language, which would have amounted to an Official Secrets Act, was omitted from the bill as introduced.

The British Official Secrets Act has always had an appeal to Americans of an authoritarian turn of mind. "We need a severe Official Secrets Act," Dean Acheson wrote when *The New York Times* began publishing the Pentagon Papers, "to prevent irresponsible or corrupt transfer of secret papers from the government to publishers." He also called for the establishment of a commission of the quality of the Royal Commission [on secrecy] recently created in Britain . . ."

The British government does indeed operate with more secrecy than the American government, but it is hardly a model to be emulated. In 1965, to take one example, the *London Sunday Times* appointed Anthony Howard, a leading young political writer, to cover the government departments in Whitehall. It was a bold departure for Fleet Street, and the Labour government responded by sending a memo to all government offices ordering that no officials speak to Howard. After about a year the *Sunday Times* gave up on its experiment of trying to have a Whitehall correspondent. The *Observer* sent Howard to Washington, where he was much happier.

It is the Official Secrets Act that provides the framework for Britain's rigid government secrecy.* The first section of the act prohibits collecting or communicating defense information "for any purpose prejudicial to the safety or interests of the State." That is the section aimed at spies. Section 2, however, prohibits any official of the crown from communicating any information to unauthorized persons. And it bars any unauthorized person from receiving official information. The ban is so sweeping that it applies to all kinds of government information, even that which is unrelated to defense or national security.

This section has been used to prosecute journalists. The mere existence of the section is sufficient threat in itself; it has provided the government with a powerful weapon to restrict freedom of the press in Britain.† Yet, when the 1920 act was passed to amend and tighten the basic secrets act of 1911, doubtful members of Parliament were assured that the law would not apply to the press.

The British journalist Jonathan Aitken has characterized the Secrets Acts as "the widest, vaguest, and most far-reaching criminal statutes ever enacted in this country." Aitken had first-hand experience in arriving at this conclusion; along with the *Sunday Telegraph*, its editor Brian Roberts, and Colonel Douglas Cairns, he was a defendant at Old Bailey in a celebrated secrets trial that took place in 1971.

The charges had revolved around a report on the Nigerian civil war which Colonel Cairns, Britain's representative on an interna-

---

*The Official Secrets Act is really a series of acts. The first was passed in 1889. The basic law was enacted in 1911 and amended in 1920 and 1939.

†Section 2 offenses may be punished by up to two years in prison and a fine. Convictions under Section 1 may be punished by imprisonment of up to seven years on each count.

tional observer team in Nigeria, had sent to his former boss, Major-General Henry Templer Alexander, in England. Aitken, a journalist and the Conservative candidate for the House of Commons, was invited to dinner with other guests at General Alexander's home at Brandsby, Yorkshire. Over port, after the ladies had retired from the dining room, the general said the Nigerians were about to win the war with Biafra; when Aitken disputed this, Alexander said he had a report from Lagos that would prove it. The general then lent the report to Aitken—the two men dispute whether it was given to Aitken in confidence—and the journalist had it Xeroxed. (Much was made at the trial about the removal of the staple and its replacement by a smaller one.) On January 11, 1970, three weeks after the dinner party, the report was published in the *Sunday Telegraph*.

In his summing up, Mr. Justice Caulfield pointed out to the jury with some glee that if Colonel Cairns was found not guilty, then Aitken could not be convicted unless General Alexander were proved guilty. And Alexander was not on trial, since the government had not seen fit to bring charges against the general.

"It may well be," said Mr. Justice Caulfield, "that prosecutions under this Act can serve as a convenient and reasonable substitute for a political trial, with the added advantage of achieving the same end without incurring the implied odium." He added: "This case, if it does nothing more, may well alert those who govern us at least to consider, if they have the time, whether or not Section 2 of this Act has reached retirement age and should be pensioned off, being replaced by a section that will enable men like Colonel Cairns, Mr. Aitken, and Mr. Roberts, and other editors of journals, to determine without any great difficulty whether a communication by any one of them of a certain piece of information originating from an official source, and not concerned in the slightest with national security, is going to put them in peril of being enclosed in a dock and facing a criminal charge."

All of the accused were acquitted on all counts, and the trial, together with the judge's charge to the jury—an exquisite legal and literary document—seriously weakened, if it did not altogether demolish, Section 2 of the act. Two weeks after the trial the Home Secretary announced the formation of a special Committee of Inquiry under Lord Franks (who as Sir Oliver Franks had served as British ambassador to Washington) to investigate the operation of Section 2 of the Official Secrets Act. After a seventeen-month study, the committee reported in September, 1972. It termed Section 2 "a mess," and called for its repeal and replacement by a new law, somewhat narrower in scope, to protect specific categories of information, including classified defense secrets the disclosure of which might cause "serious damage" to national security. Some legislative reform seemed at least possible as a result of the trial and the Franks inquiry.

Thus, ironically, at a time when American officials were pointing to the Official Secrets Act as a model for American secret-keeping, the British law, for the first time, had been significantly weakened, and the British press appeared perhaps to be moving slowly in the direction of greater freedom to report about national security affairs.

Britain's D-notice system, an important adjunct to the Act, has also been eroded in recent years by a series of controversies. A D-notice is an advisory letter circulated to news editors by a joint government-press committee, warning that certain information, or kinds of information, may well be protected from disclosure by the Official Secrets Act. While a D-notice technically has no force of law, it acts as an effective club over Fleet Street. Since an editor is warned that he *may* be breaking the law by printing a story, he is usually disinclined to take the chance; the effect is almost indistinguishable from compulsory, official censorship.

Those who defend censorship, or would seek to impose it in the United States, customarily pose the issue in its most extreme form, a situation in which human life might be endangered. Suppose a newspaper *does* print the sailing date of a troopship? What if a newspaper had published the date of D-Day in advance?

These are difficult questions; in arguing the Pentagon Papers case before the Supreme Court, the attorney for *The New York Times*, Professor Alexander M. Bickel of Yale Law School, was pushed to the wall on this point by Justice Stewart. Suppose, said Stewart, there was something in the Pentagon Papers that convinced everyone that disclosure would mean the death of a hundred young American soldiers. What should the court do? Then this exchange took place:

> JUSTICE STEWART: You would say the Constitution requires that it be published, and that these men die, is that it?
> MR. BICKEL: No, I am afraid that my inclinations to humanity [would] overcome the somewhat more abstract devotion to the First Amendment in a case of that sort.

Bickel was not about to step into the trap and go on record as favoring publication in the example posed by Stewart. Nor did the *Times* feel it necessary to argue an absolute First Amendment right to publish in order to win its own case. But Bickel did take the position that any exception required proof of direct causation between publication and the feared result. The First Amendment, he said, was part of "the risk of freedom."

In fact, Stewart's example was unrealistic. Nothing in a diplomatic history of the policies that led America to war in Vietnam in the 1960's could endanger troops in the field in 1971. The hazards posed by the government in arguing for censorship usually melt away upon closer examination. For example, the Nixon administration solemnly contended that publication of the Pentagon Papers would cause "irreparable injury" to the nation. The government lost, the papers were published, and the republic stands.

A subliminal issue in the Pentagon Papers case also illustrates the point; although it was not known to the general public, the question of whether the *Times* articles might compromise U.S. codes was the subject of an invisible battle between the *Times* and the government.

From the start, the code question posed a worrisome issue for the *Times*. Its editors and lawyers were sure that modern codes embodied the principle of "one-time" use; and that, because code patterns were constantly changing, the publication of verbatim text would not reveal the code to another country. The difficulty was that the *Times* could never get anyone in the government to stand up in open court and say so.

To deal with the problem, the *Times* hired David Kahn, author of *The Codebreakers,* as a consultant. Kahn, the leading non-government authority on cryptography, assured the newspaper that any damage to codes would be negligible. The *Times* also received several anonymous phone calls from servicemen who worked with codes. These callers also said that the publication of cables and verbatim texts of documents would not compromise security.

In tense planning sessions for the court appearances, the *Times* editors and lawyers spent hours discussing how to reply in case the government *did* accuse it of compromising codes and communications intelligence. Max Frankel, then chief of the Washington Bureau, prepared a thirty-page memo analyzing the *Pueblo* case. North Korean PT boats seized the U.S.S. *Pueblo,* an American intelligence vessel, in January, 1968. A House subcommittee began hearings into the incident in March, 1969, and the record published in July contained the verbatim texts of messages from the *Pueblo,* and from naval commands in the Pacific responding to the crisis. In addition, the North Koreans had captured code and communications equipment on the *Pueblo* itself. The Pentagon study went only as far as May, 1968, and only a handful of documents in the possession of the *Times* were dated after the *Pueblo* seizure. So if the capture of the ship, or the subsequent publication of verbatim texts by the

House subcommittee, had compromised codes, major damage had already been done.

The issue emerged in open court only fleetingly, when Judge Gurfein told Bickel, during oral argument in federal district court in Manhattan, that he was "concerned" about the lack of "paraphrase of code messages."

Bickel replied quickly that the government had not alleged that "anything the *Times* put in print broke a code, compromised a code, came within five miles of an existing code."

With all due respect, said Gurfein, "neither you nor I nor *The New York Times* is competent to pass on that subject as to what will lead to the breaking of a code." The conversation was getting difficult; the *Times* needed Gurfein and could hardly afford to antagonize him.

It was common knowledge, Bickel replied, "that the security of codes is insured by their being changed with extreme rapidity in very short order." But Gurfein was still bothered; Vietnam could be discussed, he said, "without reprinting verbatim a code message."

Throughout much of the legal proceedings, the *Times* lawyers continued to insist that codes were not at issue. But the government, by saying nothing, sought to leave the impression that perhaps codes were endangered.

Finally, during an in camera session in the district court, the issue was met head on. Gurfein, who served in the OSS during World War II, pointed out that in his day messages were slightly altered when placed in the files, in order to protect the codes in which they had been transmitted. Would not further publication of verbatim texts jeopardize codes?

Bickel was on his feet, protesting that Whitney North Seymour, the United States attorney in New York, had agreed that codes were not involved in this case. But Seymour angrily replied that he had agreed to no such thing. The *Times* was in danger of losing control of the code issue.

This dispute took place entirely out of public view, of course. One of the ironies of the Pentagon Papers case is that many important arguments took place in court sessions from which the public was barred and in "classified" briefs filed by both sides. Much of the official record of the most celebrated modern case involving freedom of the press was, and is, sealed.

As Bickel, Seymour, and Gurfein squabbled in secret over the question of compromising codes, Admiral Francis J. Blouin, deputy chief of naval operations, who had earlier appeared in open court as a witness for the government, arose. To the amazement and relief of the *Times* attorneys, Blouin, then sixty and a bluff, bemedaled veteran of World War II, Korea and Vietnam, candidly put the matter to rest.

"Judge Gurfein," said the admiral, "you and I are probably the only people in this room old enough to remember when verbatim texts compromised a code."

The attorneys and executives of *The New York Times* could have kissed him.

The controversy about codes, which bubbled just below the surface of the Pentagon Papers case, is typical of most fears that the press will, by publishing certain stories, endanger "national security." The *Times* was correct all along in its assumption that verbatim text did not compromise codes. Today codes are all computerized, one-time, and random. The random factor means that the verbatim text of one message is of no help in decoding another.

Moreover, newspapers do not publish everything they learn. There have been many instances where editors or reporters have not published stories when they believed that national security or human life was at stake. Mistakenly or not, *The New York Times* withheld information before both the Bay of Pigs invasion and the Cuban missile crisis.

And suppose the *Times*, which learned there were missiles in Cuba in 1962, had published that fact before October 22? The Russians already knew the missiles were there, of course; they were installing them. There is no way to assess what effect publication would have had, since it did not happen; the *Times* chose not to print the story. But disclosure, as Bickel suggested, is part of the "risk of freedom."

It is true that with the growth of underground newspapers, and the educational experience of Vietnam, the government can no longer rely, to the extent it once did, on voluntary restraint by the press. But this is not too great a burden in a healthy democracy. If there are risks to national security in publishing sensitive information, there are greater risks in silence. The war in Vietnam was secretly undertaken and directed, as the Pentagon Papers revealed so starkly. More than 45,000 Americans and countless Vietnamese civilians, North and South, died in the war. It was not a question of a troopship, but of a generation. Had the press published more about Vietnam, and sooner, U.S. policy might have taken a different course and lives might have been saved. More disclosure, not suppression, would have been truly in the national interest.

Americans like to believe that in a pluralistic society, all interests can be accommodated and differences smoothed over. But there is in this country an in-built tension between press and government that cannot, and should not, be reconciled. And the differences between them are intrinsic and fundamental. Government has the right to classify and attempt to protect its secrets. The press has a right to try to obtain and publish those secrets. These are two forces that will continually be in some degree of conflict.

"There is always a tendency in government to confuse secrecy with security," Robert F. Kennedy once said. Disclosure, he added, "may be uncomfortable, but it is not the purpose of democracy to ensure the comfort of its leaders."

Judge Gurfein, worried as he was about the codes from his old OSS days, genuinely troubled as he was about taking any action that might endanger national security, came squarely to grips with the issue in his courtroom in Foley Square, and understood it. He ruled that the Pentagon Papers must be published.

"If there be some embarrassment to the government . . . we must learn to live with it," he said. "The security of the nation is not at the ramparts alone. Security also lies in the value of our free institutions. A cantankerous press, an obstinate press, a ubiquitous press must be suffered by those in authority in order to preserve the even greater values of freedom of expression and the right of the people to know."

8

The Case of the Colorado Tibetans

On the morning of December 7, 1961, Henry M. Wood reported for work as usual at Peterson Field near Colorado Springs. It was a few days before his thirty-ninth birthday, but Wood anticipated no other major event in what had been up to then an ordinary week.

"Hank" Wood, as he was invariably known to his friends, was a calm, pleasant man, and in the view of his fellow employees at the Kensair Corporation, easy to get along with. A native of Columbus, Mississippi, Wood was an experienced pilot and mechanic. He was the manager of Kensair, a small aviation company that operated a flying school and sold Piper airplanes.

Peterson Field is six miles to the east of Colorado Springs. It serves as both the municipal airport and a United States Air Force base. The military has shared the field with the city since World War II; it is one of a complex of Air Force installations in and around Colorado Springs.

Kensair's hangar was located at the eastern edge of the field, adjacent to an area that the Air Force used to load and park its planes, and it was to this hangar that Wood reported, as he customarily did, at 8 A.M. He noticed that an Air Force C-124 Globemaster was parked not far away, near a small Piper Colt owned by Kensair.

The mountain air of Colorado is chilly in the early morning, and the coffee was already brewing when Wood arrived and greeted foreman Bill Watts and J. R. Smith, who ran the flight school. Lynn Boese, a twenty-year-old student pilot and Kensair's only customer at that early hour, was waiting to take out the Piper Colt.

Wood idly strolled outside to get a better look at the Globemaster, but before he could reach the plane someone yelled "Coffee's ready!" and he turned away and went back in. A moment later Bill Watts, who had also stepped outside, raced breathlessly in to the hangar. "Hank," he blurted out, "we're surrounded."

Wood put down his coffee and stared at his foreman, a reliable man not normally given to fantasies.

"There are guys out there with guns," Watts insisted. "They told us to get back in the hangar, push our airplane back in the building, and lock the door."

Incredulous, Wood went out to see for himself what was going on. He did not get far. "There was a G.I. there dressed in green battle fatigues, armed," Wood recalled. The soldier told Wood to halt. The normally unexcitable Kensair manager lost his temper. "I told him, 'You get off my property—what in hell is going on here?' "

In reply, the soldier pulled a pistol and stuck it in Wood's face. "Get back inside," he snapped.

"When he put that .45 Colt in my face," Wood said, "it looked like a fifty-five gallon barrel. That barrel looked awfully large. When he drew that pistol and pointed at me, I knew I was going to do just as he told me. He was a young kid with a very nasty manner. There wasn't any doubt in my mind that he'd pull the trigger."

Wood retreated hastily. Under orders from the soldiers, who were armed with automatics, rifles, and machine guns, Kensair employees quickly rolled the Piper Colt inside. Lynn Boese was herded into the hangar along with Wood, Smith, Watts, Kensair mechanic Harold Ravnsborg, and two secretaries, and the big front door clanged shut.

There was a telephone in the hangar, so Wood and the others now trapped in the Kensair building had a link to the outside world. Wood used it; he picked up the phone, dialed Sheriff Earl Sullivan, and identified himself. "Sheriff," he said, "we're surrounded. We can't get out."

"What do you mean you're surrounded?"

"Just what I say. There are troops out here with guns. They've got us surrounded."

Sullivan, fearful that someone at the airfield had gone berserk or was attempting to hijack a plane, quickly rounded up two deputies, Bernard Barry and Albert Moore. They jumped into a police car and roared out to Peterson Field. The car sped onto the field and got about halfway across to the Kensair hangar when it was halted at a roadblock manned by armed M.P.'s. An officer in charge politely informed Sullivan that he could go no further.

Agents of the Army's Criminal Investigation Division from nearby Fort Carson were also stopped; traffic at the roadblock was beginning to pile up. Near the eastern side of Peterson Field, a telephone repairman was up on a pole. A soldier armed with a pistol ordered him down.

Inside the Kensair building, the five men and two women peered through a window. Although they did not know it, other civilians were being held in similar fashion at the Maytag Aircraft Corporation hangar nearby. As Hank Wood strained for a glimpse through the window of what was happening, an Army bus rolled up alongside and stopped. The windows of the bus, Wood observed, were painted black.

He could hardly believe what he saw next.

"There was fifteen Orientals got out of the bus and onto the plane," Wood said. "They were wearing some type of uniform— green fatigues, just like the G.I.'s. Each one of these Orientals had a white tag around his neck. As each man got on the Globemaster, someone at the door checked the tag."

It is not every day that civilians are held at gunpoint in Colorado Springs while Oriental soldiers scramble onto a C-124 from a bus with its windows painted black, and Harold Ravnsborg thought the event sufficiently out of the ordinary to snap pictures through the hangar window.

About an hour and twenty minutes from the time that Bill Watts had first reported the Kensair hangar surrounded by men with guns, the Globemaster took off, and the armed guards departed in their jeeps. Newsmen heard about the strange goings-on at Peterson Field, and that afternoon the *Colorado Springs Gazette Telegraph* carried a brief story. The sheriff's office had received a report that "a number of civilians" had been held at gunpoint at Peterson Field. A soldier had pointed a gun at Henry Wood, manager of the Kensair Corporation. The Army had been contacted by the newspaper but a spokesman was "unable to give any further information."

Meanwhile, an Army officer from Fort Carson, "a major or a colonel," as Henry Wood recalls it, arrived at the hangar "and lined us up in my office. We had to hold up our hands and swear we wouldn't talk about it to anyone for six months." This development put Wood and the other Kensair employees in an awkward position, since some of them had already discussed the morning's events with several newspapermen. "The Army Officer had a book with him and he read the law to us. He was telling us all the things that could happen to us if we talked about it. The guy threatened us; he said we were under the highest secrecy in the world."

Harold Ravnsborg was scared. The officer from Fort Carson, he said, made it clear that "it was a federal offense" even to discuss the incident. "It was supposedly top-secret information; we were told not to talk about what we had seen." As soon as the officer had left, Ravnsborg quietly removed the film from his camera and burned it.

The next day two Denver newspapers, the *Denver Post* and the *Rocky Mountain News,* and the Colorado Springs paper all published news stories about the mysterious episode at the airport. The *Rocky Mountain News* reported that the armed military guards had kept the civilians away during the loading of "classified equipment from Camp Hale," a military installation high in the Rockies near Leadville, Colorado. The story said the camp was rumored to be the location of "a supersecret military development and research program."

The same day the Army issued an official apology. "The Army regrets the poor judgment used in handling this affair," a spokesman said, "and also regrets any repressive measures which may have been taken by Army military policemen." Brigadier General Ashton H. Manhart, the commander of Fort Carson, also apologized publicly. "We were involved in a very sensitive project," he explained. "It was a matter involving national security." But public information officers at Fort Carson and Peterson Field declined to provide any additional details.

The only clue as to the nature of the "classified equipment" being loaded on the C-124 came from Lynn Boese. The story in the *Colorado Springs Gazette Telegraph* quoted him as saying that "several Oriental soldiers in combat uniforms" had entered the plane.

On December 8 the wire services moved short stories about the peculiar episode at Colorado Springs. In Washington, a desk man in the Washington bureau of *The New York Times* handed the wire copy to a reporter and asked him to make a routine check.

It did not seem like more than a minor incident, although there was a strange James Bondian aspect to the story: some of the civilians held at gunpoint reported they had seen what looked like Chinese soldiers at the airfield. In Colorado Springs? The *Times* correspondent placed some calls to the Pentagon.

The reaction was swift and unexpected. Within minutes the office of Secretary of Defense Robert McNamara was on the phone to the *Times* Washington Bureau. The high-level Pentagon caller urgently pleaded that the *Times* kill the story; the "Chinese," he confided, were not Chinese. They were Tibetans. Moreover, the caller said, if the *Times* disclosed this fact, it would be detrimental to the national security of the United States.

The high official on the phone did not provide much further detail, but certain inferences could be drawn. In 1950, Communist China had invaded Tibet, that exotic land above the clouds and beyond the Himalayas. By 1951 China had consolidated its control over the country. In 1959, fearing for his life, the Dalai Lama, political and spiritual leader of Tibet, had fled the golden temples of Lhasa to India. In the fighting that had since erupted, thousands of Tibetans—more than 100,000, according to some reports—were killed by the Chinese, and tens of thousands of refugees escaped to Nepal, Sikkim, Bhutan, and India. Hundreds of Tibetan children were sent to resettlement camps in Switzerland. If there were indeed Tibetans in Colorado, it was possible that they were being secretly trained by the United States government as guerrillas or parachutists to go back to Tibet and fight against the Chinese Communists.

The government's request to suppress the story came near the close of what had been a year of major international crises. Eight months earlier, in April, John F. Kennedy, America's young, new President had suffered a powerful blow to his prestige when a secret operation against Cuba failed at the Bay of Pigs. In June, shaken by that experience, Kennedy had faced an uncompromising Nikita Khrushchev in Vienna; over the summer the Berlin Wall was erected and the President called up the reserves.

Against this troubled international background, the government was now asking the *Times* to forget about the incident at Peterson Field. The story obviously was potentially explosive. If published, it might raise tensions between Washington and Peking to a dangerous level. Accepting the government's plea, the *Times* chose to dig no further; it did not run the sensational story of what was apparently a secret U.S. operation based in the Rocky Mountains and directed at Communist China.

The story would not even have surfaced locally in the Colorado papers, of course, if Henry Wood had not gotten mad at the young G.I. who shoved the .45 Colt in his face. The Army was acutely aware of this, because the day after the incident, General Charles G. Dodge, the Army's chief of information, personally telephoned Wood from Washington to offer his apologies.

General Dodge did not explain to Wood what had been going on at Peterson Field. But by this time Wood had gotten wind of some additional information: "These guys had been training up at Camp Hale. They were supposed to be shock troops or guerrillas, trained for some damn invasion."

Wood did not know that the "Orientals" he had seen were Tibetans.* Nor could he have guessed at the complex chain of circum-

---

*Ironically, during World War II, Wood had flown along the borders of Tibet. He served in the China-Burma-India theater as a member of the 24th Combat Mapping Squadron of the Army Air Forces. For two years he flew back and forth over the hump between India and China.

stances, a strange mixture of Buddhism and Cold War, that brought Tibetans to Colorado.

A remote and mysterious land of 1,300,000 people, Tibet lies between India, on the south, and the Chinese province of Sinkiang on the north. Protected by the great natural barrier of the Himalayas, Tibet was for centuries cut off from the rest of the world and virtually untouched by modern civilization. Until Communist China conquered Tibet in 1951, it was the last country in the world in which the ruler was revered as a god. Even today many Tibetans consider the exiled Dalai Lama to be a manifestation of the absolute Buddha in human form. By tradition, when a Dalai Lama died, the search began for his reincarnation, who was discovered with the help of revelations seen in the sacred waters of Lhamoi Latso, a lake southeast of Lhasa, the capital.

In 1933, the Year of the Water Bird, Thupten Gyatso, the thirteenth Dalai Lama, died, and the search for his reincarnation began. According to ancient custom, a regent was appointed. Peering into the waters of the sacred lake, he reported that he saw a monastery with roofs of jade-green and gold and a house with turquoise tiles. The vision was written down but kept secret.

High lamas and officials from Lhasa then set out to all corners of Tibet to search for the buildings seen in the waters of the sacred lake. In time, the lamas made their way to the remote village of Taktser, in northeastern Tibet.

Approaching the town, the lamas had carefully noted the green-and-gold roofs of a monastery in nearby Kumbum, and in Taktser itself, they found a house with turquoise tiles. Among the seven children of the farmer who lived there was a two-year-old boy. A series of tests were given to the child; he was offered a small, rather plain drum that the Dalai Lama had used to summon his attendants, and a much larger, gaudier drum with golden straps. The boy chose the simpler drum and began to beat it. Offered two walking sticks, he first touched the wrong one, hesitated and then chose the one that had belonged to the Dalai Lama. The officials were troubled at the boy's apparent mistake, but when they investigated further, they discovered that the Dalai Lama had once briefly used the first walking stick as well.

And so, in 1940, the Year of the Iron Dragon, the child was taken to Lhasa, placed upon the Lion Throne in the Hall of All Good Deeds in the Potala Palace, and proclaimed the fourteenth Dalai Lama, spiritual and temporal ruler of all Tibet.

But after 1949, when Mainland China fell to Mao Tse-tung and the Communists, Peking began to place increasing pressure on the Dalai Lama and Tibet. China had periodically claimed Tibet as part of its territory, beginning in the thirteenth century, when Kublai Khan, the Mongol emperor of China, swept into eastern Tibet.

Beginning in 1910 the Chinese had supported the rival Panchen Lama, also an incarnate, who is regarded as second only to the Dalai Lama in religious importance. The seventh Panchen Lama, born in 1938, was educated and trained in Communist China. One year after Peking's troops conquered Tibet in 1951, the Panchen Lama rode into Lhasa escorted by Chinese Communist troops. The Dalai Lama, however, was permitted to remain on his throne.

During the mid-1950's Tibetan rebels began guerrilla warfare activity against the Chinese. In Washington, officials of the Eisenhower administration were disturbed by the Chinese pressure on Tibet, but unable to do anything about it openly. With guerrilla warfare breaking out, however, Allen Dulles, director of the Central Intelligence Agency, concluded that the situation offered an ideal opportunity for the CIA; the agency would provide clandestine assistance to the Tibetan rebels harassing the Chinese.

The CIA's plan, as it evolved, was to establish a secret training base for Tibetans within the United States. Tibetan rebels would be recruited among the refugees already trickling through the Himalayas. They would be screened, and the most promising candidates flown to the United States. They would be taught guerrilla-warfare skills, equipped with modern weapons, and then infiltrated back into Tibet.

It was important that the guerrillas be trained under conditions that most nearly approximated those in their mountainous homeland. The average altitude in Tibet is an astonishing 15,000 feet; in the United States the closest one could come to matching that height would be the Rocky Mountains of central Colorado.

Colorado is the highest state in the union; it has 1,500 peaks over 10,000 feet, including the celebrated Pikes Peak. Colorado is also the state with the highest city in the United States: Leadville (population 4,314), an old mining town 115 miles southwest of Denver at an altitude of 10,152 feet. Nearby is Mount Elbert, the tallest peak in Colorado and the second highest mountain in the continental United States. Altogether, it seemed to the CIA the ideal location to train Tibetans.

Leadville's past was as rich and colorful as the West itself. At the height of the silver boom, 40,000 people lived there, and it was a wild frontier town in the best Hollywood tradition, where law and order were the responsibility of a gunfighter who had somehow been appointed city marshal. The town's most famous citizen was H.A.W. Tabor, who arrived in Colorado in 1859 and later acquired the fabulous Matchless Mine in Leadville. Tabor longed for public recognition; he built opera houses, and even served, for one month, as a United States senator from Colorado. He married the beautiful Elizabeth "Baby" Doe; but when silver prices collapsed, Tabor was ruined. On his deathbed in 1899 he told Baby Doe: "Hold on to the Matchless." She did, living in poverty in a cabin by the mine shaft until she died in 1935, still hoping vainly that the mine would once again produce a fortune in silver.

Leadville was also the home of James J. Brown, a gold miner whose wife, "the unsinkable Molly Brown," became the most famous passenger on the *Titanic*, later to be immortalized on Broadway by Tammy Grimes and on film by Debbie Reynolds.

If the CIA's operators had researched the history of Leadville, they would have found only one incident to give them pause; during the silver boom of the 1880's the first Chinese who made their way into the town's mining camps were hanged.

But that, after all, was a long while ago. And near Leadville the CIA found a site made to order for its purposes. Fifteen miles to the north, surrounded by mountain peaks in a secluded valley at 9,300 feet, was Camp Hale, an old Army base that had been used to train ski troops during World War II.

The Tenth Mountain Division had trained there in 1942, in weather that often hit thirty below zero. The men learned to ski, to handle guns in subfreezing temperatures, and to survive in the wind and snow of the Rockies. The Tenth sailed for Italy in 1944, joined General Mark Clark's Fifth Army, and fought the Germans through the Po Valley and into the Italian Alps.

Back in Colorado, 3,500 Nazi prisoners assigned to dismantle Camp Hale in 1945 tore down most of the buildings. But a few were left standing, and in the early 1950's the Army continued to use the site intermittently for training ski troops and for winter war games. By 1957, however, the Army had virtually abandoned the old camp.

Leadville and Camp Hale not only offered ideal climatic and geographic conditions for the CIA's Tibetans, the area also offered another important asset—seclusion. Unlike fashionable Aspen to the west, Leadville was not a winter ski resort, and the tourists who did visit there in the summer to see the relics of the silver mines were not likely to wander north into the remote and well-guarded CIA base at Camp Hale.

By 1958 the first Tibetans were receiving guerrilla-warfare training from CIA instructors at Camp Hale. To supervise this highly sensitive activity, Dulles soon turned to the CIA's top man for "black"—that is, secret—operations, Richard Mervin Bissell.

A tall, brilliant Ivy Leaguer in horn-rimmed glasses, Bissell grew up in Hartford, Connecticut, where his father was president of a large insurance company. As a boy, Bissell liked to memorize railroad timetables, and in later life he retained a fascination for detail. At first Bissell embarked on an academic career as a professor of economics at Yale. But during and after World War II he served in various government posts in Washington, rising to the rank of assistant administrator of the Marshall Plan.

In 1954 Bissell joined the CIA as a special assistant to Dulles; he played a key role in developing the U-2 spy plane, which began overflights of the Soviet Union in mid-1956. Until Francis Gary Powers and his plane came crashing down on May 1, 1960, the U-2 was the CIA's most successful espionage tool for gathering strategic intelligence about the Soviet Union.

In 1959 Dulles chose Bissell to become the CIA's deputy director for plans (DDP), and as such he was in charge of its clandestine operations all over the globe. One of these was the Tibetan operation at Camp Hale. The project was particularly sensitive because, unlike CIA operations abroad, there was a much greater risk of exposure and of political fallout from an operation conducted within the United States.

In the meantime, events were moving swiftly in Tibet. On March 1, 1959, the Communist generals in Lhasa "invited" the Dalai Lama to come alone to attend a play to be given in the Chinese military camp on March 10. The Tibetan leader immediately suspected a plot to abduct him. Rumors of the invitation reached the populace, and crowds surrounded the palace to protect the Dalai Lama and prevent him from going. When the Chinese fired mortar shells at the palace, the Dalai Lama decided to flee to India.

Disguised as a soldier and accompanied by a few loyal aides and members of his family, the Dalai Lama slipped out of the palace and headed south. He made his way to rebel-held territory, and the party gradually grew to several hundred as Tibetan soldiers and guerrillas joined the caravan to protect their leader. Back in Washington, it was said within the CIA's Plans Division that a few of the guerrillas from Camp Hale were among those who helped to guide the Dalai Lama through the mountain passes and over the border to safety in India. Bissell and his clandestine operators concluded that the Dalai Lama would not have made it to safety without the help of the men who had been trained in Colorado.

The Chinese were furious when they learned the Dalai Lama had escaped from their grasp. Open warfare broke out between the Chinese army and the people of Tibet, and thousands of Tibetans were killed in the fighting. On March 28 Chinese Premier Chou En-lai ordered the Dalai Lama's government dissolved and the Panchen Lama installed in his place. Soon afterward India's Prime Minister Nehru confirmed that the Dalai Lama was in India and had been granted political asylum. The disclosure increased tension between India and Communist China.

In Washington, on April 11, President Eisenhower conferred at length on the crisis in Tibet with CIA director Dulles. This was duly reported to the press by news secretary James C. Hagerty; the CIA's role and the existence of the secret base in Colorado was, of course, not revealed (and is disclosed here for the first time).

The fighting continued inside Tibet; by late summer Chinese troops had moved across the border into Bhutan, Sikkim, and India. The border skirmishing continued throughout the year. In New York, the UN Assembly voted to express its grave concern over Chinese suppression of human rights in Tibet, and in India, the Dalai Lama announced the formation of a "provisional government" inside Tibet to wage guerrilla warfare.

With the guerrillas in Tibet taking an increasingly active role, and fighting raging throughout the country, it was clear that the training at Camp Hale would continue for some time. The risk of exposure had to be reduced. The CIA decided to improve its cover arrangements in Colorado.

On July 16, 1959, the *Denver Post* carried a front-page story, headlined "Atom Unit Making Tests Near Leadville." It reported that the Defense Atomic Support Agency was carrying out "a top secret testing program at Camp Hale high in the Rocky Mountains near Leadville," and that the "exact nature of the program is highly classified." But Rear Admiral Edward N. Parker, DASA's chief in Washington, had assured the newspaper that the program "does not include the setting off of nuclear weapons."

Admiral Parker noted that DASA would not test nuclear weapons without authority. "We don't do what the President tells us not to do," he said. However, the admiral declined to say precisely what was being tested.

Camp Hale, the story explained, was formerly the Army's center for training ski troops, but "the installation was closed two years ago when the Army disbanded its ski forces." The camp was attached administratively to Fort Carson, in Colorado Springs. But "even top officials at Carson have not been informed what is going on" at Camp Hale. Major George Martin, the Fort Carson public information officer, said DASA had been there "since last fall." He added: "I was told that a quick way of being put in jail is even to ask what they are doing. It's so secret."

Apparently the CIA has a deep-seated suspicion of repairmen up on poles, because the article concluded: "A spokesman for the Public

Service Co. of Colorado said the DASA group about July 1 told the PSC manager at Leadville that they require twenty-four hours notice any time PSC crews desire to patrol or service company power lines traversing the camp."

The CIA's problems in hiding Tibetans in Colorado must have been endless, when one stops to think about it. Nosy telephone and power-company repairmen were only the half of it; there was also the continuing problem of concealing their presence from the townspeople. It wouldn't do to have Tibetans in their distinctive fur caps wandering into the saloons of Leadville, and a run on yak butter in the local supermarket could hardly fail to arouse suspicion.

The training of the Tibetans in Colorado continued in 1960, but by the spring of that election year Richard Bissell had turned his attention to what soon became a much larger clandestine operation, the fate of which was to become linked, at least indirectly, with the future of the secret base at Camp Hale. On March 17, 1960, President Eisenhower authorized the secret arming and training of Cuban exiles. As DDP, Bissell took over the project.

Within two months the first Cubans had arrived at a CIA base established on a coffee plantation near Retalhuleu, in the Pacific slope region of southwestern Guatemala. An airstrip was constructed, and Cubans recruited in Miami were secretly flown to Guatemala from Opa-locka Airport in Miami.

Ten days after Kennedy won the 1960 Presidential election, Dulles and Bissell flew to Palm Beach to brief the President-elect on the Cuban operation. The CIA assembled a formidable air force of twenty-four B-26 bombers at Retalhuleu, recruited Cuban and American fliers, and, with the Joint Chiefs, picked a landing site: the Bay of Pigs.

Over opposition from only a few of his advisers, President Kennedy approved the invasion. But the initial air strike by the B-26's on April 15, 1961, failed to destroy all of Castro's air force, and when the Cuban exile brigade landed on the beach two days later, it was decimated. Hundreds of its members were taken prisoner. Four American CIA airmen were killed flying B-26's over the beachhead.

The U-2 affair, and now the disastrous Cuban invasion, had made much of the public aware of the CIA for the first time. And the twin disasters had badly shaken the intelligence agency. Even though President Kennedy publicly took responsibility for the Cuban debacle, it was clear in the bitter aftermath of the Bay of Pigs that changes would be made at the top level of the CIA. Dulles and Bissell would have to go.

On September 27, 1961, after a decent interval, Kennedy accepted Dulles' resignation and simultaneously announced the appointment of John A. McCone as his successor. McCone was sworn in on November 29. Slightly more than a week later the entire Tibetan operation was jeopardized when Henry Wood stared down the barrel of a pistol at Peterson Field.

Although the episode was papered over, just barely, it caused some extremely nerve-racking moments in the seventh-floor executive offices of the CIA's newly opened $46,000,000 headquarters in Langley, Virginia. The Tibetan project was clearly a high-risk operation to be run from United States territory, and the uncomfortable parallel to the training of Cubans in Guatemala was all too apparent. The operation in Colorado, in fact, had the potential of a mini-Bay of Pigs.

Coming as it did only a little more than a week after McCone had been sworn in, the episode at Peterson Field threatened to confront the new dirctor with an embarrassing and politically explosive controversy before he had been confirmed by the Senate. As it was, McCone, a Republican oil and shipping millionaire and a Cold War hard-liner, knew that he faced substantial opposition from Democratic liberals in the Senate. He would not have welcomed additional trouble in the form of a disclosure that the CIA was training Tibetans in Colorado.

Despite the risks, Bissell and his CIA colleagues believed the Tibetan operation had enjoyed some degree of success, although it was rather less than they had hoped for. Some of the men trained in Colorado were parachuted into Tibet; others went in on the ground. A few filtered out again and made contact with the CIA.

But after the Cuban disaster in April, it seemed unlikely that the Tibetan operation could survive for very long. Indeed, there is some reason to believe that the group of Tibetans being loaded aboard the Globemaster at Peterson Field on December 7 was the last contingent to come out of Camp Hale.

Ironically, it was the snow and the mountains—the very factors that led the CIA to select Colorado for the training base—that almost caused the operation to surface. The CIA had loaded the Tibetans aboard an Army bus at Camp Hale shortly after midnight for the 129-mile trip over icy mountain roads to Colorado Springs. The plan was for the men to board the C-124 at Peterson Field in the darkness, well before dawn, several hours before Kensair's employees reported for work. If all had gone according to schedule, by the time Henry Wood had arrived at the hangar, the Globemaster would have been gone. There would have been no Tibetans, no armed American troops, and no trace that the CIA had been there in the night.

But coming down from the mountains, the bus skidded off the

road in the snow. As a result of the delay caused by the accident, it was daylight when the Tibetans arrived at the field.

In December, 1961, when the Washington Bureau of *The New York Times* decided, at the government's request, not to pursue its inquiries into the strange events at Peterson Field, the relationship between press and government was very different from what it is today. Ten years later, in June, 1971, attorneys for the *Times* stood in the United States Supreme Court defending the newspaper's right to publish the Pentagon Papers. The two events, separated by a decade, were not entirely comparable, of course, and the Pentagon Papers was a much more important story. Nevertheless, the different outcomes reflected a gradual, but real, change in the attitude of the press toward government claims of "national security."

In the Tibetan case, the *Times,* or its Washington Bureau, agreed not to write a story when the government invoked national security. In the Pentagon Papers controversy, the *Times* challenged the government's claim that publication would cause "irreparable injury to the United States." The newspaper successfully argued that the First Amendment's guarantee of freedom of the press outweighed the government's case for prior restraint. The *Times'* victory meant that the public could read the Pentagon's secret history of the Vietnam war despite the effort at official censorship.

During the 1950's, and in the early 1960's, there was a much greater tendency on the part of the press to accept the government's word and to accede to its judgment on national security questions. The U-2 affair, and the realization that government lied, brought a new degree of sophistication to the press, an increased willingness to exercise independent judgment in handling stories dealing with national defense, and a deeper skepticism toward government pronouncements in general.

The degree of independence demonstrated by the news media in reporting on national security affairs still fell far short of what it might be—in 1964, for example, the great majority of the American press unquestioningly accepted Lyndon Johnson's version of events in the Tonkin Gulf. But by 1971 the changing relationships and growing tension between government and the news media, combined with the tragic war in Vietnam, had made it somewhat more difficult for government to persuade the press to withhold a story on vague grounds of "national security."

In 1961 these issues were just emerging. On January 10 of that year the *Times* ran a front-page story from Retalhuleu by Paul P. Kennedy. It did not mention the CIA, but it told of mysterious training taking place at a base there. The story indicated that the purpose was an offensive against Cuba, and that the United States was deeply involved. The *Miami Herald,* which knew much of what was going on, then printed a story confirming that anti-Castro exiles were training in Guatemala.

On April 7, ten days before the Bay of Pigs, the *Times* published a long front-page story about Cuban exile activity in Miami and Guatemala and developing plans for an invasion. In a speech in 1966 Clifton Daniel, then managing editor of the *Times,* indicated that the story, by Tad Szulc, had been toned down on the advice of the paper's publisher, Orvil Dryfoos, the managing editor, Turner Catledge, and James Reston, the chief of the Washington Bureau.*

Initially, after the disaster in Cuba, President Kennedy was furious at the press for publishing advance stories about exile training and plans for an invasion. In a speech in New York on April 27 to the American Newspaper Publishers Association, Kennedy urged that newspapers, before printing a story, ask not only "Is it news?" but "Is it in the interest of the national security?"

At a meeting at the White House soon afterward with a delegation of editors, publishers, and news executives, the President read off a list of what he considered security breaches by the press, including Paul Kennedy's story of the previous January. But President Kennedy paradoxically told Turner Catledge at the same meeting: "If you had printed more about the operation, you would have saved us from a colossal mistake." In 1962 Kennedy reportedly repeated these sentiments to Orvil Dryfoos.

Would the nation's security have been endangered if the story of the Tibetan operation had been disclosed in 1961? In the wake of the Bay of Pigs, Kennedy ordered two separate investigations of the CIA, and he struggled to take tighter control over the agency's operations by changing its top leadership. Had it been publicly disclosed in 1961 that the CIA was training Tibetans in Colorado to fight against Communist China, the result would have been a major political embarrassment for the Kennedy administration. It would also have embarrassed the CIA.

But it is not the task of the free press to save the government from political embarrassment. If the Tibetan operation had a measure of success, it was "success" very narrowly defined. The guerrillas

---

*Although details of how the story was changed remain fuzzy, apparently it was decided in New York not to mention the CIA's role in the invasion and not to indicate the date of the invasion. Daniel also said that Dryfoos was "gravely troubled" by the security implications of Szulc's dispatch. "He [Dryfoos] could envision failure for the invasion, and he could see *The New York Times* being blamed for a bloody fiasco."

infiltrated into Tibet by the CIA were attempting to harass the Chinese, not to free the country; in the long run it is doubtful that they made very much difference. Since 1961 Communist China has tightened its grip on Tibet. In 1964 Peking ended the rule of the lamas and deposed the Panchen Lama, who was publicly beaten and humiliated in Lhasa. In 1966 the Red Guards overran Tibet and smashed the temples, seeking to eliminate all vestiges of Tibetan culture and religion.*

Publication of the story of the CIA's base in the Rockies might have focused public attention on a number of important issues, including the basic question of whether tax money should be used to finance clandestine intelligence operations. Disclosure would also have raised a subsidiary issue. By law, the CIA is barred from domestic operations. It traditionally justifies its activities in the United States by arguing that they are related to foreign operations or foreign intelligence-gathering. But the establishment of a secret base in the Rocky Mountains seems rather close to the definition of a domestic operation even if it is ultimately aimed at Tibet or Peking, and it is not at all clear that Congress contemplated such shenanigans when it established the CIA in 1947.

Disclosure might also have led to a public examination of such important questions as whether President Eisenhower approved the Tibetan operation, whether President Kennedy was aware of it or approved it, and whether the four "watchdog" committees of the Congress had any knowledge of what was going on in Colorado.

One cannot be certain, but it would seem likely that if the *Times* learned today that the CIA was training Tibetans in Colorado to fight against China, it would print the story.† And a strong argument can

---

*In Dharmsala, India, the Dalai Lama still presided in 1972 over a fragmented exile community. From bases in northern Nepal, the Khampas of eastern Tibet, organized into a guerrilla force of reportedly 7,000 men, continued to harass Chinese troops across the border. According to Indian press reports, this guerrilla army is financed and supplied by the CIA.

†One technical complication that may have mitigated against the *Times* publishing the story in 1961 is the fact that the newspaper learned the nationality of the "Orientals" seen at Peterson Field only from the high official who simultaneously requested that the story be killed. By taking the *Times* correspondent into his confidence, the official took a calculated risk, but he probably reasoned that this would make it ethically difficult for the newspaper to reveal that the men were Tibetans. The stratagem is an old one, not unlike one boxer clinching with another, and the purpose is the same: to "tie up" the reporter so he cannot publish something.

be made that the *Times* would have been wholly justified in pursuing and publishing the story in 1961. The important point, however, is that the *Times,* although it heeded the government's arguments in this instance, made its own decision. That decision was not imposed from outside or ordered by a federal court.

The press does not and need not print every piece of information that comes into its possession. It can delay publication or withhold information when it is genuinely and freely persuaded that national security is imperiled. But such instances should logically be extremely rare, for in the overwhelming majority of cases, the nation, its citizens—and therefore, ultimately, the "national security"—are best served by full disclosure and open debate.

Part III

MISINFORMATION

REPORTER: In connection with Dr. Kissinger's travels and whereabouts, do you think the government has a right to lie?
MR. ZIEGLER: . . . I wouldn't make that broad, sweeping statement, no.

—*White House press briefing,*
April 26, 1972

9

The Selling of
the Government

One of the more memorable quotes of our time was uttered in his own defense by Colonel Oran K. Henderson, the Vietnam brigade commander whose troops killed somewhere between 102 and 347 men, women, and children in the village of My Lai 4 on March 16, 1968.*

During his court-martial in 1971 on charges of allegedly covering up the massacre, Colonel Henderson testified that after My Lai he never heard the name of the hamlet again—except during briefings for visitors. "The My Lai operation," he explained, "was briefed for visitors as one of our successful operations."

Colonel Henderson was acquitted of all charges. But we must be grateful for his testimony; for it is at once symptomatic and terribly revealing. That the murders at My Lai, which rank as one of the most tragic and dishonorable episodes in the nation's history, could have been "briefed for visitors as one of our successful operations," tells a great deal about the nature of government information. It also

---

*First Lieutenant William L. Calley, Jr., the sole person convicted of murder at My Lai, was charged by the government with killing 102 persons and convicted in March, 1971, of killing twenty-two. Author Seymour M. Hersh, who first reported the massacre at My Lai, noted in a book published in 1972 that a secret Army CID report placed the number of dead civilians at My Lai at 347.

explains much about why the war in Vietnam contributed so greatly to the lack of belief by Americans in the word of their government.

The Defense Information School has something of the tree-shaded, peaceful atmosphere of an Ivy League campus. It has a ninety-three man faculty and is located at Fort Benjamin Harrison, near Indianapolis. It is seldom publicized. The students are members of the Armed Forces; the school, known back at the Pentagon as DINFOS, is the place where military public relations officers receive their training. More than 30,000 persons have attended the school and its forerunners since World War II; about 2,000 information specialists "graduate" from the institution each year.

In June of 1971 *The New York Times* ran a story about the school. One of the faculty members interviewed was Captain Robert Musil, of Garden City, Long Island, an instructor in the Department of Research and Oral Communications. The captain, who was active in the peace movement, and who was seeking a discharge from the Army, expressed his view of the purpose of the school. "The essential fact," he said, "is that we give people training in how to be slippery before the press . . ."

A dissident, antiwar Army officer might, after all, be biased about the nature of government information. So we may turn to higher authority, to McGeorge Bundy, who served as assistant for national security to President Kennedy and President Johnson before departing in 1966 to become president of the Ford Foundation.

On August 1, 1971, the John F. Kennedy Library opened many of the non-classified White House files of the Kennedy era. In a page-one story in *The New York Times* the next day, reporter Henry Raymont described one document in detail, for it bore an indiscreet marginal notation that was surely never meant to be seen by the public.

In reading through the thousands of papers at the library's temporary home in Waltham, Massachusetts, Raymont had discovered a draft communiqué prepared by Presidential press secretary Pierre Salinger for release on November 20, 1963, following a cabinet-level meeting on Vietnam in Honolulu. The language of the communiqué was deliberately vague. Written in the margin, the *Times* story said, was a note in Bundy's handwriting: "Pierre: Champion! Excellent Prose. No Surprise. 'A communiqué should say nothing in such a way as to fool the press without deceiving them.' "

Eleven days later the *Times* ran another story, also by Henry Raymont, headlined "McGeorge Bundy Sets Record Straight for Press." The article was really a long correction in the guise of a news story. Interviewed by Raymont at his office at the Ford Foundation, Bundy explained that he had actually written that a communiqué should say nothing in such a way as to "feed" the press—not "fool" the press.

What had happened was as follows: After the first story was published, Bundy telephoned Abe Rosenthal, the managing editor of the *Times*. Bundy was elaborately cordial—but he wanted something done. According to Raymont, the entire matter was handled amicably; Rosenthal sent him over to interview Bundy and write the second article. Raymont had take the precaution of bringing a Xerox of the document down from Waltham when he wrote his original story. Upon reexamining it, he said, he concluded that "clearly Bundy was right." It was one of those cases Raymont said, where something could easily be misread the first time, but once you were told the correct word, there seemed no doubt about it.

It was mildly embarrassing, since good reporters do not like to misquote anyone, let alone the president of the Ford Foundation, but it did occur to Raymont afterward, that while there is undoubtedly some difference between the word "fool" and the word "feed," in the context of the draft communiqué the difference was really more one of degree than of meaning. Indeed, the clear intent of Bundy's advice to the President's news secretary and the attitude of mind it revealed seem not substantially altered whichever word one inserts in the margin. The point of Bundy's advice is that the press—and therefore the American public—should be told nothing in a way that makes it seem that they are being told something. In this case, the purpose of saying nothing was to mask the growing U.S. involvement in Vietnam. Three weeks before Bundy wrote "Champion!" in the margin of the communiqué, the South Vietnamese generals, with the help of the CIA and the advice and consent of the White House, had overthrown President Diem. Three days before Diem died Bundy had cabled Lodge that it was in the interest of the United States that a coup, once launched, "should succeed." Publicly the United States denied any involvement in the coup. Under the circumstances, what is astonishing about the "fool"/"feed" incident is that, having played a key role in the enormous deception of the press and public about Diem, Mac should have felt it necessary to call Abe.

At 9:32 A.M., on February 20, 1971, an employee of the National Emergency Warning Center inside Cheyenne Mountain, ten miles south of Colorado Springs, fed a punched tape into a teletype machine. The message was immediately transmitted via the wires of the Associated Press and the United Press International to radio and TV stations across America. It began: "This is an emergency action notification directed by the President. Normal broadcasting will cease immediately." The chilling words meant that the United States might be under impending nuclear attack.

The message was preceded by the code word HATEFULNESS, a signal to stations that it was real. According to federal regulations, upon receiving this message, the stations should have made this announcement: "We interrupt this program. This is a national emergency. Important instructions will follow in thirty seconds . . . This station has interrupted its regular program at the request of the United States government to participate in the Emergency Broadcast System . . . I repeat . . ."

Broadcasters who had checked their code instructions were horrified to find that HATEFULNESS was indeed the correct authenticating word for the day.* "I thought I was gonna have a heart attack trying to open that envelope," said the news director of WEVA, in Emporia, Virginia. In Brazil, Indiana, Chuck Kelley, program director of WWCM, took one look at the teletype and froze. "My God," he said, "it's Pearl Harbor all over again." Kelley took his station off the air.

Deep inside Cheyenne Mountain, the error was discovered quickly. Frantically, officials at the National Emergency Warning Center tried to cancel the message. About eight minutes after the false alert went out, the same civilian operator who made the original mistake sent out a cancellation. This time he forgot to include the necessary code word for a cancellation. Finally, at 10:17 A.M., forty-four minutes after the first alert, a notice to cancel, preceded by the correct code word IMPISH, clattered over the wires.

A month later, reviewing the fiasco, the FCC reported that only 487, or about 6 percent of the nation's 8,142 radio and television stations, shut down as they were supposed to do during the alert. In other words, the blunder had proven that the system was not working. In the post-mortem that followed the false alert, certain changes in procedure were made.

In the process of making these, it leaked out—but received almost no public attention—that in cooperation with the Emergency

---

*The code words are sealed inside a red envelope, which, appropriately, is officially known in federal regulations as the Red Envelope. The words appear on an Authenticator List, changed four times a year.

Broadcasting System, Civil Defense officials had prepared tapes to be broadcast immediately by radio and television stations in the event of nuclear attack. In at least one instance, in the state of Florida, the message on the tapes would have assured the public that the enemy who had attacked the United States had been hit by strong retaliatory action. The prerecorded message to the American public explained that the enemy had "struck the first blow." But it added: "Our Strategic Air Command and naval units have devastated many of his major cities and industrial centers. Our defense forces have retaliated with tremendous effectiveness and probability of victory is good."*

This might be exhilarating news, assuming that our radios were still working amid the nuclear wreckage, and that any of us were left to hear the message. It is, in any event, comforting to know that official lies are now pretaped, prerecorded, and prepackaged, ready for any eventuality, including Armageddon.

On the morning of September 2, 1970, Secretary of Defense Melvin Laird met in his office with reporters who cover the Pentagon. Coffee was served and the atmosphere informal, but it was, after all, a press conference, and an official transcript was made.

Toward the end of the interview, Laird remarked with elaborate emphasis that he did not want his answers "to create a credibility problem." He chided one reporter for writing that his remarks about American air power in Cambodia had given rise to a "credibility gap."

The transcript then read as follows:

A. I've tried to be as forthcoming on information about our activities and the use of air power in Cambodia as I possibly

---

*When the existence of the prepared messages was disclosed, the federal government's regional Civil Defense headquarters at Thomasville, Georgia, ordered officials in Miami to destroy the tapes. Recorded messages instructing the public in case of nuclear attack are distributed to radio stations throughout the country by the Defense Civil Preparedness Agency in Washington. The messages in Dade County had apparently been prepared locally. When they were discovered, national Civil Defense headquarters sent out an all-points teletype message warning local officials to destroy all tapes that did not conform to instructions from Washington. A spokesman for Region Three, which ordered the Miami tapes destroyed, claimed that no other area —as far as was known—had tapes that spoke of "retaliatory" action.

could . . . I just don't believe that anyone can find a case where I've shied away, have not given you complete and full information. I don't believe that when you give information in answer to questions or discuss it as frankly and as openly as I have that you can create a credibility gap. If there is a problem of some information that you don't have, that you want, I hope you'll ask me and I hope you'll ask me right now, 'cause I'm willing to answer those questions.

Q. How many sorties are we flying in a day?

A. The number of sorties is a matter which I have not released, and we are not releasing the sortie levels.

As these vignettes might suggest, government information is a commodity at once frightening and hilarious. Its language and style often evoke the Newspeak and doublethink of George Orwell's *1984.** But its humor is unintended; to the government, information is a tool of power.

In *The Selling of the President 1968,* author Joe McGinniss described how Richard Nixon employed television and Madison Avenue techniques in his successful campaign for the Presidency in 1968. Once in the White House, a President makes use of these same techniques to preserve and extend his power.

Unlike a candidate, whose campaign funds restrict his television, advertising, and public relations budget, an incumbent President has almost unlimited federal funds at his disposal for public relations during his four or eight years in the White House. Moreover, prime television time, so costly to a candidate, is usually free to a President between elections.

And while spending by political candidates occurs, for the most part, during campaigns, the government public relations effort is

---

*A literally Orwellian study prepared by the Nixon administration contained one recommendation that closely paralleled the frightening "telescreens" used by Big Brother to spy on the inhabitants of *1984.* Congressman William S. Moorhead, who uncovered the study, said it included a proposal that would have "required manufacture and installation of special FM receivers in every home radio and television set, boat, and automobile, which could be automatically turned on by the government to contact every citizen, whether awake or asleep." The supposed purpose would be to broadcast disaster warnings. Existing systems, the report noted, have "no wake-up capability." The White House said the study, prepared for its Office of Science and Technology, had been rejected.

continuous. The machinery serves the President throughout his term of office, not only at election time.

The vast, interlocking federal information machine has one primary purpose: the selling of the government. The machine markets its one product—the President and his administration—by distributing an official, and often misleading, version of truth to the voters. It does so with the help of the system of secrecy and classification, combined with government control over access to military and diplomatic news events. The information machine, in short, is the mechanism through which government information—and misinformation—is transmitted to the press and the electorate. The major objective is to enhance and preserve the Presidential image. In the electronic age, a political leader's image (especially his image on the television screen), is the true index of his power; imagery is a form of political energy directly convertible into votes.

Television is by far the most important public relations tool available to a President, although an American President, to be sure, operates at some disadvantage, since the government regulates, but does not wholly control, the networks and stations. There are those who lament the absence of a domestic Voice of America to broadcast government propaganda directly to the people. In secret and startling testimony before a House subcommittee in 1971, the commander in chief of the Strategic Air Command, General Bruce K. Holloway, suggested that what America needed to preserve its security was a government-controlled news program to combat media "slanting." He added: "It would have to have authenticity. You would have to have the President starting it off with a thirty-second introduction."

While it might be preferable if the commander of SAC stuck to his missiles and bombers, General Holloway quite accurately understood the fact that the President is the chief public relations officer of the government. He stands at the apex of what must surely be the largest and most formidable information complex in the world, one that includes not only his own coterie of press secretaries, communicators, and media advisers, but literally thousands of PR and information officials in the civilian and military departments of the government.

It would be wrong, however, to think of this information structure as consisting, below the Presidential level, only of public relations men. When a cabinet secretary or lesser official issues a statement, holds a press conference, appears on a TV panel show, or drafts a policy with public or political reaction in mind, he, too, is acting as a shaper and distributor of information.

Although the whole thrust of government information is to mer-
chandise the best possible image of the government and its leader,
it is a cardinal principle of public relations that this goal is never
publicly admitted. Consider, for example, Richard Nixon's appearance on the NBC *Today* show in March of 1971. Barbara Walters was
interviewing the Chief Executive:

> MISS WALTERS: . . . there has been a lot of talk, Mr. President,
> about your image and the fact that the American public—for-
> give me Mr. President—see you as rather a stuffy man and not
> a human man. Are you— Oh, dear. Are you worried about your
> image, Mr. President?
>
> PRESIDENT NIXON: Not at all. When Presidents begin to worry
> about images . . . do you know what happens? They become like
> the athletes, the football teams and the rest, who become so
> concerned about what is written about them and what is said
> about them that they don't play the game well . . . the President,
> with the enormous responsibilities that he has, must not be con-
> stantly preening in front of a mirror . . . I don't worry about polls.
> I don't worry about images . . . I never have.

Here was a President appearing on the *Today* show before an
audience of millions of voters—and simultaneously denying he was
concerned about his image. That is irony sufficient in itself, but there
is additional irony in the fact that Nixon was on the show only because his advisers had persuaded him that he was not getting across
to the public and that he needed more exposure. Suddenly, within
a period of twelve days, Nixon appeared on the *Today* show, granted
a long interview to Howard K. Smith on ABC television, and—on the
same day he taped the *Today* program—gave a long, folksy interview to a group of women reporters. During the week the newspaper reader or TV viewer could scarcely escape Richard Nixon
proclaiming his lack of concern for his image.

For a President so unworried about appearances, Richard Nixon
surrounded himself with an unprecedented number of PR men and
"communicators," some openly acknowledged and others hidden in
the White House and the Executive Office of the President under
innocuous or misleading titles.

One must begin with Harry Robbins Haldeman, the former
manager of the Los Angeles office of J. Walter Thompson, whom
Nixon appointed as his principal White House assistant. Strictly
speaking, Haldeman's job was to serve as the President's chief of staff,
but he installed Ronald L. Ziegler, his protégé at J. Walter, as press
secretary, and his deputy, Dwight Chapin, was a member of the

President's Image Committee, which has already been mentioned, so it could not be said that Haldeman was entirely remote from public relations policies.

A crew-cut all-American Boy, Haldeman unabashedly took home movies of important dignitaries in the midst of state visits and summit meetings. As a student at UCLA after World War II, he worried about the Communist Menace and became an admirer of Richard Nixon. In 1956 and 1958 he took leaves of absence from his advertising job to work for Nixon in political campaigns, and in 1960, when Nixon ran for President, he named Haldeman his chief advance advance man.*

Haldeman managed Nixon's 1962 campaign for governor of California, but their friendship survived even that disaster. Meanwhile, Haldeman was upward mobile at J. Walter, in charge of an office with clients that included Disneyland, 7-Up, and Diaper Sweet. One of his young executives, handling the Disneyland and 7-Up accounts, was Ron Ziegler, the former star fullback of Dixie Heights High School in Park Hills, Kentucky. The family had moved to California, and Ziegler, during his sophomore year at college, got a job driving the Jungle Cruise boat at Disneyland. ("Welcome aboard, folks. My name's Ron. I'm your skipper and guide down the River of Adventure . . . Note the alligators. Please keep your hands inside the boat. They're always looking for a handout.")†

While at the University of Southern California, Ziegler became active in the Young Republicans, and in the 1962 gubernatorial campaign, Haldeman recruited him as a press aide to Herb Klein. After Nixon lost, Haldeman hired Ziegler at J. Walter. In 1968 Haldeman served as chief of staff of the Nixon-for-President campaign and Zie-

---

*During the 1960 campaign Haldeman was in charge of such mundane but nonetheless important details as seeing that cars and press buses stayed close together in the candidate's motorcade, that baggage was unloaded and schedules kept. He and his equally crew-cut assistants kept in constant touch over walkie-talkies; reporters who rode the press bus can probably remember at 2 or 3 A.M., weary after a nineteen-hour day, hearing the walkie-talkie in the front of the bus crackling in the night: "Haldeman, Haldeman . . . Haldeman, Haldeman."

†It is an interesting although possibly not significant parallel, that as a teenager, Richard Nixon served as a barker for the wheel of chance at the Slippery Gulch Rodeo in Prescott, Arizona. According to biographer Earl Mazo, "Nixon barked for the legal front of the concession, where the prizes were hams and sides of bacon, which was a 'come on' for a back room featuring poker and dice."

gler was press spokesman; after the election both moved into the White House in the same capacities.

The new Presidential press secretary was a dark-haired man who chewed two sticks of gum at a time, drank Chivas Regal, wore dark-blue suits, and had the Secret Service code name Whaleboat. He was usually very pleasant, although not always, and he proved generally popular with most White House reporters.

In 1971 James M. Naughton of *The New York Times* reported, however, that some journalists were convinced that "Ziegler is hardly more than a Pinocchio puppet whose nose does not grow when he fibs." But a prominent Washington correspondent and student of the Nixon adminstration insisted to the author of this book that Ziegler possessed a "fundamental honesty" not always to be found elsewhere on the White House staff. As the correspondent explained it, however, Ziegler's honesty had to be viewed with split vision; because of the nature of Ziegler's job, the newsman said, "in his briefings he has been forced to mislead reporters, to deny things that did in fact happen and to say outrageous things. But I don't think he has ever intentionally misled me in a face-to-face interview." It was a rather fine distinction; and it was Ronald Ziegler, after all, who sought to dismiss the Watergate break-in by agents of the President's re-election committee as "a third-rate burglary attempt."

Ziegler's appointment as press secretary—the most visible position in the government information structure—gave rise to considerable speculation about why Nixon had passed over his veteran press secretary, Herb Klein, in favor of a twenty-nine-year-old advertising man with no experience in Washington or in journalism.

The answer goes back to the post-election period when Nixon was putting together his staff at the Hotel Pierre in Manhattan. As soon as Haldeman's appointment was announced, the new staff chief told reporters bluntly that in the Nixon administration, "there will be no Sherman Adams, no Jim Hagerty . . . " As a matter of fact, Haldeman added, there would be no press secretary "in the traditional sense."

All of this was interesting news to Herb Klein. In 1968 Klein, fifty-one, had served as "communications manager" of the Presidential campaign, and having resigned his job as editor of the *San Diego Union*, he was, during the Hotel Pierre phase, plainly awaiting a White House job. But as one Nixon intimate put it, "If Herb had any idea of being Hagerty, he could forget it. Nixon had his fill of that for eight years under Eisenhower. He didn't want staff people dominating."

Flowing from Nixon's determination not to have a powerful press secretary who could speak, as Hagerty did, virtually with the voice of the President, was the decision to name Ziegler, the younger man, and not Klein, as press spokesman. There was considerable pulling and hauling about all this inside the Nixon camp; two days after Haldeman announced that there would be *no* press secretary, Ziegler was named as a special assistant to the President-elect, sans press title. Not until January 13, 1969, did Ziegler announce that Nixon had told him to go ahead and use the title of "press secretary" after all.

In the meantime, three weeks after election, Klein's appointment as "director of communications for the Executive Branch" was finally announced—by Ron Ziegler. It was then that Klein declared that "truth will become the hallmark of the Nixon administration" and that the new administration would "eliminate any possibility of a credibility gap"—predictions that proved premature.

The creation of the new post of "communications director" and the appointment of Klein meant that for the first time the public relations function at the Presidential level had been split in two. One inevitable result was an increase in the cost of White House publicity as the number of people engaged in Presidential PR work proliferated. Klein soon had a staff of a dozen persons, whose salaries, added to his own annual pay of $42,500, totaled almost $200,000 a year. Ziegler had an even larger staff of fourteen—eight assistants and six secretaries.

A second inevitable result was friction between the two competing PR power centers, between Ziegler and Klein. Operating from across the street in the Executive Office Building, Klein could *see* the White House through his office window, but he was physically not as close to the throne as Ziegler, whose office was in the White House proper. Theoretically, Klein spoke for "the Executive Branch as a whole," as Ziegler put it, but in practice this meant that Klein was reduced to working with the cabinet departments; and traditionally, when any *really* important news originates in a department, the White House grabs it and the President's press secretary announces it.

"I have the President and the White House," Ziegler once pointedly told an interviewer.

Indeed he did, and within the White House, Ziegler's power and influence grew steadily. One White House official privy to the power struggles inside the palace guard gave a laconic explanation: "Ziegler is Haldeman's man."

The inbuilt tension between the communications director and the Presidential press secretary could be illustrated by a number of incidents, but one will suffice. Early in the administration, Fred Maroon, a talented photographer, and Evelyn Metzger, the Washington editor of Doubleday, approached Klein with an idea for a book, with pictures and text, that would give an inside view of the Nixon White House. Klein approved, author Allen Drury agreed to do the text, and the book, *Courage and Hesitation,* was published by Doubleday in 1971. But Ziegler, sour from the start on what he regarded as a "commercial project," cooperated as little as possible with the Klein-backed literary effort. On one occasion Ziegler left Drury cooling his heels outside his office for almost an hour. Although Drury generally admired what he saw in the Nixon White House, his book reserved a special scorn for Ronald Ziegler.

Despite Ziegler's proximity to the President, and his high visibility, Klein was not wholly without his own sources of power; these included a personal relationship with Nixon that traced back to 1946, a measure of patronage—Klein was able to place several friends in public relations jobs in the departments—and perhaps most important of all, a cordial relationship with many members of the Washington press corps.

In California, Klein liked to skin-dive near his home in La Jolla, and as communications director, he possessed some of the qualities of a cuttlefish, exuding clouds of amiability that spread out ahead of him, enveloping any potential enemy. Bland and unfailingly pleasant to newsmen, Klein, in turn, was generally well liked by the press.

Klein had weathered three of Nixon's *Six Crises*—the "Checkers" speech, the "kitchen debate" in Moscow in 1959, and the 1960 Presidential campaign. And he was at Nixon's side in 1962 when Nixon lost the election for governor of California. Klein alternated his public relations chores for Nixon with various posts on the conservative *San Diego Union*; he was named editor of the paper in 1959.

Klein has a sleepy and faintly elfin face that some might not regard as ideal for a communications director in the electronic age. (There are reporters in Washington who swear that Klein drew a backstage role at the White House because Nixon did not think he looked good on television.) But this factor is probably not as important as it might seem. Ideally, the role of a communications director calls for a Walter Cronkite sort of face—warm, friendly, and trustworthy. Yet Pierre Salinger, who closely resembles an overweight Mississippi riverboat gambler (he once played the role of a crooked lawyer on *Batman*) experienced relatively few credibility problems as President Kennedy's press secretary. By contrast, Arthur Sylvester, whose beatific countenance could pass for that of an Anglican bishop, achieved undesired fame as McNamara's press spokesman by coining the phrase the "right to lie."

From the start, however, Nixon's communications director

played an ambiguous role; on the one hand he described himself as a sort of ombudsman, whose job was to "get more information out" by persuading the departments to cooperate with the press. And Klein did win some plaudits from correspondents for opening doors within the government. But as one of the President's public relations men, Klein also joined in the Nixon administration's general attack on the news media. Appearing on a TV panel show in November, 1969, for example, he warned that unless the news media, both newspapers and television networks, reexamined their handling of the news, "you do invite government to come in." In time, it became increasingly difficult for Klein to pretend that he served two masters, the press and the President.

The communications director began to spend more time on the road, making speeches and extolling administration policies. "Klein," said one White House official, "is ambassador to the boondocks." As a sort of traveling salesman for the Nixon White House, Klein argued for the ABM, had a kind word for the military-industrial complex, and predicted Clement F. Haynsworth would make a "great" Supreme Court Justice. Before a group of college students at Northern Illinois University, he attacked Senator George McGovern's proposal to expand the food-stamp program. Food stamps, Klein explained, would not end hunger: "A lot of mothers will go out and buy a Pepsi-Cola or a Coke for their children instead of milk. Or they might buy a lot of potato chips for them to eat."

In Washington, Klein presided over Saturday morning sessions of the Image Committee, whose regular members were himself, Dwight Chapin, and Special Counsel Charles W. "Chuck" Colson, then the *eminence grise* of the White House PR operation. Lest anyone doubt the existence of such a group, it should be noted that Allen Drury, in researching his book on Nixon, was permitted to sit in on a meeting of the committee, and reported its deliberations.*

According to Drury, the committee's agenda included the question of whether information about the President's reading habits should be provided to several magazines that had requested it. The committee decided this was extremely sensitive, because if it were revealed that he read anything "frivolous," someone would surely use this as the basis for "snide criticism." The committee then turned

---

*Drury referred to the group as the Plans Committee. The panel may have been known by this euphemism when it was discussed with outsiders, but within the White House, among members of the President's staff, it was widely and better known as the Image Committee. Chapin, who was linked to political espionage in the 1972 campaign, left the White House in 1973.

to another problem: "how to counter the theme that the President is heartless and cold." The discussion, Drury reports, became vehement, and centered on the fact that "a little black poster girl had been turned away without having her picture taken with the President," a gaffe that aroused criticism in the black community. It was noted by the committee that the girl and her parents would be invited to a Sunday worship service at the White House; perhaps the picture with the President could be taken then. The meeting of the committee began at 9:30 A.M. and ended just under three hours later.

Klein also presided over occasional meetings with information officials from the departments. These were informal sessions, usually held in Klein's office over drinks and peanuts. At these PR encounter groups, the government publicists were encouraged to run ideas up the flagpole and air their collective problems. One such session was devoted to a discussion of whether a public relations man for a cabinet secretary should be seen at his boss's side when the latter holds a press conference.

"At one meeting," a participant said, "Harry Flemming [the President's assistant for personnel] was explaining how to get your own man in PR jobs. It's hard to do—there are too damn many Civil Service rules—but the way he said to do it wasn't right anyway. It seemed amateurish."

At another session, Klein stressed the importance of tipping off the White House when embarrassing news was about to break. In October, 1971, after Nixon nominated Mrs. Romana Banuelos to be Treasurer of the United States, but before she had been confirmed, U.S. immigration agents raided her Mexican food-packing plant in California and seized thirty-six Mexican workers as illegal aliens. It developed that the firm had been raided six times in four years for the same reason. Someone had called the communications director before the story broke—presumably it was a PR man for the Immigration Service—and the White House had a few hours' notice, Klein said. "I can't tell you" Klein added, "how important that is—to have some forewarning."*

At the end of 1971 Klein's office distributed to the press an amazing thirty-four-page, single-spaced mimeographed document entitled "Richard Nixon's Third Year." The prose was so glutinous in its praise of the President that the document brought snickers in official Washington and inspired an Art Buchwald column.

"In the year now ending," Klein's encomium began, "President

---

*Mrs. Banuelos' appointment was not withdrawn by the White House. She was sworn in as Treasurer of the United States on December 17, 1971.

Nixon moved vigorously on both the foreign and domestic fronts
. . . It was a year of bold initiatives . . . of large conceptions, of daring
innovation . . . a year of bold action based on meticulous preparation.
It was a good year, that promises much for those to follow . . . In its
first four months, the New Economic Policy has been enormously
successful . . . " And so on.

Upstaged by Ziegler, Klein by 1971 found himself squeezed
from a new direction in the person of Charles Wendell Colson. As
Special Counsel to the President, Colson's job ostensibly was to deal
with organized interest groups. In fact, he moved powerfully but
quietly into the field of public relations. Wheeling and dealing backstage, his hand usually hidden, Colson had succeeded by 1972 in
building a mini-public relations empire inside the White House,
unannounced and out of public view. In classic Washington tradition
—the bureaucrats call it "layering"—Colson had created a third public relations power center, wedged in above Klein and rivaling even
Ziegler.

Colson, a tough, ambitious operator, made it to the White House
via a background in Republican politics and law. A New Englander,
he went to Brown University, served as a company commander in
the Marine Corps during the Korean War, and by age twenty-seven
was administrative assistant to Senator Leverett Saltonstall, the
Massachusetts Republican. He attended law school at night, got his
degree, and in 1960 formed what is now the large Washington law
firm of Gadsby & Hannah, lobbyists for Grumman Aircraft and other
corporate interests. He played a significant role in Nixon's 1968 campaign, and in November, 1969, the President brought him to the
White House.

There, Colson quickly earned a reputation as a political mechanic and a sort of improper Bostonian. "Chuck Colson," John Pierson wrote in the *Wall Street Journal,* "is a hatchet man."* Certainly
this was true in the Tydings affair; as already noted, it was Colson who
delivered the crucial witness to *Life* reporter Bill Lambert; the
magazine's resulting exposé hastened Tydings' departure from the
Senate in the 1970 election.

Colson was responsible for other politically inspired leaks. Often
he pulled the strings and got subordinates or other White House staff

---

*Perhaps mischievously, Pierson quoted the definition of a "hatchet man"
from *The New Language of Politics* by William Safire, a Nixon speechwriter
and the nation's leading political lexicographer: "HATCHETMAN . . . the
insider who does the dirty work for a public figure." *See* William Safire (New
York: Random House, 1968), p. 185.

members to make the actual contact with a newsman; the technique made it harder to trace the story to Colson. But Colson also operated on a straight PR level; he was the official who arranged for Nixon to accept a hard hat from the leader of the construction workers union in New York.

The story is interesting. On May 8, 1970, a week after President Nixon announced that American troops had invaded Cambodia, construction workers in lower Manhattan brutally beat up a group of student war protesters. Shouting "All the way, U.S.A. . . . Love it or leave it," the construction men bloodied heads with fists, tools, and hard hats. Mayor John V. Lindsay angrily charged that the city had witnessed "a breakdown of the police." On May 20 more than 100,-000 construction workers, longshoremen and others massed at City Hall for a rally in support of the Vietnam war. The demonstrators chanted "Spiro is my hero," "Impeach the Red Mayor," and burned Lindsay in effigy.

Nixon telephoned Peter Brennan, president of the Building and Construction Trades Council of New York, to congratulate him on this peaceful rally. Colson then arranged for a delegation of workers, headed by Brennan, to come to the White House on May 26. The day before the scheduled meeting, Ziegler, in answer to a question, declined to say what the President's attitude was toward the beatings in Manhattan. At the White House, however, Brennan did have a comment. "Nobody talks about how beautiful last week's rally was," he said, "without even a punch in the nose."

The construction workers sat around the cabinet table with the President and presented him with a white construction helmet bearing the words "Commander in Chief." In a formal statement, Brennan said: "The hard hat will stand as a symbol, along with our great flag, of freedom and patriotism to our beloved country."*

Liberals, appalled at the brutality on May 8, were dismayed by Nixon's open embrace of the construction workers. But Colson, with his eye on the votes of Middle America, had understood the symbolism of the hard hat and captured it for Nixon. Given Nixon's constituency, and his desire to preempt George Wallace on the right, the hard-hat episode was something of a PR triumph. At any rate, Colson seemed to think it was, and so, one must assume, did Nixon.

Colson gradually took over more and more of Klein's functions.

---

*During the 1972 Presidential campaign, Brennan played a key role in organizing a committee of two hundred labor leaders for Nixon. The group represented construction workers, longshoremen, teamsters, and other trades. After the election, Nixon named Brennan Secretary of Labor.

Within the White House, some of Klein's critics had argued that he was too nice, and not enough of a tough political operator to handle the job of Presidential public relations. Robert B. Semple, Jr., the White House correspondent of *The New York Times*, put it this way in an interview: "If the title of "communications director" meant propagandizing for the President, then there was a need for a guy with an intensely sharp, political mind. And they have since found him—Chuck Colson."

Besides Ziegler and Klein, as Semple analyzed it, Nixon and his advisers perceived the need for a third type of operator, "a man who could conduct PR-political warfare on an activist level. They needed someone who would ask 'How do you answer John Kerry? How do you organize a citizens committee to beat the drums for Phase Two?' "*

As Colson's influence expanded inside the White House, he reached outside to strengthen his public relations power base. Colson urged Nixon to appoint a top diplomatic correspondent to handle foreign-policy image-making and advise Ziegler and Henry Kissinger. At the President's direction, Colson contacted John Scali of ABC, an experienced reporter and the secret intermediary who had helped to end the Cuban missile crisis. In two talks with Nixon, Scali was persuaded to take the job of special consultant to the President.†

Colson, who thus acted as a recruiter for the new White House post, had privately described it in blunt language: "We need a sharp PR man in the foreign affairs area who can advise Ron and Henry." Three months later, in July, 1971, Colson added a PR man to his own staff to handle domestic affairs—Desmond J. Barker, Jr., president of an advertising and public relations firm in Salt Lake City.

Colson's own image became somewhat embarrassing, however, after he was linked in the press to the Watergate bugging scandal through Everette Howard Hunt, Jr., one of the defendants, whom Colson had hired as a White House "consultant" in 1971. The two had met, the White House explained, as members of the Washington

---

*When John Kerry, a leader of a group of antiwar Vietnam veterans came to Washington in April, 1971, it was Colson who organized a competing group of veterans. After Nixon announced Phase Two of his economic policy later that year, it was Colson who set up background briefings for the press, scheduled radio-TV appearances by administration officials, and helped organize the Citizens for a New Prosperity, a group specifically created to promote Nixon's policies.

†In December, 1972, Nixon named Scali U.S. ambassador to the United Nations.

chapter of the Brown alumni club. The old school tie hastened Colson's departure, which was announced soon after Nixon's re-election.

In addition to Ziegler and Klein, their deputies and staff, and the various public relations specialists, a press staff of five women served Mrs. Nixon. Nixon also employed a speechwriting team of sixteen persons—the largest in White House history—as well as four aides to monitor the news media and compile the "President's Daily News Briefing," a private news digest of about 6,000 words prepared for the President each morning. The major speechwriters were Raymond K. Price, former chief editorial writer for the old *New York Herald Tribune*; William Safire, a writer and former New York public relations man; Patrick J. Buchanan, former editorial writer for the *St. Louis Globe-Democrat*; and the Reverend John J. McLaughlin, a Jesuit and the first Catholic priest to serve as a White House assistant.*

The President also had a television adviser—first, Roger Ailes (who was paid by the Republican National Committee), and later, director Mark Goode. The television adviser worried about camera angles, make-up, lighting, and other technical details. Finally, the White House employed a staff of official photographers. Although the White House understandably never issued a press release on the subject, a conservative estimate would be that Nixon's public relations staff, including all these categories, numbered at least sixty people.

The media-conscious Nixon administration had a particularly elaborate public relations superstructure in the White House. As in every administration, below the Presidential level there existed a large publicity and public information apparatus extending into virtually every corner of the federal government. Yet no one knew its precise size or cost.

One reason for this is that no official of the federal government has the words "public relations" in his title. Job titles vary, and in some departments an official serving as assistant to a cabinet secretary, or as an "executive assistant," is, in fact, the top public relations man. Below him, there is often a public information office that handles everyday contacts with the press. In the Pentagon, the chief public relations man was an Assistant Secretary of Defense. At the

---

*In addition to these men, Dom Bonafede of the *National Journal* reported in February, 1972, Nixon had eight "back-up" speechwriters: Lyndon K. Allin, Eliska A. Hasek, Lee W. Huebner, John K. Andrews, Jr., John McDonald, Harold Lezar, Noel Koch, and David R. Gergen. Four researchers served the speechwriters. Safire left in 1973 to write a newspaper column.

State Department, early in the Nixon administration, Apollo astronaut Michael Collins held the title of Assistant Secretary for Public Affairs, but daily relations with the press on the working level were handled by department spokesman Robert J. McCloskey. Even the CIA has a public relations director, under another title.

It is down below, in the ranks, that counting government PR men becomes soupy. Some are deliberately hidden, it is true, under uninformative job descriptions; but in addition, there is a legitimate problem of definition. Writers, editors, photographers, and others could be included in the definition of "public relations."

Quite aside from such knotty questions of definition, there is the more practical consideration that officials of the government would simply rather not estimate the size and cost of the public relations structure; the whole subject is politically sensitive.

An indication of the scope of the information machine can be found, however, in a study published by the United States Civil Service Commission in 1968, entitled *Occupations of Federal White-Collar Workers*. Buried among its 162 pages of charts, graphs, and computer print-outs are some revealing figures.

According to the study, in the category of "Information and the Arts," there were 20,380 employees working for the federal government in 1968, with an average salary of $10,742 a year.* There were nineteen occupational titles listed in this broad category, and a few had little to do with public relations, strictly speaking. For example, the list includes 165 "museum curators" and six "musical technicians." But even after these and other unrelated occupations are eliminated, the total still provides some indication of the dimensions of the information establishment.

Aware that the massive size of the government public relations machine made it vulnerable to political attack, Nixon in December, 1969, wrote a memo to Haldeman urging that the administration take "a very hard look" at the PR apparatus. "Every department is terribly overstaffed in this respect—it is one of Washington's worst self-perpetuating bureaucracies," Nixon wrote.

In November, 1970, this was followed by a formal Presidential memorandum to all departments and agencies. In this directive,

---

*Within the overall category, however, public relations workers earned more—an average of $16,200 in Washington and overseas, and $12,000 in the United States outside of Washington. The study also showed that the number of Information and Arts workers increased at a much more rapid rate than did those in any other job category in the entire federal government—zooming from 6,105 employees in 1957 to 20,380 in 1968.

Nixon ordered a "curtailment of self-serving and wasteful public relations activities." Some of these public relations efforts, the President said, represented "a questionable use of the taxpayers' money for the purpose of promoting and soliciting support for various agency activities." The cutback, Nixon said, was not aimed at "legitimate" public information activities but at "fancy publications" and "similar extravagances." (The order, did not, however, apply to the White House, which continued to augment its large public relations staff.)

The job of policing the Nixon order fell to the Office of Management and Budget. This created a problem; the Executive Branch traditionally claimed it did not know how many public relations men were employed by the government or how much was spent on such activities. How could the administration reduce a program when it did not know its size to begin with? How much would be cut from what?

OMB solved this dilemma by sending out questionnaires to the departments and agencies, asking them to report back on the cost and scope of their information programs. Based on the replies, OMB estimated that the Executive Branch employed 6,144 people in public relations (including Congressional relations) at a cost of $161 million a year.* An official of OMB who helped to compile this data at the President's request said, when interviewed: "Do you believe it?" His skepticism reflected the fact that OMB had used a fairly narrow definition of "public relations" in arriving at its totals.

After it had completed its survey, the budget office set as its target a reduction in public relations spending of $45 million. OMB then sent a new set of questionnaires to the departments asking how they had complied with the cutback order. The House subcommittee on government information sent out letters asking the same question.

The answers varied widely. The Pentagon claimed it had cut 991 people and $3.7 million from its PR budget; the Department of Health, Education, and Welfare said it had eliminated sixty-eight positions and cut its budget by $1.6 million; other agencies reported smaller reductions. Not every agency was willing to admit there was

---

*In 1967 an Associated Press team estimated that the federal government spent $425 million a year on public relations. But this total included $200 million spent by defense contractors and charged off the government, and $125 million in government printing costs. Of the balance of roughly $100 million, AP estimated that the Executive Branch spent almost $90 million and Congress about $10 million.

anything to cut; chairman Helen Delich Bentley of the Federal Maritime Commission wrote to the House subcommittee: "The Federal Maritime Commission, a relatively small regulatory agency, does not engage in self-serving promotional programs, and, accordingly, is not affected by the President's directive." John M. Maury, legislative counsel of the CIA, wrote: "The agency is not considered to be included among those agencies having public relations functions."*

Eight months after Nixon's directive was issued, OMB officials announced that 1,164 public relations jobs had been eliminated at a saving of $9.4 million. No further figures were ever released, although OMB said it "thought" the goal of $45 million would be reached.

There was a major catch to the Nixon cutback, however. To the public, it appeared that the government was saving money and trimming fat from the federal payroll. In fact, the order did not require that any public relations personnel be dismissed, and the "cutback" did not save the taxpayers a penny. It simply meant that employees were for the most part shifted to other jobs within their departments. In some cases they even continued to do the same work under new titles. And the transfers meant no overall reduction in total departmental budgets.

"The money saved on public relations," OMB official George Strauss explained, "was used for something else—perhaps something else that might not have been done. It's like squeezing a tube of toothpaste. The money remains in the tube even though it might appear at the other end."

Strauss added: "Heads of departments seek shelter for their people. If a PR man is a speechwriter for the head of an agency, he doesn't want to lose him, so they may change his job description. For example, sixty-eight positions were cut at HEW, but it did not mean they were fired. Many were clerical people. They just moved these people elsewhere and now they type for someone else. But this was not a vindictive approach to ruin people's lives or cut them from the payrolls."

Nixon's order contained an explicit Presidential warning against any department attempting to "circumvent" it. Yet the Interior Department received paid, expert advice on how to do just that. The

---

*Under Allen Dulles, the post of PR man for the CIA was held by Colonel Stanley J. Grogan, assistant to the director, and the job has been filled, successively, by Paul M. Chrétien, Joseph C. "Gus" Goodwin, and Angus MacLean Thuermer.

advice came from an astonishing source—Harry Treleaven, Jr., the advertising and media director of Nixon's 1968 Presidential campaign.

Treleaven, a gray-haired, fast-talking ad man, was another alumnus of J. Walter Thompson, where he had produced commericals for Pan Am and Lark cigarettes. During the 1968 campaign he operated from an office in New York. After Nixon's election he set up his own public relations firm in Washington, where he was closer to the honey pot. As a highly successful PR man—he had, after all, helped to elect a President of the United States—Treleaven might reasonably hope to do business with the new administration.

The Treleaven affair provides a fascinating case study of the point at which public relations, party politics, and government secrecy intersect. The story began in November, 1970, when Nixon fired the outspoken Wally Hickel as Interior Secretary. As his replacement, Nixon chose Representative Rogers C. B. Morton, the Maryland Republican who was then chairman of the Republican National Committee. Morton's deputy at the national committee was James N. Allison, Jr., a former newspaper executive from Midland, Texas, who had managed George Bush's successful campaign for Congress in 1966. It was Allison who first got Treleaven into politics; he had persuaded him to come to Texas to serve as advertising director of Bush's campaign. Morton's nomination as Secretary of Interior was confirmed by the Senate on January 28, 1971, and he was sworn in the next day. Three days later, on February 1, Allison left the national committee to join Treleaven's PR firm, which was reorganized as Allison, Treleaven & Reitz, Inc. Reitz was Kenneth Reitz, who also had close ties to the Nixon administration and the Republican Party; in 1971 he directed a study for the GOP national committee of how Nixon might best appeal to the large youth vote in the 1972 Presidential election.

On February 18, less than three weeks after he was sworn in as Secretary of Interior, Morton hired Treleaven as a $121-a-day consultant. His task was to analyze Interior's public relations and apply his Madison Avenue expertise to "streamline" and "improve the image" of the department.

Treleaven turned in an eighty-five-page report which the Interior Department adamantly refused to make public—even though public information was its subject. Requests made under the Freedom of Information Act for copies of the Treleaven Report were turned down by Mitchell Melich, solicitor of the Interior Department, on the grounds that the report was "an internal communication."

A copy obtained from another source sheds light on why Interior preferred to keep Treleaven's report secret.*

"The [President's] requested reduction in expenditures for public relations activities has everyone totally confused," Treleaven told Morton. ". . . The fact is, the information offices are finding it impossible to cut the kind of items that occasioned the request for a reduction, because they don't exist. The response, therefore, is to eliminate worthwhile items, or go 'underground'—i.e., hide expenditures in other budgets. The latter is probably the practical way out."†

It was extraordinary advice. Treleaven was paid several thousand dollars of the taxpayers' money to advise a government department on how to hide federal funds in direct violation of a Presidential order. For the taxpayer, any government public relations expenditure is an exercise in self-persuasion, since the government is using his own money to persuade him that the government deserves his support. In this case, the taxpayers paid twice.

In his report, Treleaven estimated that the department's various public relations offices "employ over two hundred persons and spend something over $2 million." But his still-secret report added: "It's virtually impossible to be precise about budgets, because many information activities are paid for by programs, or out of special permanent funds (like the Water and Conservation Fund), or are charged to administrative and operating budgets, or are privately funded. The total for the department is probably close to $4 million."

Treleaven was highly critical of Interior's public relations, however, terming its $4 million effort "bland," and "too passive, reacting to events rather than looking for opportunities." The department's work, he said, "is an almost endless source of material for news releases." What the department's lower-level PR people needed to

---

*In April, 1972, Melich released a relatively innocuous portion of the report to the House government information subcommittee, which published it, but the bulk of the report, including several portions quoted here, has not been made public by the Interior Department.

†In an interview with the author, Treleaven offered an explanation for this advice. As a result of the President's directive, he said, "there were certain things which they were going to have to cut out which we thought were useful to the public; for example, the production of maps in certain western areas which no one else is making. If people wanted to do off-road exploring, they could not if the maps were no longer produced." Treleaven was unable to provide any other examples of such beneficial activity threatened by the cutback. But there were other things, he said, and "rather than cut them out, we thought they might slip them into other budgets."

inspire them, Treleaven explained, was "a more Gung Ho attitude at the top."

In the television age, he lamented, most of the "senior people are print-oriented." Because of this, he said, "a top priority must be to develop ways of getting Interior's story on television."

Since the Interior Department's environmental responsibilities often bring it into conflict with corporate interests, Treleaven's next suggestion was startling. "The high cost of producing films has greatly restricted their use," he said. "However, some of the Bureaus (Mines, Outdoor Recreation, and Fish and Wildlife) have been able to obtain private funds for their film programs. This is a source of money which should be sought energetically and systematically by the entire department." The Bureau of Mines had forty films available for distribution and "all but two of their films were produced and paid for by industrial sponsors—including Atlantic Richfield, Goodyear, Alcoa, Phillips Petroleum, Texas Gulf Sulphur, Johns-Manville, Phelps Dodge . . . " Other bureaus "should take lessons from the Bureau of Mines in this area," the report added. If Treleaven perceived any conflict of interest in the Interior Department's accepting money from the industries it regulates, he did not say so.

A PR man's mind must be flexible, if nothing else, as Treleaven demonstrated in discussing *Children in the City,* a film produced by Interior to show how the Nixon administration had used federal funds to aid urban recreational programs. When the film was shelved, however, after Nixon failed to request a similar appropriation for 1971, Treleaven ingeniously noted that "the same film could be used with a new voice track changing the thrust to an appeal for private support of an increased recreational budget."

Most revealing of all, however, was Treleaven's description of the goals of the Office of Information of the Secretary of Interior. Among the "objectives of this office" listed by Treleaven were: "to play a key role in helping develop new programs to mold public opinion in support of the Secretary and the administration . . . and to head off or counteract adverse publicity resulting from events and activities that could put the department in a bad light (such as mine disasters, accidents in National Parks, etc.)."

This is about as candid a statement of the real purpose of government information as one will find anywhere in print. Small wonder that Interior labeled the report secret and set its lawyers babbling about "internal communications."

Treleaven's reference to mine disasters putting the department in a "bad light" was a hint of his next, and much more ambitious, project. For his three-month study of Interior's image factory, Treleaven received $11,135. But this was only the camel's nose. After finishing the study Treleaven proposed that Interior commit from $200,000 to $500,000 for a "full-scale all-media communications program" to convince coal miners that their own carelessness is a major cause of mine disasters and deaths.* The mine safety campaign proposed by Treleaven would have used lapel buttons, bumper stickers, billboards, and television commercials to "help motivate miners to do what is right."

While mine owners like to promote the theme that carelessness causes disasters, negligence by the mine operators and failure of the Bureau of Mines to enforce federal safety standards are much more important causes. On the floor of the House, Representative Ken Hechler, the West Virginia Democrat, ripped into the Treleaven proposal. Hechler noted that the head of the General Accounting Office, the Congressional auditor of government spending, had estimated that about 90 percent of coal-mine accidents "are due to failures of the mine operators rather than to the failure of the miner himself." Hechler introduced an amendment to Interior's 1971 appropriation, barring payments to "any public relations firm for any promotional campaigns among coal miners." The amendment passed. Treleaven failed in his bid for a share of a media contract that could have cost the American taxpayers up to half a million dollars.

Even without the continued services of Harry Treleaven, the Interior Department had a skilled public relations man to nurture its image. In May of 1971 Morton hired Robert A. Kelly, director of public relations for Pepsi-Cola, to be director of the Office of Communications.†

"I'm a corporate PR guy, first, last, and always," Kelly declares pridefully. In his previous job he had worked for Donald M. Kendall, president of PepsiCo, Inc., and a close friend of Richard Nixon. "Pepsi and Frito-Lay merged and formed PepsiCo, Inc., under Ken-

---

*Treleaven proposed the contract be shared by his company and the Holder-Kennedy Co., a Nashville, Tennessee, public relations firm that handled the successful media campaign of Representative William E. Brock, a conservative Republican, against Senator Albert Gore, the Democratic incumbent, in 1970. Ken Reitz, Treleaven's partner, had served as a key media adviser to Brock in that campaign and listed himself in 1971 as vice-president and a member of the board of Holder-Kennedy.

†The title was new and had been recommended by Treleaven in his report to Morton on streamlining Interior's public relations. Previously it was known simply as the Office of Information.

dall. They also have Wilson sporting goods. I was director of public relations for the Pepsi-Cola Company, which is a division of the parent company. Morton brought me in. Nixon is a great friend of Kendall, and Nixon's law firm worked for Pepsi-Cola International." During the kitchen debate in Moscow in 1959, Kelly reminded me, "Nixon and Khrushchev both drank Pepsi-Cola from paper cups. The cups had been handed to them by a Pepsi PR man."

Was selling the Secretary of the Interior any different from selling Pepsi Cola? "Different? As different as the moon. The function here is much narrower. In industry the job is to gain and hold public understanding and acceptance. In government the thrust is more on informing and much less on promoting. The function is communicating."

Secretary Morton, Kelly noted, was getting "a hell of a lot of exposure. Wednesday night he's doing the Dick Cavett Show, network; Thursday morning he's doing the CBS morning news, twelve minutes; Friday he meets with Mr. Sulzberger and the editorial board of *The New York Times*. In all of these meetings he will be communicating where he stands. At the same time this enhances his personal image. It's a natural by-product."

Kelly said he was in frequent touch with Herb Klein's office, but also with Des Barker on the White House staff. "I deal with Barker almost every day," he said. An example of coordination with Barker, he added, "was Julie Eisenhower's trip to the Big Cypress Swamp in Florida last week. Big Cypress is an important fresh-water preserve and the President has proposed that the government take it over. Morton guided her through the swamp."

Technically, all of this activity is illegal. In 1913 Congress passed a law prohibiting the government from paying any money to a "publicity expert" without Congressional approval.* The measure was introduced by Representative Frederick H. Gillett, a Massachusetts Republican, after the Civil Service Commission announced an examination for "Publicity Expert—Male" for the Office of Public Roads.

The bureaucracy easily by-passed the law by hiring "information" experts to handle public relations. The job titles under Civil Service today, for example, are "public information officer" and "public information specialist." A veteran government publicist sardonically explained the legal situation this way: "The fact is there are

---

*The law appears on the books today as 5 U.S.C. 3107: "Appropriated funds may not be used to pay a publicity expert unless specifically appropriated for that purpose."

no public relations men working for the federal government, and the words 'public relations' do not appear in the federal budget."

Below the policy level, many government information people are career civil servants who try, within the limits of their jobs, to handle information with a minimum of political distortion. And they serve a useful function; they answer questions from the press and public and prepare publications about government programs. Yet they are well aware that much government information is misleading. Mel White, a career information official at HEW, declared: "I'm with the government, and I don't believe half of what comes out of any government agency. And I resent that as a taxpayer."

Even the career people are never far removed from politics. White, for example, recalled that during the Truman administration he was ordered to draft a speech pushing socialized medicine. During the Eisenhower administration, when he worked for HEW secretary Oveta Culp Hobby, he was ordered to write a speech opposing socialized medicine. He did both.

At sixty-one, White, gray-haired and stocky, was a veteran of twenty-five years in government public relations. In his quarter of a century of bureaucratic infighting, he had learned the first principle: survival. Like an experienced old badger blinking in the sunlight, he knew how to run back into his burrow at the slightest sign of danger.

And the danger, White emphasized, is always high, because information officers are "exposed" and highly vulnerable to replacement by political appointees. The Nixon administration, White said, went to unprecedented lengths to take political control of the information apparatus. Normally, about 5 percent of government information jobs go to political appointees, he said; he estimated that under Nixon, the figure jumped to 20 percent. "I've never seen them go so deep before. Career information officers have been fired even though they are Civil Service. They abolish the job, create a new category, and move in a political appointee. They are looking for places to put people, and the information category is the weakest because it has no legal status in the first place. A budget officer or a personnel officer tends to be safe. But anybody can write, anybody can talk to the press, and anybody can keep his mouth shut."

White could afford to be so outspoken because he was protected by his seniority: "I have good efficiency ratings and strong bumping rights. I'm practically invulnerable until I'm ready to go."

Jack Rosenthal, once press secretary to Attorney General Robert F. Kennedy, divides government public relations men into three categories. At the top, he said, is the "policy-level adviser. He sits in on any important meetings, knows what is going on, and advises his boss on the public information consequences of policy." The next step down in this typology is the "faithful mechanic. He is not at the policy level, but he can get the news out, handle the press, leak stories, and build good relations with the reporters." Next is the "defensive PR man. This is the lowest rung on the totem pole. He is insecure. He does nothing but answer questions. He never does any leaking. He gives minimal answers, tries not to be quoted, and speaks on background. He is evasive and doesn't return telephone calls. He does the worst job for his boss."

At the Justice Department, Rosenthal said, he would normally handle about a hundred calls a day from newsmen. His most difficult telephone call occurred in 1962 during the riots on the campus of the University of Mississippi at Oxford. Rosenthal, like other Justice Department officials, had been in his office all night when the phone rang at 6 A.M. Joe Mohbat, the AP reporter assigned to cover the department, had a habit of imitating President Kennedy's voice, which he did rather well. Rosenthal, hearing the familiar voice when he picked up the phone, replied: "Cut out the horseshit, Mohbat."

"No, no, this is really the President."

It was JFK, calling to check on a wire-service story about the deployment of U.S. marshals at Oxford. Then he asked Rosenthal: "How is my brother doing?" When Rosenthal later informed Robert Kennedy of the President's question, he replied: "If you didn't lie, it's your job."

The Nixon administration went in heavily for a new form of electronic, fully automated government public relations. By early 1972, with little publicity, nine of the eleven cabinet departments had installed Spotmaster machines, tape units that carried brief recorded announcements such as speech excerpts by cabinet secretaries, and other canned features. Presented in the guise of "news" stories, the recordings are really blatant propaganda. By dialing special telephone numbers, radio stations around the nation are able to plug into the Spotmasters and record and broadcast the features. The tapes are usually changed daily. The system allows a small radio station in the Midwest, for example, to broadcast a "live" report as though it had a correspondent in Washington.*

---

*For example, a radio station that dialed OXford 5–6201 on March 9, 1972, would have heard the following: "This is Captain Ron Lindeke speaking for the Department of Defense Public Affairs. Following a five-second tone, Defense Audio Release for Thursday March 9. Today's release was updated at 9:30 A.M. and includes the forty-five-second story with actuality on a new

Such recordings are known in the trade as "actuality" reports.

Some of the projects dreamed up by government public relations men are almost unbelievably banal. In 1969, when the Department of Transportation was pushing the Supersonic Transport plane, it printed and distributed 50,000 copies of a seventy-three-page *Teachers Guide for SST*, designed to help indocrinate the nation's schoolchildren in the virtues of the controversial aircraft. One chapter, entitled "Supersonic Pussycat," tells the story of a rich cat name Marita whose mistress takes her to the French Riviera on an SST. "The day before we were leaving," the cat declares in the story, "I was sent to Fifi's. My silver fur was washed, brushed, and perfumed. My nails were done particularly well . . . Bright and early the next morning, Mistress and I were off the airport . . . We made ourselves comfortable in the large roomy seats and before we knew it we were airborne . . . the pilot announced we were cruising at an altitude of 64,000 feet and at a speed of 1,800 mph—faster than the speed of sound. Why, at this rate, I thought, we'd be in Paris in less than three hours. By the time I had a few slivers of liver (excellent, by the way) and watched a short movie, we had arrived."

Another story in the teachers' guide tells of Maxwell the Mouse, who was worried about sonic boom but found a house that had been soundproofed against jet noise. The booklet also encourages the students to "Play Airport." ("Have children take different roles of people concerned with an airport . . . pilots, stewardesses, traffic controllers, safety officer, etc.")

Apparently acting on the theory that it is never too soon to begin training the little PR men of the next generation, the booklet also tests the children with this question: "How would you write the advertisement for the first flight on the SST? How would you illustrate your advertisement to appeal to the interests of people?" All of this cost the taxpayers only $12,872.*

It was, of course, a relatively small expenditure as PR budgets go. For example, NASA, with a $12.2 million public relations budget and a staff of 359, ranked only third among all federal agencies in public information spending, according to figures provided by the Office of

---

lunar camera developed by the Naval Research Laboratory in Washington." The announcement, painting the development of the new camera in glowing terms, followed. The tape ended: "This concludes Defense Audio Release for Thursday, March 9. For further information on Defense news, call OXford 7-6161."

*Congress killed the SST in 1971, but a year later some of the Supersonic Pussycat guides were still in use in the nation's elementary schools.

Management and Budget.* HEW ranked second, with a public relations budget of $27.4 million and a staff of 737.

But the Defense Department had by far the largest public relations operation in the government; according to OMB figures, prior to the Nixon cutback, the Pentagon public relations budget was $44.7 million and had a public relations staff of 3,076 or just over half of all PR employees in the federal government by OMB's calculations. In 1972 the Pentagon said it had 2,274 public relations officials, of whom 1,649 were in the Armed Services. According to the Pentagon's figures, it spent $44 million on public relations in 1969, $40 million in 1970, $29 million in 1971—as a result of the Nixon order and Congressional cuts—and $25.6 million in 1972.

But Representative Jonathan B. Bingham, Democrat, of New York, charged in a 1971 speech on the House floor that in listing its public relations expenditures, the Defense Department had omitted several agencies that spent more than $48 million in 1970. Bingham made public a GAO report on these Pentagon agencies. He said it confirmed that "there are nests of public information activities and expenses in the vast Defense establishment that continue to be hidden from the Congress." Bingham said the agencies that spent the $48 million produced materials ostensibly for "internal use" by the military. The same materials, he said, "in fact are also widely distributed and presented to the public."

The GAO found that during one period in 1970, films produced by the Air Force's Aerospace Audio-Visual Service at a cost of $13.3 million were shown 26,300 times to civilian groups. According to the GAO report, one of these films, entitled *NORAD Tracks Santa*, portrayed "Santa Claus' trip from the North Pole to homes of children in the Unites States . . . as tracked by the men and equipment of the North American Air Defense Command." When such costs are added on, Bingham concluded, "the true figures" for Pentagon public relations could be twice as high as the $40 million public figure.

The Pentagon's public relations programs cover a breathtaking array of activities, ranging from VIP tours of military installations for community leaders and businessmen to providing aircraft carriers to Hollywood film makers. Since 1963 the Pentagon has even hired private firms to monitor and record all radio and television newscasts in Washington dealing with military or diplomatic events. According to a Defense Department spokesman, the purpose of this monitor-

---

*The figures, for fiscal 1971, were compiled by OMB before the reductions ordered by President Nixon went into effect.

ing, which costs about $20,000 a year, is to keep informed "on what's being said about us."

Senator J. William Fulbright, the arch-foe of the Pentagon propaganda machine, summed up his objections in a Senate speech in 1970: "There is something basically unwise and undemocratic about a system which taxes the public to finance a propaganda campaign aimed at persuading the same taxpayers that they must spend more tax dollars . . . "

Fulbright's campaign against Pentagon public relations had been well publicized. But his crusade did not arouse anything comparable to the enormous controversy touched off by the CBS documentary "The Selling of the Pentagon."

At 10 P.M. on the night of February 23, 1971, CBS presented a one-hour program about Pentagon public relations, narrated by correspondent Roger Mudd. The documentary showed children scrambling over a tank on display at an Armed Forces Day exhibit in South Carolina and included some shots of colonels lecturing on Vietnam to civilian audiences. It also showed civilians on a guided tour of military bases. One of the guests burbled: "It was fun to actually get your finger on the trigger of some of the things like the recoilless weapons . . . " The program also included clips from some of the more inane Defense Department films. It presented a brief interview with Daniel Henkin, the Pentagon's chief public relations man.* It noted that the Defense Department makes war heroes available to members of Congress for taped television reports shown back in their home districts. To illustrate the latter point, CBS ran a film clip of Representative F. Edward Hébert, the Louisiana Democrat, interviewing Major James Rowe, a Green Beret, who denounced peace demonstrators.

Considering the fact that the Pentagon's propaganda activities had long been a target of criticism, the most surprising thing about "The Selling of the Pentagon" was the intense reaction it engendered. Such is the impact of television that the CBS program overnight became a major political issue and a center of national debate. Before it was all over, it appeared—at least for a while—that Congress might try to put the president of CBS in jail.

The network made two mistakes in producing the show. First, Henkin's answers to Roger Mudd's questions were transposed, which was entirely unfair to Henkin. Second, CBS had mortally offended Eddie Hébert (pronounced A-bear), the sixty-nine-year-old powerful

---

*Both Henkin and Defense Secretary Melvin Laird resigned their Pentagon posts in January, 1973.

chairman of the House Armed Services Committee. Hébert charged that CBS had tricked him into giving the network his television film, a charge that CBS denied.

Since Hébert did not have jurisdiction over the networks, he persuaded his friend Harley O. Staggers of West Virginia, chairman of the House Interstate and Foreign Commerce Committee, to investigate the program. Staggers, partly out of loyalty to his fellow committee chairman, joined in an unwise battle with CBS and its president, Dr. Frank Stanton. Unwise because members of Congress, who must use television to get reelected, like to preserve pleasant relations with the TV networks, however much they may thunder against them in public. And unwise because Staggers, the former sheriff of Mineral County, West Virginia, permitted his personal prestige to become committed in a high-noon confrontation from which he could not retreat.

The House committee served CBS with a subpoena demanding the network's "outtakes," the filmed material not actually shown on the air. The committee claimed it needed this material to see how CBS had edited the Henkin interview and the remarks of one of the lecturing colonels. Stanton appeared before the committee, compared the outtakes to a reporter's notes, and refused to give them to the House panel, which then cited him for contempt, 25 to 13. A number of committee members were unhappy with having to cast their votes to cite Stanton, but they went along with old Harley, who might, so it was said, be planning to retire from Congress, but who was in the meantime, still in a position to control their subcommittee assignments and other perquisites. CBS mounted a massive and expensive lobbying effort to keep Frank Stanton out of the pokey in what, after all, were his golden years, and on the House floor when the crunch came it was 226 to 181 against the contempt citation.

All of this brouhaha successfully diverted attention from the major point, which is that the Pentagon does spend a disgraceful amount of our money on propagandizing us, and that CBS had performed a major public service in bringing this forcefully to the attention of a mass audience. Somehow, the vitally important questions of substance got lost in the Battle of the Henkin Outtakes.

Perhaps, when all is said and done, My Lai provides a better insight than anything else into the government information process. In his book, *My Lai 4*, Seymour Hersh reports that Jay Roberts, the Army correspondent who covered Charlie Company's attack on the hamlet, knew very well that most of the dead were civilians; he had personally counted at least fifty bodies. Roberts wrote a story based on the false, official version and gave it to the brigade press officer, Second Lieutenant Arthur Dunn, who knew it looked fishy. But

Dunn dictated a similar story for divison headquarters, and explained later: "If I had known there was a massacre and let somebody write about it, I would have lost my job."

There were even greater risks to being a public relations man in Vietnam. During Colonel Oran Henderson's trial, one witness was Ronald L. Haeberle, the combat photographer whose color pictures in *Life* convinced even the skeptics that there had been a massacre at My Lai. He was asked, on the witness stand, why he had not told his superiors about the killings. He replied that he had been afraid that had he done so, members of the public information detachment in which he served might have been shot by the men of the infantry unit that ravaged My Lai.

Part IV

THE PRESS

"Now, I want to make myself perfectly clear. I'm not asking for government censorship . . ."

—Vice-President Spiro T. Agnew,
November 13, 1969

10

Nixon vs. the Press

The President was in a good mood.

He had left Bucharest that afternoon; now his plane touched down at Mildenhall Royal Air Force Base, England, the last stop on what had been a successful journey around the world. The crowds that cheered Richard Nixon along the way had a special reason; only two weeks earlier, on July 20, 1969, the United States had become the first nation to land men on the moon.

Prime Minister Harold Wilson had gone to the Air Force base, eighty-five miles north of London, to greet the President. As he chatted informally with Wilson at a reception at the officers' club, Nixon said he planned to send moon rocks to every chief of state. At the time, there was a good deal of concern, later discounted, that germs might exist on the moon for which earthlings had no immunity. Because of these fears of a real-life Andromeda Strain, upon their return from outer space the Apollo 11 astronauts had been sealed up in a capsule and quarantined. Well aware of this, Nixon told Harold Wilson that he also had another gift in mind. He might find a few "contaminated" pieces of the moon, he said, and give them to the press.

Nixon was, of course, joking, but the story revealed with clarity his attitude toward, and relations with, the news media. Nixon's bitterness toward the press was legendary, perhaps best symbolized by his now-classic remark: "You won't have Nixon to kick around any more . . . " But some of the tight-faced men who worked for Nixon when he became President occasionally left the impression that they would very much enjoy kicking around the press. On November 6, 1968, fifteen minutes after Richard Nixon issued his victory statement, about twenty advance men gathered in the empty ballroom of the Waldorf-Astoria in New York to accept congratulations from John Ehrlichman, their chief. The happy, elated Nixon workers next heard from J. Roy Goodearle, a tall, beefy Southerner who was Spiro Agnew's chief advance man (and later the Vice-President's principal political liaison with Republican party leaders).

"Why don't we all get a member of the press and beat them up?" he asked. "I'm tired of being nice to them."*

As in the case of Nixon's comments in 1962, Goodearle's savage remark came at the end of a long political campaign, at a time when men are fatigued and their emotions frayed. It is also under such conditions, of course, that men are likely to say what they think.

After Nixon moved into the White House, the administration did not find it necessary physically to use truncheons on the press, although at one point the FBI was turned loose to investigate CBS correspondent Daniel Schorr, about which more will be said later. A wide variety of other weapons were available.

The experience of *Newsday* and several of its reporters and editors is particularly instructive. In October, 1971, *Newsday*, a major newspaper serving Long Island, ran a series about the many-sided business dealings of President Nixon's closest friend, millionaire Charles G. (Bebe) Rebozo. The series was painstakingly assembled by the newspaper's special investigative team under reporter Robert W. Greene.

The stories explored a number of fascinating business deals, including one in which Rebozo developed a shopping center for Cuban refugees in Miami with the help of the Small Business Administration. SBA's regional chief in Miami was Thomas A. Butler, who had purchased stock in Rebozo's bank in 1964, three years before the shopping-center project was begun. *Newsday* also noted that Nixon, Rebozo, and Butler were investors in Fisher's Island, a valuable piece of real estate south of Miami Beach. After Nixon became President, the paper reported, he sold his stock back to the corporation for $2 a share, or a total of $371,782, at a time when the stock was selling

---

*Unbeknownest to Goodearle, Ehrlichman, or the other advance men, Joseph Albright, then Washington Bureau chief for *Newsday*, was standing in the room and wrote down the remark. Goodearle does not deny it; Agnew's press secretary, Victor Gold, speaking for Goodearle, insisted to the author that "it was a joke." Perhaps so, says Albright, "but nobody laughed."

to others for $1 a share. The series also told about a loan granted by Rebozo's bank to an Atlanta businessman on what turned out to be 900 shares of very stolen IBM stock.* And it delved into the intricate financial affairs of former Senator George Smathers, a close friend of both Rebozo and Nixon.

When the series concluded, *Newsday* ran a blunt editorial which said, in part:

> For the past week *Newsday* has published in daily install-ments the results of a six-month-long investigation into one area of the twilight zone of American politics where private enter-prise and government meet and commingle. It is a cozy place where ethics and morality are qualities as elusive as the morning mist that swirls over South Florida . . . Rebozo's genial relation-ship with the Small Business Administration suggests one of the reasons for the disillusionment of the less privileged. Although fully capable of raising money in the private sector, he was able to build extensive Florida real-estate holdings with the help of public funds earmarked by statute for people who cannot get private loans . . . Rebozo, of course, is not unique . . . But this man is known as the closest friend of the President of the United States. We are not suggesting any automatic guilt by association. We are suggesting, however, that the President has shown a lack of sensitivity, responsibility, and care in the choice of a friend. All eyes focus on a President. His symbolic role is no less impor-tant than his executive one. He should set the moral tone of the nation by all of his actions, private and public. Let's face it: the deals made by Bebe Rebozo and the Smathers gang have tar-nished the Presidency.

This was extraordinarily daring language for a newspaper to use about the President, even under a system in which the press is consti-tutionally protected. Just how daring is illustrated by the fact that the story of Rebozo's relationship with Thomas Butler, the SBA regional chief, had been around for some time, and in 1969 had even drawn a public protest by Representative Wright Patman, the Texas Demo-crat, but had received little attention in the nation's press.

What happened next can be told in the words of Martin Schram,

*In a delightful detail, the newspaper noted that the stock was allegedly owned by a "Mr. Sturgeon," a mythical resident of the Bahamas, who, ac-cording to a subsequent federal indictment, was in reality a group of eight persons, of whom two were eminent mobsters.

Newsday's White House correspondent when the stories were published. After the series ran, he said: "I began having problems with the White House. What happened was that Ziegler wouldn't speak to me. If I was to go up and ask him something, he would tell me, 'Not now, I'm too busy,' and walk away . . . I realized I was getting snubbed, so I made it a point to call once a week, to ask for an appointment with Ron. His secretary would take down the information and I would never get a call back. None of this pettiness really bothered me, because Ziegler has never been a good source of information for me, or for anyone, as far as I know, so it was not a problem for me, except to get guidance, like travel plans—was it important for me to make this trip to Key Biscayne—that type of thing. I would have to call up other reporters to find out whether I should go to Florida or make other trips.

"Finally, in mid-January, 1972, I approached Ziegler after the morning briefing and asked if I could speak to him privately. And to my surprise, he said, 'Wait here in the lobby and I will see you.' He told the same thing to several other reporters, and Ziegler's secretary sent them in one at a time to see him and I was still sitting out there. Finally, I was the only one, and his girl came out and told me, 'Marty, I'm sorry, the President just buzzed Ron.' I said that was all right. I went through the same thing the next day, I was waiting alone in the lobby. Finally I went back to Ron's inner office and asked if he was ready to see me, and the secretary replied that he had gone for the day.

"I had really gotten ticked off. I didn't mind a lot of things, but I didn't like cooling my heels on something as obviously a snub as that. It took up my time, and I didn't like that. I called some other White House officials and told them what was going on and they acknowledged to me that it was because of the Rebozo series, and they said it wasn't intended for me personally, but at *Newsday*, and one of them said, 'Don't forget that the series hit pretty close to home.'*

---

*One article that must have been particularly annoying to the White House described at length Nixon's physical surroundings on Key Biscayne, including some touches straight out of Ian Fleming. Driving down the street toward the Presidential compound, the article said, a visitor passes a ten-foot hibiscus hedge. He is "startled by a metallic voice which rasps out of the hibiscus to inquire, 'Can I help you? What is your business?' Only then does the visitor notice the closed-circuit television cameras, electronic alarms, and loudspeakers planted at intervals in the hedge." *Newsday* also noted that a $342,000 helipad constructed by the government at Nixon's beach

"Finally, on January 27, I don't know why, but in the briefing Ziegler said, 'Good morning, Marty, how are you?' This could be a diplomatic breakthrough, I thought, so I decided maybe he is going to speak to me now. All the time that I asked to see him I didn't have anything particular to see him about, I just wanted to see if he would see me. This time I did get in to see him. I told him there had probably been some personal problems between us, and he looked at me and said, innocently, 'Problems—what problems?' He wasn't aware of any problems. I told him I had been aware of plenty of snubs due to the Rebozo series and that if there was anything personal between us he ought to speak up and lay it on the table. And he said, 'Marty, we have absolutely no personal problems between us.' "

Schram's difficulties with the White House soon became much more serious, however. A White House correspondent since Nixon's election in 1968, Schram, at twenty-nine, was representing a major newspaper in the most prestigious beat in Washington. Now a major assignment loomed, one that was potentially important to his career, and to the 450,000 readers of *Newsday*. In February, 1972, almost every correspondent in the capital was angling for a chance to go to China and cover the biggest story of the Nixon administration. There were only eighty-seven seats on the press plane, and Ziegler, it appeared to many reporters, savored the process of alloting them.

Schram had made a point of applying for the China trip in writing, which was not necessary, since he was a White House "regular," a reporter normally assigned by his paper to cover the President. "I sent the formal letter to make sure I had all my bases covered," Schram said. On February 7, 1972, the White House announced the list of newsmen who would be accompanying the President to Peking later that month. Schram and *Newsday* were not on the list.

"On the day the list for the China trip was announced," Schram said, "Ziegler called me into his office, and he called in others who were not going, and told us individually the reason. He said something like, 'Well, Marty, the reason I called you in here is because I wanted to tell you personally that *Newsday* is not on the China list and that it doesn't have anything to do with the Bebe Rebozo series.'

---

included electric eyes and devices to detect underwater swimmers. But it said the White House refused to disclose the cost of "the shark net" installed off the beach.

He then ran down a list of criteria, and we had met each one."*

On March 21, Schram recounted, three weeks after Nixon's return from China, he telephoned the White House press room and Ziegler happened to pick up the phone. "And he said, 'Marty, it's funny that I got you on here because I was just going to call you and ask if you could come in and see me this afternoon around four.' I said okay, and he said bring your bureau chief—that's Russell Sackett, they had never met—and so Russ and I got in there, and Ron said, 'Let's clear the air.' And he went on to say that he recognized there had been some problems between *Newsday* and the White House and he said something to the effect that 'We have always had a good relationship before that series, the Rebozo series, haven't we, Marty, and there is no reason why we can't pick it up again where we left off.'

"He finally admitted relations between the White House and *Newsday* had deteriorated after the Rebozo series ran, and when I asked why, he said, because 'I didn't think the series represented good journalism.' He would not admit that we were kicked off the China trip because of the Rebozo series. We didn't believe him.

"Then Sackett said he had written a letter to Jerry Warren [Ziegler's deputy] complaining about two things. Number one, we were trying to get White House passes for two of our new men, Warren Berry and Tony Marro, and we had been trying since November, and hadn't gotten any action. And second, my typewriter at my desk in the White House press room had been broken and I couldn't get a repairman through the gate to fix it. Ziegler didn't acknowledge that these were due to the Rebozo series, but he said they would take care of them immediately. And he snaps his fingers and gets the process started. He said everything would be taken care of."

Schram emphasized he had no direct knowledge of why Ziegler chose to make peace with *Newsday* early in 1972, but he added: "If I were President, I would certainly want my press secretary to make up with a reporter for an influential paper in a major state in an election year." Schram cautioned that he had no evidence of this, it was just his personal theory. "To be fair about it—I can only guess—

---

*The first criterion, Schram said, was whether a paper had previously accompanied the President on trips overseas; *Newsday* had made all three of the foreign trips. Next came domestic trips, and Schram said Ziegler conceded that *Newsday* qualified on that ground as well. "Third was coverage of the White House, and he admitted that we were there most of the time. The only time that we really did not cover the White House is when I was working on the Rebozo series—which I considered covering the White House."

it might be that deep down inside they are all really good fellows after all. They realized the errors of their ways and they wanted to repent. I don't know."

This, however, was not the end of the story. According to Robert Greene, the head of *Newsday*'s investigative team, the government's concern over the Rebozo series was not confined to the White House. While the series was being prepared, he said, the FBI displayed great interest in when it was to appear. "Tom Renner, one of our reporters who covers organized crime, said he had been called by the agent in charge on Long Island, Artie Fuss. Tom was called at home, although he was on vacation, and Fuss wanted to know when the 'Greene Team' was going to publish, and did Tom know. 'No, I don't,' Renner replied. 'Is there any way you can find out?' Fuss asked, 'I'm getting a lot of heat from Washington.' "

Annoyed, Greene telephoned an assistant director of the FBI in Washington. Was the FBI being used to find out if *Newsday* was going to run a series damaging to Nixon? Greene wanted to know. The FBI declined comment for the record. But *Newsday* knew that the FBI was investigating George Smathers, who had recently been nominated by Nixon for a peripheral government post, and who also figured prominently in the *Newsday* investigation. So it was possible that the FBI, in the course of a background check, wanted to know the publication date of the *Newsday* series so it could read what the newspaper had to say about George Smathers.*

David Laventhol, the editor of *Newsday*, said that when Greene's reporters were researching the series the newspaper had great difficulty gaining access to records of the Defense Department and other government agencies. "They put up a stone wall," he said.

After the series ran, Greene and Arthur G. Perfall, a *Newsday* executive who had edited the series, were interested in the possibility of publishing the articles as a book. *Newsday* is owned by the Times-Mirror Company, which also owns the *Los Angeles Times* and a hard-cover book division, the World Publishing Company. Laventhol entered into discussions with Peter Ritner, the chief editor at World. The project must have reached a fairly advanced stage, since

---

*Whether or not this was the case remained an open question in Greene's mind. Smathers had been nominated by the President to be a member of the Arms Control and Disarmament Agency's advisory committee. Two weeks after the *Newsday* series was published, Smathers wrote the President a personal letter; his schedule was very busy and he really did not have the time to serve on the committee. Smathers' name was quietly withdrawn by the White House, with no public announcement.

lawyers for World read the manuscript for libel and their written comments were forwarded to Perfall.

But then the project collapsed. There is some disagreement among the principals over the reason; Ritner said it was World's decision; checking the legal questions, he said, would have "taken a long time." However, William Attwood, the publisher of *Newsday,* said that the decision was his. "I thought it was a good newspaper series," he said. "The book would have come out in 1972. It would have looked like a campaign hatchet job. It would have looked like we were going out of our way to stick the shiv into one of the candidates—namely, Nixon. We explained this to Los Angeles because World books was a subsidiary. It was just the wrong year." No one interviewed cited any evidence of administration pressure about the book against either *Newsday* or the parent company of the *Los Angeles Times.* Attwood said he knew of none.

Since *Newsday* owned the copyright on the series, and the reporters who compiled it were employees of the newspaper, they were not in a position to try to publish the book elsewhere. Art Perfall quit *Newsday;* the collapse of the book project was reportedly one of several reasons he did so. Although each of the participants in these events cited a somewhat different reason, it seems clear that a major newspaper decided it would be the better part of wisdom not to publish a book about Bebe Rebozo in the spring of 1972.

During and after the preparation of the Rebozo series, Laventhol's income tax was audited by IRS, for the first time. Robert Greene's returns were audited, as were the tax returns of William Attwood. And IRS accountants were at *Newsday* itself, auditing the newspaper's financial records. *Newsday* officials said they had no evidence, of course, that any of this activity was related to the Rebozo series. But all things considered, it would appear that under the Nixon administration, when it came to a newspaper writing an exposé of the President's best friend, the White House was not prepared to Let a Thousand Flowers Bloom.

But that might be expected. And Nixon's difficulties with the press, after all, did not begin as President, but traced back to early in his career. It was the newspapers that broke the story in the 1952 campaign of the "Nixon Fund"—the $18,235 collected from wealthy contributors to pay for his political expenses, "to enable me to continue my active battle against Communism and corruption." As pressure mounted over the fund, Eisenhower threatened to force Nixon to resign as the Republican nominee for Vice-President. Nixon prepared to deliver his famous televised "Checkers" speech.

"My only hope to win," he wrote in his book, *Six Crises,* "rested with millions of people I would never meet, sitting in groups of two or three or four in their living rooms, watching . . . me on television. I determined as the plane took me to Los Angeles that I must do nothing which might reduce the size of that audience. And so I made up my mind that until after this broadcast, my only releases to the press would be for the purpose of building up the audience which would be tuning in. Under no circumstances, therefore, could I tell the press in advance what I was going to say or what my decision would be . . . This time I was determined to tell my story directly to the people rather than to funnel it . . . through a press account."

And so Nixon went before the television cameras. He invoked Pat's Republican cloth coat, his little girl, Tricia, and his little black and white spotted cocker spaniel dog ("regardless of what they say about it, we are going to keep it"). The public response was overwhelmingly favorable; Nixon flew to Wheeling, West Virginia, to meet Eisenhower, wept on Bill Knowland's shoulder, and stayed on the ticket.

But the lesson of all this was not lost on Nixon: the newspapers had threatened his political career; television had saved it. The words in *Six Crises* remained a manifesto and guideline to his dealings with the press. The way to deal with newspapers was to tell them very little, build up suspense, and then go over their heads to the people via television. This was precisely the formula that Nixon followed in 1968 and in the White House as President.

Nixon's relations with the press were particularly bad in the 1960 Presidential campaign. The atmosphere aboard the Nixon campaign plane was joyless, the staff edgy and even hostile toward the press. Nixon traveled in his forward compartment, frequently granting interviews to Willard Edwards of the conservative *Chicago Tribune,* but to almost no other reporters. As Theodore H. White has put it, Nixon and his staff considered the press "a hostile conspiracy."

The Kennedy press plane, by contrast, was a happy ship, with a jovial press secretary, Pierre Salinger, making every effort to accommodate reporters. Kennedy had his own plane, the *Caroline,* but at airport stops he made a point of frequently chatting with newsmen, often greeting them by their first names.

The tactics were shrewd, and by and large Kennedy was personally much more popular with the newsmen covering the campaign. And there were things that Nixon said and did that grated on the press. There was, for example, the matter of the pies, the strawberries out of season, and the hamburgers.

Faced with a millionaire opponent, Nixon repeatedly emphasized his own poor origins, to the point where reporters covering the campaign would groan quietly when he launched into his dietetic log-cabin routine. In Chester, Pennsylvania, for example, on October

22, he told a crowd: "I grew up in a little country store. Saturday was a long day because that's the day we started at 8 A.M. My mother used to get up at 5 A.M. and bake pies. Lemon . . . cherry was my favorite. Boy, she could make the best."

Half an hour later at another rally, he had inexplicably switched to apple pies. His mother's pies, said Nixon, were "mighty good." It cost only "twenty-five cents for the best green-apple pie you could possibly put in your mouth." The poverty in which he grew up, Nixon added, meant that customers in the little grocery store would buy "hamburger rather than steak, stew meat rather than the chuck roast that was a little more expensive, no strawberries out of season." Nixon continued to emphasize the poor-boy theme as he whistle-stopped through Michigan and Illinois on his campaign train.

By the time he reached Danville, Illinois, he was grinding the hamburger himself: "You know, one lady would come in and there would be nice hamburger. I ground it myself, incidentally—no suet in it, all meat—and it was mighty good, incidentally, only twenty-two cents a pound then—but here would be some nice hamburger and over here would be a fine roast beef. So the lady would buy the hamburger, because she had a big family."

In another speech he remembered how when he was about ten years old "we didn't have too much but . . . I wanted to get an automatic train, not an electric train, but just one that would wind up," and his brother desperately wanted a pony, but his father had to say no. All that day, as Nixon campaigned through Illinois, he invoked the heartrending story of the pony. His older brother "wanted a pony . . . He wanted it more than anything in the world," but his mother and father could not buy the pony, because there would not be enough money for groceries, or "the shoes that my other brothers needed."

Now, Nixon could not be faulted for praising apple pie and motherhood, since these are traditional American values, but the whole performance struck many reporters as maudlin, and of a piece with the cloth coat and the Checkers speech. Moreover—and this was perhaps the heart of the matter—to many newsmen it seemed a cynical appeal to the emotions of the voters, since Nixon was far too intelligent a man, and far too sophisticated, to believe that the mouth-watering qualities of his mother's pies, or the number of ham-burgers he ground, or the hardships of the little grocery store in Whittier, or the little wind-up train, or the pony denied had very much relevance to his qualifications to be President of the United States in the nuclear age.

And Nixon displayed an insensitivity and awkwardness in his personal relationships with the press in 1960 that are perhaps best illustrated by an incident that occurred along the campaign trail on a Sunday night in Billings, Montana. The local citizenry had arranged a party for the press at a private establishment called the Petroleum Club. A group of reporters, including Thomas B. Ross of the *Chicago Sun-Times* and columnist Art Buchwald, was standing at the bar with two stewardesses from the chartered press plane, who were out of uniform. The girls, Republicans and staunch Nixon admirers, were thrilled to be along on the campaign.

Their excitement increased when Nixon, along with Herb Klein, arrived at the club. As the Republican candidate approached, Buchwald said: "Mr. Vice-President, these are the stewardesses on our plane. They've been so nice to us. I'd like to introduce them."

Nixon stared at the girls. "Stewardesses?" he said. "I thought they were B-girls."

After this pleasantry, the candidate moved on, leaving behind two highly upset young women on the verge of tears. Klein, apparently realizing that Nixon had left the group in a state of shock, soon reappeared and announced that the Vice-President's comments were off the record. Besides, Klein explained with a ha-ha, "he didn't mean B-girls, he meant *Billings* girls."

Nixon clearly did not have any easy way with newsmen. Moreover, he was quick to claim that the press was conspiring against him. I can give personal testimony to this as a result of one classic episode in the 1960 campaign in which I was involved.

I traveled aboard the Nixon press plane as a newspaper correspondent in the final days of the 1960 campaign. The candidate's advisers and staff were gloomy; Nixon was behind in the polls, and his aides did not bother to conceal an air of impending defeat. Nixon had pledged to campaign in all fifty states—a pledge that he later conceded had been a mistaken waste of his energies and time—and to keep this commitment on November 4, he ordered his chartered American Airlines 707 jet to land in a blinding snowstorm at Casper, Wyoming. He had known the weather conditions in Casper before leaving from Fort Worth. Nevertheless, Nixon kept his campaign promise—Wyoming was the forty-ninth state, leaving only one, Alaska, to go. With the candidate, his wife, and ninety-eight newsmen and staff members aboard, the big plane banked steeply and made two unsuccessful passes at the field. Each time, at the last moment, the pilot pulled away, flaps up. The snow was too thick, and visibility was reduced to four hundred feet. On the third approach, the jet came in for a perfect landing on instruments. Charles W. Bailey II, then Washington correspondent of the *Minneapolis Tribune*, who occupied the seat next to me, was softly singing "Nearer My God to Thee."

Reporters were so shaken by the experience that after Nixon had delivered his speech in Casper and the plane was airborne again, the pilot, at the request of the Nixon staff, sauntered back to talk to the press, picked up a microphone in the cabin and announced that this is your pilot speaking, and there had been no danger, folks, and he would not have landed it had it been otherwise, since he had a wife and children back in Brentwood, California. Most of the reporters were unconvinced.

An instrument landing in the Rockies in a howling snowstorm to fulfill a campaign promise seemed worthy of mention, and I duly reported it in detail in the dispatch I filed that day to the *New York Herald Tribune,* which ran the story on page one. Later Nixon cited the story, in bitter complaints to the newspaper and to Republican friends, as an example of the biased, unfair reporting of which he claimed to have been the victim in 1960.

The theme of candidate-as-victim emerged even more strongly in 1962. On the morning of November 7, 1962, as Nixon sat in his room at the Beverly Hilton, Herb Klein informed him that the press was downstairs waiting for him to concede defeat to Governor Edmund G. "Pat" Brown. Jules Witcover reports in his book, *The Resurrection of Richard Nixon,* that Nixon stared at Klein and replied: "Screw them."

According to Witcover, he repeated this phrase several times in answer to the repeated entreaties of his aides that he face the reporters and concede. Finally Klein went down and made the concession statement. No one was more surprised than Klein when, in the midst of this, the velvet drapes parted behind him and out popped Nixon.

"Good morning, gentlemen," he began. "Now that Mr. Klein has made his statement, and now that all the members of the press are so delighted that I have lost, I'd like to make a statement of my own . . . for once, gentlemen—I would appreciate if you would write what I say . . .For sixteen years, ever since the Hiss case, you've had a lot of fun—a lot of fun—that you've had an opportunity to attack me . . .I think that it's time that our great newspapers have at least the same objectivity . . . that television has. And I can only say thank God for television and radio for keeping the newspapers a little more honest.

"The last play. I leave you gentlemen now and you will now write it . . . But as I leave you I want you to know—just think how much you're going to be missing.

"You won't have Nixon to kick around any more, because, gentlemen, this is my last press conference and it will be one in which I have welcomed the opportunity to test wits with you . . . I hope that . . . the press . . . recognize that they have a right and a responsibility, if they're against a candidate, give him the shaft, but also recognize if they give him the shaft, put one lonely reporter on the campaign who will report what the candidate says now and then."

The reporters were stunned. No modern political figure had ever said anything like this in public—it was well before the age of Spiro Agnew—and Nixon had obviously unburdened himself of his innermost feelings only because, at the time, he believed that it really *was* his last press conference.

When he ran for President six years later, Nixon dealt with the media in accordance with the formula laid down in *Six Crises.* With Harry Treleaven's professional guidance, he reached the public through a series of carefully controlled televised question-and-answer sessions in local communities. He went over the heads of the press.

Having learned from 1960, the Nixon press staff went out of its way to assist reporters during the campaign. But the basic hostility toward the news media was there, it surfaced on election night in Roy Goodearle's "beat the press" suggestion, and it was to characterize the Nixon Presidency.

Even before he was inaugurated, Nixon revealed his feelings during a closed meeting with his cabinet appointees and their wives at the Shoreham Hotel in Washington. According to James Keogh, a former executive editor of *Time,* who served for two years as chief of Nixon's speechwriting team, the essence of what the President said went like this: "Always remember, the men and women of the news media approach this as an adversary relationship. The time will come when they will run lies about you, when the columnists and editorial writers will make you seem to be scoundrels or fools or both and the cartoonists will depict you as ogres . . . "

As President, Richard Nixon unleashed, and personally participated in, the strongest, most highly coordinated, and, ultimately, the most dangerous attack on the nation's constitutionally protected free press since the Alien and Sedition Acts of 1798. The Nixon administration not only placed a wide range of unprecedented pressures on the press, it made a concerted effort to undermine public confidence in both the print and electronic news media.

Should this seem overstated, consider a few of the elements: a constant drumfire of attacks upon the press, not only in the inflammatory rhetoric of Vice-President Agnew, but by the President himself, by the chairman of the Republican National Committee, and by a rather large number of other high White House and administration officials; the attempt—unprecedented in the history of the republic —to censor the nation's leading newspapers from printing the history of the Vietnam war; direct threats by White House officials of government action against television networks and stations whose news broadcasts are too liberal; dozens of subpoenas issued to newsmen by law enforcement agencies; a Chief Executive whose press conferences were only slightly less a rarity than those of Charles de Gaulle, and, on the working press level, reprisals, obstacles, and pressures at every turn.

A study of the Nixon administration and the press conducted by the American Civil Liberties Union in 1971 concluded: "Attacks on the press by officers of the government have become so widespread and all-pervasive that they constitute a massive federal-level attempt to subvert the letter and spirit of the First Amendment."

This enormous, organized assault on the news media reflected more than the deeply felt attitudes of the President, although obviously those attitudes provided a crucial framework and support for what occurred. The attack had a larger and more calculated purpose: to erode public confidence in the credibility of the press in order to divert public attention from the credibility of the government.

The "credibility gap" had helped to send Lyndon Johnson back to the ranch, and Richard Nixon, who had wanted the Presidency as desperately as he had once wanted a wind-up train, who had lost it once (by very little), and who had finally achieved it, was determined to avoid Johnson's fate. The public, therefore, must be persuaded that if it was being lied to, the lying was being done, not by the government, but by the press. Moreover, it was the press, and particularly television, that for several years had been bringing the bad news that disturbed Richard Nixon's Middle America—the news of war, of pot, of hard drugs, of rock music, of long hair and easy moral behavior, of crime, of racial tension—and of change. In the turbulent twentieth century old values were crumbling, and the frustrations of coping with such rapid change hardly required much official encouragement to find a target in the news media. As the administration discovered, there was political advantage to be gained by blaming the messenger who brought the bad news. And if the so-called silent majority could be convinced that the news industry was in the hands of a remote, faintly alien Eastern establishment (the "Seaboard media," in one of Spiro Agnew's favored phrases), so much the better. The attacks on the press, in short, could serve the dual purpose of diverting public attention from the question of the government's credibility to the question of the news media's credibility, while at the same time building political support and enlarging the size of Nixon's constituency.

It was Spiro Agnew who became the unlikely instrument of this dual policy. During the 1968 campaign Agnew's "Fat Jap" and other blunders had earned him the image of a buffoon. In the early months of the Nixon administration Agnew did nothing to dispel the belief that he was a modern Alexander Throttlebottom, the Vice-President in the 1931 musical *Of Thee I Sing,* who spent his time feeding pigeons in the park.

In the fall of 1969, however, all this changed. On October 15, Moratorium Day, hundreds of thousands of students and other Americans gathered in Washington and across the nation in a massive, generally orderly protest against the war in Vietnam. Four days later, in New Orleans, Agnew excoriated the leaders of the demonstration and suggested that it had been encouraged by "an effete corps of impudent snobs." On November 3 President Nixon delivered a major address on Vietnam, designed in part to counteract another antiwar demonstration set for November 15. As was customary, newsmen on the three major television networks commented briefly on the address when the President had concluded. Then, in Des Moines on November 13, Agnew delivered the most famous speech of his political career, assailing the "small band of network commentators and self-appointed analysts" who had dared to subject the President's speech to "instant analysis." A week later, in Montgomery, Alabama, Agnew extended his attack to include *The New York Times* and the *Washington Post.*

One of the more wondrous events in Washington, in retrospect, was the debate that occurred over whether Spiro Agnew spoke for President Nixon in attacking the networks and the news media. Of course he did. Vice-Presidents, historically, have not been celebrated for independence of action—especially if they hope to be renominated or run for President some day—and in this case, Agnew's attacks on the press coincided with Nixon's own views.

Yet Ronald Ziegler insisted that Agnew spoke for himself. This required the ludicrous assumption that the Vice-President of the United States, occupying what is theoretically, at least, the second highest elective office in the land, was independently crisscrossing the nation delivering his gloriously alliterative, inflammatory speeches while the White House and the President stood by, helpless to stop him. Ziegler did go so far as to concede that Patrick J. Buchanan "may have, and I think did have, some thoughts" on the text of the Des Moines speech. Since Buchanan was the President's speechwriter, it was a not unimportant admission by Ziegler, and in a press conference on December 8 Nixon himself said that Agnew had "rendered a public service in talking in a very dignified and courageous way" about the news media.

Largely unnoticed in all of this discussion was the fact that two days before Agnew's Des Moines speech excoriating network analysts, communications director Herb Klein had voiced amazingly similar criticism, albeit in more restrained language.* And Klein, by virtue of his position, spoke for the President and the administration.

After the President's November 3 broadcast, Klein said, "Three networks came on and made comment immediately thereafter. The public response to this was very negative, and the interesting thing has been to look through the wires which have come in from the silent Americans expressing this overwhelming wave of support which has come forth for the President—to find intermixed in those, criticism of some of the commentary which perhaps come on too quickly . . . Sometimes I think a discussion which becomes too one-sided . . . erodes the confidence the public has in the network and its commentators. Credibility isn't just the problem of the government. I think it is a problem with the media as well."

Klein, although nobody noticed, had given the game away. One can almost visualize the scene: The President's media advisers reading the telegrams after the November 3 address, the dawning realization that here, in the public's discontent with the television analysts, was an issue that could be exploited; Agnew chosen to bell the cat, and given the services of the President's personal speechwriter.

Agnew continued his attacks upon the news media, and any thought that he had acted independently was soon dispelled when other high officials voiced similar complaints. Dean Burch, Nixon's appointee as chairman of the Federal Communications Commission, praised Agnew's "thoughtful" speech. Senator Robert Dole, chairman of the Republican National Committee, accused all three major television networks of biased news reporting. Network correspondents, he complained, were "liberal" and "antiwar." Bob Haldeman joined the chorus in 1971, declaring that Nixon had "a more hostile press corps" than previous Presidents and that most reporters were Democrats. Richard Kleindienst, later to become Attorney General, assailed "the so-called liberal press," and in 1972 Pat Buchanan— speaking for himself, of course—raised the specter of government antitrust action against the television networks if they continued to "freeze out" opposing viewpoints in their news programs. Shortly before Nixon named L. Patrick Gray III to be acting director of the FBI, following the death of J. Edgar Hoover, Gray delivered a speech in Orange County, California, in which he charged that American newspapers had begun to sacrifice "accuracy and objectivity to parti-

---

*The Klein interview, over the National Educational Television network, was taped on November 11, but not released until November 13, the day of Agnew's speech; as a result, Klein's comments were buried in the avalanche of press copy reporting on the Agnew blast.

san bias and prejudice." He singled out NBC, CBS, *The New York Times,* and the *Washington Post* for criticism in a speech interlarded with phrases such as "news distortion," "blatant news fabrication," "phony information," "grossly unfair," and "hatchet job." In the spring of 1972 Kenneth W. Clawson, Klein's deputy communicator, objected publicly to the content of Anthony Lewis' dispatches from Hanoi in the *Times.*

Nixon himself continued to proclaim his lack of concern over press criticism. "I expect I have one of the most hostile and unfair presses that any president has ever had," Nixon told Allen Drury, "but I have never called a publisher, never called an editor, never called a reporter on the carpet. I don't care. And you know? . . . That's what makes 'em mad. That's what infuriates 'em. I just don't care . . . the press will never irritate me, never affect me, never push me to any move I don't think is wise . . ."

Despite such comments, Nixon, in his March, 1971 interview with Howard K. Smith over ABC television, personally criticized the networks for their coverage of the South Vietnamese invasion of Laos, and assailed both television and newspaper reporting of the invasion of Cambodia by U.S. forces in 1970. He added: "It doesn't prove that the press was trying to deliberately make America look bad." It was a classic example of innuendo, of raising an issue by denying it.

In another interview that same month, Nixon first accused CBS correspondent Daniel Schorr of telling a "lie" in a news report dealing with the ABM, then softened this to say probably it was just "wrong information." A President, Nixon added, had to have people around him who were unperturbed by "the lousy column or the terrible cartoon." But, Nixon said in the same interview, "I am never concerned about opinion, criticism and opinion."*

These elaborate disclaimers of concern over what is written about him form an obbligato to Nixon's comments on the press, unconvincing by their very repetition. Along with Nixon's inelegant but revealing choice of language when discussing the news media ("the lousy column," "give him the shaft"), the impression conveyed is the opposite of that intended: both before and after he became President, Nixon's words have always suggested a man excruciatingly

---

*In this interview with women reporters on March 11, Nixon also struck an old, familiar theme: "My mother was a marvelous pie baker. We used to, Pat and I, before we were married, love to eat those pies she made. She baked them and sold them in a store and helped put me through law school that way and college, too."

concerned with what was written and said about him by the news media. So, one should add, are most Presidents, but some have felt less compelled to deny it.

The Nixon administration's broad-gauge attack on the news media was not limited to rhetoric. The pervasive attitude of hostility toward the press was reflected as well in deed.

The most spectacular act, the effort to prevent *The New York Times* and the *Washington Post* from printing the Pentagon Papers, was, one suspects, more than an attempt by Attorney General John Mitchell to protect the national security at the expense of the First Amendment. It also offered a good chance to teach the *Times* and the *Post* a lesson they would remember. Similarly, the months of ominous rumblings about Neil Sheehan emanating from the federal grand jury in Boston raised speculation that what the Justice Department really wanted was not an indictment, or at any rate, not an indictment right away, but a club to hold over the head of the *Times* in a Presidential election year. If an injunction could not succeed in curbing the *Times,* then perhaps the prospect of prosecution of one of its star reporters, and possibly a number of its editors and executives as well, might make the paper more cautious in writing about the administration.

In large ways and small, the pressures were felt. Even the physical changes instituted in the White House press facilities were symbolic of the administration's view of the news media. The Presidential living quarters are in the center section of the White House, but the Oval Office and staff offices are located in the West Wing. As long as anyone could remember, the press had access to, and could move freely within, the large lobby at the Pennsylvania Avenue entrance of the West Wing.

This meant that unless visitors were specifically instructed to use some other, more discreet entrance to the White House, the press was able to record who came and went and sometimes interview them. A small press room off the lobby contained cubicles for reporters, typewriters, and telephones; the room was cramped, but most newsmen were willing to put up with the crowded conditions as the price of access to the lobby.

Ron Ziegler did not like the setup. Early in 1969 he broached to James Deakin, the White House correspondent of the *St. Louis Post-Dispatch,* the suggestion that an "auxiliary" press room be built in the Executive Office Building across the street. There would, Ziegler went on solicitously, be lots more room, they could put in sandwich and coffee machines, and "pipe in" the west lobby by closed circuit TV. Deakin, suspicious of Ziegler's zeal for enhancing the comfort of the White House press corps, asked why the change was necessary.

It was too crowded in the West Wing, Ziegler explained; the idea was not to "eliminate" the press room, but to supplement it. You had better not eliminate it, Deakin replied.

Nothing came of Ziegler's plan for an auxiliary press room, but in April, 1970, the press corps was moved en masse out of the west lobby and into luxurious new quarters built over what had been the White House swimming pool and sauna. The new two-level press area, known officially as the West Terrace Press Center, was decorated in motel modern, with deep-pile beige carpets, tufted suede chesterfield sofas, upholstered red ottomans, Currier and Ives prints, and lamps in the shape of hunting horns. In the words of *Washington Post* reporter Don Oberdorfer, the briefing room "resembled the lobby of a fake Elizabethan steak house." The White House declined to reveal the cost of the new center. But the Muzak and the décor could not obviate the fact that under the new arrangement, reporters no longer had free access to the west lobby. Two polite Marine guards in dress uniform now barred the way, and the press was required to use a different entrance to its new quarters.

"You are prevented from going in the old West Wing entrance," said Hugh Sidey, chief of the *Time* magazine Washington Bureau. "So you cannot see who is coming and going to see the President. The whole purpose is to cut the press off from the flow of visitors to the White House.* You are barred from going out on the driveway. If you loiter by the West Wing, the guards tell you to go back." The new press center, Sidey added, was both opulent and comfortable, with "coffee machines and what not, all designed to keep the press happy."

Ziegler instituted another change that Sidey considered significant. Hagerty, Salinger, Reedy, and other recent press secretaries held the twice-daily news briefings in their office with reporters clustered around the desk. A reporter who waited around after the

---

*The process of physically isolating the press, as Edward T. Folliard, former White House correspondent for the *Washington Post,* pointed out, actually began during the Eisenhower administration, when a wall was erected at the south end of the west lobby, blocking the view of the comings and goings of staff assistants. During the Kennedy and Johnson administrations Presidential visitors often, but not always, used other entrances. Folliard, who began covering the White House in the Coolidge administration, recalled that "under FDR and Truman, you could see the visitors when they emerged. There was none of this side-door business. Many of the stories I wrote were based on interviews with White House callers. It was very important."

briefing had concluded could usually have a word with the press secretary. Sometimes the secretary's reply, or even his reaction, would provide the missing piece in what might be an important news story the reporter was developing. Sidey noted that Ziegler continued to use the same office his predecessors had used, but "you can't wander into Ziegler's office any more as in the old days." Since Ziegler went to the briefing room in the new press center to meet with newsmen, "you can't hang around with questions after the briefing. He may linger a bit, but when he wants to go, that's it. It's indicative."

Although the reporters were physically isolated, the White House did not lack interest in their activities. Robert Semple, Jr., the White House correspondent of *The New York Times*, said that when a reporter contacted a member of the Nixon staff, the press office quickly became aware of it. Semple would occasionally go to see George Shultz, who served in the White House for two years as director of the Office of Management and Budget before becoming Secretary of the Treasury. "When I saw Shultz," Semple said, "Ron knew." Ziegler, he added, "is supposed to know what reporters are doing. It is all highly organized; I've very rarely seen anyone in this administration without Ron knowing about it."

The Nixon White House kept close tabs not only on whom reporters were seeing, but on what they wrote. When Herb Klein was appointed communications director, his staff prepared a thirteen-page, single-spaced document for internal use entitled: "Press Reaction to Herb Klein Appointment as Director of Communications." The analysis characterized editorials as "favorable," "very favorable," or "unfavorable." It described a *New York Post* profile as "a warm appraisal of HGK the person, the professional." It also analyzed the three major news magazines. *Newsweek,* the document said, "Zaps into RN's relations with the press as nonexistent." *Time's* coverage was called "fairly non-partial," but *U.S. News and World Report* provided "completely non-partial coverage of appointment" and was "complimentary."

Columnist Joseph Kraft elicited the sharpest language in the analysis: "Kraft, in an extremely cynical article, says Nixon is clever to have let the right people believe that Rockefeller, Brooke, and Clifford turned down jobs, thus pacifying liberal Republicans and coalition-minded Democrats." Kraft had commented on Klein's appointment in the same column.

On at least one occasion, Bob Haldeman, the President's chief of staff, figuratively donned his green eyeshade and played editor. At a private lunch in his White House office with Robert J. Donovan, David Kraslow, and Stuart H. Loory of the *Los Angeles Times,* Haldeman complained about the amount of coverage given to Nixon by the newspaper. He had marked up a copy of the *Los Angeles Times* and a copy of *The New York Times,* Haldeman said, and he found that *The New York Times* gave the President more space than his hometown newspaper.

Nixon himself could keep track of what the networks and news media were saying about him through the "President's Daily News Briefing," the highly detailed private digest prepared for him by his speechwriting staff.* Copies were not meant for public consumption, of course, but when the President was in China in February, 1972, a reporter got hold of one, and it showed that—even in Peking— Nixon could read what was being written and said about him in fantastic detail.

Television reports, for example, had obviously been clocked with a stopwatch, since the precise number of minutes and seconds of each network story was given, e.g.: "NBC led with 5:20 from the banquet . . . 1:30 of RN toast and 1:20 by Chou." Translated, this meant Nixon could tell by a glance at the summary that American viewers watching NBC-TV got ten seconds more of Nixon than of Chinese Premier Chou En-lai. The log, which covered February 25, went on to say that NBC's Herb Kaplow had done a two-minute report from the Forbidden City. "Both better film and audio of RN than was the case in live coverage." For "2nd night in a row," the summary noted somewhat sourly, "CBS led with busing story . . ."

In discussing coverage by CBS—not the Nixon administration's favorite network—the digest said: "Still frustrated in getting news was Cronkite . . . as he said reporters were again turning to sightseeing . . ." White House correspondent Dan Rather, the log said, did a report on acupuncture. "We saw a fellow under lung surgery—no pain. Then Dr. Dan in his operating room outfit concluded if it was all as it had been demonstrated, and he gave no reason to cause one

---

*The length of the news summary varied. In a five-page letter of complaint to the editors of the *Washington Post* in November, 1970, Pat Buchanan, the Presidential speechwriter in overall charge of preparing the summary, said it ran "between twenty and fifty pages on an average day" and went to the President and fifty White House assistants. Buchanan's letter criticized in great detail a column by Marquis Childs, who reported that Nixon was said to get his news from a one-page summary. In 1972 Buchanan said the news summary had been streamlined and reduced to an average length of twenty-one pages. Although widely distributed inside the White House, the cover of the daily summary was prominently marked: "Eyes Only for the President."

to think it was otherwise, the witnessed operations were 'amazing.' "
The sardonic reference to Rather as "Dr. Dan" implicitly questioned
his ability to make medical judgments; and the tone of the President's news summary suggested that Rather had clearly been taken
in by acupuncture and these clever Chinese. The log concluded with
several single-spaced pages of reports on newspaper coverage of the
trip, quoting headlines and going into great detail about news play,
photographs, cartoons, and editorials.

One can only speculate about the cost, the tremendous effort,
and the man hours it must take to monitor the television networks
and dozens of newspapers in such minute detail, every day, then boil
it down into written form, assemble it and—when the President is
out of Washington—transmit it to him.

But the system is efficient, as Stuart Loory can attest. In Rome
with Nixon on a trip to Europe in 1970, Loory, then White House
correspondent of the *Los Angeles Times*, reported, far down in his
story—in the twentieth paragraph, to be precise—that the Pope had
given Nixon a cool reception.* The next day the President was in
Yugoslavia. President Tito held a reception for Nixon, and afterward,
as Loory was descending the steps of the presidential palace in Belgrade, Haldeman came over.

"There was just ice in his eyes," Loory said. He recalled their
conversation as follows:

"Stu, where did you get the idea that the President's reception
was cool?"

"Bob, all you have to do is read the statement put out by the
Vatican."

"That's incredible. That's just incredible."

The point, Loory said, was that quite aside from the dispute over
the degree of papal warmth shown to the President, "Haldeman had
a report back on my story twenty-four hours later. Loory's offending
paragraph had traveled from Rome to Los Angeles, from there to
Washington, and then back across the Atlantic to Belgrade.

Loory got off easily. Nicholas Thimmesch of *Newsday* did not

---

*Loory reported that although the Italian government had reacted with
warmth toward Nixon's visit, the Pope's reaction was "polite coolness." To
back up the point, Loory quoted from a statement issued by the Vatican after
the two leaders met. The statement, Loory noted, contained "no praise" for
the U.S. role in the Middle East, warned of the risk of "disappointing the
hopes" that had been raised by the prospect of negotiations, and urged that
the negotiations resume. The Pope also hoped that there might be peace in
Southeast Asia.

fare so well. In the spring of 1972 Thimmesch was invited to a private screening of *The Godfather* at the Washington headquarters of the Motion Picture Association of America. Seated in the small theater, Thimmesch suddenly felt someone grab his hair from behind and yank his head back sharply against the seat.

When Thimmesch was able to turn around he saw that the hair-puller was Haldeman, about whom Thimmesch had recently written a somewhat critical profile.* Apparently Haldeman did not approve of the length of Thimmesch's hair.

"Oh, pardon me," said the President's chief of staff, "I thought it was a girl sitting there."

Thimmesch sat through the picture, but he did not entirely appreciate Haldeman's idea of a joke. In the movie, there is a scene in which a huge gangster is garroted in a bar; the next morning his boss, the Godfather, receives two fish wrapped in a bulletproof vest —the mob's way of letting him know that his lieutenant was "sleeping with the fishes." When the screening ended, Thimmesch sidled up to Haldeman. "You pull my hair again," he said, "and you sleep with the fishes."

The administration's keen interest in the press was not confined to the White House. In 1971 Pentagon reporters were disturbed to learn that their press room had been searched overnight by the PCF, the Pentagon Counterintelligence Force.

The PCF went through the room on the night of November 16, but its agents were thoughtful enough to leave little cards on the desks of the correspondents for *Time* magazine and the *New York Daily News,* which said: "An inspection of this office area by the Pentagon Counterintelligence Force revealed no violations of security regulations." Reporters were understandably upset at the thought that the counterintelligence agents might go through their notes or learn the names of their news sources. It was a reasonable fear, since administrations are forever trying to plug unauthorized leaks, and sometimes the government launches full-scale investigations designed to find and punish the leaker.

A Pentagon spokesman said that Daniel Henkin, the Assistant Secretary of Defense for Public Affairs, "was very distressed to know that this happened." The spokesman said Henkin had been told by

---

*The article termed Haldeman's manner "brusque" and "clinical," and quoted Haldeman as saying: "I guess the term 'sonofabitch' fits me." Haldeman's crewcut, the profile added, "hasn't changed since the beginning of the cold war." Despite this column, Thimmesch was held in exceptionally high regard by the Nixon administration.

the security officials that it was "an inadvertent check" and would not happen again.* Although Henkin did not deny that the PCF had been through reporters' desks, David O. Cooke, the assistant secretary in charge of Pentagon security, claimed in a memo to Henkin that the PCF had not peeked into desks or looked at "files, notes, and draft news stories." The PCF, Cooke said, simply wanted to be sure there were no intruders in the press room.

It was during the Nixon administration as well, that growing numbers of news reporters found themselves subpoenaed by federal, state, and local prosecutors to give evidence in legal proceedings. Historically, the courts had held that the First Amendment did not exempt reporters from giving testimony. Newsmen who wished to protect confidential sources had to go to jail, and some did.

Summoning news reporters to testify before grand juries, or in other official proceedings, raised a complex constitutional issue of immense importance. The government argued that the duty to give evidence was fundamental to the system of justice. But newsmen pointed out that where a confidential relationship existed, the law already recognized several classes of persons exempt from this requirement—husband and wife, attorney and client, priest and confessor. The press contended that if newsmen were forced to give evidence, their confidential sources would dry up, reducing the flow of information to the public. Freedom of the press would be abridged within the meaning of the First Amendment.

These issues crystallized in the case of Earl Caldwell, a reporter for *The New York Times*. Caldwell, a black, gained the confidence of the Black Panthers in the San Francisco area and wrote a series of articles for his newspaper. In 1970 he was subpoenaed to appear before a federal grand jury to testify. He refused. The U.S. district court in San Francisco ruled that the First Amendment might protect Caldwell from testifying, but he did have to appear before the grand jury. The judge found Caldwell guilty of contempt and ordered him to jail. But Caldwell appealed. He argued that his mere appearance before a jury would destroy his relationship of trust with

---

*There was a very peculiar sequel to the story. The day after the press room had been searched, the wife of one of the reporters who worked in the Pentagon telephoned her husband in the press room from their home. She hung up, made a call to their daughter, then picked up her phone to call someone else. Instead of getting a dial tone, she could hear her husband having a conversation in the press room with another person. During the entire conversation her husband's telephone was resting on its cradle in the Pentagon.

the Panthers. A federal appeals court upheld his position, ruling that the government could not "convert news gatherers into Department of Justice investigators." Unless the government could demonstrate a "compelling need" for Caldwell's presence, he did not have to go before the grand jury.

As the Caldwell case moved through the courts, Attorney General John Mitchell attempted to defuse the issue by promulgating a series of "guidelines" to govern the issuance of subpoenas to newsmen; Mitchell promised that henceforth the Justice Department would negotiate with the press first, and subpoena later. Even so, late in 1971 CBS and NBC disclosed that in the first two and a half years of the Nixon administration, they had received an unprecedented 122 subpoenas, more than one-third from federal, state, and local governments. During the same period the *Chicago Sun-Times* and the *Chicago Daily News* received thirty subpoenas, mostly from the federal government.

In 1972 the Supreme Court handed down its decision in the Caldwell and two related state court cases.* President Nixon's four appointees, joined by Justice Byron R. White, were enough to swing the balance against the press in the 5-to-4 decision. The court ruled that the First Amendment gave journalists no right to refuse to disclose to grand juries relevant confidential information or the names of their sources.

The decision was a major blow not only to Earl Caldwell and *The New York Times,* but to the press and the public's right to know. Eighteen states had statutes extending some degree of protection to newsmen in regard to confidential sources, and efforts were immediately renewed in Congress to pass a federal immunity law for journalists. But the decision against the press was consistent with the conservative trend of Supreme Court decisions resulting from Nixon's appointments.

Caldwell did not actually go to jail, since the term of the federal grand jury seeking his testimony had expired by the time the Supreme Court ruled. But three months after the Caldwell decision, Peter J. Bridge, a Newark, New Jersey, news reporter, was sent to jail for twenty days for refusing to give a county grand jury information that went beyond what he had already published about an alleged

---

*In one, Paul M. Branzburg of the *Louisville Courier-Journal* had refused to disclose to a state grand jury the names of drug sellers and users he had written about. In the other, Paul Pappas, a New Bedford, Massachusetts, television newsman, declined to tell a grand jury about his night at Black Panther headquarters.

bribe offer to a housing commissioner. Soon, other reporters were jailed for protecting news sources.

Sentencing a reporter to jail, as in the case of Earl Caldwell, or exploring with a grand jury the possibility of sending him there—as in the case of Neil Sheehan—amounts to government pressure on the press in rather extreme form. Even a Pulitzer Prize may not be worth going up the river, and reporters frequently have wives and families who may take a dim view of their prolonged absence.

The Nixon administration had a whole range of milder options available to it, however. As the experience of *Newsday* and Martin Schram indicated, a reporter and a newspaper could simply be frozen out at the White House. At first glance this would not seem to be a total calamity; after all, one could not *prove* that *Newsday*'s microscopic attentions to Bebe Rebozo had cost Schram a visit to Peking and deprived his newspaper's readers of direct coverage, and if his typewriter repairman could not get past the gate, at least there was no effort to keep Schram himself out.

But a correspondent's standing at the White House, by some mysterious process, does become rather quickly known within a widening circle of Presidential advisers, and if official displeasure is great enough, assistants to the President may stop answering their phones when the reporter calls, and official sources may be permanently out to lunch. A resourceful reporter can perhaps continue to find good stories despite the chill, but in time there is always the danger that his coverage may suffer, and his editors, even if they are aware of the reason, may begin to wonder if it is not time to change White House correspondents.

There are other small, but effective ways for the White House to retaliate against reporters who do not "go along." One such device is the White House press "pool." Because of the size of the White House press corps, only a few reporters at a time are permitted to travel with the President on Air Force One, or to cover certain events, or to ride near the President in a motorcade. The AP and UPI reporters are permanent members of this pool, but correspondents for newspapers are assigned on a rotating basis. The reporter chosen represents his colleagues; he types up his notes and makes them available to the others. It is important to be chosen for the pool, because sometimes it offers a correspondent his only opportunity for direct contact with the President, or with his top assistants. Key Presidential aides may sit down and talk with the pool reporters on Air Force One, for example. As a matter of administrative convenience, the President's press secretary makes the pool assignments.

Stuart Loory of the *Los Angeles Times*, whose aggressive reporting was a source of special irritation to the Nixon administration, said he had the constant feeling that he was "losing pools" when he covered the White House. During the 1970 campaign, when the President would arrive in a city, normally the reporter from the paper serving that area would draw the pool. It was logical to do so, and it might also serve to give the reporter a little added prestige in the eyes of his editors. On a major campaign swing to California, Loory failed to get the pool going into Los Angeles.

But when Loory did not go on a Presidential trip, he said, the correspondent of the *Los Angeles Times* filling in for him "just coincidentally would be drawn for the pool. This happened several times."

On Nixon's journey to Europe in 1970, however, Loory was extremely pleased with his pool assignment; he was to go by helicopter out to the aircraft carrier *Saratoga*, where the President would be piped aboard for a visit to the Sixth Fleet. The night before, Loory ran into Ziegler at a bar in Rome.

Ziegler asked how Loory liked his pool assignment *this* time. Loory said he liked it.

"I had to tell them you got seasick to get it for you," Ziegler said. The press secretary hastily added that he was only joking.

But Ronald Ziegler did not always hesitate to remind a reporter of his power, as James H. McCartney of the Knight newspapers discovered. McCartney wandered into the White House press room one afternoon in March, 1972, shortly after Nixon had returned from China. The President had gone to Key Biscayne at noon, and, as McCartney noted, "under those circumstances the press room was usually deserted. Well, I came in and the place was full of people who had been on the China trip, most of whom I know and recognized . . . it was obvious that something was going on."

What was going on was that Henry Kissinger had briefed reporters that morning. The background session had been organized by Peter Lisagor of the *Chicago Daily News*, and it had been held outside the White House, at the Federal City Club. The reporters were now back at the White House, awaiting an official transcript.

The briefing had been limited almost entirely to reporters who had accompanied the President to China. McCartney was disturbed that the Knight papers had been left out, since their Washington Bureau chief, Robert Boyd, had been on the China trip but had not yet returned, as he had remained for a time in China and the Far East. McCartney went in to see Ziegler, and asked for a transcript. Ziegler waffled, so McCartney requested that Ziegler call him later to let him know whether a transcript would be forthcoming.

"In an hour and a half there was no call," McCartney said, "so I called his office and his secretary said Mr. Ziegler left town an hour ago, that he was gone on vacation and that we don't expect to see him for several days." McCartney then told the secretary that the Knight organization would not feel bound by any "ground rules" governing the backgrounder.

"My editors were very disturbed by the whole procedure. I was specifically told, 'Well, let's not play their ball game, why don't you leave and let's write a story about what they are doing.' So I started to leave the White House." At that point, McCartney said, the transcript was ready, but he refused a copy offered by Lisagor, because to have accepted it would have bound him to the ground rules for attribution, which meant shielding Kissinger's identity as the source.

McCartney filed a story about the circumstances surrounding the backgrounder, and he named Kissinger. "At 8 P.M. Ziegler's secretary called me and said Ron wanted to talk to me. I had written my story by this time, and in our organization, it's very hard, since its a big organization, to make changes late in the evening. She gave me his number, he was on vacation, in a hotel in Florida at Lake Buena Vista. I had to get the room number right, because he was under a different name, and he said, 'Jim, I understand that you have refused this transcript, and I want you to know that this is not going to do our relationship any good.'

"I said it was true we were offered the transcript finally, but hardly as a result of any efforts attributable to you; and that I didn't think our relationship was worth preserving—which I must say is a personal opinion, but a strong one. Whereupon, he ended the conversation by saying, 'Well, I'll see ya in five years,' which, if I interpret Nixonesque diplomatic language accurately, means 'Don't count on us for anything if we get reelected,' which of course is a sort of reprisal. Ziegler then took it upon himself to call John S. Knight, the chairman of the board of the Knight newspapers, and he also called Lee Hills, the president of the Knight newspapers. Whatever happened, I was told down through the chain of command that the calls had taken place and that the instructions to the papers were to handle the story on its merits, and don't worry about any of this nonsense."

The job of Presidential press secretary seemed not to have taken the slightest toll in Ronald Ziegler in almost four years—in an interview in his office in 1972, he was just as smooth-faced, and seemingly relaxed, as the day he moved into the White House. In his early thirties he retained something of the easy style of a high school jock who has just scored the winning touchdown. Despite his youthful appearance, Ziegler somehow suggested a figure from an earlier era; he could easily be the handsome hero of a 1938 Warner Bros. campus musical, or perhaps a Frank Merriwell character suddenly come to life. Richard Nixon's Dink Stover.

Sitting at his curved executive desk in the White House, occasionally interrupting to say a few words on his gold-and-white telephone, Ziegler was disarmingly direct, his manner ingenuous. He was terribly pleasant, ready to concede that various incidents had occurred with reporters, but dismissing them as of no importance.

He did not dispute James McCartney's recollection of their conversation.* It was true, he said; he had gotten "mad" at Jim McCartney, and he had telephoned John Knight and Lee Hills.† As for *Newsday*, the Rebozo series "was a bad, lousy series, a rehash . . . full of innuendo," and he had indeed been "cool" to Marty Schram afterward, but the fact that *Newsday* did not get to go to China "had nothing to do with the Rebozo series."

He did not, Ziegler continued, engage in "reprisals . . . To cut through it all, there can be no legitimate statement made by any network or any individual journalist where they have been intimidated or where there was any effort to hurt them professionally." There were, he said, some incidents that merely *"looked* that way."

As for attacks on the press by administration officials, again Ziegler said, there had been no "intent" to intimidate. "Unless the press can point to efforts on the part of the government to restrain them, they shouldn't care. I suppose if we were in a debate, someone would point to the Pentagon Papers. I feel the government had to take that view, do what they did." Ziegler paused. "And after all," he said, "the Pentagon Papers were published."

Since the Nixon administration fought against publication of the Pentagon Papers all the way to the Supreme Court, that the President's press secretary could, in effect, claim credit for having lost the case boggles the mind. One came away from an interview with Ronald Ziegler with the feeling of having sunk slowly, but hopelessly, into a quagmire of marshmallows.

At least Ziegler, unless a newsman was out of favor, was accessible to the press. To an unprecedented degree in the modern Presidency, Nixon was not. The institution of the Presidential press conference has often been compared to the "question time" in the

---

*He insisted, however, that he was registered at the hotel in Florida under his own name. "I was at Disney World for a three-day vacation with my family after the China trip," he said.

†If Richard Nixon had "never called a publisher since I have been President," as he claimed in his March 22, 1971, interview with Howard K. Smith on ABC-TV (and to Allen Drury), the same, obviously, was not true of his press secretary. And Ziegler clearly spoke for the White House and the President.

British House of Commons, in which ministers respond to inquiries by the opposition or members of their own party.

The press conference is not directly comparable, but, for all of its shortcomings, it is the *only* way that the press can put questions directly to the Chief Executive. As such, it can be a vital channel of information to the public and an important element in the democratic process. If the press conference is televised, the voters can see for themselves how the President handles difficult questions of public policy. They can draw their own conclusions.

Richard Nixon shunned the naked exposure of the press conference. In his first four years as President, he held only thirty-one press conferences. By contrast, Kennedy held sixty-four in slightly less than three years; Johnson held 126 in slightly more than five years; Eisenhower had 193 in eight years; Truman had 322 in almost eight years, and Roosevelt had 998 in just over twelve years.

The question of news conferences aside, under Nixon, reporters complained that the President and his staff were generally remote and isolated from the press. The open administration turned out to be closed.

"Nixon resolved to keep us all at arm's length," Robert Semple, Jr., of *The New York Times* declared. "He was going to be impartially invisible. The White House staff people, most of whom grew up with Nixon's distrust of the press, said, 'Why should we have to talk to these guys?' They felt that was the job of Ziegler and Klein. The result was that after a while it became almost impossible to see senior White House officials like John Ehrlichman."

In three years Hugh Sidey of *Time* saw Nixon privately only once. "I saw Kennedy once a month, if you averaged it out," Sidey said. "Sometimes twice a week. But that's not important. When I saw Ted Sorensen, or Larry O'Brien, I had confidence in what they said. In this administration you can go out and have lunch with Bob Finch, and the next day, completely the opposite of what he told you will happen. Because he doesn't know. There are some exceptions; Kissinger and Ehrlichman do know what is going on. But most of the White House staff don't know. They just don't *know*. Ron is not unpopular personally, but it is a worthless exercise. It's a non-news operation, a laborious waste of time."

The administration saw political advantage in attacking the press, Sidey added, "but don't discount their general hostility toward the press. It bubbles to the surface all the time. I once asked JFK what ever possessed him to call the steel men S.O.B.'s. He said, 'Because it felt so good.' Some of that is here in the attacks on the press."

"Under Truman, Eisenhower, Kennedy, and Johnson, the staff guys would bitch and moan about us, but there was always a sense of public trust, that they were awed by the responsibility given to them, and they understood this and would talk about what they were doing. They would talk about things. You could talk, write about, or disagree with them, but at the end of the day you could have a drink with them. There is no sense of that with these people.

"This crowd came in like an occupying army. They took over the White House like a stockade, and the Watergate, and screw everybody else. They have no sense that the government doesn't belong to them, that it's something they're holding in trust for the people."

Tom Wicker, associate editor and columnist of *The New York Times* was equally critical. "We all feel the general pressure," he said. "No administration in history has turned loose as high an official as the Vice-President to level a constant fusillade of criticism at the press. The Pentagon Papers case was pressure of the most immense kind. You have the Earl Caldwell case. If they indict Neil Sheehan, it will be pressure. In a sense, even the Ellsberg indictment is a form of pressure.

"There is a constant pattern of pressure intended to inhibit us. What the lawyers call a chilling effect. To make us unconsciously pull in our horns." In December, 1971, Wicker said, he had received a telephone call from James Reston: "'Scotty called me from Washington. I was in New York, and something had come up about the Sheehan case. I said, 'I don't think we ought to talk about this on the phone.' I don't know if they were listening. But if they can make us feel that way, hell, they've won the game already."

11

Television

The executive suite on the thirty-fifth floor of the Columbia Broadcasting System skyscraper in Manhattan is a tasteful blend of dark wood paneling, expensive abstract paintings, thick carpets, and pleasing colors. It has the quiet look of power.

Over breakfast in the small private dining room of the executive suite, Frank Stanton, the president of CBS for twenty-five years, talked candidly about the relationship between government and the television industry. I was interested, I explained, in pressures by government on the TV networks. I particularly wanted to know about telephone calls from Presidents; I recognized that this was a delicate subject, but I assumed that as head of CBS he had received some. He had, as it turned out, from several Presidents.

"I had a curious call from LBJ," he said. "It was one night back in 1968, at the time of the Democratic platform committee hearings in Washington." Johnson called on a Tuesday, Stanton said; it was August 20, and Dean Rusk was scheduled to testify at an evening session of the committee. As Stanton recalled the conversation, it went as follows:

> LBJ: Are you going to cover Dean Rusk tonight?
> STANTON: Yes. We're covering the whole thing.
> LBJ: No, I mean are you going to cover it *live?*
> STANTON: Why?
> LBJ: Rusk has an important statement.

STANTON: If you're saying Rusk is going to have an important statement, we'll cover it live. But he has to be there on time.
LBJ: Okay, just tell me the time—I'll have him there.
STANTON: Well, 9 P.M. But you really have to get him there on time. We'll be cutting into the Steve Allen show, and people are going to be furious if there is nothing going on.

Stanton knew that the Steve Allen show (which on that night starred Jayne Meadows and the Rumanian National Dance Company) began at 8:30 P.M. and ran for one hour; viewers would naturally be disappointed, he reasoned, if time was preempted for a political broadcast and the screen showed an announcer doing "fill." The CBS president had visions of the Secretary of State arriving late and the television audience getting nothing: no Steve Allen, no Jayne Meadows, no Rumanian dancers, not even Dean Rusk.

The conversation with President Johnson continued:

STANTON: How long will Rusk speak?
LBJ: Not long—why?
STANTON: We've got a special on blacks coming on at 9:30 P.M. and I don't want Rusk to collide with that.

The President assured Stanton there was no need to worry; the Secretary of State would be there on time, and he would be off before the special.*

Johnson was true to his word. Precisely at 9 P.M. CBS correspondent Roger Mudd began introducing the broadcast from a booth in the hall. "Suddenly," Stanton said, "you could see Mudd look up, startled. Rusk was starting in right at 9 P.M., straight up."

The President of the United States had called the President of CBS and sweet-talked Steve Allen off the air and the Secretary of State on the air, in prime time, for a specific political reason, which he did not share with Stanton. That afternoon supporters of the late Robert F. Kennedy, with the backing of other Democratic liberals, had circulated a draft plank calling for a halt to the bombing of North Vietnam. Lyndon Johnson wanted Dean Rusk on nationwide television, at an hour when he would have maximum exposure, to head off the inclusion of any such plank in the Democratic party platform.

Rusk followed his marching orders. "We hear a good deal about

---

*"Of Black America: In Search of a Past." The program, one of a seven-part series on the role of black Americans, showed three black high school students from Washington, D.C., on a visit to Ghana.

stopping the bombing," he said. ". . . If we mean: Let them get as far as Dupont Circle but don't hit them while they are at Chevy Chase Circle, that would be too rude, let us say so." The party platform, Rusk said, should "state objectives" but not outline "tactics or strategy." In other words, no antibombing plank.

Rusk, in fact, made no important announcement; but presumably Johnson had to tell Stanton *something* to justify handing over the network to the President at 9 P.M. As it turned out, however, viewers were treated to a drama that was entirely unexpected, even by the President. Just as Rusk was finishing his twenty-five-minute statement, he was seen being given a piece of wire copy announcing the Soviet invasion of Czechoslovakia.

In plain view of the television audience, Rusk huddled with committee chairman Hale Boggs for a moment, and then announced: "I think I should go see what this is all about." And he hurried away.

Stanton, of course, had been watching CBS, waiting for that important statement. About twenty minutes later he got a call from the President. Did Rusk show up on time? Johnson wanted to know. Yes, said Stanton, hadn't the President been watching?

"No. Dobrynin came in to tell me what happened [in Czechoslovakia], and I've been tied up. I've just convened the NSC."

"Can I use that?"

"Yes."

"Excuse me, I want to tell our people this."

Stanton hung up and passed on his scoop to CBS News.

It eventually became known that a summit meeting between Johnson and the leaders of the Soviet Union was to have been announced at the White House the next morning, August 21. But the Czech invasion killed the projected meeting, to Johnson's bitter disappointment, and there was never any White House announcement that it had even been contemplated. In retrospect, Stanton harbored some suspicion that Rusk had planned to announce the summit meeting that night on CBS. Stanton was an old friend, and a close friend of Lyndon Johnson, and he was understandably reluctant to think that the President might have been fibbing to him about Rusk having an "important statement."*

---

*Johnson's personal relationship with Stanton dated back to the early 1940's. Johnson, then a congressman, went to New York looking for a network affiliation for KTBC, the Johnson family radio station in Austin. No one at CBS was too enthusiastic about adding a small-power station in Austin to the network. At the time stations in Dallas and San Antonio covered Austin fairly

But Dean Rusk said in an interview with the author: "The announcement, whatever the President had in mind, was not the Czech invasion—I did not know the invasion had occurred until I heard about it at the platform committee." Rusk said he could not recall anything that would fit LBJ's description to Stanton of an "important statement." As for the summit meeting, "we had agreed with the Russians on the hour and date of the meeting, to be announced simultaneously in both capitals," so he could not have disclosed it that night. Moreover, Rusk pointed out, "it would have been inappropriate for me to announce a major diplomatic development at a partisan forum." Rusk said he was puzzled by the reference to an important statement; frankly, he could recall nothing of that nature in his speech.* So one is left with the conclusion that either there never was to have been any important statement, or that, to Johnson, Rusk's opposition to an antibombing plank was the important statement, important enough, at least, to justify his call to the President of CBS.

It is an illuminating little story. Quite aside from the incongruities of the President of the United States and the head of CBS dickering like Hollywood producers over how much prime time the Secretary of State could steal from Steve Allen, it shows the way things really work.

Television is a regulated industry, regulated by the government, and when the President of the United States wants network time, he calls up and gets it. Or he has one of his assistants call. Not only Lyndon Johnson, but *all* modern Presidents have had a consuming interest in television. The medium has a fascination for Presidents, an interest that is easily understood, since so much of their political success, or failure, depends on the skill with which they use it.

A telephone call from a President to the publisher of *The New*

---

well. Stanton was then in charge of research for CBS; it was his job to know whether stations overlapped or did not. Stanton pointed out that Austin filled in just a little crack between San Antonio and Dallas. KTBC got its valuable CBS affiliation; later, in 1952, it acquired a television channel (also a CBS affiliate) and Johnson became a multimillionaire. The radio and TV station formed the cornerstone of the Johnson family fortune.

*The text of the speech is consistent with Rusk's memory; it contains nothing startling. Rusk is positive that he had not planned to announce the summit meeting during his testimony. He added: "That night, when we heard about the Czech invasion, I had to call the Soviet ambassador and urge him to call Moscow to tell them not to announce the summit meeting. I remember taking considerable pains to do that."

York Times, for example, is not an unknown event, but one cannot, somehow, picture Lyndon Johnson calling up Arthur Ochs Sulzberger and saying: "Punch, Dean Rusk is going to have an important announcement tonight, and I want y'all to give it page-one treatment, eight-column head with full text and pictures. What time does your Late City close?"

But when a President calls the head of CBS, or NBC, or ABC, it is not easy, or even advisable, to brush him off. In the fall of 1971 Julian Goodman, the president of NBC, went to Rome for a staff meeting of NBC's correspondents in Europe. One of the reporters at the private meeting complained that Nixon was "using" the television networks to speak to the American people whenever he pleased, for free; he had done so something like fourteen times up to that date.

Yes, yes, I know, said Goodman, I know. But the correspondent persisted. "Julian, what is your attitude toward President Nixon's requests for television time?"

"Our attitude," said Goodman evenly, "is the same as our attitude toward previous Presidents: he can have any goddamn thing he wants."

A television network may also find it prudent to be cautious in covering a candidate for President—since he may win. During the 1960 Presidential campaign, Stanton said, he had some difficulties with Senator John F. Kennedy. Although Stanton was an intimate of Lyndon Johnson, his relations with Kennedy—at least during the campaign—were considerably less smooth.

That spring, as Stanton recalled it, CBS had selected some sample precincts in Wisconsin to measure the impact of the religious factor and the farm vote. Wisconsin was the first major primary contest between John F. Kennedy and Hubert Humphrey; as a Catholic, Kennedy's vote in rural, Protestant areas of the state would be closely watched. On election night CBS put Elmo Roper on the air from Madison, and Roper analyzed the returns. Kennedy had won, but not decisively; the religious question remained unsettled.

The Kennedy forces were not happy with the CBS telecast. Senator Abraham Ribicoff telephoned William S. Paley, chairman of the board of CBS, and Kennedy himself called Stanton.

"Jack called from the airport in Fort Wayne," Stanton said. "His voice was very strident. He objected to the CBS analysis of the primary vote in Wisconsin and said that we had raised the religious issue." Yes, Stanton said he told Kennedy, "but have you looked at the editorials? This isn't something we invented. The papers are commenting on the religious issue, too."

"But, said Jack, 'this is different. You're licensed.' That raised my blood pressure. I raised my voice. Finally I asked if he had seen the broadcast—I had to find a way out of what was an escalating conversation. He said no. I offered to send him a print, and did. That eased the atmosphere of the conversation."

Stanton said CBS received further complaints from the Kennedy camp in 1960. At one point, Stanton said, Kennedy complained to CBS correspondent Blair Clark in such forceful terms that Clark— an old friend of Kennedy from Harvard days—interrupted his coverage of the campaign to fly back to New York from the Midwest to alert the CBS president to impending danger. According to Stanton, Clark quoted Kennedy as saying: "Wait till I'm President—I'll cut Stanton's balls off."*

Stanton assumed that his difficulties with Kennedy stemmed from the network's coverage the night of the Wisconsin primary. But when Kennedy won the Presidency, the climate changed. After election, Stanton said, "Evelyn Lincoln called in December and asked whether I could come to see Kennedy in Georgetown.† Before I went I got out all my notes of incidents during the campaign because I figured this was the day I was going to have my balls cut off. But he couldn't have been more charming; never once did he get into any troubles we had during the campaign."

While Kennedy was President-elect, Blair Clark flew to Palm Beach, and Kennedy offered him the post of ambassador to Morocco; Clark reluctantly passed it up to become vice-president of CBS News. After inauguration Kennedy's relations with CBS warmed considerably, although Clark said that the President "sometimes called to complain about items on the CBS Evening News." Clark thought Kennedy might have called four times during the period that he managed CBS News. Clark left the network in 1964.

Newton Minow, the Chicago attorney whom Kennedy appointed as chairman of the Federal Communications Commission, recalls that the President on at least one occasion also expressed dissatisfaction with NBC News. The FCC, which licenses and regulates radio and television stations, is by law an independent agency,

---

*Although Clark said he did not precisely recall how Kennedy had phrased his remark, "I would not challenge Stanton's recollection. Stanton has a memory like a Xerox." Clark said he clearly recalled that JFK "wanted me to express his displeasure to Stanton."

†As President-elect Kennedy still lived in his house on N Street in the Georgetown section of Washington.

but its members are appointed by the President. So the degree of "independence" of the commission, and of its chairman, is always relative.

One night in April, 1962, Minow said, in the midst of Kennedy's fight with the steel companies, the Huntley-Brinkley show on NBC included "a long speech by somebody who took the President apart. I happened to have watched it. We were having a small dinner party at home and I was getting dressed when my wife said, 'The President is on the phone.' " As Minow recalled the conversation, it went this way:

> JFK: Did you see that goddamn thing on Huntley-Brinkley?
> MINOW: Yes.
> JFK: I thought they were supposed to be our friends. I want you to do something about that. You do something about that.

Minow said that the President definitely did not, as the story later got around in the television industry, ask that the FCC chairman take Huntley-Brinkley off the air. But, said Minow, the President "was mad."

Minow added: "Some nutty FCC chairman would have called the network. Instead I called Kenny O'Donnell [Kennedy's appointments secretary] in the morning and I said to him, 'Just tell the President he's very lucky he has an FCC chairman who doesn't do what the President tells him.' That's about the only time anything like that happened. But I got plenty of calls like that from Congress all the time."

One night at the Indian embassy in Washington, Minow recalled, "Nehru was giving a party. The President was there; it was early in the administration. He started shaking his finger at me off in a corner and saying you ought to be doing this, and you ought to be doing that. My wife, who has a big mouth anyway, heard all this and said to the President, 'You'd make a wonderful chairman of the FCC.' "

Kennedy looked at Mrs. Minow and said, "I think I make a pretty good President."

Minow remembered one call from Kennedy the day after Jacqueline Kennedy had starred in a televised tour of the White House. "The President called and said, 'Can you do me a favor and find out the rating of the program?' " Minow telephoned Stanton, who explained that the ratings would not be available for about two weeks; the next day, however, Stanton called back with some preliminary figures. Minow passed these along to the President. Perhaps sensing that Kennedy wanted to twit his wife about her ratings, he warned: "I just want you to know—it's higher than your press conference."

When Johnson was President he telephoned the president of CBS so often that it got to be a standing joke around the Stanton household on Manhattan's East Side; if the phone rang after 7:30 P.M., Stanton's wife would say: "It's Lyndon."

John Chancellor says he received fifteen or twenty calls from Johnson during the period he covered the White House for NBC; sometimes the calls were chiding, at other times the President would invite Chancellor to come to the ranch.

One typically Johnsonian call stands out vividly in Chancellor's recollection. NBC News in New York had telephoned Chancellor at the White House press room to ask him to check a report that Maxwell Taylor was about to be replaced as ambassador to South Vietnam. Chancellor tried Presidential assistant Jack Valenti, who gave a noncommittal reply. Chancellor then telephoned New York to say that his source would not confirm the story, but had not knocked it down either. "A few moments later the telephone rang in my cubicle in the White House. It was the White House operator. 'Mr. Chancellor, the President is calling. Just a moment.' I thought, Oh, brother, I am really going to get bawled out. He came on *bellowing:* 'What is this about Max Taylor?' " Chancellor told the President about the report NBC had received, and as Chancellor recalls it, the following conversation took place:

LBJ: That's not true.
CHANCELLOR: I'll report that, sir. May I quote you?
LBJ: Of course. It's not true. Why didn't you call me? I'm just down the hall from you.
CHANCELLOR: Mr. *President*, you have to run the country.
LBJ (dead silence, during which Chancellor swears he could almost hear Johnson saying to himself: "By God, I *do* have to run the country"): Well . . . don't you do that again.

By happenstance I witnessed a personal confrontation between President Johnson and Chancellor in May of 1965. Johnson led a group of reporters on a walking backgrounder during the height of the Dominican crisis. As we circled the lawn, Chancellor asked the President at what point he had learned that Communists had taken over the revolt in the Dominican Republic. It was a sensitive question, since Johnson had misled the public on that very point.

The President stopped in his tracks, glowered at Chancellor, and pushed his face close to the NBC correspondent's nose. "At no point," Johnson said angrily.

The answer seemed contradictory, since Johnson had told the nation on television the previous night that the Communists had indeed taken over.

"When did you become six foot one?" Johnson demanded.

"When I stopped being six foot one-half inch," Chancellor responded.

The two men stood toe to toe, slugging it out verbally, neither giving ground. But apparently Johnson had respect for Chancellor; a month later he named him director of the Voice of America.

When any President desires to make a television broadcast, there are standing arrangements to handle his request, procedures worked out between the White House and the Washington bureaus of the major networks. At the time Johnson was President, the networks told the White House they needed six hours to make the technical arrangements for a White House broadcast; they could do it in three, they said, but could not guarantee a good picture, or any picture. Despite this, Johnson often demanded instant access to the networks and got on the air within one hour.

Johnson used TV so frequently that finally he asked for, and the networks agreed, to provide "hot cameras," manned throughout the day in the White House theater, with continual crews at the ready. Johnson could then walk into the theater and go on the air live, immediately. During the Dominican crisis Johnson went on television on such short notice that he burst into the regular network programming with almost no introduction, startling millions of viewers.

"Once Johnson went on the air so fast," an NBC executive recalled, "that we couldn't put up the Presidential seal. When a network technician said we need a second to put up the seal, Johnson said, 'Son, I'm the leader of the free world, and I'll go on the air when I want to.'"

Another Johnson television story circulated among the top echelon of NBC News executives during the 1964 Democratic National Convention. The network was devoting extensive coverage to what was really the only news at Atlantic City: the fight over the seating of black delegates from the Mississippi Freedom Democratic Party. The President, so the story went, called Julian Goodman, later president of NBC and then an official of NBC News, to complain that there were "too many black faces on the tube."

There is a seeming paradox in Richard Nixon's view of television. On the one hand, as already noted, television saved his political career in 1952, and he has often had kind words for the medium. Recall for example, that in his 1962 false exit, he stated: ". . . thank God for television and radio for keeping the newspapers a little more honest." As President, he told columnist Cyrus L. Sulzberger of *The New York Times* in 1971: "I must say that without television it might have been difficult for me to get people to understand a thing."

On the other hand, as President, Nixon criticized the networks —for example, for filming those South Vietnamese troops who were having a little difficulty in Laos. And it was with Nixon's blessing that Spiro Agnew launched his celebrated attack on network news analysts. His administration has made systematic efforts to cow the networks and destroy the credibility of the press, including television news.

There is no inconsistency, however, if one understands that in Nixon's view, television ideally should serve *only* as a carrier, a mechanical means of electronically transmitting his picture and words directly to the voters. It is this concept of television-as-conduit that has won Nixon's praise, not television as a form of electronic journalism. The moment that television analyzes his words, qualifies his remarks, or renders news judgments, it becomes part of the "press," and a political target.

In discussing Nixon and television, therefore, one must carefully distinguish between television as a mechanical means of communication and television as an intellectual instrument. "Pure" television is okay, television news is not. As President, Nixon's use of television flowed logically from these basic premises; thus, at every opportunity, Nixon solemnly addressed the nation, but he usually avoided the give-and-take of the televised news conference. Only in the first setting did Nixon have total control—except for the analyses afterward by network newsmen, which Agnew's attacks were specifically designed to discourage. In short, to Richard Nixon, television ideally was the mirror, mirror on the wall.

Some of Nixon's love-hate relationship with television could be glimpsed in his personal relations with TV newsmen; the same President who could permit his Vice-President and other high officials to excoriate the networks occasionally went out of his way to ingratiate himself with individual television personalities.

After one major Nixon address to the nation, John Chancellor and NBC correspondent Robert Goralski stopped for a drink on the way home at a saloon called Mr. Henry's near NBC's studio in Washington. Chancellor had told his wife, Barbara, where he would be. At 11 P.M. Nixon telephoned Chancellor's house; his wife took the message and in turn telephoned the bar.

Rather than call the President from a saloon, with juke-box music, clinking glasses, and bar noise in the background, Chancellor went across the street to a pay phone on the sidewalk, dropped in his dime, and got the President. There seemed to be no particular reason for the call; Nixon just wanted to chat. "I don't watch TV," he told Chancellor, "but my daughter Tricia does and reports to me." The conversation continued along these lines, and Chancellor formed the impression that Nixon was trying to find better ways to get along with the news media. A few other reporters received similar calls.

Ever since the Lazy Shave make-up he wore in his first televised debate with John Kennedy in 1960 caused him major embarrassment, Nixon has sought and received expert technical advice on his use of television. Early in his administration the advice was provided by producer Roger Ailes. It was Ailes, according to author Joe McGinniss, who privately remarked during the 1968 campaign: "Let's face it, a lot of people think Nixon is dull . . . They look at him as the kind of kid who always carried a bookbag . . . Now, you put him on television, you've got a problem right away. He's a funny-looking guy. He looks like somebody hung him in a closet overnight and he jumps out in the morning with his suit all bunched up and starts running around saying, 'I want to be President.' I mean, this is how he strikes some people. That's why these shows are important. To make them forget all that."

After that quote was published in McGinniss' widely read book, *The Selling of the President 1968*, it is amazing that Nixon let Ailes anywhere near the White House, but for a time, at least, Ailes continued to advise the President. When Nixon addressed the United Nations in September, 1969, Ailes flew in from Cincinnati at the President's request and briefed him on the special television hazards of the General Assembly. He warned the President not to touch the button on the lectern, because it activated a hydraulic lift that would cause the platform, and therefore the President, to rise up or sink down. The overhead lighting was very strong, and Ailes also advised the President to stand back from the lectern so the lights would not deepen the shadows of his eye sockets, turning him into an animated Herblock cartoon.

In a 1969 interview in *The New York Times*, Ailes made no further mention of Nixon sleeping in closets. He praised the President as a man who knew television "cold," adding: "I can talk to him in technical language and he knows it all. He can time himself perfectly, better than most newscasters. He won't be more than a second or two off, if he knows he has to go one minute or two minutes. He's like clockwork. He understands the medium better than any politician I know."

Later Nixon hired his personal TV producer, Mark Goode, as a special assistant to the President and a member of the White House staff at a salary in the $35,000 range. Before becoming the President's television director, Goode directed comedian Pat Paulsen and singer Johnny Cash on ABC-TV. Goode banished the center aisle at Presidential news conferences in the East Room and placed a camera directly in front of Nixon. This eliminated the side-angle shots that displayed the President's profile, so often caricatured by newspaper cartoonists.

Nixon, as Roger Ailes had suggested, understood the medium, and he used it, although the public was not always conscious of that fact. For example, Nixon's triumphant returns in 1972 from both China and the Soviet Union were carefully timed to occur at an hour when the largest possible television audience would be watching. When Nixon flew back from his historic summit meeting in Peking on February 28, Air Force One, renamed "The Spirit of '76" touched down at Andrews Air Force base just after 9 P.M.—prime time on the networks. Nixon's return from Moscow on June 1 was an even more dramatic television spectacular. From Andrews, he flew by helicopter, landing, as no President had done before, at the floodlit East Front of the Capitol at precisely 9:30 P.M. to address Congress and the nation.

While cosmetics and expert technical advice could help Nixon's television image, they could not influence news judgment. But political pressure might.

The Agnew assault on the networks and the continued barrage of criticism by Agnew and other high administration officials were intended, in part, to serve as a public reminder to the networks that television is a government-licensed industry. They were also, in Walter Cronkite's words, a clear indication on the part of the administration "of a grand conspiracy to destroy the credibility of the press."

Dean Burch, who had served as chairman of the Republican National Committee during Barry Goldwater's 1964 Presidential campaign, was appointed chairman of the FCC by Nixon two weeks before the Agnew attack. Burch did more than praise Agnew's speech; he also telephoned the heads of the three major networks to demand transcripts of the commentaries on Nixon's November 3 Vietnam speech. To the networks, the signals were plain enough; by his words and actions, the theoretically independent chairman of the FCC was supporting the Vice-President.

While Agnew's attack was dramatically visible, the administration applied continuous behind-the-scenes pressure on the networks and individual newsmen in ways that the industry was aware of but the public, for the most part, was not. The pressures included a steady stream of complaints from Ziegler, Klein, Colson, and others to network executives. By telephone, letter, and personal visits, the administration made its displeasure known.

In April of 1971 John Ehrlichman, the President's chief assistant for domestic affairs, complained in person to Richard S. Salant, the president of CBS News, about Dan Rather, the network's White House correspondent. Ehrlichman was in New York to appear on the CBS Morning News with correspondent John Hart. Afterward Hart and Ehrlichman adjourned for breakfast at the Edwardian Room of the Plaza, where they were joined by Salant. Over eggs Benedict, the President's assistant brought up the subject of CBS's White House reporter.

"Rather has been jobbing us," Ehrlichman said. Salant, seeking to inject a lighter note into the conversation, told how Rather had been hired by CBS in 1962 after he had saved the life of a horse, an act of heroism that resulted in considerable publicity and brought him to the attention of the network.* It was then that Rather went to work for CBS News as chief of its Southwest Bureau in Dallas. When President Kennedy was assassinated in that city, Rather went on the air for the network, and his cool, poised coverage of the tragedy gained him national recognition. After Dallas, Salant explained to Ehrlichman, CBS brought Rather to Washington, in part because the new President, Lyndon Johnson, was a fellow Texan.

"Aren't you going to open a bureau in Austin where Dan could have a job?" Ehrlichman asked Salant. Although he said this in a jocular tone—the Nixon people were great jokers—his intent was clear. Ehrlichman then accused Rather of never coming to see him in the White House, and he suggested it might be beneficial if Rather took a year's vacation. While he was at it, Ehrlichman also accused CBS correspondent Dan Schorr of being unfair to the administration; Schorr, he said, reported what the critics said about Nixon's domestic programs, but not the administration's side.

That evening, following a Presidential press conference at the White House, Ziegler cryptically told Rather that President Nixon's obvious failure to recognize him at that conference had "no connection" with something that "you are about to hear."

Rather heard the next morning. Salant telephoned William Small, head of the CBS Washington Bureau. Small called Rather in and told him about the breakfast at the Plaza; he assured Rather that his standing with CBS was not affected. He said he was mentioning

---

*Rather, a reporter for KHOU-TV, Houston, was televised while standing on a hummock surrounded by rising flood waters. As he talked, he walked down the hill and rescued the horse.

the episode simply because sooner or later Rather was bound to learn about it. Rather told Small it was true he had not seen much of Ehrlichman at the White House—because Ehrlichman would not see him.

Now, however, Ziegler began urging Rather to see Ehrlichman and talk the situation over. Rather was reluctant at first, but ultimately a meeting did take place, in Ehrlichman's office in the White House.

When Rather walked into Ehrlichman's office, he found Haldeman waiting there as well. The conversation, with just the three men present, was blunt on both sides. As Rather reconstructed it, the dialogue proceeded as follows:

EHRLICHMAN: I wanted to tell you to your face I wasn't in New York for this purpose . . . I didn't know there was going to be a breakfast. When the conversation went in the direction it did, I told them what I thought, which is I think you're slanted. I don't know whether it's just sloppiness or you're letting your true feelings come through, but the net effect is that you're negative. You have negative leads on bad stories.
RATHER: What's a bad story?
EHRLICHMAN: A story that's dead-assed wrong. You're wrong 90 percent of the time.
RATHER: Then you have nothing to worry about; any reporter who's wrong 90 percent of the time can't last.
HALDEMAN (breaking in): What concerns me is that you are sometimes wrong, but your style is very positive. You sound like you know what you're talking about, people believe you.
EHRLICHMAN: Yeah, people believe you, and they shouldn't.
RATHER: I hope they do, and maybe now we are getting down to the root of it. You have trouble getting people to believe you.
EHRLICHMAN: I didn't say that.

At one point Ehrlichman complained that "only the President, Bob, and sometimes myself" knew what was going on, and "you're out there on the White House lawn talking as though you know what's going on."

Haldeman accused Rather of not seeking information from "high-level" White House sources. Rather replied that if Haldeman was available, he would come to see him. Backing off, Haldeman then said he had to be careful not to see reporters too much because he did not like to mislead anyone and "I know an awful lot."

Ehrlichman's comments to Salant did not succeed in dislodging Rather from the White House beat. But it was a blatant attempt at government pressure on a major television network. Rather noted that there are "a thousand ways" that an administration can make things difficult for a network. "Frequently the President comes out of a meeting and walks right over to the microphone of another network. In the nature of our screwy business, this can be devastating. When the word gets around that you are *persona non grata*, the network gets the message: We like CBS but we don't like this guy."

It is interesting that Ehrlichman, at the Plaza breakfast, also singled out Dan Schorr, for a few months later Schorr was under investigation by the FBI. Early on the morning of August 20, 1971, Ellen McCloy, Salant's secretary, received a telephone call at CBS News headquarters on West 57th Street in Manhattan. The call was from one Tom Harrington. "He's the CBS FBI man," Miss McCloy explained. "He always opens up his conversations by saying 'Tom Harrington FBI.'"

He did so on this occasion, explaining to Miss McCloy that she would be getting a call from another FBI man "who is checking on Dan Schorr." Salant was not in yet, so his secretary called him at home to alert him to the fact that the FBI was on the trail of a CBS correspondent. When the second agent called Miss McCloy, she gave him Salant's listed number in New Canaan, Connecticut. "He was in a big rush," Miss McCloy recalled. "He gave the impression he had to have the information right away." The FBI man then called the CBS News president at his home, asking for the names of people who knew Dan Schorr. In the meantime Miss McCloy called Bill Small in Washington, Schorr's boss, to let him know what was happening.

The FBI agent called Miss McCloy back twice. With Salant's permission, she provided the names of other officials for him to talk to at CBS. Salant confirmed that the FBI agent who telephoned him presented the matter as "very urgent." The sort of questions he was asked about Schorr, Salant said, were: "Was he loyal? Did he go around with disreputable people?"

Schorr, a gray-haired, bespectacled family man of fifty-five, and a veteran of eighteen years at CBS, definitely did not have the reputation of hanging around with disreputable people. A serious, hardworking newsman, he specialized in covering health, education, welfare, the environment, and economics.

As Schorr recalls the sequence of events, it began on Tuesday, August 17, when Nixon, in a speech to the Knights of Columbus, promised that "you can count on my support" to help parochial schools. The producer of the CBS Evening News—the Walter Cronkite show—called Schorr and asked for a follow-up story. Schorr went to see a source, a Catholic priest active in the field of education, who told him the administration was doing nothing to aid Catholic schools.

Wednesday night Cronkite ran a film clip of Nixon's speech promising to aid parochial schools, then cut to Schorr saying there was "absolutely nothing in the works" to help these schools. On Thursday, Alvin Snyder, Herb Klein's deputy for television, telephoned Schorr, asking him to come to the White House because "Peter Flanigan and others thought I didn't have the facts." Late in the day Schorr met at the White House with Pat Buchanan, Terry T. Bell, deputy commissioner of education, and Henry C. Cashen II, an assistant to Charles Colson. "They began reading figures off very rapidly," Schorr said. He suggested they put their main points down on paper; he would try to get it on the air.

On Thursday, the same day that Schorr was summoned to the White House, a member of the White House staff, who has never been identified by name, requested the FBI to investigate the CBS correspondent.

On Friday morning Schorr reported to the CBS studios in Washington. An FBI agent was already there questioning Small, who declined to answer until he knew the reason. "I don't know except it has to do with government employment," the FBI man said. Not having learned much from Small, the agent then wandered over to Schorr's desk and started asking routine questions—age, family, occupation?

Without thinking, Schorr began answering, then suddenly stopped and said he would not say any more until the agent specified what employment he was talking about. Since the agent would not or could not, Schorr refused to answer any more questions.

"Is that what you want me to report?"

"Yes."

"Do you mind if I ask other people about you?"

"Yes."

Schorr explained to the agent that he was in a "highly visible" occupation; it would soon get around that he was being investigated and it might seem as though he was looking for a job. And that, Schorr explained, could be harmful to his reputation and position at CBS.

"All the rest of the day," Schorr said, "calls came in from all over from people who said they had been approached by the FBI. Fred Friendly [the former president of CBS news] called from his vacation home in New Hampshire. They had telephoned him and asked to see him, but he said he would not talk to them without checking with me. They called Bill Leonard and Gordon Manning, both vice-presidents of CBS News. They called Ernie Leiser, the executive producer of CBS specials. Sam Donaldson of ABC was called. Irv Levine of NBC, who was with me in Moscow, was called; they wanted to know how I carried on as a correspondent in Moscow.

"They even checked with my brother's neighbors. The following week I was in Aspen on vacation, and my eighteen-year-old nephew telephoned. My brother, Alvin Schorr, is dean of the School of Social Work at New York University. They live at 3 Washington Mews in the Village. They were on vacation in Europe at the time, but my nephew, Kenneth, was home from college. He said, 'Hey, Danny, what does the FBI want with you?' "

Kenneth then explained that Alvin Schorr's neighbors had been questioned by the FBI. The agents wanted to know "who comes and goes at the Schorr house." When the neighbors asked why the FBI was making these inquiries, they were told that Dan Schorr was being considered for a high government post, a position of trust.

Back from vacation, Schorr, who lived in Georgetown, discovered that "the FBI had talked to my neighbors, including Marjorie Hunter of *The New York Times.*" One neighbor reported that Schorr's home had apparently been under surveillance. By now Schorr was determined to know more. "There were two theories at CBS: first, that it was a real employment investigation, and second, that it was an adverse investigation as a result of my stories on Catholic school aid. But if there was a job involved, where the hell was it?"

Schorr knew that the federal government in general wasn't hiring; Nixon's Phase One economic controls included a 5 percent cut in federal employment and a pay freeze. But the Cost of Living Council, set up by Treasury Secretary John Connally to administer the economic controls, needed people. "This was the only outfit hiring," Schorr said, "so it seemed if there was a job, it would have to be with Connally."

Through an intermediary, Schorr privately contacted Connally's press secretary, the late Cal Brumley, and asked if Brumley could find out informally whether he was under consideration for a government post. "Cal asked IRS if they had been asked to run a check on my tax returns. Brumley explained that an employment investigation had to include a check on tax returns, and if there were no such check ordered, then it could not be an employment investigation. The answer came back from IRS—negative. So it was purely an FBI investigation."

Washington is a big city, but in terms of people in the upper levels of the government and the press, it is in some ways a small town; everybody knows everybody. As it happened, on Lupine Lane in McLean, Virginia, across the Potomac from Washington, there lived two officials of rather different political persuasion. One was William C. Smith, staff director of a Senate committee, a Harvard graduate and liberal Democrat, who had directed George McGovern's Senate investigation of hunger in America.

His neighbor across the street was Frederic V. Malek, a Republican and chief of personnel in the Nixon White House. Malek, a thirty-four-year-old West Point graduate, had an unusual background. He grew up in a lower-middle-income suburb of Chicago and attended high school in Cicero. Malek is sensitive if anyone refers to his father as a "beer salesman"; he was a beer *distributor*, Malek is quick to point out. After serving in Vietnam with the Army Special Forces, Malek enrolled in Harvard Business School. In 1967 he and two partners invested $50,000 in a small hand-tool manufacturing plant in Orangeburg, South Carolina. Two years later, at age thirty-two, Malek was a millionaire.

As personnel man in the White House, Malek earned a reputation as "the Cool Hand Luke" of the Nixon administration. Critics called him a barracuda, ruthless and cold, but then, the nature of his job required a certain detachment. After Nixon fired Interior Secretary Walter Hickel in 1970, Malek personally fired five of Hickel's aides.

Despite partisan differences, the Smiths and the Maleks got to know each other, since they were neighbors and their children played together. On October 8 the Smiths invited five couples, including the Maleks, to a dinner party. Among the guests were Daniel Schorr and his wife. The dinner was something of a disaster, since Malek was politically out of place, and some of the guests were giving him a hard time.

Over Gretchen Smith's leg of lamb, within earshot of the other guests, Schorr confronted Malek. Was he being considered for a job? Why was he being tracked down by the FBI?

The FBI's investigation of Dan Schorr had not yet surfaced in the press, so the dinner-table question was a shocker. Malek, embarrassed, professed to know nothing about it. He said he would check into it and let Schorr know. Schorr had to go on television that night, and left immediately after dinner. Malek left early, too.

Schorr heard nothing further from Malek, but a month later, on November 11, the *Washington Post* published a detailed front-page story about the FBI investigation. The story said the probe had been initiated by the office of Frederic V. Malek.

The storm broke over Ronald Ziegler at the White House morning press briefing. Schorr, Ziegler told newsmen, was being checked for a job in "the area of the environment." Malek, Ziegler added, was in charge of searching "across the nation" for "qualified people." Claiming that "I am trying to be forthright with you," Ziegler nevertheless repeatedly ducked the simple, direct question of who had ordered the FBI investigation. He kept saying that ". . . it was part of the Malek process." But the transcript of the briefing does include this exchange:

Q. Is it your understanding Mr. Malek was aware that an FBI check was under way?
ZIEGLER: Yes.

The *Post* reported that Schorr had encountered Malek at a dinner party at which Malek had denied any knowledge of the investigation. How, the reporters wanted to know, did that square with Ziegler's indication that Schorr was investigated by the FBI at Malek's instigation? Ziegler, squirming by now, replied: "I talked with Fred this morning and his point was that he was surprised that Mr. Schorr did raise the matter with him and that he felt that he would not be responsive to Mr. Schorr's question at that time in fairness to Mr. Schorr . . . it was just Malek's judgment at the cocktail party not to be responsive to his question." When reporters persisted, Ziegler said: "It would be a natural human reaction to respond the way he did."

In plain English, the press secretary to the President of the United States was saying that the assistant to the President for personnel had lied to Daniel Schorr of CBS. Malek not only knew about the FBI probe, he was responsible for it.* No wonder he left the Smiths' house early.

Ziegler also said there was no FBI probe of Schorr "for any other purpose than the process which I have just described to you." There was, he said, no "intent to intimidate." Ziegler also said that the White House had not ordered an "extensive" investigation of Schorr. But in an interview published the next day Malek seemed to imply that there had been a full field FBI probe. Malek said someone on his staff—again unidentified—had asked the FBI to investigate Schorr but "the message somehow got bungled. Somehow something went wrong. Either I wasn't clear on what I wanted or the staff wasn't clear or the FBI. A breakdown occurred."

Something indeed had gone wrong, and Senator Sam J. Ervin of

---

*Reporters who attended Ziegler's briefing were told "on background," that "Fred told me . . . he had requested a complete background or biog rundown on Mr. Schorr . . ." But reporters were unable to quote Ziegler directly on this key point. Some of Malek's friends insist that the Schorr investigation was actually ordered by Charles Colson and that Malek "took the rap." Ziegler, however, denied that Colson had ordered the FBI probe.

North Carolina, a Southern defender of constitutional liberties, announced a Senate investigation of the episode.

"Job or no job," Schorr told the Ervin committee, "the launching
of such an investigation without consent demonstrates an insensitivity to personal rights. An FBI investigation is not a neutral matter. It has an impact on one's life, on relations with employers, neighbors, and friends."

Considering the administration's protestations of innocence, it
was surprising how little cooperation Ervin received. The President
declined to let any member of his staff testify—Malek, Klein, and
Colson all refused invitations—but the White House sent a letter to
Ervin, saying that Schorr "was being considered for a post that 'is
presently filled.' " The letter was signed by John W. Dean III, Counsel to the President. Nixon, the letter added, had decided that such
job investigations in the future would not be initiated "without prior
notification to the person being investigated."* On the same day the
letter was published, the *Post* quoted an unnamed White House
official as saying that the job for which Schorr had been investigated
was that of assistant to Russell E. Train, the chairman of the Council
on Environmental Quality. The story indicated that the administration thought Schorr might produce a series of television programs on
the environment.

The leak was not entirely convincing, since Train had no assistant producing TV shows, and the White House letter to Ervin dis-
tinctly said the job was "presently filled." In fact, the council had no
one with the title or duties of assistant to the chairman, and no such
job existed; the closest anyone came to that description was Jayne

---

*Until the Schorr case surfaced, however, there had never been any public
indication that the FBI had previously conducted full field investigations of
prospective federal appointees without their knowledge. Matthew B. Coffey,
who was executive assistant to John Macy, chairman of the Civil Service
Commission under Presidents Kennedy and Johnson, said that under both
administrations, *"The candidate was always aware ahead of time before they
[the FBI] went into a full field investigation."* [Emphasis added.] Coffey said
the procedure was to draw up a list of half a dozen people for a job. The FBI
would be asked to perform a "name check" on each. This meant the FBI
would check its own files and those of nine other federal agencies, but would
not talk to persons outside the government. When the President selected
one name, the candidate, after some preliminary discussion, would be offered the job. "If the person agreed, we would get a resumé from him and
order the FBI to make a full field investigation going back fifteen years,
covering previous jobs and residences."

Brumley, Train's press secretary (whose husband, Cal, had checked for Schorr and discovered that IRS had not been asked to provide his tax returns).

The most damning single piece of evidence against the administration in the Schorr affair was the fact that the White House never took the one step that could help to lay suspicions to rest. It never publicly and specifically identified the job for which Schorr was supposedly under consideration. The administration would not tell Senator Ervin. It would not tell the press; the report in the *Post* about the job being Russell Train's assistant, was, after all, entirely unofficial.*

There was some effort to whisper to reporters that the reason the job was not identified was that it was filled, and this would embarrass the incumbent; but this degree of concern and sensitivity on the part of the White House for the feelings of the unknown incumbent, while heartwarming, scarcely seemed consistent with Fred Malek's reputation. And since, if one believes the story at all, the poor fellow was about to get the boot anyway to make way for Dan Schorr, it really does strain credibility to argue that the administration would not get itself off the hook and end the controversy because of its tender regard for an official it was trying to replace.†

Months after the matter had died down, the Nixon administra-

---

*On January 18, 1972, before the *Post* story appeared, Malek called in NBC reporter Ron Nessen and offered him a $35,000-a-year job as special assistant to Train to produce a series of weekly half-hour TV programs extolling Nixon's record on the environment. Malek waved what he claimed was a letter from John Macy, then president of the Corporation for Public Broadcasting, agreeing to air the programs on public television. Malek told Nessen that this was the job "we really had in mind for Dan Schorr."

Here the plot thickens. Matthew Coffey, Macy's assistant, says Macy never wrote a letter to either Malek or Train, and had never committed public broadcasting to air any films produced by the environmental council. Nessen, who considered the films, as described by Malek, to be outright propaganda timed for the Presidential election, turned the job down. The more he pondered the interview, the more he felt he had been used in an elaborate scheme to spread the word around town that there really had been a job for Schorr.

†Dan Rather, for one, considered it most unlikely that Schorr was ever considered for an administration job, in view of the open hostility toward Schorr in the White House. Rather noted that Haldeman and Ehrlichman "always refer to Schorr as Daniel P. Schorr." Schorr's middle initial is "L," but he does not use it professionally. Curious, Rather asked Ehrlichman one day what the "P" stood for. "Prick," Ehrlichman replied.

tion privately offered Schorr yet another explanation of the FBI probe, one that directly conflicted with the White House letter to Senator Ervin saying the job for which Schorr had been considered was "presently filled." On August 14, 1972, Ziegler replied to a letter from Schorr, who had asked for an official explanation. Ziegler wrote Schorr that he had been considered for a job as assistant to the chairman of the Council on Environmental Quality, with broad responsibility to coordinate and supervise "public affairs in the area of the environment" for the council, the Environmental Protection Agency, and the Interior Department. And the job, Ziegler wrote, had never been filled.

Although Malek had considered Schorr for about ten days, Ziegler added, "Fred subsequently concluded that you and the job were not really matched . . ." No "comprehensive" FBI report was prepared, the press secretary added. "The preliminary report, which was entirely favorable, and which was forwarded to the White House, has subsequently been destroyed."

Schorr, who had a good deal of time to think about the whole thing, reached his own conclusion. The probe, he believed, was "meant to let me know I was being investigated or to get something on me."

The FBI did not confine its attentions to CBS. In 1971 J. Edgar Hoover had bitterly—albeit privately—criticized the National Broadcasting Company. On June 1 NBC's *First Tuesday* aired a segment about the FBI. The broadcast, filmed under the direction of NBC producer Eliot Frankel, included an interview with John Shaw, an FBI agent who was transferred from New York to Butte, Montana, after he had written a paper criticizing the bureau and Hoover.*

In the interview, Shaw called the FBI's new headquarters building in Washington "a monument to Mr. Hoover . . . He studies blueprints. He stands at his window and observes each slab of marble going in place." Correspondent Garrick Utley, who narrated the FBI segment, noted that the building was very secure and would even have a moat. Former FBI agents were also interviewed, and the program quoted from some of the embarrassing documents stolen from the FBI in Media, Pennsylvania, in 1972. With devastating effect, the program also interviewed John J. Rooney, Brooklyn

*Shaw, a student at the John Jay College of Criminal Justice in New York, made the mistake of having the paper typed in the FBI's New York office. Shaw resigned rather than accept the transfer to Butte, which, he indicated, was the FBI equivalent of Siberia for agents who had fallen from grace with Hoover.

Democrat and Congressional champion of the FBI; Rooney said the FBI had wiretapped Martin Luther King and then leaked information about King to him, and, as Rooney put it defiantly, "why not?"

Hoover, who was not pleased, wrote a letter to Julian Goodman, president of NBC, attacking the network, the program, the liberal news media in general, and Utley in extraordinary language seldom used by a public official. The three-page letter, dated June 3, 1971, was not made public, either by Hoover or Goodman, which is not surprising considering its contents.

The FBI director wrote that he had seen the "venomous and malicious" broadcast which had featured former FBI employees "who were either malcontents or cry babies." Only "one person, namely Honorable John J. Rooney . . . rendered a forthright statement upon the work of the bureau." Utley had even said that while the Attorney General in theory controlled the FBI, "in practice I am my own boss. Nothing could be farther from the truth . . ."

Hoover added: "The liberal communications media has certainly desperately tried to represent the FBI for some time as an American Gestapo. This is simply not true." At a time when the news media "should be supporting law enforcement, certainly the National Broadcasting Company has gone out of its way to besmear it . . ." NBC had indulged in "reckless attacks upon this bureau and your moderator did a top muckraking job."

The last phrase seeped out within the confines of NBC, and caused a good deal of quiet merriment, since among newsmen, "a top muckraking job" would be considered high praise, even though it was obviously not intended as such by Hoover.*

Like the Hoover letter to NBC, much of the pressure by government on the networks takes place out of public view. The telephone calls from White House assistants and the visits to network executives by Presidential aides are seldom publicized. For the most part, however, it was CBS that felt the greatest pressure during the Nixon administration. The official who bore the brunt of that pressure was Richard Salant, the president of CBS News.

Salant, a lawyer-turned-news-executive, occupies a high-pres-

---

*The term "muckraker" was not meant to be complimentary when President Theodore Roosevelt applied it in 1906 to reporters who were crusading against big business. But Lincoln Steffens, and others who have followed in his footsteps, did not mind the term at all, and over the years muckraker became a term of approval rather than approbation, describing reporters who exposed scandal and wrongdoing among public officials.

sure job; he wears glasses, has receding hair, and chain-smokes. Unlike some network executives, he is unusually outspoken. Salant maintains that the Nixon administration's pressures have at the very least had an adverse psychological effect on the networks. Noting that the government licenses television stations, Salant proceeded to reel off a long list of complaints, pressures, and contacts with CBS emanating from the Nixon administration.

In February of 1971, he noted, CBS did a segment on Agnew on the program *60 Minutes*. Narrator Mike Wallace reported that Agnew's grades at Forest Park High School "were mediocre at best." CBS asked to see the grades, Wallace added, "but school principal Charles Michael told us Agnew's record was pulled from the file when he became Vice-President." The program, tracing Agnew's early career, also noted that he once served as personnel director at a supermarket and, like other employees, "Agnew often wore a smock with the words 'No Tipping Please' on it."

After the broadcast, Salant said, the President's director of communications telephoned him. "Klein called and said he wanted to see me. He came to New York and came to my office and made small talk. Then he got around to the point; he said the Vice-President didn't see *60 Minutes*, he never looks at those things. *But Mrs. Agnew saw it and didn't like it.*"

Salant told Klein that *60 Minutes* had broadcast letters from viewers who did not like the Agnew program; CBS would be happy to receive a letter from Mrs. Agnew.

CBS had problems with the Nixon administration from the very start. On March 4, 1969, Salant related, *60 Minutes* broadcast a commentary on a televised news conference Nixon had held earlier in the evening to report on his trip to Europe. The commentators were Bill Moyers, former press secretary to President Johnson and, at the time, publisher of *Newsday*; Emmet J. Hughes, former adviser to President Eisenhower; and Michel de St. Pol, Washington correspondent for Agence France-Presse, the French wire service.

Their comments were not flattering—Moyers, for example, thought there was some danger that Nixon would "become boring" —and as soon as the program went off the air, a telephone call came into the control room from the White House. It was Klein, and the call was taken by Gordon Manning, vice-president of CBS News. Said Klein: "You've got Moyers; he's a Democrat. You've got Hughes; he's a liberal. And the Frenchman was a Democratic sympathizer."

Although it was eight months before Agnew's attack on the networks, the complaint was similar—television had analyzed the President's performance in critical terms, and the White House didn't like it. After Nixon's November 3 speech on Vietnam, Klein telephoned the CBS affiliates in Minneapolis and Los Angeles to ask whether they planned editorials and, if so, what they intended to say. Later that month Klein acknowledged to a group of broadcasters that he did call stations sometimes to ask about their editorial treatment of the President, but it was only to ask "which side are you on, or something like that." The stations, Klein said, had "seemed pleased" at the White House interest.

Salant, for one, did not seem pleased. Nor was he pleased when Ronald Ziegler took issue with the editorial views of WCBS, the network's radio station in New York City. In March of 1971 Ziegler wrote to Joseph T. Dembo, general manager of the station, about an editorial dealing with Agnew's attacks on the news media: "One portion of the editorial aroused my curiosity. I would appreciate your outlining for me in the most specific terms what you consider to be the Nixon administration's 'embarassing failures' at home and in Indochina."*

Sometimes, the White House employed a friendlier approach. In 1970 Frank Stanton, along with executives from NBC and ABC, attended a background briefing given by Nixon at San Clemente, California. As the network executives trooped in for lunch, they were each given a token of Presidential esteem—a box of golf balls. Salant had declined his invitation to San Clemente, because he felt news personnel should not fraternize with the President. But he was told he had not missed much; it was, according to Salant, "a rambling stream of banalities and the golf balls . . ."

In mid-1971 Stanton and other CBS executives were invited to the White House by Klein. The group met with the President, Colson, Klein, and Ziegler. Two or three times the President said, "Chuck, make a note of that," and the CBS officials came away with the distinct impression that Colson outranked the other image makers at the meeting. Stanton invited Colson to let him know if he had any complaints, and Colson took the CBS president at his word; he

---

*On one occasion John Chancellor was still on the air broadcasting the NBC Nightly News when Ziegler called the program's producer, Wallace Westfeldt, in the control room. Ziegler did not like what Chancellor was saying —namely, that the White House was under pressure to name a woman to the Supreme Court, but "only men are under consideration." At his briefing, the President's press secretary complained, he had used a phrase indicating that women were also under consideration.

Name one, said Westfeldt. Ziegler said he couldn't; and Westfeldt, a burly, combative Southerner, allowed as how there was really nothing more to discuss.

called several times, at least once to complain bitterly about Dan Schorr.

Once Klein telephoned Reuven Frank, president of NBC News, to protest a broadcast by David Brinkley. Frank became so furious that he stormed next door into the office of Richard C. Wald, the vice-president of NBC News, to let off steam.

"Relax," said Wald, "he gets *paid* to call you."

A few days later on a Saturday morning, the White House telephoned Frank at home. Frank was annoyed since he was kept waiting interminably on the line, it was his day off, and he hadn't had his breakfast yet. He started to do a slow burn again. Finally Klein came on. He was calling, he announced cheerily, to say he had seen something he *liked* on NBC; he just wanted Frank to know.

It may be that no single example of government power directed at television news means very much—Dan Rather survived John Ehrlichman's bemoanings, Salant's sympathy for Judy Agnew was limited, and so on—but taken together, such incidents constitute a pattern of pressure that has dangerous implications. It is implicit in such contacts that political leaders attempt to use the leverage of the federal regulatory power over broadcasting to influence the presentation of the news. One purpose of pressure, after all, is to try to skew the news to put the government in the most favorable light, in order to preserve and extend the power of the political leaders who are applying the pressure.

The First Amendment clearly protects the written press. But the Founding Fathers, after all, did not foresee the advent of television, and the degree to which broadcasting is protected by the First Amendment has been subject to shifting interpretation. Technology has outpaced the Constitution, and the result is a major paradox: television news, which has the greatest impact on the public, is the most vulnerable and the least protected.

Only economics limits the number of newspapers and magazines that may be published. But the number of radio frequencies and television channels is finite; the rationale for government regulation is that stations would otherwise overlap and interfere with each other. Cable television may one day erode the technological argument for government regulation by opening up an unlimited number of channels, but for the moment the networks remain under government supervision and Dean Rusk will continue, when necessary, to replace Steve Allen and the Rumanian dancers on short notice.

In pondering to what extent the Constitution protects television, the Supreme Court has spoken in a rather indistinct voice. In 1964 a radio station in Pennsylvania, operated by the Red Lion Broadcasting Company, carried a broadcast by the Reverend Billy James Hargis and his "Christian Crusade." The program attacked Fred J. Cook, the liberal journalist and author, and he demanded free time to reply under the FCC's "fairness doctrine." The doctrine requires that in reporting on controversial public issues, broadcasters must afford "reasonable opportunity for the presentation of contrasting viewpoints." It also provides for the right of reply to personal attack. In upholding the FCC's fairness doctrine, the Supreme Court, in *Red Lion Broadcasting Co., Inc. v. Federal Communications Commission,* declared in 1968 that stations did not possess "an unabridgeable First Amendment right to broadcast comparable to the right of every individual to speak, write, or publish."

So the court, in *Red Lion,* held that broadcasters had only limited constitutional protection. In 1971, however, the court appeared to take the opposite view when it ruled against George Rosenbloom, a distributor of nudist magazines in Philadelphia. A local radio station had reported Rosenbloom's arrest for possession of obscene literature; Rosenbloom was acquitted in state court, and sued the station for libel. The Supreme Court, in *Rosenbloom v. Metromedia, Inc.* decided for the station. The court, in the *New York Times v. Sullivan* and later decisions, had already ruled that public officials or public figures could not recover damages in libel suits against the news media, unless actual malice could be proved. Now the court extended the same rule to private persons like George Rosenbloom who happened to be involved in public events. The First Amendment, the court said, required freedom to report the news. Here the court seemed to be saying that the Constitution did, after all, apply to broadcast news. But, who knows.

Moreover, in recent years, the FCC has increased its enforcement of the fairness doctrine. Literally thousands of complaints have been received by the FCC from groups demanding access to the airwaves under the doctrine. By 1972 the networks were busily attempting, at enormous legal expense, to justify the fairness and editorial balance of their news programs and of documentaries on subjects ranging from airline pilots to fallout shelters. Because broadcasters must comply with complicated FCC procedures in responding to such complaints, the fairness doctrine gave the government enormous power to harass the networks.

Julian Goodman, the president of NBC, said the government places pressure on a television network for much the same reason that a baseball player argues with the umpire: "They don't expect to win the argument but they hope to make us think twice the next time."

Government pressure, Goodman declared in an interview, is

often subtle, because "government operates by a set of hand signals. Nobody sends a memo saying do this or do that; but the tone set by those at the top has a decided effect upon the actions of those below. When Agnew makes speeches, people down the line take it as a signal.

"When a tone is set by public statements or actions of administration officials, it is regarded throughout the government establishment as a policy, and it can stimulate repressive action in a variety of quarters, from staff people up. No other words need be spoken."

The government's ultimate power over radio and television is its ability to take away a license at renewal time and give it to someone else. The fact that the FCC has rarely done so does not entirely diminish the threat. Goodman said that broadcasters worried less about losing licenses than about such things as the extent to which the fairness doctrine "will be used to control news." On the other hand, according to Richard Salant, although few television licenses have been taken away by the government, "the stations are worried to death about it."

Salant accused the White House of attempting to exploit the natural tensions between the networks and their often more conservative affiliates around the country. In 1970, he said, the White House was behind a movement by CBS affiliates to send a delegation to Vietnam to dramatize their discontent with CBS coverage of the war. Salant was able to dissuade them from going through with the plan, but just barely.

As for government power over licenses, Salant noted that shortly after Agnew delivered his speech lambasting the networks, and a second speech attacking the *Washington Post*, a group including friends and former associates of President Nixon applied for the license of Channel 10, Miami, a station which happened to be owned by the *Post*. The chairman of the group attempting to take control of the station was W. Sloan McCrea, Nixon's former partner, along with Bebe Rebozo, in Fisher's Island. This sort of thing can make a broadcaster nervous.*

A little more than a month after Nixon's overwhelming re-election in 1972, the administration openly threatened to make televi-

---

*The group headed by the President's former partner eventually withdrew its challenge. Larry Israel, board chairman of the Post-Newsweek Stations, said he did not "attach any political significance" to the takeover attempt. In January of 1973 ownership of the Post-Newsweek TV station in Jacksonville, Florida, was challenged by a company whose president was Nixon's Florida finance chairman in the 1972 Presidential campaign.

sion license renewals dependent on the nature of a station's news broadcasts. Clay T. Whitehead, Nixon's director of telecommunications, warned: "Station managers and network officials who fail to act to correct imbalance or consistent bias in the networks—or who acquiesce by silence—can only be considered willing participants, to be held fully accountable . . . at license renewal time."

Public television, dependent on Congress for funds, is even more susceptible to government intervention than the networks. The Nixon administration made no secret of its discontent with public television. In July of 1972 Nixon vetoed a bill to increase the budget of the Corporation for Public Broadcasting. Nixon's ire was not directed at Bert, Ernie, and Big Bird—he specifically exempted *Sesame Street* from his criticism—but at public television news and documentaries. Nixon noted "widespread concern" that control over public television was becoming centralized instead of remaining in the hands of local stations. But the argument over centralization versus local autonomy masked the administration's real complaint—that public television was run by a bunch of Eastern liberals and high-salaried former network newsmen. Put Agnew on every night, instead of Bill Moyers and Sander Vanocur, the White House seemed to be saying, and you will have no trouble getting your funds.

All of this was complicated by the fact that government does have a legitimate role in regulating broadcasting in the public interest. Questions of fairness and of access to the airwaves for the powerless necessarily involve government intervention on behalf of the public. At the same time regulation means that both private and public television are acutely vulnerable to government pressure. The dilemma is insoluble; what is regulated cannot also be free.

"The pressure," according to Walter Cronkite, "is on the affiliates—this is where it hurts, pressure on the little guy who can be harassed right out of business. He doesn't have a full-time legal service, the way the networks do. If his congressman is unhappy with the way the station is handling its political reporting, it's got to give the station owner or manager pause. He can't *afford* to be called to Washington. By the same token, the advertising pressure can be particularly powerful when a station is operating on a thin margin of profit. It can lose that margin with the loss of one advertiser. The advertiser who has reason to get along with Washington—because of postal rates, or truck permits, or other reasons—this guy is called by a congressman or by the White House; that's where the pressure is."

Cronkite believes the Nixon administration attacked the news media "to raise the credibility of the administration. It's like a first-year physics experiment with two tubes of water—you put pressure on one side and it makes the other side go up or down." He added:

"I have charged that this is a 'conspiracy.' I don't regret my use of that word."

By applying constant pressure, in ways seen and unseen, the leaders of the government have attempted to shape the news to resemble the images seen through the prism of their own power.

The men who produce and broadcast television news are understandably reluctant to admit that they have been influenced by this pressure. But since they are human, it would be hard to conclude they have not. The administration's attacks, Richard Salant acknowledged, have "made us all edgy. We've thought about things we shouldn't think about."

12

The Government
and the Press:
Leaks and Techniques

On the night of July 27, 1971, Albert R. Hunt, a young economic reporter for the Washington Bureau of the *Wall Street Journal*, received a telephone call from the White House.

The caller was DeVan L. Shumway, an assistant to the Nixon administration's director of communications, Herb Klein. "I have something that will interest you," Shumway told Hunt.

The *Wall Street Journal* correspondent went immediately to Shumway's office. "He started to read some handwritten notes," Hunt said, "and told me the information was only attributable to White House officials."* Shumway told Hunt that Nixon "has under serious consideration" asking Congress to "bring the Federal Reserve [Board] into the Executive Branch." The President, Shumway said, was "furious" with the Fed's chairman, Arthur F. Burns, for repeatedly calling for a wage-price review board to control the economy. Moreover, said Shumway, still consulting his notes, Burns was "hypocritical"; while talking about anti-inflation measures, he was "trying to get his own salary raised" from $42,500 to $60,000.

---

*Although Hunt readily discussed the episode related here, professional ethics did not permit him to identify the White House aide by name or position. Through other sources, however, the author was able to make positive identification of Shumway as the official.

The following conversation then took place:

HUNT: This is a hell of a story!
SHUMWAY *(innocently)*: It is?
HUNT: Yes . . .

Hunt then pressed Shumway for more information. The White House aide provided it, assuring Hunt that the *Journal* had the story exclusively. The next morning Hunt arrived at his office early to write his piece. He was stunned to find that UPI had a story on the wire saying that Nixon was considering enlarging the size of the Federal Reserve Board and that Arthur Burns wanted a salary increase.

Furious, Hunt telephoned Shumway, who soothingly explained that the part about packing the board was incorrect, and that Hunt had the story right. Hunt wrote his story, but not the way the White House had calculated. The administration, he wrote, was "escalating its war of nerves" with the board; the previous night "a White House aide summoned a reporter" to say that the President was thinking about ending the board's independence, and that Burns was seeking a pay raise. The purpose of the maneuver, the story said, was to silence Arthur Burns.

The White House had bungled a leak, and the story had backfired.

What had happened was that Shumway, before meeting with Hunt, had summoned to his office another reporter, Norman Kempster of UPI. For three years in the late 1950's Kempster had worked for UPI in Sacramento, California. His boss there, the head of the state capital bureau, was DeVan Shumway.

Shumway, a short man with thinning hair and black horn-rimmed glasses, had never expected to get mixed up in *this* sort of thing when he left UPI. He had resigned from the wire service in 1970 to take a job in Washington as deputy public relations director of the Department of Health, Education, and Welfare, but suddenly the job dissolved. Klein, presumably feeling some sympathy, and perhaps some responsibility, for Shumway's having burned his reporting bridges behind him, invited the former UPI man to become his assistant. Now Shumway had a story for Kempster, and he came directly to the point.

"Burns has been making speeches calling for wage controls," Shumway told his former associate. "It may interest you to know that Burns himself has been seeking a salary increase. His arguments on wage controls are so persuasive that the President is starting with Burns. He is disallowing his salary increase."

Kempster (who also declined to identify Shumway to the author) returned to his office armed with what was clearly a scoop. As he was preparing to write it, Shumway telephoned him with more information. The Federal Reserve Board, he said, has been too much of a "closed club," and "only by doubling its size can it really function reliably." Kempster had planned to lead with the Burns salary increase, but on reflection he thought that enlarging the board was a better story; it could be compared with Franklin Roosevelt's attempt to pack the Supreme Court in 1937. He moved that up into the lead and handed in his story. It went out across the United States on the A-wire around 3 A.M. under Norman Kempster's byline.

Hunt, determined to find out the background of the anti-Burns leak—which was more than normally malicious—checked with several sources. "To a man they came back and told me it was Colson who had instigated the leak. There is no doubt in my mind that Colson instigated this." Other sources independently confirmed to the author that it was Colson who had instructed Shumway to leak the story.*

"They just wanted to intimidate Arthur Burns," Hunt said. "Burns was making it very uncomfortable for them. He was talking every week about the need for a tough wage-price policy." Although Burns had been Nixon's counselor and economic adviser before the President appointed him to the Federal Reserve Board, Hunt added, "he did not get along with the Germans on the White House staff, and he had disdain for their intellectual capacity. The White House felt that Burns was not increasing the money supply fast enough."

Hunt assumed that the White House decided to leak the story as a sort of one-two punch, with a wire-service exclusive followed up by an in-depth analysis in the prestigious *Wall Street Journal.* "They not only did it in a clumsy way," he said, "but on the salary raise, they lied. It just wasn't true."

An administration official with knowledge of the background to the leak said that while there had been some discussion within the White House of raising the salary of the chairman of the Federal

---

*Poor Shumway. In 1972 he went to work for the Committee for the Re-election of the President, and it fell to him to try to explain to the press why the committee's security chief was one of five men arrested in June, 1972, for bugging the Watergate headquarters of the Democratic National Committee; and why two of the suspects had address books listing the name of Everette Howard Hunt, Jr., the former CIA official who had been hired as a White House consultant by—Charles W. Colson. Hunt was later indicted in the bugging case and pleaded guilty.

Reserve Board and of the director of the Office of Management and Budget to match cabinet salaries, Burns himself was *not* requesting this.

And Nixon said as much. On August 4 Nixon held a press conference. He was asked if he was still "resolutely opposed" to wage-price controls. He replied that the question gave him a chance "to set the record straight with regard to some greatly blown-up differences that I am supposed to have with my very good friend Arthur Burns." Burns, the President went on, had been the victim of "a very unfair shot." OMB had recommended that the chairman of the Federal Reserve Board receive a pay increase, Nixon said, but "Dr. Burns . . . indicated that neither he nor any other individual in a high position in government should take a salary increase" at a time when the President was limiting pay increases for blue-collar government workers.

As far as wages and prices were concerned, Nixon added, "guidelines in this country have always failed. They have never worked."

Eleven days later Nixon stunned the nation by going on television to announce a ninety-day freeze of wages and prices. In October he announced Phase Two of his economic plan—a sweeping program of wage and price controls administered by an elaborate new structure of boards and commissions. It was a startling reversal of traditional Republican opposition to government controls, and of Nixon's own pronouncements. Nixon had adopted the very policies that Burns had been proposing all along.

The Burns affair demonstrated that the Nixon administration did not hesitate to use political sabotage techniques even on a Republican—an official who held one of the more prestigious posts in the federal government and who had served as the President's personal adviser. The episode left at least one unanswered question: Had Charles Colson acted on instructions from the President when he ordered Shumway to leak the story?

The White House effort to damage the Chairman of the Federal Reserve Board told a great deal about the process of official leaking in Washington: the leak was initiated at a high level—Colson was one of the most influential operators in the Nixon White House—it was politically motivated, and given to the press on condition that the leaker's identity be concealed. At the same time attribution to "White House officials" was permitted so that the story would carry authority.

Since the leak was anonymous, it could be denied if trouble arose —and in this case the denial came from an unusually high source, the President himself. The technique had an additional advantage; even if it became necessary to issue a denial, the original charge would remain in the public's mind. For months afterward Burns and his associates found it necessary to assure people that the chairman of the Federal Reserve Board had really not been pushing for a salary increase.

Normally the leaker can count on competitive pressures within the news media to insure publication of the story. The reporter who believes he possesses an "exclusive" is usually impelled to write it.

The news leak is a major weapon used by government for a variety of purposes: to mislead, to silence a political opponent, to test public or Congressional reaction to a program under consideration, to signal the leaders of another nation, to marshal public support for a President, or a policy, to deny an embarrassing story, and, in various other ways, to influence and manipulate the news and the electorate.

The practice is even older than the republic. The only news to be released by the framers of the Constitution during their deliberations at Philadelphia in 1787 came in the form of a statement leaked to the *Pennsylvania Herald* in August. The delegates had been meeting in secret, and as a result, there were all sorts of rumors about what they were doing, including one report that the convention intended to establish a monarchy. "Tho' we cannot, affirmatively, tell you what we are doing," the leaked statement said, "we can, negatively, tell you what we are not doing—we never once thought of a king."*

Another kind of leak—unofficial and unauthorized—usually has as its goal embarrassing the administration, or attacking a particular program, political leader, or bureaucrat. A White House assistant, for example, calls in a reporter to throw cold water on a rumored cabinet appointment. (He may, of course, act out of conviction that he is helping the President, because he believes the appointment will create political problems.) The Pentagon Papers and the Anderson papers, which revealed NSC-level discussions during the India-Pakistan war, are examples of spectacular unofficial leaks.

In 1968, during the Johnson administration, a leak counter to official policy had a significant impact on domestic political events and the course of the war in Vietnam.

---

*Like a number of modern leaks, the statement was not entirely accurate, although it was generally correct. Two months earlier, on June 18, Alexander Hamilton did propose a virtual monarchy in the form of a lifetime President. "The English model was the only good one," he told the delegates. And everyone knew what "the English model" meant. Hamilton's plan won no support. But the phrase, "we never once thought" is, at the very least, ambiguous.

The story of the leak began in the most unlikely of settings, a small gathering of Washington members of Skull and Bones, the most prestigious of the Yale University secret societies. The party was held March 1 at the home of Representative William S. Moorhead, the Pittsburgh Democrat, and among the guests were his classmate, Edwin L. Dale, Jr., Washington economic correspondent of *The New York Times*, and Townsend Hoopes, the Under Secretary of the Air Force. All three were members of "The Bones."* At the party, Dale learned from casual conversation with Hoopes that he and other Pentagon officials were opposed to sending great numbers of additional troops to Vietnam.

Dale reported this conversation to the Washington Bureau of the *Times*, and Hedrick Smith and Neil Sheehan went to work on the story. From Congressional sources they learned the size of a specific troop request pending before President Johnson. On March 10 the *Times* published a story headlined: "Westmoreland Requests 206,-000 More Men, Stirring Debate in Administration." A headnote said the article had been written by Smith and Sheehan, assisted by Max Frankel and Dale.

The story broke on a Saturday night, during the white-tie dinner of the Gridiron Club, an annual ritual gathering of journalists and government officials, and it caused a sensation in the grand ballroom of the Statler-Hilton as the word of the story spread. The recent Communist Tet offensive had already shaken public confidence in the ability of the United States to achieve a military victory in Vietnam. Following as it did so soon after the news of Tet, the story of the huge troop request came as a near mortal blow to the Johnson administration. Two days later Senator Eugene McCarthy made an unexpectedly strong showing in the New Hampshire Presidential primary. Four days after that Robert Kennedy announced his candidacy for the Democratic nomination, and on March 31 Johnson stunned everyone by announcing he would not run for President again.

Johnson was furious at the leak. He wrote in his memoirs that he suspected it had come from "Pentagon civilians" with "more than a little political motivation behind their action, since the article appeared two days before the New Hampshire primary." A dissident official, Johnson wrote, "has no right to sabotage his President and his own government from within." Johnson also insisted he never intended to send anything like 206,000 men.

---

*Hoopes was admitted to "The Bones" in the class of 1944 and was a member of the group that "tapped" Moorhead and Dale.

In 1971 Philip Potter of the *Baltimore Sun,* a veteran reporter who enjoyed the confidence and respect of Lyndon Johnson, wrote a story identifying Hoopes as the source of the *Times* article. The Potter story said that Hoopes had mentioned to Dale a specific "request" by General Westmoreland for 206,000 troops.

After this version of the leak was repeated in a column in the *Washington Post,* Hedrick Smith and Neil Sheehan took the unusual step of jointly writing the *Post* to say that Hoopes "did not provide the controversial figure" to the *Times.* Hoopes sent a letter to the *Post* as well, confirming his dinner-party talk with Dale, but insisting he had not disclosed "the dimensions or details of any troop request."

In an interview with the author, Hoopes said he is certain he did not mention a specific figure to Dale; and he doubts that he mentioned that any troop request was pending, although he said he cannot recall the conversation with sufficient clarity to rule out that possibility.* According to Dale, however, Hoopes did not mention that a specific request was pending and gave no figures.

The Vietnam troop leak was an echo of an earlier controversy over leaks that occurred during the Eisenhower administration. In 1956 the Pentagon was a sieve, as the Army, Navy, and Air Force competed for greater power and a bigger share of the defense budget by leaking their arguments to the press. On May 19 Anthony Leviero of *The New York Times* revealed the dimensions of the inter-service rivalry and quoted from staff papers. Secretary of Defense Charles E. Wilson called a press conference and denied everything. Then on July 13 Leviero disclosed that the Joint Chiefs were considering a proposal to cut back American military manpower by 800,000 men.

That did it. Wilson appointed what may have been the only official United States government committee on leaks.† He named three retired generals and a retired admiral to the committee, and

---

*Hoopes provided a revealing account of the events of March, 1968, the troop request, and the reversal of Johnson's policy of escalation in Vietnam in his book *The Limits of Intervention,* published in 1969. The book infuriated Johnson and some of his intimates; Jack Valenti, the President's former aide, took the trouble to find out how many times Hoopes had been in the White House—presumably he was able to consult Secret Service logs or other records—and went around town citing the infrequency of Hoopes' presence in the Executive Mansion as proof of the book's unreliability. It was an entirely new standard for judging historical accuracy.

†Officially it was known by a more dignified title: the Committee on Classified Information.

as its chairman, he appointed Charles A. Coolidge, a Boston lawyer and a former Assistant Secretary of Defense.

The Coolidge committee reported in November, and among its more ominous recommendations were the convening of special "courts of inquiry" inside the Pentagon in case of "serious" leaks— Coolidge did not say whether they would be manned by kangaroos —and the use of federal grand juries to force reporters to name their sources. But the committee also reached some unexpected conclusions that Wilson could not have welcomed: it found that "overclassification has reached serious proportions" in the Defense Department and that such excessive secrecy was, in itself, responsible for leaks.

It is hardly necessary to add that the Coolidge committee did not stop any leaks. The practice is too well established, and too much a part of the government information process, to be rooted out by a committee.

"There is an art to leaking," according to Jack Rosenthal, a former practitioner as press spokesman for the Department of Justice. "One kind of leak is the weak story which might not get much play, but if leaked to the right reporter it will get printed and force other papers to pick it up. Every professional will know how to do that. He'll know who's the guy's competitor, so when he comes in to bitch about the story, he'll have something ready for him."

Often, as the more sophisticated Washington observers are aware, the way to spot the person who has leaked a story is to see which official is most indignant about it or denies its accuracy most vigorously. To cover their traces, leakers have even been known to launch official investigations into the source of a news story, privately hoping, of course, that the investigators will not go so far as to uncover the culprit.

Sometimes the investigations of leaks smack more of a police state than of a democracy. In September, 1971, lie detectors operated by CIA agents were used on State Department employees, and the FBI was turned loose, in an effort to find out who had leaked information to *The New York Times.* When the story broke, State Department spokesman Robert J. McCloskey confirmed that the FBI was questioning State Department personnel to find the source of "stories harmful to the national interest."

The next day Secretary of State William P. Rogers held a news conference and implied that the leaks had violated the Espionage Act. The FBI was apparently concentrating on two *Times* stories, one by William Beecher, disclosing U.S. negotiating strategy at the SALT talks, and another by Tad Szulc about arms shipments to Pakistan. "Is there anything wrong with investigating a crime when it occurs?" Rogers blustered. He brushed aside a question about lie detectors, saying he did not want "to go into any investigative techniques."*

While the news leak may be used to distort the truth and mislead the public—as the White House tried to do, for example, in hatcheting Arthur Burns—paradoxically the device, especially the unofficial leak, is one of the most important tools available to reporters covering the government. Washington is fragmented. Not only are there three branches of government, and the quasi-independent regulatory agencies, but within the executive and legislative branches there are hundreds of departments, bureaus, and Congressional committees. Outside of the government, but closely interacting with it, are the interest groups and lobbyists. Because there are so many competing coalitions of power, which Douglass Cater has called "subgovernments," the Washington correspondent is often able to obtain information that would not be available in a more orderly, homogenized political system.

In a widely discussed article in *Commentary* in March, 1971, Daniel P. Moynihan, who served Presidents Kennedy, Johnson, and Nixon, criticized the American press at length. One of his targets was the news leak; Washington reporters, he said, "depend heavily on more or less clandestine information from federal bureaucracies which are frequently, and in some cases routinely, antagonistic to Presidential interests." And leaks were very upsetting to officials, Moynihan added. "I have seen a senior aide to a President, sitting over an early-morning cup of coffee, rise and literally punch the front page of *The New York Times.*"

One might argue that the number of front pages punched by government officials in Washington could be regarded as a pretty good index of whether the press is doing its job. (In some less tolerant societies, it is the reporters who are jailed and punched, or worse.)

Moynihan asserted that the leak process "means, among other things, that the press is fairly continuously involved in an activity that is something less than honorable. Repeatedly it benefits from the self-serving acts of government officials who are essentially hostile to the Presidency . . . Too much do they [the press] traffic in stolen goods, and they know it."

---

*Although the FBI was ordered to conduct the investigation at the State Department, the CIA experts were called in to administer the lie-detector tests. FBI director Hoover, in a letter to the *Washington Post,* indignantly denied published reports that his agents had used lie detectors. He did not mention, nor did the Secretary of State, that the tests had been administered by another agency of the federal government. It made little difference to those who were wired to the polygraphs.

Although Moynihan did not raise it, there is a legitimate question buried in this: that of the moral responsibility of a government official to speak out if he sees corruption or gross waste and inefficiency. The official in this position is in a dilemma; he is torn by loyalty to the government and the administration, and loyalty to the American people. There are no easy formulas to apply when this happens, and each public servant must follow his own conscience when the dilemma arises. The personal cost may be high. A. Ernest Fitzgerald, the Air Force official, exposed a two-billion-dollar-cost overrun in the C-5A aircraft program, and was hounded out of his job in return. Would anyone seriously argue that reporters should ignore or suppress similar information when it is offered to them?

Even in more routine cases, Moynihan's view of the dynamics of relations between the American government and the American press is surprisingly narrow. A reporter who develops news sources within the bureaucracy which help him to inform the public is not involved in an activity that is "less than honorable." He is engaging in an occupation that is essential to the functioning of a democratic system, and therefore, one would hope, honorable.

In a published reply to Moynihan, Thomas B. Ross, chief of the *Chicago Sun-Times* Washington Bureau, took exception to the phrase "stolen goods." Noting that the press depends on leaked information, Ross asked: "Who, after all, owns the government and its store of information? The President or the people? . . . The press will continue to rely on the leak, its lifeline to unauthorized truth . . ."

When a leak takes place in a group setting, it is called a "backgrounder." Both reviled and defended, the backgrounder remains a major institutional link between press and government. There are two kinds: the background session called by a government official, to which reporters are invited, and the background meeting initiated by the press.* The type of news that results from each may vary somewhat; the backgrounder initiated by an official is usually held to

---

*Beginning in 1966 during the Johnson administration, and continuing under Nixon, officials regularly attended breakfast meetings with the press organized by Godfrey Sperling, Jr., national political correspondent of the *Christian Science Monitor.* These sessions, generally on the record but sometimes on background, were held in the Federal City Club and attended by about twenty correspondents. Several other such groups existed. Some are transitory; others, like the Overseas Writers, which holds regular "deep background" lunches, are long-established.

discuss a specific policy or a developing situation; the news emanating from a background breakfast or luncheon sponsored on a regular basis by a group of reporters is likely—although not always—to have more of a random quality.

The official who holds a backgrounder is, by mutual agreement, not identified by name, although sometimes his identity becomes known and is published. The form of attribution varies. The information may be attributable to "administration officials" or, somewhat less vaguely, to "White House officials," "State Department officials," or officials of some other department of government. At the other end of the scale is no attribution at all, usually known today as "deep background" and among older Washington reporters as "the Lindley rule," so named in honor of Ernest K. Lindley, a former *Newsweek* correspondent. Under this rule, the reporter must state the information on his own authority.

Woodrow Wilson frequently demanded that reporters attribute his statements to an "official spokesman," and Calvin Coolidge's press conferences were, in effect, boring backgrounders. Coolidge would drone on at great length about inconsequential affairs of state, but his comments were attributable only to a mythical "White House spokesman" whom Coolidge had invented. Other officials held backgrounders from time to time in Washington prior to World War II, and the practice became firmly established during the war, when General George C. Marshall and Admiral Ernest J. King met informally but anonymously with newsmen on a regular basis. Douglass Cater has written that the backgrounder grew "almost haphazardly. Admiral King agreed to meet with a few reporters at a relative's home in Alexandria, Virginia. It was early November, 1942, a time when continued Japanese sinking of Navy ships was creating a national morale problem. King, though ordinarily a hard-bitten and taciturn naval officer, came to enjoy these informal get-togethers and, according to one who attended, 'learned to make use of the press with the skill of a public relations counsel.'"

After the war the backgrounder gradually became accepted as an almost daily channel of communication between government and press. President Eisenhower held background dinners and meetings fairly frequently; President Kennedy, on occasion; President Johnson, almost compulsively; and President Nixon, hardly at all. Some recent Secretaries of State and Defense—Rusk and McNamara, for example—often met the press on a background basis. Laird avoided backgrounders and Rogers held them infrequently. In the Nixon administration it was Henry Kissinger who emerged as the principal background briefer. Kissinger held lengthy and frequent background sessions, the transcripts of which sometimes ran to fifty pages.*

During the Eisenhower administration Admiral Robert B. Carney held a backgrounder that touched off a major war scare and vastly embarrassed the President. On March 24, 1955, the admiral, an Indochina hawk before his time, met with a group of reporters over dinner in a private room at the Statler Hotel. On "deep background," and not for attribution, Carney told the newsmen that Communist China could capture the Nationalist-held offshore islands of Quemoy and Matsu. "They will probably initiate an attack on Matsu in mid-April," he said.

A reporter persisted: "What we face then in April is a general war?"

"Very possibly," said Carney, "unless they are convinced we mean business."

The next day Anthony Leviero of *The New York Times* filed a long story, which led the paper, and was headlined:

U.S. EXPECTS CHINESE REDS
TO ATTACK ISLES IN APRIL;
WEIGHS ALL-OUT DEFENSE

POLICY RESTUDIED

Eisenhower May State
Get Tough Decision
at Coming Talks

Within a few days Carney's identity as the source of the war scare had leaked out and been published. Presidential press secretary James C. Hagerty, fighting fire with fire, held a counter background dinner, at which he told newsmen that Eisenhower did not agree with Carney's prediction. Majority Leader Lyndon Johnson arose in the Senate to attack "some who are talking war." In a prescient, if

---

*The transcript of Kissinger's briefing at Hartford, Connecticut, on October 12, 1970, which runs to fifty-one legal-sized, single-spaced pages, is marked: "BACKGROUND BRIEFING . . . may be attributed to administration officials. Direct quotation not permitted." This was one of a series of regional backgrounders held for local editors and newsmen. Herb Klein, in introducing Kissinger, declared that the meeting would be on a background basis, attributable to "administration sources, or White House sources, but probably administration sources would be the best phrase."

unwitting, description of his own later involvement in Vietnam, Johnson declared that "it would be folly to jeopardize our future through an irresponsible adventure for which we have not calculated all the risks."

On March 30 Eisenhower held a press conference and rebuked Carney by saying that anyone—Eisenhower mentioned no names— who predicted war in the Formosa Strait in April had information "that I do not have." A week later Carney, falling back on the oldest dodge in town, told a Senate committee that he had been misquoted. Unfortunately for the admiral, Robert L. Riggs of the *Louisville Courier Journal* had recorded the entire Carney backgrounder in expert Gregg shorthand. Riggs was outraged that the Chief of Naval Operations could predict war and, under the background rules, not be identified. Moreover, under those rules, Riggs himself could not quote from his shorthand notes to refute Carney's denial. He discussed his despair with Robert Roth of the *Philadelphia Bulletin* and showed him his stenographic record. "I don't suppose you'd let me have it?" asked Roth helpfully.

Riggs decided he would. Roth, who had not attended the dinner and was therefore not under any restrictions, wrote a story for his paper quoting Carney verbatim and at length. The admiral was permanently piped ashore by Roth; it had been expected that Carney would be reappointed to the Joint Chiefs, but two months later Eisenhower replaced him as CNO with Rear Admiral Arleigh A. Burke.

At the beginning of the Kennedy administration a backgrounder held by Defense Secretary Robert S. McNamara proved almost equally disastrous. In the last two years of the Eisenhower administration a controversy had swirled in Washington over whether the United States lagged behind the Soviet Union in the development of strategic missiles.

Senator John F. Kennedy of Massachusetts announced his campaign for the Democratic Presidential nomination on January 2, 1960. In a confidential memo to Kennedy dated the same day, Professor Walt W. Rostow of MIT outlined his ideas for Kennedy's campaign strategy. As his first point, he urged that the senator stress the "missile gap." Said Rostow: "The military issue is decisive for two reasons: first, nothing is more likely to swing votes than the conviction that the Republicans have endangered the nation's safety . . . This is truly a gut issue if it can be developed in detail . . . The missile gap can be used as the Charles Van Doren of the Republican administration."

This line of attack, Rostow argued, combined with an assault on the Republican slogan of peace and prosperity, might goad Nixon into breaking ranks with Eisenhower. And that, said Rostow, would be "the ultimate rag of Tricky Dick—letting down the boss who made him . . ."

Kennedy seized the "missile gap" issue and turned it into a major campaign theme. Deirdre Henderson, the coordinator of Kennedy's Cambridge group of academic advisers, prepared a thirty-page draft of a defense speech, based on material submitted by several of the academic advisers. The draft referred to the "missile gap," and said it would not end until the United States had "a sufficient force of solid fuel, mobile missiles." In a speech on the floor of the Senate on February 29, Kennedy attacked the missile gap, using portions of the draft. In September and October, during the Presidential campaign he repeatedly charged that America faced a "missile gap."

On the evening of February 6, 1961, less than three weeks after Kennedy's inauguration, Defense Secretary McNamara invited Pentagon reporters to his third-floor office in the E-ring. Over cocktails and dinner, with the floodlit dome of the Capitol visible through the window, McNamara talked on background about a number of defense problems, including the relative missile strength of the United States and the Soviet Union.

The next morning stories were widely published saying that the Pentagon had tentatively concluded there was, after all, no "missile gap." McNamara, fresh from his $400,000-a-year post as president of the Ford Motor Company, was not yet wise in the ways of Washington; he had inadvertently touched off a major political crisis for the new President. At the White House, press secretary Pierre Salinger huddled with public relations experts from the Pentagon and the State Department, then called in newsmen to announce that no such finding about the nonexistence of the missile gap had been made.

It was an open secret in Washington that McNamara was the source of the embarrassing story. The next day Kennedy held a news conference. He had talked with McNamara, he said, and no conclusion had been reached "as to whether there is a missile gap or not." Republicans pounced on this, asking how Kennedy had, in that case, been so sure of a gap during the Presidential campaign. Eventually the controversy faded from the front pages, but it was an excruciatingly awkward affair for both McNamara and the new administration.

For Lyndon Johnson, the backgrounder was an art form, and it was in this relaxed, informal setting that Johnson was at his best: anecdotal, alternately funny or moody, earthy or dignified, but above all, himself. Up close, and free of the formality of a press conference, Johnson was a fascinating personality, far more attractive for all of his warts than the pious, false persona he presented on television.

Early in 1964, after he had been President for about six weeks, he invited a few Washington reporters for a long evening at the ranch. Johnson talked expansively about subjects ranging from the defense budget to his boyhood in Texas. He had already notified Scoop Jackson and Dick Russell, he said, that he was curtailing production of atomic warheads. The weapons manufacturers would like to go on making missiles forever if they could. "Hell, that's like me. I'd like to sell four hundred thousand steers, not four hundred."*

He talked about the responsibilities of his office, how the United States had the nuclear capacity "to kill a hundred million people in thirty minutes, and so do the Russians." No, he had not really had a chance to study Vietnam in detail yet, but he was thinking of relieving General Paul Harkins. "You wind up with fourth-stringers out there because first-class men don't want to go. They don't want to go down with a sinking ship."

Now he was talking about how he had persuaded a reluctant Chief Justice Warren to head the investigation of President Kennedy's assassination. At first Warren told a Presidential emissary that he couldn't possibly do it. So he had replied: "Well, tell him to come on down here and say it to me face to face." And when Warren had come to the White House, he told the Chief Justice he knew he had been a first lieutenant in World War I, and he knew Earl Warren would walk across the Atlantic Ocean to save the lives of *three* Americans, and possibly a hundred *million* lives were at stake here, the future of the whole country, and he had concluded: "I'm putting you back in that uniform; and never mind what some puny-faced associate justice might say." And so Warren, after all that, could hardly say no. The President said that he had already asked Senator Russell to serve on the commission, and Russell had agreed. But when the senator from Georgia learned that the Chief Justice of the integrationist Supreme Court was to head the commission, he told Johnson: "I wouldn't sit in the same room with him." And Johnson added with a big grin: "So I went ahead and appointed him [Russell] anyhow."

---

*This and subsequent Johnson backgrounders quoted here took place during the period when the author was chief of the Washington Bureau of the *New York Herald Tribune*. A newsman who accepts information on a background basis is clearly under obligation not to disclose its source contemporaneously. At some point, however, a President's private musings to the press become part of the historical record; although the rules of backgrounders are ill-defined on this question, I do not believe anyone would seriously contend that they extend indefinitely into the future, long after a President is out of office.

An accomplished raconteur, Johnson began to tell political anecdotes. He recalled how old Magnus Johnson, a Swedish congressman from Minnesota, once arose in the House and proclaimed: "The only t'ing to do is to grab the bull by the tail and look the situation in the face."

When he was a boy, LBJ recounted, he had competed in a declamation contest with a German lad named Walter Peter. Johnson had represented Stonewall, and he still remembered how he had ended his own speech: "The most glorious sight these eyes ever beheld was the flag in a foreign land." Walter Peter had spoken broken English, but the judges were German and they gave the first prize to Walter Peter. He had that in mind when he told Ludwig Erhard, the Chancellor of Germany, that he didn't want to run against him in Fredericksburg.*

Then he was talking about Nixon's 1950 Senate campaign against Helen Gahagan Douglas; all she wanted to do was feed hungry people, "and Nixon had called her a Communist. She was no more a Communist than I was." That was one of the dirtiest campaigns ever run.†

He recalled Kennedy's last words to him in the hotel room in Fort Worth: "There are two states in the union I know we're going to carry, Massachusetts and Texas."

In a fatalistic mood, Johnson stared out of the window at the ranch house and talked about Diem and Trujillo, both of whom had also died violently: we took care of them, Johnson said;‡ maybe this

---

*Erhard had visited the LBJ ranch December 28–29, 1963. Johnson took him to Fredericksburg, which had been settled largely by German immigrants, and to a barbecue lunch at Stonewall.

†At the very least, Nixon and his aides charged that Mrs. Douglas, whom they depicted as the "Pink Lady," was sympathetic toward, and soft on, Communism. The most famous episode was the distribution by Nixon's campaign director, Murray Chotiner, of the "pink sheet," a leaflet linking Mrs. Douglas' voting record with "the notorious Communist party-liner, Congressman Vito Marcantonio of New York."

‡Johnson did not elaborate; but his meaning was clear. The deep U.S. and CIA involvement in the overthrow of President Diem is described in Chapters 3 and 6. General Rafael L. Trujillo, dictator of the Dominican Republic, was assassinated in May, 1961, by a group of Army officers. Since no Pentagon Papers have been released concerning the Dominican Republic, the U.S. role is murkier. The Kennedy administration was aware for several months before the assassination that various plots were brewing against Trujillo, and the U.S. mission was friendly to anti-Trujillo elements. Henry Dearborn, the U.S. consul and the senior American diplomat in the Dominican Republic

[the Kennedy assassination] was some kind of terrible retribution.

Johnson held most of his backgrounders at the White House. He particularly savored the moment when he informed Robert Kennedy that he would not be on the ticket in 1964 as Johnson's Vice-Presidential choice. And he regaled reporters with details of the confrontation on a background basis. On July 31, four days after his meeting with Robert Kennedy, Johnson invited Tom Wicker of the *Times*, Douglas Kiker of the *Herald Tribune*, and Edward T. Folliard of the *Washington Post* to lunch at the White House. Over sherry, broiled half lobster, tomato salad, watermelon, and iced tea, the President described his version of the episode. Johnson said he had telephoned Bobby on Monday and told him he would like to see him on Tuesday; he could tell by the way Bobby's voice had changed that he knew something was up; "I've been in the same position myself." In a little while Bobby called him back and said: "Mr. President, I've got a meeting of the Kennedy Memorial Library scheduled for Tuesday. Should I cancel it?"

"I said, 'No, Bobby, it's nothing important. Wednesday will be fine.'"

When the meeting took place, Johnson said, he had his statement all written out. "I told him, 'Bobby, I appreciate the fact that you want to perform public service, and I think you've got a great future ahead of you. But I have decided that it is inadvisable of me to recommend your name to the convention as Vice-President. And when I said that he swallowed." The President then illustrated this by gulping for his luncheon guests.

That the President of the United States could *gulp* on background was an extraordinary innovation. The luncheon performance was probably either the high, or low, point of the Washington backgrounder since World War II.*

---

during this period, was in very close contact with the officers plotting against Trujillo. Dearborn says that he did not know the date, time, or place where the attack would occur. "My job was to know what was going on," he said. "I had very good connections with the underground . . . I did not know when it [the assassination] was going to happen. But I had a feeling it was going to happen and so reported."

*Johnson was so enamored of the story that he told it again, in part, to a group of Washington bureau chiefs at a later background session on August 12. Johnson said he informed Robert Kennedy: "'I ought not let you run right up to the convention. I'm big enough to tell you. I don't want you to tell me I should have told you earlier' . . . I was watching him like a hawk watching chickens."

With two other persons, I had a three-hour conversation with Johnson early in December, 1964, a month after he had been elected President in his own right. It is conventional wisdom that Johnson did not realize that Vietnam would pull him down until perhaps 1967 or 1968, when it was too late. But on this evening in 1964 he appeared to know that Vietnam was a trap, and that he was probably doomed to failure no matter what policy he adopted. He likened his situation to standing on a copy of a newspaper in the middle of the Atlantic Ocean. "If I go this way," he said, tilting his hand to the right, "I'll topple over, and if I go this way"—he tilted his hand to the left—"I'll topple over, and if I stay where I am, the paper will be soaked up and I'll sink slowly to the bottom of the sea." As he said this, he lowered his hand slowly toward the floor. Two months later Johnson ordered the sustained bombing of North Vietnam.

De Gaulle had criticized Johnson's Vietnam policy, and Johnson made it clear that the French president was a difficult man to deal with. But he was deliberately allowing De Gaulle's criticisms to go right past him; he was just like a batter standing at the plate and letting all the screw balls go by; he was not trying to hit them or get in their way.*

He was almost sorry Khrushchev had been deposed; he kind of liked him or had at least gotten used to him. "We took a loss when Khrushchev was bounced." What did Johnson think about J. Edgar Hoover's attack on Dr. Martin Luther King? That, Johnson said soberly, was a very bad business; it wouldn't do to have Hoover stirring up twenty-five million Negroes. He had done everything he could to get Hoover and King together, but . . .

Then Johnson talked about the cabinet. Rusk was "broke" and would soon be leaving the government; McNamara was a "human computer" and one person who was indispensable; "I'd hate to run the government without him." He wanted to bring Frank Stanton into the cabinet, but Stanton's wife had told him, "you must choose between me or Johnson," and so he had to choose his wife.

People joked about his campaign to turn off the lights in the

---

*Although Johnson did not expand on his remarks, he may have had in mind more than De Gaulle's public statements. The White House had received a report that De Gaulle was firmly convinced the United States was behind the failure of his recent trip to South America. De Gaulle had visited nine countries there in September–October, 1964. According to the intelligence available to Johnson, the French president believed that Washington had the CIA cable its agents in South America to prevent a big turnout of crowds.

White House, but he had saved "four or five thousand dollars." When he was a boy he was told never to leave the lights on in a room if they weren't being used, and his mother never wanted to run the bill up beyond twenty-four kilowatts, because then there was an extra charge. He wondered if he could keep the budget below $100 billion next year, but he didn't think so . . .

And Kennedy, always John Kennedy. In almost every conversation, Johnson would make a critical reference to his predecessor. Kennedy had a fine style, granted, and when the New Frontier started, there was a lot of excitement, "but *we're* getting the bills passed." And he listed them.

It was obvious that President Kennedy's appearance and style still rankled Johnson a year after the assassination and even after his own landslide election over Barry Goldwater. Later in December, near the end of a background session with several reporters, Johnson said: "Now some of you newspaper people go around saying"—and here Johnson put his hand to his mouth and spoke confidentially, behind the back of his hand—"looks to me like he doesn't have any style or class." It was clear that Johnson resented reporters who compared his personal style unfavorably to that of JFK.

Stylistically, Kennedy *was* a difficult act to follow, but Johnson himself was responsible for much of the adverse comment. As though to prove that he did not care about his lack of Ivy League refinements, Johnson would deliberately go out of his way to be crude in front of reporters. Thus, Senator Harry Byrd "had us where the hair was short" on the tax-cut bill. A well-known Washington columnist "couldn't find his ass with both hands." Strolling around his ranch in March, 1965, Johnson remarked to reporters that he planned to invite the members of the Senate to the White House in three groups, but he did not know if there would be receptions or dinners; "I'll tell you one thing, though, I'm tired of eating bologna sausage at these receptions. I told Ladybird the other day, that stuff was just raising hell with my belly."

Johnson backgrounders could be held in the calm of the second-floor living room, over drinks, or almost anywhere. The "walking backgrounders" were frenetic; the one in early May of 1965 in which Johnson quarreled with John Chancellor was typical of these. Around and around the White House lawn went the President and the reporters. Johnson was under the pressure of the Dominican crisis, and it seemed to relieve the pressure when he talked, and talked, and talked, with newsmen.

"I knew that if I acted to send in the troops," he said, "I couldn't live in the hemisphere, and if I didn't, I couldn't live in this country."

It was as candid a statement of Presidential concern over domestic political reaction to foreign policy as one is likely to hear.

As we circled the lawn, Johnson pulled a letter out of his pocket from President Eisenhower. (Johnson's pockets were an inexhaustible supply of letters, memos, polls, and reports; he could produce paper from his pockets with the flourish of an expert conjurer, and one almost expected to see the document followed by a long chain of silk handkerchiefs, or perhaps a white rabbit.) The Eisenhower letter supported Johnson on Vietnam. Out popped another piece of paper, and Johnson read from it: there had, he said, been 24,000 Viet Cong deaths since December 1, 1963.

Admiral William F. Raborn would not be director of CIA for very long, Johnson was saying. Raborn didn't want to come back to the government from California. His idea of how to live was to work until 1 P.M., go home, have a bowl of soup and a nap, and play golf in Palm Springs for the rest of the afternoon. Dick Helms would eventually take over and replace him, that's why he told Raborn to bring Helms every time that Raborn came to the White House and briefed anyone. But Raborn had come in the middle of the difficult Dominican crisis and had handled himself very well.

Johnson spied some tourists at the East Gate. He was there with a few long strides, shook hands and exchanged tie pins with one. How y'all? Mighty nice to see you folks. At various times Bill Moyers or Jack Valenti trotted over and handed the President pieces of paper, which went into his pockets. Props for the next trick. He praised Moyers: "That boy has had his stomach cut up but he works from 8 A.M. to midnight."

The President was perspiring in the hot sun. Suddenly he was talking about General William F. McKee, whom he had just appointed head of the Federal Aviation Agency six days before. "Even though he's a four-star general, he was shaking like this [LBJ wobbled his hands] when he came to see me. 'Why does the President want to see me so suddenly?' So I told him I needed him to run the FAA."

We continued our travels around the lawn. "Where are we going?" columnist Mary McGrory was moved to ask. "Wherever I go," the President responded benignly. He asked her whether she knew the old Baptist hymn "Where He Leads I Will Follow." Then, in an off-key voice, Johnson began singing the hymn softly, almost to himself, several times, as the reporters trailed along. He was still singing as he walked up the path to the Rose Garden and went back into his office.

One of President Nixon's rare experiments with a background

briefing led to a flap, with international repercussions. On Thursday, September 17, 1970, Nixon was in Chicago and visited the offices of the *Chicago Sun-Times* and the *Daily News*, both published by Marshall Field. Bailey Howard, president of the parent Field Enterprises, opened the session by assuring Nixon it would be off the record. The President sipped tomato juice and coffee and for two hours reviewed the world situation with the editors of the two papers. At the time King Hussein of Jordan was battling to preserve his power against Palestinian guerrillas; the United States feared that Syria might intervene (which it did, the next day).

When Nixon began talking about the Middle East he prefaced his remarks by saying: "Now, I suggest you get out your pads and pencils and take this down." David Murray, a *Sun-Times* reporter who was in the room, started to take notes. As James Hoge, editor of the *Sun-Times*, listened, it seemed clear to him that Nixon expected a story to emerge from the meeting. That afternoon the *Sun-Times* led the paper with an article headlined: "U.S. Ready to Act to Save Jordan King." The story, written by Murray, said the United States was "prepared to intervene directly in the Jordanian civil war" if Syria and Iraq entered the conflict. It gave no source, but a story on page two told of Nixon's visit to the paper and said the President had discussed "foreign policies, particularly the Middle East."

The *Chicago Tribune*, which had also received a visit from Nixon that afternoon, was distressed to read the story in the *Sun-Times*. The White House was soon alerted to David Murray's story. Clayton Kirkpatrick, the editor of the *Chicago Tribune*, telephoned a protest to Herb Klein, and when he asked whether his own paper was free to write a similar story, he was told no. Ziegler and Klein then placed a telephone call to the *Sun-Times* from Air Force One, as the President's plane was winging its way back from Chicago to Washington. As a result of this discussion, the story was revised and toned down. ("U.S. Action Is Possible" said the late-edition headline.) Later the editors of the *Sun-Times* and the *Daily News* disagreed whether Nixon had spoken on background, in which case the story had not violated any rules, or off-the-record, in which case it had.

There was a peculiar sequel to the whole thing, which suggested that Nixon had wanted the story out, after all, as a warning to both Syria and the Soviet Union. Ten days after his visit to Chicago, Nixon left for a trip to Europe. In Ireland, he encountered *Sun-Times* reporter Morton Kondracke at a reception. "I want you to know that your paper handled that story just right," the President said (he seemed to mean the first edition, not the second). The publication of the U.S. warning, Nixon indicated, had been very helpful in the resolution of the crisis.*

Whatever the reasons, the Syrian tanks had pulled back, and the Soviet Union, under pressure from the United States, had apparently urged restraint on the part of its Arab clients. Hussein agreed on a cease-fire with the guerrillas.

A little more than six months later, at the governors' conference in Colonial Williamsburg, Spiro Agnew invited nine reporters up to his suite for post-midnight drinks and talk. An American ping-pong team had recently visited China, a signal of changing U.S. relations with Peking. Agnew complained that the young players on the American team might have given the U.S. public a false impression of life inside China; at a recent National Security Council meeting, he said, he had opposed any détente with Peking. The ping-pong matches were a bad business, Agnew concluded, and America had taken a propaganda beating. Although the meeting was supposed to be off the record, reporters who had not been there heard about the Vice-President's comments and wrote stories.† Agnew's remarks could not have come at a more inappropriate time. The administration was moving toward a historic shift in policy toward Communist China; in mid-July, Nixon revealed that he would visit Peking.

For the most part the President left the background briefings to Henry Kissinger, who conducted them regularly. In a typical session, reporters gathered in the East Room of the White House on the afternoon of Friday, September 25, 1970.

About halfway into the questioning, Kissinger let drop a major

---

*Nixon's words had reached their major intended target. Within minutes of the time the *Sun-Times* story hit the streets in Chicago, Leonid N. Zhegalov, a Washington correspondent for Tass, the Soviet news agency, appeared in the Washington office of the *Sun-Times*. (Tass had offices on the second floor of the National Press Building, and the *Sun-Times* bureau was on the thirteenth floor.) Zhegalov tried to find out the source of the *Sun-Times* story from Tom Ross, the newspaper's Washington Bureau chief. Nixon had visited the paper, the Tass man said—was he also the source of the story? You can draw your own conclusion, Ross told the Russian.

Soon afterward Zhegalov was expelled by the State Department in retaliation for the Soviet expulsion from Moscow of *Newsweek* correspondent John Dornberg.

†Only the nine reporters who had been invited to Agnew's suite were bound by the rules and unable to file stories. In the press room, as Jules Witcover reported in *White Knight: The Rise of Spiro Agnew,* someone wrote in chalk on the bulletin board: "Free the Williamsburg Nine."

news story. "With respect to Soviet naval activity in the Caribbean," he said, "we are, of course, watching the development . . . of possible construction there . . . The Soviet Union can be under no doubt that we would view the establishment of a strategic base in the Caribbean with the utmost seriousness." Kissinger's statement led to disclosures of a round of secret diplomacy designed to prevent the Russians from basing nuclear-missile submarines in Cuba. Three weeks later the administration apparently decided to switch tactics and play down the submarine and missile scare; it leaked a story to the *Times* saying that the construction at Cienfuegos was not a submarine base after all, but a recreation area for Soviet sailors, including a soccer field and a tennis court.

The massive mimeographed transcripts of the Kissinger back-grounders emerged as important foreign policy source material in the Nixon administration. But members of the Senate Foreign Relations Committee couldn't get copies for a long time. This was true despite the fact that correspondents for Tass and other reporters from Communist nations regularly attended the Kissinger back-grounders. Even Republican members of the Foreign Relations Committee were denied the transcripts; in the fall of 1970 Senator Clifford P. Case of New Jersey, a liberal, it is true, but a Republican nevertheless, exchanged letters with Kissinger. ("Dear Henry: . . . If possible I would like to be included on a regular distribution list." "Dear Cliff: . . . I must plead that the ground rules for these sessions and the distribution of transcripts are determined by the press secretary and not myself . . .")

The situation got so ludicrous that at one point the Committee on Foreign Relations of the United States Senate was able to read the contents of a Kissinger backgrounder only by obtaining it from a sympathetic official of the British embassy. (They must have enjoyed *that* in Whitehall.)

Finally, after a protracted struggle, the Foreign Relations Committee was cleared to receive the Kissinger transcripts. Even then, the committee first had to find out that a backgrounder had been held, and then request it specifically.

Kissinger was an effective background briefer, but in the fall of 1971 a series of misadventures plagued him. First, Senator Barry Goldwater got hold of a briefing held by Kissinger on December 7 and inserted it into the *Congressional Record* two days later for all to see.

Kissinger's embarrassment was compounded when columnist Jack Anderson released transcripts of secret NSC subcommittee meetings. In the published text of the December 7 press briefing, Kissinger had denied that the United States was "anti-Indian." That, he said, "is totally inaccurate." But the Anderson documents revealed that on December 3, four days before his backgrounder, Kissinger said: "I am getting hell every half hour from the President that we are not being tough enough on India. He has just called me again. He does not believe we are carrying out his wishes. He wants to tilt in favor of Pakistan." Naturally, this created the impression that Kissinger had not been wholly candid in his background comments.

An even bigger fuss over a Kissinger backgrounder arose after Nixon flew to the Azores later in December for a meeting with French president Georges Pompidou. The trip was part of a series of little summits to reassure American allies about the President's forthcoming visits to Peking and Moscow. The weather in Azores was lovely, the skies blue and sunny, and the weather warm. But the war was raging between India and Pakistan, and it was very much in the mind of David Kraslow when he boarded the President's plane for the return trip to Washington. Kraslow, then the chief of the *Los Angeles Times* Washington Bureau, had been chosen as one of the pool men for the return leg. Midway into the flight, Kissinger agreed to talk to the poolers. He came back and stood in the aisle in his shirt sleeves and took questions for about fifteen minutes, with his answers on background. Several times Kraslow pressed Kissinger on whether Nixon might cancel his trip to Moscow if the Soviet Union failed to exercise a restraining influence on India. Finally Kissinger said he would speak under "the Lindley rule, deep background."

When Kissinger had concluded, Kraslow typed up the pool report on his Olivetti portable. Kissinger was asked whether the war might affect Nixon's trip to Moscow, and the report said he replied on deep background "not yet but . . . we would have to wait to see what happens . . . plans for the President's trip might be changed . . . the entire matter might well be re-examined."* Kraslow gave the report to Presidential aide Dwight Chapin, who took it forward to Kissinger. Kissinger crossed out the word "matter" and wrote above it "U.S. Soviet relationship." Copies were run off on the plane and

---

*The pool report also contained this intriguing paragraph: "When Kissinger said he would talk to us on background, he was reminded of his India-Pak backgrounder. He appeared clearly irritated that the backgrounder had been published, and he denied that he had anything to do with getting a copy to Goldwater. He said he would never play that kind of game, that the whole purpose of doing the briefing on background was to prevent inflaming the issue. He said he had not tracked down how the backgrounder had gotten to Goldwater but suggested it was done by some eager beaver in the White House."

distributed at Andrews Air Force base when the rest of the press corps landed, and at the White House. Kraslow went to his office, filed his story, and went home.

The next morning, when Kraslow took the *Washington Post* out of his mailbox in Silver Spring, Maryland, he learned that the newspaper had identified Kissinger by name; the President's adviser, the story said, had warned "in a background briefing" that Nixon might cancel his trip to Moscow. In an accompanying box, the *Post* claimed that it had "learned Kissinger's identity independently."

Upset, Kraslow telephoned Benjamin C. Bradlee, the executive editor of the *Washington Post*, and informed him that he intended to criticize the newspaper publicly for breaking the rules. "I'm sick and tired of diplomacy by backgrounder," Bradlee replied.

Later in the day, in the course of a White House news briefing, Kraslow assailed the *Post* for "unprofessional, unethical, cheap journalism." Bradlee, a leading foe of backgrounders, issued a statement charging that background briefings had become a way for government "to use the press . . . without taking responsibility for what it is saying." The public, he said, "has suffered from this collusion between the government and the press." Henceforth, Bradlee ordered, *Post* reporters would seek full attribution at briefings and the paper's editors would decide how to handle material when the reporters' request was refused. A.M. Rosenthal, the managing editor of *The New York Times*, said the paper would issue no flat rules, but that its reporters would be "a lot more selective" about attending background sessions. Ron Ziegler said it was "a problem for the journalistic community" to solve. But he added that the administration planned no change in its policy on background briefings.

The dispute soon died down, however, and there was no substantial drop in the number of backgrounders being held in Washington. Some newsmen felt the controversy had achieved at least some results, however. Richard Harwood, national editor of the *Washington Post*, noted that in the months after the dispute, Kissinger's briefings were almost entirely on the record. Robert H. Phelps, the news editor of *The New York Times* Washington Bureau, also detected a slight decline in the number of backgrounders in other parts of the government, although not in the intelligence community where "they still expect you to carry the ball for them." Bernard Gwertzman, who covered the State Department for the *Times*, thought Kissinger's new visibility was not so much a result of the Azores affair specifically as it was "due to the realization by the White House that Kissinger's identity could no longer be successfully hidden." On balance, Gwertzman added, "not much has really changed."

At various other times individual newspapers, Washington bureaus, and reporters have taken a stand against background information, or announced policies under which information on background will or will not be accepted for publication. But these policies, sometimes proclaimed with considerable fanfare, tend after a time to melt away, and the relationship between press and government slips back again into familiar patterns. While the debate over backgrounders continues, so do the backgrounders.

Only six months after the Kissinger affair Secretary of State Rogers held a background session in Moscow that turned into a total embarrassment. Although Rogers generally spoke on the record, he sometimes talked for background on overseas trips. During Nixon's summit meeting in Moscow in May of 1972 Rogers invited a select group of reporters to a background chat at the Rossiya Hotel. Asked whether Nixon and Soviet party chief Leonid I. Brezhnev were making any headway on Vietnam, Rogers indicated that there had been no real discussion of that subject; every time the President raised it, Brezhnev veered away from it. The trouble was, as reporters soon learned, at the very moment that Rogers was saying this, Nixon, Brezhnev, Soviet Premier Alexei N. Kosygin, President Nikolai V. Podgorny, Foreign Minister Andrei A. Gromyko, and Rogers' principal rival, Henry Kissinger, were holding a lengthy discussion about Vietnam at Brezhnev's dacha in a birch forest at Barvikha, fifteen miles from Moscow. The meeting was preceded by a hydrofoil trip on the Moskva River. Rogers was not invited to either event; he had literally missed the boat.

The general problem of backgrounders, of course, was not new; in 1964 the subject had even received Congressional attention. In that year the House subcommittee on government information conducted a staff study of backgrounders. The staff reached two conclusions: that the anonymous news source "can be useful in making more information available to the public," or it can be "a self-serving device to convey distorted information which the public seldom can evaluate."

The staff study had neatly formulated the problem. The rationale for background briefings is that they permit officials to explain sensitive foreign policy matters, or domestic programs, with more candor, and perhaps in greater depth, than might be the case if they were forced to speak for attribution. Public officials will be more relaxed about what they say if their words cannot be quoted, attributed, and used against them politically, so the argument runs; it is only human nature that this would be the case.

There is substantial truth to this, but it is equally true that officials who are able to hide behind a cloak of anonymity may be more than normally tempted to lie, or to disseminate self-serving propaganda, than if held publicly accountable for their words. It has also been argued that by agreeing to the rules for background sessions, the press enters into a sort of conspiracy of concealment with the government.

Both arguments have merit, and there remains a considerable division of opinion within the Washington press corps about the propriety and usefulness of backgrounders.

A persuasive case can be made that the "Lindley rule" should be retired. A group of reporters attending a briefing should no longer accept any information on "deep background," a practice that particularly lends itself to abuse, because their readers receive no indication of the source, which might help to evaluate the information. Furthermore, a reporter who accepts information under such restrictions is either required to believe that it is true, or risk his professional reputation by printing information that may not be accurate. He may be tempted to publish it, even so, because of the pressure of competition. He knows that other reporters who were present may file the story; then his editors will soon be asking why he missed it. ("AP and UPI has it; where the hell were you?")*

Similarly, reporters at background briefings could reject information with only vague attribution, such as "administration officials," or "government officials." Information attributable to officials of a particular department or unit of the government might be acceptable, since it would, to a great extent, meet the objection of vagueness and anonymity. Such attribution would at least permit the newspaper reader or television viewer to know a more specific source of the story originating at a backgrounder and to draw his own conclusions about its possible motivation and accuracy.

Competitive pressures make it unlikely that even such partial reforms will be adopted. Since there is no general agreement about backgrounders within the Washington press community, news organizations or reporters with strong views can boycott such sessions only at the risk of missing information that their competitors will obtain. Lacking unanimity, it is difficult for the press to bring about changes.†

Although it is fashionable to assail backgrounders as the root of

---

*As the House subcommittee study put it: "Competition pressures the conscientious newsman to file all information. What he feels is questionable may be headlined in other papers."

†To illustrate the complexities of the problem, if a newspaper does boycott a background briefing, but the wire services attend and move a story based upon it, should the editor of the paper then suppress the wire story? If he does, he deprives his readers of information they might wish to have. If he uses the story, he might as well have sent his own reporter in the first place.

all evil in the press-government relationship, such a view suggests preoccupation with form rather than substance. Since a leak to a single reporter is normally acceptable and an everyday occurrence in Washington, a group leak, or backgrounder, is not necessarily in and of itself nefarious. It should be emphasized that the best stories usually result not from such group sessions or from individual reporters being called in and handed information, but from a newsman seeking out information and carefully piecing together facts that fit a pattern and lead to a conclusion.

Granted that the government can use backgrounders to shape the truth, there are other factors that may lead to news distortion. Misinformation may result not only from government manipulation but from the shortcomings and failures of the press itself.

No institution is without flaws, or exempt from criticism. Much of the recent criticism of the press, however, has arisen from suspect motives and has tended to focus on false issues. The Nixon administration's attacks on the press have been politically motivated; they are designed, as previously suggested, to destroy the credibility of the news media, build political support, and influence the content of the news, especially news broadcast over radio and television.

The most frequent charge made against the press by Spiro Agnew and other Republican critics is that it is biased, and that reporters are Eastern "liberals" incapable of writing fairly about the Nixon administration, or about Republican or conservative policies. Pat Moynihan, in his article in *Commentary*, expanded on this theme, charging that journalists were Ivy Leaguers, part of an "adversary culture," recruited from "middle- and upper-class backgrounds and trained at the universities . . ." In Washington, said Moynihan, the upper levels of the press constituted a social elite and a "leisured class." The press, he said, was increasingly influenced "by attitudes genuinely hostile to American society and American government." He did not explain what he meant by that, nor did he come right out and use the word "un-American."

It is true that the great majority of reporters today are college graduates, but that is scarcely a cause for alarm. The news about government is so complex that trained, educated, and intelligent reporters are a necessity; if anything, journalism suffers from a lack of reporters with graduate degrees and expertise in such specialized fields as economics and foreign policy. Some of the color and romance of the news business have disappeared, and perhaps they are missed, but the day of the defiantly anti-intellectual police reporter who wore his hat in the office is past. Hildy Johnson is dead, as Moynihan, a Harvard professor who holds a B.A. degree from Tufts

University, and an M.A. and a Ph.D. from the Fletcher School of Law and Diplomacy, must surely have noticed.

Graduates of Ivy League colleges are a minority among reporters in Washington, and until fairly recently the salaries of newsmen in the capital were scandalously low, much lower, for example, than pay for roughly comparable jobs in publishing, advertising, and public relations. Even today a Washington correspondent for a major paper who earns between $18,000 and $25,000 a year is hardly in the same leisure class with a member of Congress, who earns $42,500, or a cabinet secretary who earns $60,000. In fact, many reporters go into journalism because of a sense of idealism and a desire to contribute to society; they often make a conscious choice to pass up higher incomes that might be available in corporate or professional careers. As children come, and family and financial pressures increase, a reporter's biggest problem may be resisting the temptation to "sell out" and take a public relations job at higher pay. The Washington reporter's life style is hardly that of the idle rich.

What about political bias? That is rather difficult to measure, and there exists no great mass of survey data about even the party affiliation or political views of Washington correspondents. It is usually assumed that a majority of reporters in the capital are Democrats, and it may be so, but this cannot be demonstrated by the limited statistics available.*

Reporters in Washington, unlike those in other American cities, represent newspapers from all over the country. Their political opinions vary, just as do those of members of Congress from differing constituencies. But at the top, among influential senior members of

---

*William L. Rivers of Stanford University, in a study published in 1965, found reporters who identified themselves as Democrats a distinct minority in the Washington press corps. About half of the reporters in the capital called themselves Independents. That was an unusually high percentage of Independents, and it may have reflected the fact that many reporters felt their impartiality might be questioned if they enrolled in a political party. Among the remaining 50 percent, Democrats outnumbered Republicans about 3 to 1 (which translates roughly into 38 percent Democrats to 12 percent Republicans). But in the country at large, studies of party identification showed that the Democrats also outnumbered Republicans. And using Rivers' data, there were fewer Democrats among Washington correspondents than in the general voting population. In 1966, for example, shortly after the Rivers study, a Gallup poll showed that 48 percent of voters identified themselves as Democrats, 27 percent as Republicans, and 25 percent as Independents.

the Washington press corps, there is a strong streak of conservatism. The Washington bureau chiefs of the *Daily Oklahoman,* the *Indianapolis Star,* and the *Birmingham News* will not be found out picketing with the SDS.

The Gridiron Club, a group comprised of fifty bureau chiefs and other senior newsmen in Washington, is generally regarded as an organization that epitomizes establishment values. In its annual musical entertainments spoofing political leaders, it is Eugene McCarthy or George McGovern who is likely to be needled the most, not Richard Nixon or Melvin Laird. Music for the show is provided by the United States Marines. In 1968, at a time when many other Americans were beginning to develop doubts about the wisdom of Lyndon Johnson's course in Vietnam, the Gridiron Club closed its show with an astonishing hymn to Dean Rusk's untiring efforts for peace. This in a year, it will be recalled, when Rusk was calling for bombing them at Chevy Chase Circle before they got to Dupont Circle.

When Tom Wicker speaks of "peer group pressure" in the nation's capital, he does not mean fellow liberals. "There are some colleagues in the Washington press corps who practically won't speak to me," Wicker said. "There have been slurs, and I feel almost ostracized at the Gridiron Club. I could say it doesn't really matter, but these things do matter. There is a mainstream of journalism as in everything else, and if you get out of the mainstream, if you get off the reservation, you feel it. I feel more support today from the public, and less from among my peers in the press corps."

So the Washington press corps is by no means monolithically liberal—far from it. But even if this were the case, the issue is largely irrelevant. A reporter's political views are, for the most part, beside the point; the real question is whether news *as reported to the public* is biased.

All of the analysis and criticism that focus on the economic, social, educational, and political background of the press make the unproven assumption, the quantum leap, really, that a reporter's copy predominantly reflects his personal opinions. No one lives or works in a vacuum and no one is wholly free of past experience or a point of view, reporters no more than jurists, doctors, scholars, or others who daily are called upon to make "objective" judgments. And much of what a reporter does is necessarily selective—what subjects he chooses to write about, what events he chooses to report, and how he organizes his story. But in my experience, most reporters make a conscious effort to report the facts and to write the truth; their professional standards require it and many of their editors and publishers demand it.

Washington reporters must suceed in this to a great extent, for if, as the Nixon administration has charged, they are preponderantly biased, liberal, and Democratic, it is impossible to explain why Presidents Kennedy and Johnson both complained bitterly about the coverage of *their* administrations.

Times are changing, however, and it may be argued that the new movement, if it is one, toward "advocacy journalism" has eroded traditional standards of news fairness. The concept of advocacy journalism arose partially as a form of revolt against the sterile neutrality that mistook mathematical balance in a news story for truth. In a political campaign, for example, quoting one man for two paragraphs and his opponent for two paragraphs may achieve "balance" but it may bring the reader nowhere near the truth. The reporter himself may have to provide that.

And I am not sure what advocacy journalism really means. Does it mean a story reporting on the scandal of hunger in America? On the plight of migrant farm workers? Or the continuing racial discrimination in America against blacks and other minorities? Stories of this kind are not so much advocating—even if the reporter's motivation is to bring about social change—as they are reporting on important social issues that go to the heart of the question of what kind of society America is or may choose to be.

At the moment, however, the standard to which the great majority of Washington reporters aspire is not "advocacy," but objectivity. If at times they fall short of this goal, the situation is perhaps balanced by the fact that reporters, no matter how liberal they may be, generally work for conservative or Republican newspapers. With the exception of 1964, when most publishers favored Johnson over Goldwater, in every election since 1932 close to 60 percent of American newspapers have editorially supported the Republican candidate. Roosevelt, Truman, and Kennedy were elected despite newspaper opposition.*

Newsmen were debating the problem of bias versus objectivity long before the Nixon administration raised the issue. Bias lies in the eyes of the beholder, and so does "objectivity." We tend to say that what we agree with is objective and what we do not agree with is "biased."

---

*Truman was elected in 1948 with the support of only 15.4 percent of daily newspapers, and Kennedy had almost precisely the same, 15 percent. In 1968, 60.8 percent of Republican papers supported Nixon, 14 percent backed Hubert Humphrey, a division that was typical of the pattern since the days of the New Deal.

Almost everyone concurs that reporters should get "the facts" right; if an administration reports that troops have been withdrawn from Vietnam, the press should, and does, report it. The controversy arises when the press attempts to set "the facts" in a meaningful context, so that they reflect reality. How many troops did the administration secretly put into Thailand during the same period? What was the increase in the size of U. S. naval forces off Vietnam? How much was air activity stepped up?

To take another random example, on November 2, 1970, one day before the midterm Congressional elections, the Pentagon announced that Vietnam casualty figures for the previous week—thirty Americans killed in action—would hit a five-year low. Normally, and during all other weeks, the Pentagon released these figures on Thursday. So reporters asked Jerry W. Friedheim, the second-highest Pentagon spokesman, how come he was putting them out on Monday. Because, said Friedheim "it was very significant." Could it be, reporters asked, that the announcement was related to the fact that there would be an election the next day? Friedheim, who apparently had little stomach for his task, replied: "Why don't we leave it where I am?"

In this case "objectivity" required that the news story emphasize the obvious political timing of the Pentagon's release of the casualty figures. A story that simply reported the figures without explaining the unusual timing would actually be a distortion of what had happened, for it would not reflect the truth of the event. The interpretation, the additional information brought to the story by the reporter, was integral to understanding the whole.

The press, I think, can be criticized usefully not for bias, or slanting the news, but for failure to provide enough of this kind of interpretation and background, to place the news in meaningful context, and to explain what the official spokesman has neglected to mention. The sins of the press are, by and large, sins of omission.

Wicker has argued that the press has tended, for example, to give far too much weight to official sources, and he is right. "The whole method of news operation," he said, "tends to give the government the advantage. Anything that is an institution gets quoted—government, or a corporation, or a university. But it's hard to get the other side."

Although I have emphasized government pressures on the press, there are other sorts of pressures that may cause news distortion—pressure on a reporter from a publisher or from an editor who may seek to cater to a publisher's political views, or pressure on a television network, or a station, by a major sponsor.

But two other kinds of pressure are more powerful than those of advertisers, publishers, or editors. These are internalized pressures, often deeply felt by the reporter but seldom understood or articulated. They are, first, competitive pressure for information, and second, the pressures created by a reporter's conscious or unconscious identification with the values of his society.

Competitive pressure or career pressure means simply that reporters seek to excel for reasons of pride, recognition, and financial reward. Conventional wisdom holds that technology and television have made the scoop obsolete. It isn't true. There is still great self-generated pressure on a reporter to break the big story, to get the news *first,* and to gain recognition by, if not the Pulitzer jury, at least the public, his peers, and his employers. The press is in the business of selling newspapers, the networks in the business of selling time, and the news reporter is not unaware of the economics of his business. He knows that the big story helps circulation and ratings. Beyond that, he likes to see his name in the paper or to get his filmed report on the CBS Evening News. At 7 P.M. on any given day in Washington, the question on the mind of scores of newspaper correspondents is not "What fresh insights into the endless adventure of government did I bring to my readers today?" but "Did I make page one?"

These career pressures, in turn, mean that reporters may be susceptible to the self-serving or even false leak by a government official; they mean that, at times, a newsman may, alas, be more interested in "knocking down" the story of a rival reporter than in following it up. Career pressures cause the press to enter into a symbiotic relationship with the government. For its own purposes, the government leaks information to the press. For different purposes, the press seizes upon the proffered information and sells it to the public. Before reaching the consumer, the wares may not be sufficiently tested for truth-in-packaging.

The second set of pressures, those stemming from a reporter's identification with societal and community values, has led to much too great a reliance by the press on the truthfulness of the government. Far from being "hostile" to American society, as Pat Moynihan would have it, most reporters are very much a part of it; they did not grow up in Outer Mongolia, after all, they were politically socialized in the good old U.S.A. As a result, particularly during the Cold War era, the American press tended to confuse government claims with established truth. The jolt of the U-2 incident did bring an increase in the sophistication of the press, but it has been slow in developing. Reporters generally accepted the Lyndon Johnson-Robert McNamara version of the events in the Tonkin Gulf—and they therefore helped to mislead the public—because the reporters were

American citizens; like other Americans, they tended, at least in 1964, to believe what they were officially told. When the flag is attacked, or reporters are told it has been attacked, their reaction is not likely to be very different from that of any other citizen. Besides, it is vaguely unpatriotic to dispute the official version of events. The hate mail received by Seymour Hersh, who had the courage to unmask the My Lai massacre for the American public, is a case in point.

Reporters are not immune from such pressures. Usually the matter of national pride remains half submerged, but sometimes it is openly invoked by officials in their dealings with the press. At a news conference in Saigon in the early 1960's, Admiral Harry D. Felt, the commander in chief of the Pacific, was displeased with a question asked by Malcolm Browne of the Associated Press. "So you're Browne," the admiral remarked. "Why don't you get on the team?"

In a similar vein, after the Communist Tet offensive early in 1968, Dean Rusk held a background meeting with reporters. Why, he asked, must the press always take such a negative attitude? "There gets to be a point," Rusk said, "when the question is whose side are you on. I'm the Secretary of State, and I'm on our side."

There is, of course, only one side that a constitutionally free press can be on, and that is the side of truth. But to fulfill that role requires a singular tough-mindedness. The press, despite criticism from political leaders, needs to question, probe, analyze, and interpret more, not less. It should resist government pressures and self-generated pressures. It must not succumb to the seduction of power, nor automatically accept government handouts and leaks as fact. If the press acts as a mere transmission belt for government pronouncements, then it contributes to the credibility gap, and to the erosion of trust that has already divided the people from their government.

13

The President
and the Press

"I mean I'm as human as anybody else," President Nixon said in June of 1972. "I like to get a good press."

Richard Nixon chose an incongruous setting to make this remark: his first televised news conference in more than a year. Robert Pierpoint, a CBS White House correspondent, had bluntly asked Nixon why he avoided live press conferences.

"It isn't that I'm afraid to do it," Nixon insisted. "I have to determine the best way of communication . . . Every President has got to make a decision when he enters office about his relations with the press . . ."

Nixon's own decision had become apparent long before 1972. *No* modern President held fewer press conferences; through 1972 Nixon had thirty-one news conferences in four years, and of these, only sixteen were televised so that the public, as well as a few hundred privileged Washington correspondents, could watch. During this period Nixon averaged approximately eight press conferences per year. By contrast, President Truman held an average of forty-two press conferences per year, Eisenhower and Johnson averaged twenty-four per year, and John F. Kennedy, twenty-one per year.*

---

*For comparative figures on the number of press conferences held by Presidents since Franklin D. Roosevelt, see page 246. Nixon's news conferences through 1972, with the number televised in parentheses, were:

As a result, under Nixon, the press conference threatened to become a vanishing institution, the political equivalent of the whooping crane. Nixon, convinced that the press was hostile, decided from the outset to avoid frequent live exposure to questions from reporters. He much preferred the controlled setting of a televised address to the nation. In that format Nixon could ask the questions—a rhetorical device he has always favored—and provide the answers as well.

But in the electronic age, the televised press conference, for all of its faults, can serve as a vital link between the President and the people. No other forum offers an opportunity for millions of Americans to watch their elected leader address himself to the problems confronting American society.

Nixon's failure to hold regular news conferences, however, was part of the administration's general pattern of hostility toward the press. Although the organized assault on the news media reached an unprecedented level under Nixon—at least among modern Presidents—he was certainly not the first Chief Executive to complain about the press.

George Washington wrote that he was tired of being "buffited in the public prints by a set of infamous scribblers."* John Adams grumbled that he had been "disgraced and degraded" by the press, and he personally ordered his Attorney General to prosecute William Duane, an opposition editor, under the infamous Alien and Sedition Acts. Thomas Jefferson, although eloquent in his defense of a free press, could also write: ". . . even the least informed of the people have learnt that nothing in a newspaper is to be believed . . . the press ought to be restored to its credibility if possible."

Abraham Lincoln occasionally complained about news stories, but he was adroit at cultivating reporters and editors and had a well-developed sense of public relations.

Grover Cleveland had his problems with the press, notably in the midst of the campaign of 1884 when the *Buffalo Telegraph* published the story of his supposed illegitimate son, under the headline: "A Terrible Tale—A Dark Chapter in a Public Man's History."

1969:	9	(8)	1971:	9	(3)
1970:	6	(4)	1972:	7	(1)

*A history of the American Presidency and the press is outside the scope of this book. For a detailed work on this subject, *see* James E. Pollard, *The Presidents and the Press* (New York: Macmillan, 1947) and, by the same author, *The Presidents and the Press, Truman to Johnson* (Washington: Public Affairs Press, 1964).

Theodore Roosevelt went so far as to have Joseph Pulitzer and his *New York World* indicted for criminal libel after the newspaper charged that corrupt promoters had made millions in connection with the digging of the Panama Canal. Pulitzer cruised offshore on his yacht, appropriately named the *Liberty*, to avoid arrest. Ultimately the case was dismissed. William Howard Taft told his assistant not to show him any more clippings from *The New York Times:* "I only read the headlines and the first sentence or two. I don't think their reading will do me any particular good, and would only be provocative of . . . anger and contemptuous feeling."

Woodrow Wilson wrote to one senator: "I am so accustomed to having everything reported erroneously that I have almost come to the point of believing nothing that I see in the newspapers." Early in his administration, and long before the invention of a director of communications for the Executive Branch, Wilson seriously thought about creating a central federal publicity bureau. In 1914 he wrote to the President of Harvard:

> We have several times considered the possibility of having a publicity bureau which would handle the real facts, so far as the government was aware of them, for all the departments. The real trouble is that the newspapers get the real facts but do not find them to their taste and do not use them as given them, and in some of the newspaper offices news is deliberately invented.

Franklin D. Roosevelt was masterful in his relations with the press, and he was the first modern President fully to understand its workings. Even so, FDR invented a Dunce Cap Club, to which he would banish reporters whose questions annoyed him. He frequently lectured newsmen at his press conferences, and once awarded an Iron Cross to John O'Donnell of the *New York Daily News*, whose stories, Roosevelt felt, were aiding the Nazis.

Harry Truman was personally popular with reporters, but his relations with the press were erratic. He berated Paul Hume, the music critic of the *Washington Post*, who had failed to appreciate his daughter Margaret's singing voice; if he ever met up with the critic, Truman indicated, Hume would "need a new nose and plenty of beefsteak."

Eisenhower was clearly irritated, and had great difficulty controlling his temper, when reporters pressed him about the activities of Senator Joseph McCarthy. But Eisenhower did not grumble much in public about the press. He had little need to do so; he enjoyed the overwhelming editorial support of most newspapers and great public popularity. As a result, to some extent, Washington correspondents concluded that Eisenhower was untouchable; there was not much point in writing unfavorable stories or digging up scandal, because it would be difficult to get it into the paper. This attitude did not always prevail; the story of Sherman Adams, Bernard Goldfine, and the vicuna coat was fully, indeed lavishly, reported in the press.

Probably no President since FDR was more adept at press relations than John F. Kennedy, but he frequently complained about individual news stories. Kennedy lectured the newspaper industry after the Bay of Pigs, and he canceled his subscription to the *New York Herald Tribune*. In 1962 he was asked how he felt about the press, and he made his famous reply: "Well, I am reading more and enjoying it less . . ."

Lyndon Johnson was almost continually disenchanted with the press, particularly when it reported his personal idiosyncrasies, such as pulling on beagles' ears, speeding at the LBJ ranch while sipping beer from a paper cup, or yelling "Yahoo!" in the Taj Mahal to test the echo (the latter experiment was performed as Vice-President). But Johnson's unhappiness with the news media was inevitable; he kept a dozen different newspapers on his hall table, devoured each new edition, cast a careful eye on the news tickers, and watched three news shows at once on specially built triple TV monitors in his office. Anyone who consumed that much about himself was bound to find a few things he did not like.

Presidents, in short, have always complained about the press, but each in his own way has had to cope with the press. Not until relatively recent times, however, was the relationship formalized. In the McKinley administration, reporters used to gather around the great white pillars of the White House portico and waylay callers as they came and went. By unwritten rule, they never approached the President unless he voluntarily stopped to talk. Theodore Roosevelt, so it is said, saw the reporters standing out in the rain one day, invited them in, and had a small room set aside for their use. This was the first White House press room.

It was Woodrow Wilson, however, who inaugurated the modern Presidential press conference. He met reporters twice a week at first, but gradually became displeased with their aggressive questions. When newspapers published stories speculating about the engagement of his daughter, Wilson expressed outrage that the press had dared to write about "the ladies of my household." After 1915 Wilson held few press conferences.

Harding restored the regular press conferences that Wilson had begun, and held them twice a week. But Harding once inaccurately described the provisions of a treaty; after that major blunder he required that all questions be submitted in writing, in advance.

Coolidge continued the custom of written questions, and in his sour, dour manner, held regular press conferences that were notable for their lack of news content. Herbert Hoover held a moderate number of press conferences—sixty-six in four years—and although he also insisted on written questions, he sometimes allowed direct quotation of his remarks.

But if Wilson was the father of the Presidential press conference, it was Franklin Roosevelt who institutionalized it and used it as a regular channel of communication with the American people. In his twelve years in office, Roosevelt held 998 press conferences, an average of about 1.5 per week. Roosevelt ended the practice of written questions. He established three categories of attribution: direct quotation, on occasion; indirect quotation; and deep background. In addition, he sometimes made off-the-record comments that could not be used or published in any form. The reporters would gather around Roosevelt's desk, and his news conferences had an air of intimacy and give-and-take.

Truman met with the press almost once a week. To make room for more reporters, he moved his news conferences across the street from the White House Oval Office into the Indian Treaty Room on the fourth floor of the Executive Office Building. But Truman lacked Roosevelt's skill in handling questions. On November 30, 1950, after Communist China had entered the Korean War, Truman told a news conference that the United States would take all necessary steps to meet the military situation.

"Will that include the atomic bomb?" a reporter asked.

"That includes every weapon we have."

". . . Does that mean that there is active consideration of use of the atomic bomb?" the reporter persisted.

"There has always been active consideration of its use," Truman snapped.

After the press conference the White House issued a "clarifying statement," but it was too late. Truman seemed stunned that news stories went around the globe reporting he had threatened to use the atomic bomb in Korea. The story is often cited to illustrate one of the undoubted risks of the Presidential press conference—that a Chief Executive may make a verbal slip or give an ambiguous answer to a question, with dangerous international repercussions. This has seldom actually happened, however, and the risk of error is scarcely sufficient reason to forgo news conferences in a democracy.

Eisenhower held press conferences twice a month. It was during his administration that technology influenced the institution of the Presidential press conference and made it accessible to the public through radio and television. The first tape-recorded news conference was held by Eisenhower on December 16, 1953. The tape of the President's voice was made available to radio and television stations, and because of this, it was the first time reporters were free to quote all of a President's words directly. Even more important, Eisenhower allowed press conferences to be filmed and—after they were edited by news secretary James C. Hagerty—shown on television. The first filmed news conference was held on January 19, 1955.

Kennedy held the first "live" televised Presidential press conference on January 25, 1961. Gone were the restrictions of the past—written questions, indirect quotation, sanitized film, background replies, and the rest. Now the public could watch the news conference as it was actually occurring. Kennedy could afford to take the risk of live TV exposure because he was extraordinarily effective and very quick on his feet; his press conferences were virtuoso performances, in which he combined humor with an impressive grasp of government programs, often reeling off detailed statistics in reply to a question. He was also unusually photogenic; along with his facile style, this gave Kennedy a great advantage in the television age. More than any other President since TV became a factor in American politics, Kennedy was at home with the medium. Kennedy moved the press conference from the Executive Office Building into the modernistic State Department auditorium, which was better suited to television, and much roomier, than the old Indian Treaty Room.

Once Kennedy had taken the plunge into live television, it became awkward for his successors to ignore this precedent. Lyndon Johnson disliked full-dress televised press conferences, in which he usually came across badly, and he held very few. He preferred informal sessions, often called on short notice, and occasionally held in his office in the manner of his political idol FDR.*

Nixon's avoidance of regular news conferences was a source of continuing frustration to Washington reporters. (One can almost hear Nixon saying: "That's what they hate—when the President won't talk to 'em.") But Nixon and his staff could never agree on the reasons for this Presidential inaccessibility; the explanations kept shifting.

For example, in December, 1970, Herb Klein wrote in *The New York Times:* "Let's face it: A Presidential news conference—with

---

*But times had changed. I recall one such LBJ news conference in the Oval Office; there were so many reporters crowded into the room that we were standing ten-deep, like sardines. Johnson decided to whisper his answers— he sometimes did this for reasons best known to himself—and it was impossible for a great many of the reporters to hear what he was saying.

three hundred reporters clamoring for their moment on camera and with fifty million viewers watching—is not the ideal format to reveal policy to world powers or to explain it in depth to the nation." John Ehrlichman gave another reason. In an interview broadcast over KNBC, Los Angeles, in June of 1972, Ehrlichman said: "He goes in there for half an hour; he gets a lot of flabby and fairly dumb questions, and it doesn't really elucidate much."

At a news conference (untelevised) in his office soon afterward, Nixon was asked whether he agreed with Ehrlichman that the press asked "dumb and flabby questions."

"You are not dumb and flabby," Nixon replied, carefully off the point. But, he added, "I have found that these smaller sessions do provide an opportunity for members of the regular White House press, who study these issues day by day and who know what is relevant and what is not relevant . . . I think that the possibility of dumb and flabby questions is much less."

While this may have been flattering to the White House reporters, it is highly debatable. The newsmen who regularly cover the President are necessarily generalists, since they must write about a wide range of subjects in which the President is involved. One of the advantages of a large press conference, called with adequate advance notice, is that it permits other reporters who are specialists in foreign policy, defense, and other areas, to question the President.

Then, on June 29, in his first televised news conference in thirteen months, Nixon gave still another reason: "I concluded that in the very sensitive period leading up to the Peking trip and the period thereafter, and in the even more sensitive period, as it turned out to be, leading up to the Moscow trip and the period immediately thereafter, that the press conference, even no-commenting questions, was not a useful thing for the President of the United States to engage in."

Here the implication, clearly, was not that questions were dumb and flabby, as Ehrlichman seemed to believe, but that they were too astute and penetrating to be asked and answered during a period of delicate diplomatic negotiation. A "very sensitive period" that lasts thirteen months, however, would seem a bit too long a time for the President to avoid facing reporters in an arena where those fifty million people that Herb Klein was so disturbed about can watch.

As with any institution, there are definite drawbacks to the live televised press conference. Perhaps the most serious problem is its random quality and lack of follow-up questions. Normally, correspondents do not bore in and pursue a point; when the President answers a question and then recognizes the next reporter, his question usually deals with a new subject. The reasons for this are not unrelated to the presence of television. A number of reporters are instructed to ask certain questions by their editors or publishers. They know their employers are watching, and if they are told to ask about a new power project back in Dry Forks, they had better ask about it, and not try to follow up on Marvin Kalb's question about the Middle East. Many reporters, indeed most reporters, are not so instructed, but they come with a specific question, or at least a general subject, in mind. Sometimes a reporter will write down his question so that he will have something to read if he develops stage fright when he is recognized by the President and the camera swings on him. A reporter who has rehearsed his question for the President while shaving that morning is unlikely to abandon it to follow up a previous question. And the laws of chance make it unlikely that the President will call on two or three correspondents in a row who have framed questions on the same topic.

Some Presidents may find the pace, and the format, harder to handle than others. And the jack-in-the-box effect, as newsmen pop up and shout "Mr. President!" to get the attention of the Chief Executive, may disturb some viewers as lacking in majesty. This custom does not, however, seem to disturb the Presidents who have been exposed to it, and it would be difficult to arrange any other way for reporters to be recognized, unless they were to take numbers like shoppers at a supermarket meat counter.

There is no doubt that live television has tended to give the Presidential press conference something of the quality of a "show" or a performance in which both President and press are actors. The fact that there is a large unseen audience has several definite psychological effects on the reporters.

Although critics sometimes argue that the televised press conferences lead to ham acting, there is relatively little of that. But the medium does encourage reporters to play a role. For example, for the benefit of the television audience, reporters find themselves almost unconsciously prefacing their questions with long explanations and recitals of fact. Since the President and the other reporters in the room are generally perfectly well aware of the background to the question being asked, the padding is entirely directed at the television audience. This may be helpful to the viewer at home, but it does slow things down, and the press conference loses some of its basic function—to elicit information—and takes on more of the quality of an entertainment.

On an elementary human level, the fact that the conference is televised means that many reporters are somewhat nervous. The reporter knows that not only his editor, or publisher, but his wife, family, and friends may be watching. Television correspondents are used to being televised, but members of the writing press, who are, after all, not paid TV performers, may face the red eye of the television camera with some trepidation. Standing up before twenty or fifty million people and asking the President of the United States a question, possibly a very pointed question, can be somewhat nerve-racking, even for experienced reporters.

There is, in fact, considerable tension in the air at a Presidential press conference, and a viewer with a sharp eye and a keen ear can detect a little tremolo in the voice of even veteran Washington correspondents when they rise to face the President of the United States. There is always the horrible possibility that under pressure the newsman will forget what he was going to ask. Or he may botch the question, his words becoming so tangled or rambling that his colleagues start to laugh. Worse yet, he may be subject to Presidential ridicule, one of the sharpest weapons a President possesses at a news conference.

"For a brief time the President is exposed," Douglass Cater has written of the press conference. "He knows his moment of truth as clearly as any matador."

The image is apt, but it is equally true that the reporter is exposed to the matador, and in the corrida, the bull usually loses. The President, not the press, has the greater degree of control over the news conference. The choice of whether to hold one at all is his. He sets the date, time, and format. He can avoid and evade questions by a "no comment." Or, as is more often the case, he may use the question merely as a takeoff point for something he wishes to say, and never really respond.

If the heat is rising too rapidly, he can call on a friendly correspondent for a puffball question. He can put a reporter down in various ways: by challenging the premise of a question, turning the tables and asking the reporter a question, or bawling him out.

Moreover, Presidents customarily prepare for their meetings with the press, and with good staff work, they can anticipate a high percentage of the questions that will be asked. "It requires hard work in preparing for it, I can assure you," President Nixon said. President Kennedy also prepared carefully. For example, in a typical pre-conference session on March 15, 1961, Kennedy had breakfast at the White House at 8 A.M. with Pierre Salinger, Dean Rusk, Theodore C. Sorensen, and McGeorge Bundy. Over omelettes, the five men discussed the likely topics that would be brought up at the President's televised news conference set to begin at 10 A.M. Salinger, consulting a pad, played the part of a reporter and asked questions. The President tried out his answers.

At the news conference that morning Kennedy was asked

twenty-two questions. "We had not anticipated six," Salinger said later. "They were on atomic energy, a national sales tax, Defense Department research corporations, a shorter work week, the New York highway program, and a metal extrusion plant at Adrian, Michigan. We usually do a little better than that."

Sometimes press secretaries do a little better than that by planting questions or topics with reporters. This is not to say that the Presidential news conference is like one of those rigged quiz shows of the 1950's. But occasionally a Presidential press secretary will call in a newsman and quietly suggest that if he asks the President about this or that, he might get an interesting response.

Salinger did this at times, and in a 1966 interview over public television stations, Bill Moyers confirmed that he "planted" questions with newsmen on "two or three subjects" at President Johnson's news conference of August 29, 1965. "I did suggest to some reporters that the President had on his mind certain problems," Moyers declared, "and that I was certain he was prepared to deal with those questions if they came up . . . But the purpose was simply to make sure that the news got out that day."

In a similar interview, Herb Klein at first denied, but then indicated, that the Nixon administration engaged in similar practices. Appearing on the same public television interview series in 1969, Klein was reminded that Moyers had "confessed that he sometimes did plant some" questions. "Do you and Mr. Ziegler plant questions?"

A: No, we do not.
Q: None at all?
A: No, sir.
Q: . . . aren't you tempted at least to say to a reporter, I think if you raise this subject you might get an interesting answer?
A: I think an occasion like that might arise, yes, and I wouldn't think that it was wrong if we suggested to a reporter that if he wanted to ask on a particular topic it might make some news.

Apparently Klein was attempting to draw some distinction between planting questions and planting topics, but that hair does not split very well. If a press secretary tells a reporter, "Why don't you ask the President his views about going to Moscow for a summit meeting?" the press secretary may comfort himself with the thought that he has planted a topic—summit meetings—but he has also planted a question. Obviously, only the most ham-handed Presidential press secretary would give a reporter a question all written out for his reading pleasure; it isn't done that way.

One classic example of a slightly rehearsed question occurred at a Nixon press conference in 1970. On July 29 Garnett D. Horner, the White House correspondent of the *Washington Star,* approached Ronald Ziegler at the bar of the San Clemente Inn near the Western White House. A press conference was scheduled for the next day.

"What's on the President's mind?" asked Horner.

"I'll let you know," Ziegler replied.

The next day Ziegler suggested to Horner that a question about Nixon's efforts to bring government to the people might prove fruitful.

Horner, who does not have a reputation for needlessly antagonizing Presidents, arose near the end of the news conference:

HORNER: Mr. President, this press conference in Los Angeles is sort of a climax to a series of activities that you have described as bringing the government to the people, such as your recent meetings in Louisville, Fargo, Salt Lake City, and your work at the Western White House at San Clemente. What benefits do you see to you and to the country from such activities?

THE PRESIDENT: Well, I hope there is benefit to the country. I believe there is benefit in bringing the White House to San Clemente or to Fargo or to Louisville . . . I think it is very important for the people of California, for example, to know the White House, to participate, for example, like this in a Presidential press conference . . .

Since Presidents cram for their press conferences, often anticipate questions with a high degree of precision, and sometimes have their public relations men plant them, it might be concluded that the institution is less spontaneous, and therefore less useful, than it appears. But no amount of rehearsal can prepare the President for every question that may be asked, and in any case, in these confrontations the President reveals not only his policies, but himself. The quality of a leader, his performance under pressure, his character and personality—these are important to the voters no less than issues. And the press conference, more than any other institution, permits voters to glimpse the human being who occupies the Presidency, the man behind the seal, the olive branch, and the arrows.

Although the President's news secretary is often a pivotal figure in Presidential press relations, his influence and importance varies with administrations and individual secretaries. Hagerty was a key policy-level adviser to Eisenhower, for example, a role that Ronald Ziegler was not required to fill. When Eisenhower suffered his heart attack in Denver in September, 1955, it was Hagerty, more than

Vice-President Nixon, to whom Eisenhower turned to keep the affairs of the nation running. Lyndon Johnson, who ran through press secretaries like they were going out of style—he had four in a bit more than five years—overshadowed all of them. Johnson believed that there was a knack to press relations; he could solve all his image problems if only he had a smart PR man. So he tended to blame his press secretaries for his troubles. He never fully understood that his problems with the press were really problems with the public, caused by his own political decisions and actions.*

After Johnson became President, he called in all the public relations men from the various government departments and read them the riot act. They were not, he made it plain, generating enough news about Lyndon Johnson. He might have to get a couple of high school boys from Johnson City to take over their jobs, the President added; they couldn't do any worse. Presidential press secretary George Reedy, who patiently suffered through this meeting, could hardly believe Johnson's performance, thoroughly loyal though he was to the President.

Most Presidential press secretaries have had redeeming features. Hagerty made up in efficiency what he may have lacked in charm (although he was not totally without the latter); he made the press buses run on time. Salinger, one of the brightest of the New Frontiersmen, had an irreverent wit that disarmed his adversaries in the press corps. A somewhat Hogarthian figure, he liked women, drank, smoked huge cigars, bet on horses, dogs, jai alai, and almost anything that moved, played poker, and was, at all times, intensely human. What might have seemed vices in another man somehow seemed perfectly natural in Salinger. Beneath George Reedy's substantial girth and ponderous briefing style was a mind most comfortable in the realm of ideas. An intellectual, Reedy in 1972 found his true calling and was named Dean of the College of Journalism at Marquette University. Bill Moyers, a self-defrocked Baptist preacher —he worked his way through divinity school as a PR man—won the respect of the press corps in part because of his impressive ability to articulate and summarize complex problems and issues. He had the gift of clarity. George Christian was amiable enough, and even Ron Ziegler, who fit in so well with the plastic men of the Nixon administration, had a puppyish, tail-wagging quality, a continuous desire for approval that made it difficult for even the meanest reporter to be permanently angry at him.

---

*In his book *The Twilight of the Presidency*, George Reedy, one of Johnson's press secretaries, is particularly instructive on this point.

The press secretary may be a valuable news source, judiciously leaking a story here, an item there. Since he is closer to the newsmen than any other administration official, he may be tempted to utilize that proximity to protect his own power within the White House. Once, during the Johnson administration, the President chanced to be out in the driveway of the White House and became irritated when he noticed photographers popping their flash bulbs and reporters recording the arrival of some official at the Executive Office Building. Waving his hand in the general direction of West Executive Avenue, which divides the White House from the Executive Office Building, Johnson muttered: "We ought to build a wall there to stop that." Presidential aide Marvin Watson, a literal-minded and security-conscious Texan who tended to be suspicious of the press anyway, heard the President's comment and took due note of it. The next morning Bill Moyers drove into West Executive Avenue. While parking his car, he noticed some workmen with concrete blocks and mortar.

"What are you fellows doing?" the press secretary asked curiously.

"We're building a wall, sir," came the reply.

Investigating, Moyers was appalled to find out that Watson had ordered the construction of a twelve-foot wall to run the length of the street. Besides blocking the reporters' view of the Executive Office Building, Watson apparently felt the wall would create an excellent "security corridor" through which visitors to the White House would have to walk. Moyers feared that if built, the structure would be ridiculed and compared to the Berlin Wall. The unfavorable publicity could only create problems for him as press secretary. He ordered the work halted and leaked the story to Douglas Kiker of the *New York Herald Tribune,* who published it. The story was indignantly denied by other White House officials, but, of course, it was true.

The press secretary obviously plays a key role in setting the overall tone of the Presidential press relations. He is the most important point of contact between the President and the correspondents who cover the White House. And at times he may even be drawn into delicate matters involving national security.

On July 1, 1960, a U.S. Air Force RB-47 reconnaissance aircraft with a crew of six, flying from England on an electronic intelligence mission, was shot down by the Soviet Union over the Barents Sea. Only two members of the crew survived. Both parachuted to safety and were imprisoned by the Russians.

About 10 P.M. on January 24, 1961, four days after Kennedy's inauguration, the *Herald Tribune* Washington Bureau became aware that something unusual was afoot within the government. I was then the newspaper's White House correspondent. Bureau Chief Robert J. Donovan asked Warren Rogers, Jr., and me to try to find out what was going on; Donovan had learned that the White House might have an important announcement at 2 A.M. From my apartment I telephoned the White House, and was put through to Salinger's home in Lake Barcroft, Virginia. I asked him the nature of the big announcement. Salinger sputtered like a Roman candle in a light rain; where had I heard such a thing and don't you tell anyone about this, it's a matter of the highest security and I have no comment. There were further phone calls, and Warren Rogers was able to bluff confirmation from a news source of what we suspected—that the two fliers were about to be released. I called Salinger again. I told him what we had and that the paper had stopped the presses in New York so that the story could be carried in the maximum number of copies of the Late City Edition.

Salinger did not try to deny the facts; but he argued that publication of the story would be inimical to the national interest. He said the two Americans were still inside the Soviet Union, that an agreement had been reached for simultaneous announcement of their release, and that premature disclosure might blow up the deal.

I told Salinger I would get back to him. The position was difficult. The *Herald Tribune* had an exclusive story of major importance. On the other hand, relations between the Soviet Union and the United States had become frozen after the U-2 incident and the summit collapse of 1960. Now Soviet Premier Nikita S. Khrushchev had obviously reversed course; his release of the fliers might conceivably be the beginning of a détente between the two great nuclear powers. If so, did I or my paper really want to take an action that might jeopardize or upset the first diplomatic breakthrough between Washington and Moscow, four days after the inauguration of a new President?

All of these rather grandiose thoughts were running through my head at about 1 A.M. when I telephoned Donovan to relay Salinger's reaction. As we discussed the situation, I strongly urged that we hold off publication; if our information was correct, the two fliers were still in Moscow, and that fact alone made publication too risky. Human life was involved.

Donovan agreed. He telephoned Fendall Yerxa, the *Trib*'s managing editor in New York, who concurred. I called back Salinger, who had said that he was speaking on behalf of the President in his plea to us. I said carefully that if, as I understood it, the President was asking us to delay publication in the national interest, we would, having weighed the facts, agree to the request.

The Late City resumed its run, with no story about the two fliers.

There was no 2 A.M. announcement. The fliers were to have been released at that hour, but KLM Flight 300, bound for Amsterdam with the two men aboard, blew a tire as it was taking off from Moscow. The plane finally took off at 5 P.M. EST, an hour before Kennedy's press conference.

At 6 P.M. Kennedy walked into the State Department auditorium and began speaking before a televised audience of sixty million persons. He made two announcements on other subjects, and then came the third: "I am happy to be able to announce that Captain Freeman B. Olmstead and Captain John R. McKone, members of the crew of the United States Air Force RB-47 aircraft who have been detained by the Soviet authorities since July 1, 1960, have been released by the Soviet government and are now en route to the United States." As Kennedy was making this statement in Washington, the Russians announced the news in Moscow. That night Kennedy directed Salinger to send a telegram to John Hay Whitney, publisher of the *Herald Tribune,* thanking him for delaying publication of the story.

Before many months had passed, Kennedy's praise for the *Herald Tribune* was to turn into displeasure. In February of 1962 the Billie Sol Estes story began to surface. Estes, a financial manipulator from Pecos, Texas, with high political connections in Washington, had built an apparent financial empire in cotton acreage allotments, grain storage, and elusive fertilizer tanks. But in March, Estes was arrested by the FBI. Earl Mazo, Richard Nixon's biographer and the national political correspondent of the *Herald Tribune,* jumped on the story and began writing it hard. The Kennedy administration watched with growing dismay.

On May 18, 1962, a month after Kennedy had faced down the steel industry and rolled back prices, he flew to New York City, where he was joined by Pierre Salinger, who had just returned from an extraordinary mini-summit meeting with Khrushchev at the Soviet premier's dacha near Moscow. I rode into Manhattan from the airport with Salinger. He said Khrushchev had been a convivial host and had even shown him a Russian science fiction movie, called *The Amphibious Man,* whose protagonist had gills grafted on to him so he could breathe underwater. At 7:30 A.M. the next morning the telephone rang in my room at the Hotel Commodore. It was Pierre, calling from the President's suite at the Carlyle, and he sounded like the Amphibious Man coming up for air. "I just wanted you to know the President's reaction to this morning's *Herald Tribune,*" he said. I asked what it was. Salinger replied: "The fucking *Herald Tribune* is at it again." The cause of the President's ire, Salinger explained, was a page-one cartoon by Fischetti; it pictured Salinger reporting to Kennedy as they strolled along outside the White House: "Mr. Khrushchev said he liked your style in the steel crisis."

Salinger asked if I would be kind enough to convey the President's comments personally to Jock Whitney. I said that I was always happy to pass on the thoughts of the President of the United States to my publisher.

I did not have to wait long for an opportunity. Whitney invited me to join him and a few *Herald Tribune* executives for lunch in a private dining room at the newspaper. As the luncheon neared its end, Whitney leaned back expansively and asked: "Well, David, how are we doing in Washington?"

"I'm glad you asked that question," I replied. "Only this morning the President's press secretary called and asked me to pass on to you the President's reaction to the Fischetti cartoon."

"And what was that?"

I hesitated until a waitress finished clearing away the dishes and stepped out of the room. My reply shattered the calm of the executive suite.

Eleven days later, on May 30, it was revealed that Kennedy had canceled all twenty-two White House subscriptions to the *Herald Tribune.* Salinger announced that the President simply wanted to "diversify" his reading. But he singled out for criticism the paper's handling of a Senate subcommittee investigation of the federal stockpile, which was aimed at very high figures of the Eisenhower administration, including its prime target, former Treasury Secretary George Humphrey.*

The *Trib*, Salinger said, had "ignored" important disclosures made at a hearing of the subcommittee, which was only partly correct, since the story in question ran in the late edition. The unstated implication was, of course, that the *Trib* had been vigilant in covering Billie Sol Estes, a Democratic scandal, but had deliberately omitted reference to a Republican scandal.

Kennedy's cancellation of the *Herald Tribune* was extensively criticized, and inspired a rash of political cartoons (including one by the errant Fischetti, depicting a small but pugnacious newsboy

---

*On June 1, 1962, the day after Salinger confirmed the cancellation of the *Herald Tribune*, Eisenhower became so vexed with the Senate probe, he publicly declared: "If Secretary Humphrey ever did a dishonest thing in his life, I'm ready to mount the cross and you can put the nails and spear in me." The Roman Catholic *Pilot* immediately rebuked Eisenhower for invoking the terms of the crucifixion to defend George Humphrey.

hawking the *Herald Tribune* outside the White House under the beady eye of a guard).*

A President's image, in considerable measure, is shaped not only by such public acts, but by his personal, informal contacts with the press corps, particularly the "White House regulars." Even if newsmen cannot report certain details for one reason or another—a Presidential remark not suitable for a family newspaper, for example—the overall impression that a President makes filters out and, in time, reaches the public. White House reporters still recall one memorable conversation with Lyndon Johnson in September of 1964. Senator Barry Goldwater had been criticizing Johnson for allegedly weakening the NATO alliance. To counter this sort of talk, Johnson decided on a little inspection trip. He flew out to SAC headquarters in Omaha with Manlio Brosio, the precise, aristocratic secretary general of NATO. On the return trip to Washington, Johnson strolled up the aisle of Air Force One and sat down at a table with the press pool, whose members included Alvin Spivak of UPI and John Chancellor of NBC. As he chatted with the newsmen, Johnson doodled on a pad. He wrote the word *Peace* and surrounded it with doodles.†

"Peace is the important thing," the President declared soberly. "Compared to peace, everything else is chicken shit."

More than most Presidents, Lyndon Johnson was obsessed with the press. His consuming interest in reporters and what they wrote led in 1965 to a chain of events so bizarre as to rival the Marx Brothers at their best. The plot involved the President of the United States, the assistant White House press secretary, the nation's highest economic officials, reporters for two great newspapers, and quite a few other people. Before it was over, the stock market was shaken,

---

*Banishing a newspaper was obviously a political mistake, and later the story gained currency that the cancellation was actually the work of an overzealous aide. Perhaps, but the phone call I had received at the Commodore eleven days earlier led me to believe otherwise.

†Chancellor, eying Johnson's note pad, thought to himself: I'm going to steal that thing. Chancellor considered the doodle a superb example of Presidential graffiti. When Johnson headed aft with the reporters to introduce them to Brosio, Chancellor went halfway down the aisle, then pretended he had forgotten something, and turned back to the table. "Just as I reached for the doodle," Chancellor recalled, "a great hairy hand came out of nowhere and clamped down on my arm." The President, who was very shrewd about people, had suspected what was in Chancellor's mind and had followed him silently back up the aisle. Johnson tore off the doodle from the pad and pocketed it without a word to Chancellor.

the Federal Reserve Board had raised the discount rate, and the nation appeared, at least briefly, to be in the grip of a serious economic crisis.

For Joseph Laitin, it all began when his telephone rang one night in November at the Driskill Hotel in Austin. The voice, with its deep Texas accent, was unmistakable. As President Johnson's assistant press secretary, Laitin had come to expect—and to dread—the almost nightly telephone call from the ranch. The President had flown to Texas to recuperate from his famed gall-bladder operation, and Laitin and the White House press corps were quartered, as was customary, at the Driskill. Regularly, around 11 P.M., the phone would ring in Laitin's room.

"What's going on?" Johnson would ask casually. "What's new?" But Laitin knew what the President really wanted to hear: the latest gossip about the White House press corps, the earthier and juicier, the better. It was an uncomfortable role for Laitin. The short, gray-haired, and bespectacled Presidential assistant was something of a rarity in Washington—a government public relations man with a reputation as an honest and decent person. He had been a war correspondent in the Pacific for Reuters during World War II; later he covered the Nuremberg trials and the atom bomb tests at Bikini. He moved to Hollywood after the war, worked in radio and television, then came to Washington as a public information official in the Johnson administration. Press Secretary George Reedy brought Laitin over to the White House from the Budget Bureau to be his assistant. Now, in Austin, in the fall of 1965, Laitin was in a quandary over the President's telephone calls. Many of the newsmen covering the President were his friends, and Laitin felt trapped between his loyalty to the President and his loyalty to his former profession and to the reporters he worked with each day.

On this particular night, when the President called, Laitin happened to mention the name of Douglas Kiker, then the White House correspondent of the *New York Herald Tribune*. Suddenly Johnson was very attentive; he wanted to know more. "I could hear him," Laitin said in relating the incident much later, "licking his chops over the phone." Like Johnson, Kiker's roots were in the rural South, and LBJ regarded Kiker with the special wariness that male members of the same species reserve for their own. In some primordial, atavistic manner, the two men understood each other.* Kiker, the son of a

---

*They had begun at the White House on the same day. I became chief of the *Herald Tribune* Washington Bureau on November 18, 1963. At my urging, Kiker had resigned from the Peace Corps to join the Washington Bureau.

cotton-mill hand, grew up in Griffin, Georgia, thirty miles south of Atlanta in the rolling hill country of Spalding County. The red clay soil of the Georgia Piedmont is poor for farming; the hard caliche of Lyndon Johnson's Texas hill country is not suitable for farming, either. Both men had left home and headed North. Kiker was a shrewd, energetic reporter and a gifted writer who had published two novels. His news stories often seemed to reveal the complex fellow Southerner who occupied the White House better than those written by reporters from more urbane Eastern backgrounds. Indeed, some of Kiker's White House stories captured vintage Johnson in a way that nobody else could. And some got under Johnson's skin the way nobody else could. Secretly the President may have grudgingly admired Kiker's professional skill and ability to penetrate the Johnsonian psyche (there is, in fact, some evidence for this). But to his aides, Johnson enjoyed complaining about the *Herald Tribune*'s White House correspondent.

As Johnson knew, Kiker found life almost continually exhilarating, and he had the reputation of enjoying a drink, good talk, and pleasing company as well as any man. With Johnson pressing for more details, Laitin suddenly realized he had found the key to his problem: Kiker stories. Rather in the manner of Scheherazade, Laitin began regaling LBJ with stories of Kiker's supposed exploits in the *boîtes* of Austin. He told Johnson the wildest tales, never making them up out of whole cloth, but embellishing them and adding spurious details, spinning long fables of Bunyanesque drinking and roistering.

It was a nice arrangement while it lasted—Johnson loved the gossipy stories and Laitin was relieved of the unpleasant task of talking about other White House reporters. Douglas Kiker, or so it seemed, had solved the problem of Laitin's bedtime stories for the President of the United States.

That is, until a day late in November when the President, sounding puzzled, called Laitin. The night before Laitin had spun out a

---

When I mentioned that we needed someone to go to Texas with President Kennedy, Doug had volunteered. He was in the motorcade in Dallas on November 22 and wrote the story of the President's assassination. Filing the story by telephone from Love Field, Kiker wept. Since he was so new on the job, the newspaper's operator in New York was unfamiliar with his name. "It's all right, Mr. Kyber," she cut in each time he broke down, "go ahead and cry." After Dallas, Kiker remained on, logically, as the White House correspondent. In 1966, when the *Herald Tribune* ceased publication, he joined NBC as a television reporter.

Kiker story, adding the usual embellishments to please the President. "I thought you said Kiker was down here carrying on," said Johnson, "but the story in today's *Herald Tribune* is by someone named Richard Dougherty." Trapped, Laitin realized with a sinking sensation that the story he had told the previous night was based on an incident that had taken place some time earlier; Kiker was not on *this* trip to Austin—a fact Laitin had neglected to check. Thinking fast, and possibly drawing on his experience as a Hollywood scriptwriter, Laitin gulped out a reply: "Mr. President, Kiker was behaving so badly, his paper had to recall him. They sent down Dick Dougherty instead."

Johnson chuckled, pondered this news for a moment, then told Laitin: "Okay, here's what I want you to do. Let's leak a story to the new man to show the *Herald Tribune* they don't need Kiker down here." Once the scoop appeared, Johnson explained, the paper's editors would surely conclude that "Kiker never got a story like this."

Dubious, but hardly in a position to disagree, Laitin asked LBJ what he had in mind.

"Tell Dougherty the President has summoned the quadriad to the ranch for conversations."

One of those unfortunate bureaucratic additions to the language, the quadriad served as Presidential shorthand for the government's four top economic officials—at the time: Treasury Secretary Henry H. Fowler; Gardner Ackley, chairman of the Council of Economic Advisers; Budget Director Charles L. Schultze; and William McChesney Martin, Jr., chairman of the Federal Reserve Board.

Laitin assured the President he would leak the story. But he was reluctant to act; he did not know Dougherty very well, and if he simply called him in and gave him the exclusive, it would seem odd. Furthermore, Laitin well knew that some of Johnson's aides had gotten into difficulty by taking the President too literally. He decided to do nothing, hoping that Johnson would forget the whole thing, which often happened. But Johnson did not forget.

The following day, November 30, Johnson again called Laitin, demanding to know where the story was. By now, as Laitin recalls, "I was sweating bullets." Already tangled in his own web, Laitin became even more deeply ensnared. He assured Johnson he had placed calls to the chairman of the Council of Economic Advisers and the Secretary of the Treasury. "I need more details to flesh the story out," he told the President. "I'm working on it, don't worry."

As Laitin, in a near-panic by now, wondered what in the world to do next, fortune smiled. He got a telephone call from the unsuspecting Dougherty.* The Labor Department, Dougherty informed Laitin, had just announced that the Consumer Price Index had risen 0.2 percent to a new record high. Did the White House have any reaction?

"Well, as a matter of fact," Laitin said in his most confidential tones, "you can't attribute this to me, or to the White House, but the President has summoned the quadriad to the ranch. I'm sure they'll be discussing this and other economic problems."

"Gee, thanks, Joe," said Dougherty, somewhat bewildered by his sudden turn of good luck. This is an interesting news story, Dougherty remembers thinking at the time. I wonder why he told me? Oh well, I thought, it pays to ask. As it happened, Dougherty knew that his immediate rival, Robert B. Semple, Jr., the *New York Times* correspondent assigned to cover the President, was going to the movies that night. If I write this, Dougherty thought, when the *Trib*'s first edition comes out around 11 P.M., the *Times* will really land on Semple's head. Underneath a highly cosmopolitan, witty, pseudo-Gaelic exterior, Dougherty is really a decent sort. He recalled many occasions when *Times* reporters had been kind to him. He decided to share the news with Semple. At the bar of the Driskill, he confided that Johnson had summoned his economic advisers to the ranch. Then both went off and filed their stories to New York.

Around midnight the White House correspondent for the Associated Press, who was in Austin with the rest of the reporters to cover Johnson, telephoned Laitin at the Driskill. "We got a rocket from New York," the AP man complained, "saying that the quadriad is coming down. Is it true?" Laitin was highly pleased; he assumed that Dougherty's story in the *Herald Tribune* was being picked up by the wire services and played nationally. The President would be impressed with how deftly he had handled the leak. He confirmed the story to AP, again without attribution to the White House. A few minutes later the UPI man called with the same question, and again Laitin confirmed the news.

The next morning President Johnson, in a fury, called Laitin from the ranch. "I told you to leak that story to the *HERALD TRIBUNE*," he roared, "not to the *TIMES!*"

Incredulous, Laitin now learned what had happened. *The New York Times* had decided to combine the cost-of-living increase with

---

*Dougherty, later the New York correspondent of the *Los Angeles Times*, left that newspaper to go to work for Senator George McGovern and served as his press secretary during the 1972 Presidential campaign.

the dramatic news from the ranch, and Semple's information about the quadriad was incorporated in a story out of Washington under the byline of David R. Jones. The story was prominently displayed as the "off-lead"—the article in the left-hand column at the top of page one:

CONSUMER PRICES
AT A RECORD HIGH;
JOHNSON WORRIED

———

Rise of 0.2% in October Is
Viewed as Inflation Threat
—Food Costs Stable

———

PRESIDENT CALLS AIDES

———

He Will Press His Economic
Advisers to Coordinate
Policies in Price Field

The story went on to say that "it was learned" that Johnson, recuperating from surgery at his Texas ranch, planned to call in his four top economic advisers. No date for the meeting had been set, but it was understood that one of the purposes would be to coordinate government policies in the price field.

This, and not the Dougherty story, Laitin now realized in dismay, was what AP and UPI had picked up.* The wires services, Johnson informed Laitin testily, were playing the story big. "You make it look like I'm in a panic," Johnson fumed. "You better straighten this out at the morning briefing. You straighten it out—and don't quote me."

Before facing the reporters, Laitin got off a call to Dougherty. "Look, you're new around here," he snapped. "Next time I give you a story, keep it to yourself."

At the morning briefing, Laitin struggled manfully to undo the damage. President Johnson, he said, was not feeling "undue concern" over inflation, and that was not why he had summoned the

———

*Dougherty's story, like Semple's, was absorbed into another. Written in New York, the story appeared on page one of the *Herald Tribune* under the byline of Terry Robards, and the headline: "Living Costs at New High, Johnson Calls in Top Men." The wires, however, decided to carry *The New York Times* account.

members of the quadriad. The economic advisers would be moseying down to the ranch for a "regular, periodic" session. They hadn't, after all, had a chance to meet with the President since before his gall-bladder operation in October. "We don't consider inflation a major threat at this time," Laitin added.

But Laitin could not stem the tide. The next morning, December 2, once again the story was the off-lead in the *Times:*

3 U.S. AIDES MOVE
TO OFFSET WORRY
OVER INFLATION

Meeting Called by Johnson
With Economic Advisers
Termed Merely Routine

PUBLIC CONCERN NOTED

Beneath the byline of Edwin L. Dale, Jr., the *Times* economic correspondent in Washington, the story began:

> The Johnson Administration struck back on three fronts today to counter what appeared to be growing public concern over the threat of inflation.
>
> In Austin, Tex., Joseph Laitin, the assistant White House press secretary, in contrast with reports from the Texas White House yesterday, said the President was not showing "undue concern" over inflation . . . This was an apparent reversal of the word given to some reporters in Austin yesterday about the President's attitude of concern following the announcement of another increase in the Consumer Price Index . . . The administration again today sought to calm public fears . . .

The story went on to explain that Secretary of Labor W. Willard Wirtz, in a San Francisco speech, and Commerce Secretary John T. Connor, in Toronto, struck similar themes in an apparently coordinated effort "to avert any outbreak of inflationary psychology."

In its lead editorial, the *Times* thundered. The Johnson administration was dangerously "downgrading the dangers of inflation . . . The statement in Austin yesterday that the White House does not consider inflation a major threat at this time, and the supplementary remarks by Secretaries Wirtz and Connor, only reinforce the government's air of easy optimism."

On Wall Street, bond prices fell sharply. Analysts attributed the drop to concern over rising interest rates, despite administration reassurances to the contrary.

In Austin, the President telephoned his assistant press secretary again. "Laitin," the President said, "you've thrown the country into chaos."

The hapless Laitin, with visions now of being held responsible for plunging the nation into financial ruin, could manage only a feeble reply. "How did I know," he said weakly, "that Macy's tells Gimbels?"

This time Johnson made it clear to Laitin he was taking no chances. He would personally take command of the situation. From Austin, Johnson telephoned a soothing statement to the Business Council; the unofficial advisory group of business leaders happened to be meeting in Washington that day.

Once more, the *Times* put the story on the front page, and this time Robert Semple finally got a byline:

JOHNSON PREDICTS
NEW YEAR OF BOOM
WITH NO INFLATION

Address to Business Council
Seeks to Allay Fears of
Instability in Economy

"President Johnson," Semple's story began, "took a personal hand today in the administration's apparent effort to allay fears of inflation . . . Mr. Johnson thus became the fourth member of his own administration to comment on prices since Tuesday . . ."

But the snowball wouldn't stop. Wall Street responded erratically to the conflicting sounds emanating from the ranch. The Dow-Jones industrial average dropped 3.01 and the *Wall Street Journal's* market column explained: "Brokers attributed the hesitancy in the market to uncertainty about the business outlook next year despite President Johnson's statement yesterday that he expects record prosperity without inflation in 1966. Worry about rising interest rates was another factor, brokers added."

Johnson scheduled his by-now well-advertised meeting with the quadriad for Monday, December 6. On Friday, before the meeting could take place, the Federal Reserve Board acted. Defying Johnson's easy-money policies, the Board of Governors increased bank interest rates to the highest point since March, 1930. Word of the action was disclosed on Sunday, December 5. When the board's chairman, William McChesney Martin, Jr., flew into Texas to join the other quadriad members for the meeting with Johnson, the atmosphere was, to say the least, strained.

"He didn't address himself to changing my mind," Johnson tersely told newsmen afterward, "and I didn't address myself to changing his." The Federal Reserve Board, Martin assured the press on his part, had not intended "in any way to defy the President or the administration." But the repercussions continued. Major banks across the country raised their prime rates. Savings and loans officials warned of higher interest rates on new mortgages; in Washington, the directors of the Federal Deposit Insurance Corporation met to consider whether to allow state banks to follow the Federal Reserve Board's lead. Across the border, the Bank of Canada raised its discount rate to match Washington's action. On Capitol Hill, Representative Wright Patman, chairman of the Joint Economic Committee, announced a Congressional investigation of the decision. Senator Russell Long, the Louisiana Democrat, also proposed an investigation. But even Congress could not have guessed how it all began. As for Douglas Kiker, he continued to enjoy life, totally and blissfully unaware that he had been the central figure in one of the zaniest scenarios since *A Night at the Opera*.

The American President is more powerful than he should be and less powerful than he is thought to be. Nevertheless, he remains the focal point of American power and the object of unequaled attention by the press. Because of this, he retains enormous capacity to set the mood and the standards for the total political environment. He can tell the truth to the American people or he can lie. He can operate behind a shield of official secrecy or he can be open with the electorate. He can retreat in the magnificent isolation of the Presidency, making solitary decisions that affect the lives of millions, or he can communicate regularly and directly with the people in the free forum of the press conference.

"I think it is important for our democratic system of government," Harry Truman told his last news conference in 1953, "that every medium of communication between the citizens and their government, particularly the President, be kept open as far as possible.

"This kind of news conference where reporters can ask any question they can dream up—directly of the President of the United States—illustrates how strong and how vital our democracy is. There is no other country in the world where the chief of state submits to such unlimited questioning . . .

"Perhaps succeeding Presidents will be able to figure out improvements and safeguards in the procedure. I hope they will never cut out the direct line of communication between themselves and the people."

Part V

A CONCLUSION

" . . . when information which properly belongs to the public is systematically withheld by those in power, the people soon become ignorant of their own affairs, distrustful of those who manage them, and—eventually—incapable of determining their own destinies."

—*President Richard M. Nixon,*
March 8, 1972

14

Summing Up

Apparently a substantial number of Americans—it is difficult to estimate their number with any precision—do not believe that their government landed men on the moon.

On June 14, 1970, the Knight newspapers published an astonishing story based upon interviews with 1,721 persons in six cities—Philadelphia, Miami, Akron, Detroit, Washington, and Macon, Georgia—and in several communities in North and South Carolina. The people interviewed were asked whether they really believed that U.S. astronauts had been to the moon and back. The article emphasized that no attempt had been made to reach a cross section of the population; since the survey was not based on the standard polling technique of random sampling, the percentage of disbelievers could not be taken to reflect opinion nationally, or in each community.

Nevertheless, the interviews did indicate that substantial numbers of Americans do not believe the single most widely publicized action ever taken by their government in peacetime. In Macon, 19 percent of those interviewed doubted the moon landing had taken place; in Charlotte, North Carolina, 17 percent; in Philadelphia, 9 percent; in Miami, 5 percent; in Akron, 4 percent; and in Detroit, 2 percent.

"I'll never believe they walked on the moon," said Mrs. Ann Dix, a housewife interviewed in a West Philadelphia supermarket. "Not the moon I see shining in the sky at night."

A man in Macon insisted that the pictures of the moon walk shown on TV were actually taken "in a petrified forest in Arizona." A lady in Macon explained that her television set could not pick up New York City stations; how, then, could she really be getting televised pictures from the moon?

A housewife in Charlotte declared that if God wanted man to reach the moon, He would have made it easier. "He would have made steps," she said.

When the skeptics were asked why such an enormous hoax would be perpetrated, they generally replied either that the government had done it to fool the Russians and the Chinese, or that it had been done to justify the great cost of the space program. A few thought the government had a bread-and-circuses motive, to make people forget their troubles.

No doubt the overwhelming majority of citizens understand that NASA, whatever its deficiencies, really did put men on the moon. But the doubts are indicative, suggestive of a deeper ailment. As Frank Mankiewicz, national coordinator for the McGovern campaign, remarked in 1972: "There are a generation of Americans whose instinctive reaction to a public statement is that it is false."

Government deception, supported by a pervasive system of official secrecy and an enormous public relations machine, has reaped a harvest of massive public distrust. This deep distrust of government, and the word of the government, has altered traditional political relationships in America. It has shattered the bond of confidence between the government and the people. And it has diminished our confidence in ourselves and in our ability as a people to overcome the problems that confront us.

Lying is not a new phenomenon in American history or politics, but there is, after all, a question of degree and frequency, and surely nothing in our past has matched, in scale and quality, the grand deception of Vietnam. What Max Frankel has termed "the *habit* of *regular* deception in our politics and administration" is something new, and shameful. Systematic deception as an instrument of highest national policy is, God knows, hardly a cause for national pride.

What else but such a policy could result in the horror of My Lai being briefed "as one of our successful operations"? What else but such a policy could produce a General John D. Lavelle, the head of the Seventh Air Force, who commanded 400 fighter-bombers and 40,000 men, and whose pilots bombed North Vietnam at least 147 times without authorization between November of 1971 and March of 1972? Some of them filed false reports claiming they had been fired upon, for General Lavelle had made it plain to his pilots that they could not report the air strikes had taken place without enemy provocation. At one point Lavelle assigned three men, he later explained to a Congressional committee, "to try to find out how we could continue doing what we were doing but report it accurately." But the reports required so much detail that "we couldn't find a way."*

The deception in Vietnam was symptomatic. The emergence of the United States as a world power during and after World War II proportionately increased the opportunities, the temptations, and the capacity of the government to lie. The expansion of American power resulted in the growth of a vast national security establishment and an often unchecked intelligence bureaucracy. Covert operations of the CIA required official lies to protect them, and the standard in such cases became not truth, but whether the government's actions were "plausibly deniable." In other words, whether the government's lies were *convincing*.

As a concomitant of expanded American global power, the government has increasingly gained control over channels of information about military, diplomatic, and intelligence events. Frequently the press and public, unable to check the events independently, can only await the appearance of the President on the television screen to announce the official version of reality, be it the Bay of Pigs, Tonkin Gulf, or Laos, or Cambodia, or Vietnam.

Because of official secrecy on a scale unprecedented in our history, the government's capacity to distort information in order to preserve its own political power is almost limitless. Although General Lavelle could not find a way to convert lies into truth, the government has been more successful. Increasingly in recent years it has used the alchemy of power to brew synthetic truths and to shape our perception of events to fit predetermined policies.

If information is power, the ability to distort and control information will be used more often than not to preserve and perpetuate that power. But the national security policy makers, the crisis manag-

---

*Lavelle insisted to the Senate Armed Services Committee that he had not fought a private war, and that his deputies had received tacit encouragement from his superiors, including the staff director of the Joint Chiefs of Staff. This was denied by Admiral Thomas H. Moorer, chairman of JCS, and other officers. The Nixon administration tried to cover up the scandal. The Air Force originally announced that Lavelle had retired for reasons of "health." Later General John D. Ryan, Air Force Chief of Staff, said he had relieved the general as a result of the bombing raids. Ryan testified that he had recommended that Congress be told the truth, but was overruled—by Defense Secretary Melvin Laird.

ers of the nuclear age, are frequently men of considerable intellectual abilities who have gone to the right schools. They pride themselves not only on their social graces, but on their rationality and morality. For such men, the preservation of partisan political power would not be a seemly rationale for official deception (although it might be entirely sufficient for the President whom they serve). National security provides the acceptable alternative, the end that justifies all means, the end that permits men who pondered the good, the true, and the beautiful as undergraduates at Harvard and Princeton to sit in air-conditioned rooms in Washington twenty years later and make decisions that result in blood and agony half a world away. It is the rationale that permits decent men to make indecent decisions.

The excuse for secrecy and deception most frequently given by those in power is that the American people must sometimes be misled in order to mislead the enemy. This justification is unacceptable on moral and philosophic grounds, and often it simply isn't true. Frequently the "enemy" knows what is going on, but the American public does not.

For example, for several years, until details were publicized by a subcommittee of the Senate Foreign Relations Committee, the United States government waged a secret war in Laos. Secret, that is, from the American public, because presumably the Pathet Lao and the North Vietnamese were under no delusions about the American role. Apparently it was thought necessary, in this case, to mislead the American public in order to reveal the truth to the enemy.

When Lyndon Johnson issued his National Security Action Memorandum of April 6, 1965, which ordered that the commitment of American combat troops in Vietnam be kept secret, his actions were patently not designed to fool Hanoi or the Viet Cong, who would find out quickly enough who was shooting at them; it was designed to conceal the facts from the American electorate. The memorandum ordered that the troops be deployed "in ways that should minimize any appearance of sudden changes in policy," a concern that was clearly tailored more to domestic audiences than to public opinion in Hanoi, where there are very few American voters. Again and again the government has taken actions designed to mislead not an enemy, but the American public—just the opposite of the stated rationale for deception.

The elitists who make national security policy have combined "the arrogance of power," as Hannah Arendt has noted, with "the arrogance of mind." They have increasingly come to feel that they alone possess the necessary information and competence to deal with foreign policy crises and problems. Leslie H. Gelb, director of the task force that produced the Pentagon Papers, has written that "most of our elected and appointed leaders in the national security establishment felt they had the right—and beyond that the obligation—to manipulate the American public in the national interest as they defined it."

The elite policy makers have thus found an easy justification for both deception and secrecy. They are the only ones who "read the cables" and the intelligence reports and "have the information." Ordinary citizens, they believe, cannot understand complex foreign policy problems; ergo the policy makers have the right, so they think, to mislead the public for its own good.

In its baldest terms, this philosophy has been stated as "the right to lie." Even if officials feel compelled to mislead the public—and it is unlikely that total virtue will ever find its way into the councils of government—to proclaim that right is to place an official imprimatur on a policy of deception and distrust.

"It is sophistry to pretend that in a free country a man has some sort of inalienable or constitutional right to deceive his fellow men," Walter Lippmann has noted. "There is no more right to deceive than there is a right to swindle, to cheat, or to pick pockets."

The result of more than two decades of deception has been to shred the fabric of trust between people and government. It is not only that people no longer believe what a President tells them; the mistrust has seeped outward. It has spread, and pervaded other institutions. In the courts, for example, the government has discovered it increasingly difficult to convict peace activists or others who dissent from established policy because juries tend to disbelieve the uncorroborated testimony of government witnesses.

Within the Executive Branch itself, the lying has had an insidious effect, for in time, policy makers begin to believe their own lies. The deception designed for the public in the end becomes self-deception, as the lesson of Vietnam illustrates. To read the Pentagon Papers in detail is to perceive a group of men at the highest level of the government marching in lockstep toward certain disaster. They had begun to believe their own memoranda, "options," and "scenarios"; for them, reality had become the reflection in the fun-house mirror.

One of the most damaging aspects of government lying is that even if the truth later emerges, it seldom does so in time to influence public opinion or public policy. The extent of the government's deception over Tonkin Gulf did not begin to emerge until late in 1967 and early 1968, almost four years after the event. By then, it was too late.

And the effect of lying is cumulative; it is doubtless true, and possibly comforting, that the American public is less gullible today than twenty years ago, because it has learned that the government is not always credible. But this increased public sophistication has been earned at a terribly high price; there is now a tendency to disbelieve the government even when it is telling the truth. Like the reaction of the jury to the witness who admits perjury but insists that his new testimony is the absolute truth, the public responds to the government: "Yes, but when did you stop lying?"

Unfortunately, the remedies for government deception and secrecy are as much in the realm of morality as of politics. The only "solution" to government lying is for government to tell the truth. But given the combination of factors that has led to government deception in America on such an unprecedented scale, merely wishing it to go away will not help very much.

Any hope of change, therefore, must come through the political process. The need is to make the political cost of lying too high; to make political power rest, at least in some measure, on truth. The process of public education that began with the U-2 affair is perhaps slowly leading in that direction; paradoxically, the "credibility gap" may contain the seeds of its own destruction. The disclosures of the Pentagon Papers and the gradually dawning realization by the public that it has been systematically misled may in time have beneficial political consequences. If political leaders come to realize, through mass opinion and election returns, that deceiving the public carries greater political risks than telling the truth, the politics of lying may gradually be replaced by the politics of truth.

This may seem entirely too optimistic, and perhaps it is, but there are some signs pointing in this direction. Lyndon Johnson's low credibility quotient certainly helped to bring about his retirement. Government deception, truth, and trust were low-key issues in the 1968 Presidential campaign, but they were considerably more visible issues in 1972, despite George McGovern's failure to convert them into votes.

The fact that an issue is discussed in a Presidential campaign does not, of course, automatically guarantee any change whatsoever. In 1968 Richard Nixon seemed to recognize credibility as an important political issue; he promised to provide open government and tell the truth. After his election he followed much the same manipulative policies as had his predecessor, Lyndon Johnson. Nixon widened and deepened the credibility gap while warning against it.

Unless deception and secrecy are clearly recognized and identified as political issues of major importance, unless the President of the United States and his successors take personal steps to bring about and sustain a new atmosphere of candor and trust, there is little possibility of change, and there will be continuing danger to our political institutions.

During hearings in 1971 of the Moorhead subcommittee, Representative Paul N. McCloskey, Jr., wondered whether it might be possible for Congress to pass a law that would make it a crime for government officials to "willfully deceive" Congress—and, by implication, the public. As McCloskey noted: "People who submit deceptive income tax returns or willfully mislead the government when they submit information are subject to criminal sanctions." Why not turn this principle around, he asked, and apply it to the government? The proposal would create monumental enforcement problems, since government officials would be unlikely to prosecute and jail themselves for fibbing.

Still, McCloskey was right to raise the issue. Political leaders must come to understand that no government can arrogate to itself a higher right to deceive its people for their "own good." The doctrine of deception in the public interest must be rejected.

As Anthony Lake, a former White House official, has so aptly put it: "The essential first step is for the government to realize that it cannot lead the public while misleading it."

The classification and secrecy system, combined with the other factors discussed above, has resulted, I have suggested, in a system of institutionalized lying. Never before in our history has the American public accepted a classification system in peacetime that permits dozens of civilian agencies to stamp documents secret and to control information. The secrecy structure that has been allowed to take root and flourish since 1951 has given the Executive Branch unprecedented and dangerous power to conceal and mislead. As we have seen, whole categories of intelligence classifications have sprung up that are, of and in themselves, supersecret.

There have been suggestions that the United States abolish the classification system entirely. A strong argument can be made that the new technology, such as overhead reconnaissance by satellites, and the universal nature of scientific knowledge make the whole concept of government secrecy obsolete or obsolescent—at least insofar as it applies to science, and to weapons research and deployment.

A Pentagon task force reviewing the government's classification policies reported in 1970 that no matter how stamped, protected, and locked up, "on vital information, one should not rely on effective secrecy for more than one year." The task force also reported: ". . . it is unlikely that classified information will remain secure for periods as long as five years, and it is more reasonable to assume that it will become known by others in periods as short as one year through independent discovery, clandestine disclosure, or other means." The panel was headed by Dr. Frederick Seitz, a leading physicist, and its members included Dr. Edward Teller, who is usually described, unenviably, as the "father" of the hydrogen bomb.

While the task force believed that "more might be gained than lost" if the United States were to abolish—unilaterally if necessary— all secrecy, it concluded that this was "not a practical proposal at the present time." But the panel recommended "major surgery" of the classification system. It estimated that the volume of scientific and technical information that is classified could be decreased "by perhaps as much as 90 percent."

The task force also suggested that in one vital area, excessive classification was actually weakening the national security. ". . . the laboratories in which highly classified work is carried out have been encountering more and more difficulty in recruiting the most brilliant and capable minds." One member of the task force predicted that "if present trends continue for another decade, our national effort in weapons research will become little better than mediocre." Thus the mania for classification may be having an effect that is the opposite of what its designers intended.

One member of the panel, paraphrasing physicist Niels Bohr, noted that "while secrecy is an effective instrument in a closed society, it is much less effective in an open society in the long run; instead, the open society should recognize that openness is one of its strongest weapons . . ." The report also observed, accurately: "We believe that overclassification has contributed to the credibility gap that evidently exists between the government and an influential segment of the population." The report was a more than usually candid and thoughtful document, which makes it all the more unfortunate that it was given an administrative classification and kept semisecret by the Pentagon.

Although the classification system veils information from the public and permits the Executive Branch to distort the truth and shape events to fit policy, the secrecy label—and the doctrine of "executive privilege"—is also used to conceal information from Congress. Secrecy gives the President a powerful psychological advantage in his continuing power struggle with the Legislative Branch. Since national security information is highly classified, it is not only some members of the public who may assume that the President alone "has the information" and knows what is best. The same attitude is deeply rooted in Congress.

Nothing could be more dangerous in a democracy, however, than for its citizens and the legislature to abdicate foreign policy judgments to the Executive. The record of the past decade would suggest that the presumed superior knowledge of the President is often a mirage. Kennedy erred at the Bay of Pigs, Johnson plunged the country into a disastrous ground and air war in Vietnam, Nixon stumbled in Laos—all with the benefit of literally tons of classified information.

To stamp a document Top Secret does not, alas, insure that it is accurate, and because a President possesses great quantities of secret information does not mean that the information is correct, or that even if it is, he will necessarily act with wisdom.

Not only does secrecy and classification conceal data from the public and Congress, it conceals information from officials of the Executive Branch itself. The Bay of Pigs might not have taken place, for example, if knowledge of the operation were not restricted so tightly to a small group of Presidential advisers and intelligence operators. Compartmentalization and excessive secrecy increases the likelihood that a small number of policy makers, talking only to each other, may make irreversible mistakes. Potential disaster rides the access and distribution lists, and the secrecy stamps.

One previously unpublished illustration will suffice: early in the Kennedy administration Dr. Jerome B. Wiesner, the President's science adviser, was shocked to learn that U.S. Air Force jets were flying "on the deck," straight at the Soviet Union, then pulling up sharply at the border to activate Soviet radar and electronic defenses. Appalled at the potential dangers of this secret, highly classified operation, Wiesner requested a briefing from the Pentagon—and was refused. Only after he alerted Kennedy and McNamara did Wiesner succeed in getting briefed. Eventually, after Kennedy, in turn, was briefed on the dangerous flights, the practice was stopped.

In this instance, a military intelligence operation involved the potential risk of touching off World War III. Yet a high White House official, the President's chief scientific adviser, was unable to break through the screen of official secrecy without Presidential intervention.

My own view is that the present classification system should be junked. I doubt there is any need for a formal system of official secrecy in the United States. We have only had such a system for a bit more than two decades, and there is nothing in our traditions or history that requires its continuation. It is a relic of the Cold War. It breeds concealment and mistrust; it encourages the government to lie.

It is unrealistic, however, to think that Congress and the Executive Branch would agree to end all official secrecy. As an alternative, there could be substituted a system under which a sharply limited number of documents might be protected, for a much shorter period, solely by agencies directly concerned with national security and foreign policy.

For example, in place of the present system, the following limited arrangement might be adopted: in a few rare instances, if it is felt to be absolutely vital to the national safety that a document be specially protected, it could be stamped Secret. If a document needs to be secret, it can be marked that way; there is no persuasive need for any other classification or for gradations of official secrecy. There may be theoretical reasons for such degrees of secrecy, but the process breaks down when one attempts to set standards defining what information should be stamped at which level. It can't be done, and the proliferation of classifications, levels of secrecy, secret classifications, and access lists has led to bureaucratic chaos. Power to classify a document as secret would rest only with the President or the head of a department or agency, and it could not be delegated to anyone. After three years the secret label would lapse. Only action by the President personally could keep the document classified. The three-year limit is not a wholly arbitrary figure; it would mean that a document classified in the first year of a President's term would be declassified before the end of his first term; and in any event, a document classified any time during his first term would be declassified before the end of his second term. This would make it more difficult for a President who hoped to be re-elected to use the secrecy label to conceal his actions; the chickens would be more likely to come home to roost while he is still in office. And the shorter period of secrecy would encourage greater accountability.

But the President, it may be protested, has little time to classify or to review documents to see whether they should, for some compelling reason of state, be kept secret. That is precisely the point; under such an extremely limited system as proposed here, very little material would be classified to begin with—cabinet secretaries and agency heads are also busy men—and even less would be classified more than three years, since bureaucrats would be leery of going to the President to ask for an extension. This does not mean that the Pentagon, the State Department, or the CIA would be helpless to keep certain information from the public domain. It could do so by the normal practice of restricting physical access to its buildings and files, rather than by the mumbo jumbo of an elaborate, formal system of classification. Since the declassification does not automatically mean disclosure—a distinction so often overlooked—even such a rigorously limited system would not in itself guarantee a greater flow of information to the public. But abolishing the present unworkable system would create a healthier atmosphere, since the mere existence of the present system encourages and supports a secrecy syndrome throughout the government. It would be a major step in the direction of sanity and the restoration of trust between the people and their government.

There have been proposals that Congress step into the classification quicksand and attempt to legislate a new secrecy system. There is, perhaps, a hidden danger in this approach. The various suggestions that Congress establish an independent or quasi-independent review board or commission to set secrecy and classification standards entail a new kind of risk. The courts might look unkindly on newspapers that published stories relating to national security without first clearing the information with the commission. Thus, a body created to reduce secrecy might end up as a board of censors. And traditionally, the establishment of standards by legislation is accompanied or soon followed by sanctions. If Congress attempts to legislate secrecy, if its own prestige becomes involved in defining standards, it could open the door to a law prohibiting the press from publishing what Congress has defined as secret. This in turn might mean the press could not disclose whatever a government official in the Executive Branch had decided to stamp Secret. Once this line is crossed, or even if existing espionage statutes are applied to the press, the First Amendment—and the American system—would be dangerously diminished. The seeds of possible movement in this direction were planted by the Nixon administration when it attempted to prevent *The New York Times* from publishing the Pentagon Papers, and by the restrictive opinions of Justices White and Stewart when the case reached the Supreme Court.

Along with the widening of the credibility gap and the growth of official secrecy, the government's domestic propaganda capability, as the Pentagon might put it, has also burgeoned. Although the President and senior policy makers are ultimately responsible for the information released to the public, the government public relations machinery plays a significant role. The PR man is much more than a mere transmission belt; he must sell truth within the limits of established policy. Often he is as much a part of the process of information distortion as the decision makers.

Since the precise size and cost of the government's information machinery are unknown—except that in general terms it employs thousands of persons and spends many millions of dollars—the first requirement would seem to be an honest count, beginning with the White House. It should not be beyond the ingenuity of man, in the computer age, to tell the taxpayers how many public relations and information officials work in the White House and in the Executive Branch, and how much it costs.

The Nixon public relations "cutback" was a farce, a budgetary exercise in sleight-of-hand, carried out with the reluctant complicity of the Office of Management and Budget. But if the true size and cost of the selling of the government can be ascertained, the next step could be a genuine reduction in the price of federal image-making, particularly in the Pentagon.

As a first step, the more Orwellian features of the government's public relations programs could be abolished—the spending of federal monies to convince schoolchildren of the virtues of the SST, for example.

The old 1913 federal law making it a crime to hire publicity experts should be repealed, since it has not been notably observed. Career information officials, who are under Civil Service, would then at least feel that they were not engaged in an illicit activity.

In an age of mass communication, it can be expected that Presidents and administrations will continue to employ large numbers of public relations experts. Since the government PR men are here to stay, the only possibility of reform is at the top; this might come if, as the political cost of deception sinks in, a policy of candor is set by whoever is the President. Should that happen, the government information machine would, presumably, find it just as easy to disseminate the truth as to propagate misinformation, perhaps even easier.

The Nixon administration's effort to attack the press to divert attention from the government's own lack of credibility, whatever the dubious short-run partisan benefits, must ultimately be viewed as a dangerous practice. The public depends on the press for its news about government. When a President condones, and participates in, an effort to weaken public confidence in the press, in the long run the increased mistrust is bound to boomerang and reach back to the government as well.

The government's relationship with the television industry offers special problems. Television, as Ben Bagdikian has noted, is "the President's medium." Like Everest, television will be used by Presidents because it is there. It offers frightening opportunities for Presidential deception and manipulation. Television has not only increased the impact and speed of communication, it has made it much easier for the government to mislead the public. A President can go on television during a crisis, real or imagined, and rally substantial public support for military actions taken without regard to Congress or the Constitution. At the same time, as the only federally licensed medium of communication, television is uniquely vulnerable to government pressure and intimidation. It might be useful, and could even have a deterrent effect, if the press as a whole would quickly and prominently report cases of government pressure directed at the news media, and particularly at the television networks. Such pressures are legitimate news; there is no reason that they should remain the province of cocktail gossip among network executives and editors.

While no one can force a President to hold frequent press conferences—the news conference, like the cabinet, is an extralegal institution, not provided for in the Constitution—since 1932 the public has come to expect that the President of the United States will meet the press on a regular basis. The Presidential press conference, called with adequate advance notice and televised whenever possible, should be restored to its traditional place in the political process.

The reassessment by the Washington press corps of the institution of the "backgrounder" may, perhaps, lead to the publishing of more attributed information from government sources. That is by no means clear, but it is certainly time that Washington correspondents end the group practice of accepting wholly unattributable information on "deep background."

More important than this, however, is that the press—particularly at a time when it has been under government pressure and attack—continue to question, probe, analyze, and interpret the statements and actions of the government. The press, of all our institutions, must surely have learned over the past two decades that what the government says may not be true. If there is any one major shortcoming of the American press over recent years, it has been the tendency to accept the word of the government despite repeated evidence that—particularly in the national security area—the government may be lying.

Shortly before he died, Hugo Black wrote a memorable opinion in the case of the Pentagon Papers. "In the First Amendment," he wrote, "the Founding Fathers gave the free press the protection it must have to fulfill its essential role in our democracy. The press was to serve the governed, not the governors . . . The press was protected so that it could bare the secrets of government and inform the people. Only a free and unrestrained press can effectively expose deception in government."

Lying and secrecy have no place in a democracy. It is possible to debate the meaning of "the consent of the governed" and the role of public opinion in a democracy. It may be that the public, in one sense, can express its consent only by voting, but few would argue that the public should not have some influence on government policy between elections. "Unless mass views have some place in the shaping of policy," the late V.O. Key, Jr., has written, "all the talk about democracy is nonsense."

For democracy to work, however, the governed must know to

what they are consenting. If they are misled, if the truth is concealed from them by the same government that demands their sons, their loyalty, and their treasure, then the American experiment is doomed to end in repression and failure.

Possibly it has been put best by Sam Gibbons, a plain-spoken congressman from the Florida Gulf Coast. In June of 1971 Sam Gibbons, who served with the 101st Airborne Division, jumped into France on D-Day, and fought at Bastogne, was testifying at a House subcommittee hearing on the Pentagon Papers, and he had a question.

"How can you give your consent to be governed," he asked, "when you are misled and lied to?"

Author's Note

One winter night more than fifteen years ago, I arrived in Washington as a young newspaper correspondent. As the train from New York approached Union Station, I caught a glimpse of the United States Capitol. The sight of that great white dome filled me with a sense of awe and excitement, for it seemed a magnificent symbol of freedom and power, and a promise of personal adventure.

When I see the Capitol today, I still experience some trace of that same excitement and I admire its architectural beauty. But in fifteen years of reporting and writing about Washington under four Presidents, I have learned something. This book is about what I have learned.

It is also, in a very direct sense, an outgrowth of three previous books, written with Thomas B. Ross. I first examined the problem of government deception and secrecy in a democracy when we wrote *The U-2 Affair* in 1962. As we went about gathering material for that book, we realized that we were seeing only one small aspect of a much larger intelligence structure. We attempted to describe the whole in *The Invisible Government*, which raised questions about how a secret intelligence apparatus can be controlled by or reconciled with democratic government. Later we turned to both U.S. and international intelligence operations in *The Espionage Establishment*.

I think it is reasonable to say, in retrospect, that we were among the first to recognize and point out the dangers to American democracy of official lies told to protect covert operations. In time, the "credibility gap" of the 1960's turned into the massive mistrust of the 1970's.

In writing about the U-2, the Bay of Pigs, and American intelligence, I continued to be troubled by the underlying problem of government deception and official secrecy, and the role and responsibility of a free press in reporting on national security affairs. I was not sure—and am still not sure—how the American political system, based upon the consent of the governed, can continue to enjoy the confidence of the electorate at a time when the governed do not always know to what they are consenting.

In part, this book is based on my work as a Washington correspondent and political writer. During 1970–71 I was able to pursue further research in the general area of government information, secrecy, and the press as a Fellow of the Woodrow Wilson International Center for Scholars in Washington, D.C. I am grateful to the Center for its support and for the many courtesies shown me by its entire staff and by my colleagues there. After leaving the Center in November, 1971, I conducted additional research and began writing this book early in 1972. The Woodrow Wilson Center was established to encourage independent scholarly inquiry into public policy questions. Clearly, it bears no responsibility for the contents of this book; the views expressed, and any errors, are entirely my own.

Much of the information in the book was gathered in the course of some two hundred interviews during 1971 and 1972 with officials and former officials of the United States government, news reporters in Washington and elsewhere, executives of the television networks in New York, and other individuals.

As explained in the beginning of the Chapter Notes, not all of those interviewed wished to be identified or quoted. But I am indebted to all of those who helped me and who were willing to be interviewed.

I do wish to express my thanks in particular to Benjamin H. Read, director, and Albert Meisel, deputy director, of the Woodrow Wilson International Center for Scholars, and the Center staff, especially Helen Clayton, Louise Platt, and Becky Musser. I am also indebted to several colleagues at the Center who helped, including Stuart H. Loory, George E. Reedy, Townsend W. Hoopes, Robert E. Lane, Robert E. Stein, Donald L. Horowitz, and Alton Frye.

The list of those within the government who assisted me is long, but perhaps—in the words of Nathan Detroit—things being how they are, I can thank them best by omitting their names here. Many individuals can be thanked, however. I am especially grateful to James Kronfeld of the staff of the Foreign Operations and Government Information Subcommittee for his invaluable advice and assistance. I also wish to thank Representative William S. Moorhead, the subcommittee chairman; William G. Phillips, staff director; Norman G. Cornish, deputy staff director; and Martha M. Doty, for the many courtesies afforded me by the committee.

A number of persons outside the government were helpful in explaining the relationship between the security classification system and the espionage laws, and I am indebted to them: Professor Thomas I. Emerson of the Yale Law School; Professor Norman Dorsen of the New York University School of Law; Hope Eastman of the Washington office of the American Civil Liberties Union; Mitchell Rogovin, Walter Slocombe, and Charles Goodell. Samuel J. Archibald, director of the Freedom of Information Center of the University of Missouri School of Journalism, is a fount of information on all aspects of government and the press, and kindly opened the files of his Washington office to me.

Many television executives and newsmen were especially helpful, and I wish to express my thanks to Frank Stanton, the president of CBS; to Richard S. Salant, the president of CBS News; to Gordon Manning, vice-president of CBS News; to Walter Cronkite—delightful as always to interview; to E. Kidder Meade, Jr., vice-president of CBS; to Dan Rather, Daniel Schorr, John Hart, and Fred P. Graham of the CBS Washington Bureau; to William Small, chief of the Washington Bureau; and to Ellen McCloy, former secretary to Richard Salant.

At NBC, I am indebted to Julian Goodman, the network's president; to Richard C. Wald, president of NBC News, whose guidance was invaluable; to Reuven Frank, Douglas Kiker, Wallace Westfeldt, Eliot Frankel, Robert Kasmire, and especially to John Chancellor, who answered my questions on numerous occasions with patience above and beyond the call of duty and friendship. I also owe thanks to David C. Adams, chairman of the board of NBC, who took the trouble to explain to me the facts of life about the workings of the television industry. My thanks go as well to Bill Downs, Nick George, and Tom Tait of ABC.

The list of friends and colleagues in the Washington press corps who helped me is lengthy. It includes Robert J. Donovan of the *Los Angeles Times;* David Kraslow of the *Washington Evening Star News;* Max Frankel, Tom Wicker, Jack Rosenthal, Robert B. Semple, Jr., Seymour M. Hersh, Edwin L. Dale, Jr., Bernard Gwertzman, and Robert H. Phelps of *The New York Times;* Dom Bonafede of the *National Journal;* Hugh Sidey of *Time;* Mel Elfin of *Newsweek;* Don Oberdorfer, Richard Harwood, and Carroll Kilpatrick of the *Washington Post;* Albert R. Hunt, Richard Levine, and John Pierson of the

Wall Street Journal; Charles W. Bailey II, now editor of the *Minneapolis Tribune;* Martin J. Schram of *Newsday;* Norman Kempster of United Press International; James H. McCartney of the Knight Newspapers; Robert Roth of the *Philadephia Bulletin;* Frederick H. Farrar of the *Chicago Tribune;* Morton M. Kondracke of the *Chicago Sun-Times;* and Muriel Dobbin of the *Baltimore Sun.*

I also wish to thank William Attwood, David Laventhol, and Robert W. Greene of *Newsday;* Aaron Latham of *Esquire;* Jonathan Aitken of the Associated Newspapers Group Limited; Anthony Howard and Alan Watkins of the *New Statesman;* Peter Kihss of *The New York Times;* Aaron Asher of Holt, Rinehart and Winston, Inc.; Peter Ritner of World Publishing Co.; Clayton Kirkpatrick of the *Chicago Tribune;* Ben Bagdikian, Edward T. Folliard, Joseph P. Albright, Richard Dougherty, Robert L. Riggs, Fendall Yerxa, Clayton Knowles, Henry Raymont, Blair Clark, William Lambert, Theodore F. Koop, Dean Rusk, and Matthew B. Coffey. Chapter 6 could not have been written without the assistance of the two protagonists, Roger Hilsman and John P. Roche, both of whom were generous with their time and assistance, as were other actors in that drama—Jeremy Rifkin, Robert B. Johnson, Tran Van Dinh and Tran Van Zung.

A number of libraries and reference sources were helpful. I wish to express my gratitude to Mrs. Mae N. Bowler, long associated with the library of the *New York Herald Tribune* and now retired, who graciously assisted me many times in the course of my research; Rosie Frank, of the Denver *Post;* Mary Anglemyer, librarian of the Woodrow Wilson International Center for Scholars, and Phyllis Carr, formerly of the library staff; Richard A. Baker and Judith Kolberg of the *National Journal;* the research staff of *Congressional Quarterly;* William A. Hifner of the *Washington Post;* Mrs. Lucy W. Lazarou of the Washington Bureau of the *Los Angeles Times;* and David A. Brewster of the Washington Bureau of *The New York Times.*

But I am indebted most of all to the persons directly involved in the preparation of this book; first, to Susan M. Soper, my principal research assistant, whose energy, competence, and cheerfulness over many long months were unflagging, and to Stephen Collins, whose research help was also valuable and much appreciated; to Mrs. Connie de Launay, who expertly typed most of the manuscript; to Marianne Frederick, who also helped type the manuscript; and to Maria Gomez, who kept me current by clipping the daily newspapers.

In particular, I wish to express my deep appreciation to Robert D. Loomis, my editor at Random House on this and three previous books, all of which benefited enormously from his judgment and rare creative talent. I was very fortunate as well to have Bertha Krantz of Random House serve as manuscript editor.

I am especially indebted to Thomas B. Ross for reading the manuscript and giving me his advice and counsel. Finally, the manuscript benefited greatly from the wisdom and editorial skill of my wife, Joan, to whom I am enormously grateful for that, and so much else.

David Wise
Washington, D.C.
January 30, 1973

Chapter Notes

Much of the material in this book is the result of interviews with about 200 persons, many of them officials or former officials of the federal government. Where the persons interviewed spoke entirely or in part on the record, their names are listed in the following notes. Often, however, those interviewed asked that they not be identified by name, and they are not. Where the source of information is neither clear from the body of the book, therefore, nor cited below, it can be assumed that the information was given to the author in confidence. Because the notes that follow for the most part cite public source material, they do not provide attribution for all of the information in the book. This was, under the circumstances, unavoidable.

The interviews referred to below were by the author, unless otherwise indicated. Where the date of a Presidential press conference is clear, it will not be cited here, since these transcripts are easily available in *The New York Times, Public Papers of the Presidents,* and other publications.

1. The Politics of Lying

George "Steve" Lowry's account of the dinner at the White House on Thanksgiving Day, 1970, and of President Nixon's remarks were made in a telephone interview from his home in Rockville,

Maryland, on February 1, 1972. Aaron Latham's story in the *Washington Post*, November 27, 1970, p. 1, also reports that President Nixon described an air raid on a military installation near Son Tay at the dinner, and attributes this information to Army Sergeant Corris Sworn. In a telephone interview from his office at *Esquire* magazine in New York on February 1, 1972, Latham said all of the servicemen he contacted after the dinner, including Lowry and Sworn, agreed that the President had discussed this air raid. Much of the background to the Son Tay raid is from Stuart H. Loory's detailed account in the *Los Angeles Times*, February 2, 1971, p. 1. Melvin R. Laird's explanation of the choice of Son Tay is from *Hearing*, Senate Foreign Relations Committee, November 24, 1970, p. 9; his other comments to the committee appear at pps. 3, 6, 13, 22, and 27; his acknowledgment of only a "fifty-fifty chance" of returning with prisoners is from *Hearings*, Senate Foreign Relations Committee, December 11, 1970, p. 92. His press conference comments are from the official Defense Department transcript, November 23, 1970. His comments to the House committee are in *Hearings*, House Foreign Affairs Committee, November 25, 1970, pp. 50, 60, 62, and 67. Aaron Latham's role was described by him in the telephone interview (*idem*). Daniel Z. Henkin's statements are from *The New York Times*, November 28, 1970, p. 1. Senator J. William Fulbright's comments are from *Face the Nation*, CBS Transcript, November 29, 1970, p. 6. Laird's comments to the press are from the Defense Department transcript of his news conference of November 30, 1970.

William Lambert's exposé of Senator Joseph D. Tydings, "What the Senator Didn't Disclose," appeared in *Life*, August 28, 1970, pp. 26–29. His statement that he first spoke to Paul Bridston from the White Office office of Charles W. Colson, and that Colson placed the call, was made in a telephone interview from his office at *Life*, in New York City, on January 11, 1972. That Colson told Bridston to cooperate with *Life* is clear from the secret transcript of an interview with Colson, August 25, 1970, by investigators for the State Department's office of the Inspector General of Foreign Assistance. The transcript, a copy of which I was able to read, is an unpublished appendix to a report of November 12, 1970, by Scott Heuer, Jr., the Inspector General of Foreign Assistance. Ronald L. Ziegler's denial that the White House had been involved with *Life* in connection with the Tydings story is from the official White House transcript of his news briefing in San Clemente, California, at 12:05 P.M. on August 22, 1970.

General John W. Vogt's remarks to Pentagon reporters appear in "Background Briefing, Wednesday, February 10, 1971, Pentagon," a seventeen-page non-public transcript that was made available privately to me. The quote from the American helicopter pilot is from Tom Wicker, "Kick Them Off the Skids," *The New York Times,* March 23, 1971, p. 35.

President Nixon's remarks on how he would avoid the credibility gap were made in a campaign broadcast over NBC and CBS radio, September 19, 1968. Herbert G. Klein's statements on truth and credibility are from "Rough Transcript of 11 A.M. Briefing of November 25, 1968," which was prepared from a tape recording of Ziegler's press briefing at the Hotel Pierre in New York City. Ronald L. Ziegler expressed the President's regret that "Chuck is leaving the administration" at a morning news briefing at Key Biscayne, Florida, on December 2, 1972. The quotation is from the text of Ziegler's announcement in *Weekly Compilation of Presidential Documents,* December 11, 1972, p. 1728. The Tom Wicker quote on "press box mentality" is from an interview in Washington on December 4, 1971.

2. Remember the Alamo

The text of Johnson's speech at Camp Stanley appears in Lyndon B. Johnson, *Public Papers of the Presidents,* 1966 (Washington: U.S. Government Printing Office, 1967), Book II, pp. 1286–88. Details of Johnson's day in South Korea and his conversation with Choi Si Jong are from the story filed by Charles W. Bailey II to the *Minneapolis Tribune,* November 1, 1966. Johnson's encounter with the Pakistani camel driver occurred in May of 1961; a fuller account appears in Eric F. Goldman, *The Tragedy of Lyndon Johnson* (New York: Knopf, 1969), pp. 389–90. The genealogical exploration of President Johnson's great-great-grandfathers is from Rebekah Baines Johnson, With an Introduction by President Lyndon Baines Johnson, *A Family Album* (New York: McGraw-Hill, 1965), pp. 12–13, 107–46. George Christian's resourceful explanation of Johnson's Alamo remark appears in his book *The President Steps Down* (New York: Macmillan, 1970), p. 219; on p. 220, Christian reports that Johnson only later realized his Alamo claim was a "misstatement" and told reporters that he "had gotten carried away" when he made it. Eric Goldman's discussion of the origins of the term "credibility gap" appears in *The Tragedy of Lyndon Johnson* (*idem*), p. 409. Johnson's claim that Bobby Baker was "no protégé of anyone" is from Lyndon B. Johnson, *Public Papers of the Presidents,* 1963–64 (Washington: U.S. Government Printing Office, 1965), Book I, p. 365. The Mason Locke Weems letter is from Daniel J. Boorstin, *The Americans: The National Experience* (New York: Random House, 1965), p. 341. The Andrew Jackson, James K. Polk, and William McKinley quotes are from John M.

Blum, *et al.*, *The National Experience* (New York: Harcourt, Brace, 1968), pp. 232, 284, and 531. Lincoln is quoted in Richard Hofstadter, *The American Political Tradition* (New York: Vintage, 1948), p. 111: "My first impulse would be to free all the slaves and send them to Liberia, to their own native land." Hofstadter's analysis of the Emancipation Proclamation appears at p. 132. Woodrow Wilson's warning that a Republican victory would mean war was made in his famous "Shadow Lawn" speech on September 30, 1916, and is from Arthur S. Link, *Wilson: Campaigns for Progressivism and Peace* (Princeton, N.J.: Princeton University Press, 1965), p. 106. Franklin D. Roosevelt's 1940 campaign pledge, "Your boys are not going to be sent into any foreign wars," is from James MacGregor Burns, *Roosevelt: The Lion and the Fox* (New York: Harcourt, Brace, 1956), p. 449.

Gallup Poll data comparing Nixon and Johnson's credibility record on the Vietnam war is from *The New York Times*, May 23, 1971. Data on public trust in government is from "Election Time Series Analysis of Attitudes of Trust in Government," Center for Political Studies, University of Michigan, 1971, and *The New York Times*, November 5, 1971, p. 48; Dr. Warren Miller's comment is from *The New York Times, ibid.* McGeorge Bundy's remark that "Pleikus are streetcars," is from Townsend Hoopes, *The Limits of Intervention* (New York: McKay, 1969), p. 30. Data on reporters who accompanied Nixon to China is from *The New York Times*, February 8, 1972, p. 5. William B. Macomber, Jr.'s remark is from NBC News Special Report, June 30, 1971, *Transcript*, p. 11. His testimony is from *Hearings*, House Foreign Operations and Government Information Subcommittee, Part 3, July 7, 1971, pp. 916–17.

3. The Anatomy of Deception

Nixon's assessment of Eisenhower's personality is from "Remarks of the President During an Interview with Women Members of the Press," March 13, 1971, White House transcript, p. 12. For a fuller account of the U-2 episode, see David Wise and Thomas B. Ross, *The U-2 Affair* (New York: Random House, 1962); the reference to Allen Dulles' knowledge of pilot concern over the destruct mechanism is at p. 18. Francis Gary Powers' discussion of the destruct unit is from his book with Curt Gentry, *Operation Overflight* (New York: Holt, 1970), pp. 34–35, 51–52. President Eisenhower's comments on the U-2 are from Dwight D. Eisenhower, *The White House Years, Waging Peace: 1956–1961* (New York: Doubleday, 1965), pp. 546, 549. Lincoln White's denial of a deliberate overflight is from *The U-2 Affair (idem)*, p. 93. It has been argued that the U-2 incident did not cause the collapse of the summit meeting, and that Khrushchev merely used the episode as a pretext to walk out. This logic has always seemed tortured to me, for it requires one to assume that had there been no U-2 incident, the summit meeting would nevertheless have collapsed from other, unidentified, causes. The deletion of Eisenhower's comment from the CBS interview was originally reported (*ibid.*), p. 263*n*. Eisenhower's description of the cover story as an error appears in his memoir, *The White House Years, Waging Peace: 1956–1961* (*idem*), p. 558. The Kraslow quote is from "Government Information, The Media and the Public" (Washington, D.C.: Woodrow Wilson International Center for Scholars, 1971), transcript of a symposium held May 20, 1971, Washington, D.C., p. 164. Kraslow's interview with Eisenhower appeared in the *Washington Post*, December 23, 1962. For details of the CIA coup in Guatemala, *see* David Wise and Thomas B. Ross, *The Invisible Government* (New York: Random House, 1964) pp. 165–83; Lodge is quoted at p. 178 and Dulles at p. 181. For an account of the CIA operations in Indonesia, *see ibid.*, pp. 136–46; the Dulles comment is at p. 140; Eisenhower's "soldiers of fortune" remark is quoted at p. 137, and Ambassador Jones is quoted at p. 136. For further details of Adlai E. Stevenson's role in the Bay of Pigs, *see ibid.*, pp. 16–17, and Arthur M. Schlesinger, Jr., *A Thousand Days* (Boston: Houghton Mifflin, 1965), pp. 271–72. Kennedy's comment about Stevenson's integrity is from *ibid*, p. 271. Schlesinger reports that he and Barnes briefed Stevenson on April 8. Schlesinger also states that he discussed the Bay of Pigs with Stevenson over lunch at the Century Club, *ibid.* Thomas B. Ross and I interviewed Stevenson at the Waldorf Towers, October 17, 1963. The quotations from Stevenson are from a five-page typed transcript of our notes.

Pierre Salinger relates the warning that President Kennedy "might have to develop a cold" in his book *With Kennedy* (New York: Doubleday, 1966), p. 251. President Kennedy's calls to James Reston and Orvil Dryfoos were reported by Clifton Daniel, then the managing editor of *The New York Times,* in a lecture to the World Press Institute in St. Paul, Minnesota, June 1, 1966. The full text appears in William McGaffin and Erwin Knoll, *Anything But the Truth* (New York: Putnam, 1968), pp. 197–208. The text of the Pentagon statement of October 19, and Arthur Sylvester's admission that he knew at the time that the statement was false, may be found in Arthur Sylvester, "The Government Has the Right To Lie," *The Saturday Evening Post,* November 18, 1967, p. 10; Sylvester's "arsenal of weaponry" comment is from *Hearings*, House Foreign Operations and Government Information Subcommittee, March 19, 1963, p. 15; the "right . . . to lie" is from the transcript of Sylvester's speech as published in the *Congressional Record—Senate,* June 24, 1963, p. 859; for Sylvester's later explanations of this celebrated remark, see his *Saturday Evening Post* article *(idem);* House subcommittee hearings *(idem),* pp. 146–47, 151, and *Congressional Record—Senate,* March 14, 1963, pp. 3991–4001.

Kennedy's statement that "independence" was U.S. goal for South Vietnam is from his press conference May 5, 1961. Kennedy's NSAM 52 quoted in *The Pentagon Papers, The New York Times* edition (New York: Bantam, 1971) hereafter referred to as PPNYT, p. 126; details of the coup plotting against Diem and the CIA role are from the Senator Mike Gravel edition of the Pentagon Papers, *The Pentagon Papers, The Defense Department History of the United States Decisionmaking on Vietnam,* Volume Two (Boston: Beacon Press, 1971), hereafter PPG, II, pp. 218, 258–59, 769, 793; the assurance that the plan of operation would be turned over to the CIA "for Lodge's review" was given to Lieutenant Colonel Lucien Conein, the CIA's emissary to the generals planning the coup, by Major General Tran Van Don, a key figure among them, during a meeting on the night of October 24, 1963, *ibid.,* p. 218; the quote "for Lodge's review" is from the narrative of the Pentagon history, *ibid.,* p. 259. The Henry Cabot Lodge interview is from *The New York Times,* June 30, 1964, p. 14. Ambassador Maxwell D. Taylor's comments on the U.S. role in the Diem coup are from "CBS Morning News with John Hart," Transcript, pp. 26–27, June 17, 1971.

Johnson's statement and events of April 28, 1965, are from Lyndon B. Johnson, *Public Papers of the Presidents of the United States, 1965* (Washington: U.S. Government Printing Office, 1966), Book I, p. 461, and "Off the Tightrope at Last," *The New York Herald Tribune,* May 1, 1965, pp. 1, 6; Johnson's May 4 comment is from David Wise, "Dilemma in 'Credibility Gap,'" *The New York Herald Tribune,* May 23, 1965; Johnson's statement that the Communist rebels were led by "men with a long history of Communist association and insurrections" is from a contemporaneous White House transcript of his remarks, May 4, 1965, pp. 5–6. It appears in Lyndon B. Johnson, *Public Papers of the Presidents of the United States, 1965 (idem),* p. 490, as "communistic association and insurrections." Johnson's explanation of his remark about beheadings is from Lyndon B. Johnson, *The Vantage Point* (New York: Holt, 1971), p. 194. Senator Fulbright's exchange with W. Tapley Bennett, Jr., is from an unpublished transcript, *Hearings,* Senate Foreign Relations Committee, May 3, 1966. Material on the Tonkin Gulf incident is based primarily on three sources—Joseph C. Goulden, *Truth Is the First Casualty* (New York: Rand McNally, 1969), a superb account of the incident which should be required reading for anyone interested in Tonkin

Gulf and the larger issue of government credibility; *The Gulf of Tonkin, the 1964 Incidents, Hearing,* Senate Foreign Relations Committee, February 20, 1968; and David Wise, "Remember the *Maddox!" Esquire,* April, 1968. Herrick's crucial cable is from *Hearing,* Senate Foreign Relations Committee (*idem*), p. 55; The discussion of the tape recording is at pp. 56, 59–61. The urgent "Who were witnesses . . .?" cable to the *Turner Joy* is quoted in *Truth Is the First Casualty (idem),* pp. 157, 276; Senator Albert Gore is quoted at p. 202.

Johnson's Eufaula, Oklahoma, and Akron speeches are from Lyndon B. Johnson, *Public Papers of the Presidents of the United States* 1963–64 (Washington: U.S. Government Printing Office, 1965), Book II, pp. 1126, 1128, and 1391. His later explanation is from *The Vantage Point (idem),* p. 68. Ambassador Taylor's cable is from PPG, III, p. 199; William P. Bundy's memo is quoted *ibid.,* p. 562. Background to Operation Plan 34A is from PPNYT, pp. 235, 260; Robert S. McNamara's exchange with Fulbright is from *Hearing,* Senate Foreign Relations Committee (*idem*), pp. 29, 31. The chronology of the decision to bomb North Vietnam is from PPG, III, pp. 249, 257. NSAM 328 appears in full in PPG, III, pp. 702–3. The White House statement on the role of U.S. ground combat troops is from PPNYT, p. 411.

Vice-President Agnew's comment on supporting Lon Nol is from the *Washington Post,* August 24, 1970, p. 1. Nixon's pledge of no U.S. air support in Cambodia is from *Congressional Quarterly 1970 Almanac,* p. 97A; Laird's explanation is from the *Washington Post,* January 21, 1971, p. 1; Laird's comments on the fuel pipe are from "News Conference by Secretary of Defense Melvin R. Laird and Lt. Gen. John W. Vogt at Pentagon, February 24, 1971," Transcript, pp. 5–6. The data from the Cornell University study on bomb tonnage are from *The New York Times,* November 8, 1971, p. 6.

Henry Kissinger's background remarks to the press on India and Pakistan are from the *Congressional Record—Senate,* December 9, 1971, pp. S21012–16. The Jack Anderson transcript containing Kissinger's explanation that Nixon wished to "tilt in favor of Pakistan" is from the *Washington Post,* January 5, 1972, p. A8. The Nixon interview with Howard K. Smith is from White House Transcript, March 22, 1971, pp. 1–8.

4. Top Secret

The exchange between Senator Fulbright and Secretary of Defense Robert S. McNamara, in which members of the Senate Foreign

Relations Committee learned of the existence of secret intelligence classifications for the first time, is from "The Gulf of Tonkin, the 1964 Incidents," *Hearing,* Senate Foreign Relations Committee, February 20, 1968, pp. 35–39. Virtually no other published literature exists on this layer of classified classifications above and beyond Top Secret. For a concise history of the Executive Orders on classification, see *Security Classification as a Problem in the Congressional Role in Foreign Policy,* a study prepared for the Senate Foreign Relations Committee by the Foreign Affairs Division, Legislative Reference Service, Library of Congress (Washington: U.S. Government Printing Office, 1971). A useful discussion of security classification is contained in the printed record of the hearings held by the House Foreign Operations and Government Information Subcommittee during 1971 and 1972, particularly Parts 1–3, 1971, and Part 7, May, 1972. Executive Order 10501, issued by President Eisenhower in 1953, appears in Part 1, *ibid.,* pp. 61 ff. President Nixon's Executive Order 11652, issued in 1972, is published in Part 7, pp. 2312 ff.

Senator Albert Gore's bewilderment—"I thought Top Secret was Top Secret"—and McNamara's explanation of the classification system is from *Hearing,* Senate Foreign Relations Committee (*idem*), pp. 38–39. I interviewed William M. Franklin at the State Department Annex on December 27, 1971. The reference to the Top Secret classification on President Roosevelt's cable to Prime Minister Churchill is from Francis L. Lowenheim, "Roosevelt and Stalin: A Revelation," *The New York Times,* March 27, 1972, p. 33. President Truman's 1951 Executive Order is quoted in *Security Classification as a Problem in the Congressional Role in Foreign Policy* (*idem*), p. 4; the espionage laws and the Internal Security Act of 1950 are discussed at pp. 6–10.

The history of the Truman Executive Order, and the changes made by Eisenhower on January 9, 1961, are from House *Report 2456,* Special Government Information Subcommittee, September 21, 1962, pp. 2, 11. Stewart Udall's assurances to the Migratory Bird Commission are from House *Report 1257* of the same subcommittee, September 22, 1961, pp. 109–10; the discussion of how the bow and arrow was classified, and the quote from General J. H. Michaelis on "silent flashless weapons" is from House *Report 1884* of the same subcommittee, June 16, 1958, pp. 174–75; the shark repellents are discussed at p. 125. Congressman Clare Hoffman's attack on his colleague John Moss over the space monkeys is from *Congressional Record—House,* April 10, 1959, p. 5681; Robert Dechert's letter is from *Congressional Record—House,* April 15, 1959, pp. 6017–18. Hoffman accuses Moss of injecting the religious issue *ibid.,* p. 6018. The *Washington Post* story appeared April 4, 1959. Moss's reply is from *Congressional Record—House,* April 16, 1959, p. 6166.

President Kennedy established the group numbers for automatic downgrading and declassification by Executive Order 10964, September 20, 1961. George MacClain's affidavit attempting to clarify the intricacies of the group numbers is from the *Washington Post*, June 22, 1971, p. A11. The existence of the Pentagon's classified 1912 contingency plan is discussed in *Hearings*, House Foreign Operations and Government Information Subcommittee, Part 7 (*idem*), p. 2477; special access controls such as LIMDIS are referred to *ibid.*, p. 2736.

The disclosure during the controversy over the Pentagon Papers that President Nixon had named a secret committee in January, 1971, to study the classification system was made by Ronald L. Ziegler at his news briefing of June 22, 1971, at 4:45 P.M., White House Transcript, p. 6.

Jack Rosenthal was interviewed in Washington on December 8 and 29, 1971. The "flower series" and related code names for the secret Vietnam peace negotiations that took place during the 1960's appear in the four so-called "diplomatic" volumes of the Pentagon Papers not leaked to the press with the other volumes in 1971. Some of these documents were obtained from columnist Jack Anderson by the *Washington Post* and published on June 27, 1972; the discussion of the code names is *ibid.*, p. A13. The Defense Department's stringent rules about nicknames are contained in Department Directive 5200.1, June 1, 1972. This and other departmental regulations carrying out President Nixon's 1972 Executive Order were published in the *Federal Register*, Part III, August 3, 1972; the reference to nicknames is at p. 15685. Congressman William S. Moorhead's exchange with David O. Cooke is from *Hearings*, House Foreign Operations and Government Information Subcommittee, Part 2, June 29, 1971, pp. 655–57. Nicholas deB. Katzenbach was interviewed by telephone at his office in Armonk, N.Y., on December 29, 1971. The story of the confrontation between President Johnson and Robert Kennedy is from the Katzenbach and Rosenthal interviews (*idem*); from William vanden Heuvel and Milton Gwirtzman, *On His Own: Robert F. Kennedy 1964–1968* (New York: Doubleday, 1970), pp. 236–39; David Kraslow and Stuart H. Loory, *The Secret Search for Peace in Vietnam* (New York: Random House, 1968), pp. 200–4; *The New York Times*, February 6, 1967, p. 1, and *Newsweek*, February 13, 1967, p. 34, February 20, pp. 31, 32. Edward Weintal was interviewed by telephone at his office in Washington on December 13, 1971.

The data on combination locks and physical transmission of classified information are from the *Federal Register* (*idem*), p. 15637, and *Hearings*, House Foreign Operations and Government Information Subcommittee, Part 7 (*idem*), pp. 2327–28. The Pentagon regulations on glued bindings and classified typewriter ribbons are from

Defense Department Directive 5210.47, December 31, 1964, pp. 139–40. The 1972 Pentagon directive, published in the *Federal Register* (*idem*), p. 15670, is similar but adds: "As an exception to the foregoing, any typewriter ribbon which remains substantially stationary in the typewriter until it has received at least five consecutive impressions shall be treated as unclassified." My favorite paragraph in the Defense Department regulation, however, concerns the packaging of classified material, and appears *ibid.*, p. 15676: "If the classified material is an internal component of a packageable item of equipment, the outside shell or body may be considered as the inner enclosure."

The Arthur J. Goldberg quote is from his testimony in *Hearings*, House Foreign Operations and Government Information Subcommittee, Part 1, June 23, 1971, p. 28. Robert E. Stein told me about his classified dream in an interview in Washington on December 2, 1971. The Pentagon directive on pulverizing or mutilating classified documents is from the *Federal Register* (*idem*), p. 15677. The description of the awesome abilities of the Somat Macerator is from the author's personal observations. State Department security officials were kind enough to allow me into Room B527 to observe the Macerator chewing up official secrets.

Foy D. Kohler was interviewed by telephone at his home in Jupiter, Florida, on November 18, 1971. Averell Harriman's statement doubting that the Great Seal of the United States was bugged at the time he got it is from Kathleen Teltsch's story in *The New York Times*, May 27, 1960. The account of the boys who cut the Hot Line and of how Joe Washburn eavesdropped on Air Force One are both from articles by me in *The New York Herald Tribune*, May 17, 1965, p. 1, and February 16, 1966, p. 1. John Chancellor was interviewed in New York City on October 12, 1971 and in Washington on November 23, 1971.

5. "The President Is Sort of Outside the Law"

General Robert L. Schulz was interviewed by telephone on January 7, 1972, at his office at 716 Jackson Place. In answer to questions, he confirmed President Johnson's request for declassification of his secret documents but was reluctant to go into details. Later that day General Schulz telephoned and asked that I put all my questions in writing. Accordingly, I wrote to Schulz on January 17. He replied in a two-page letter, dated February 16 and quoted below.

Joseph Califano, Jr.'s 1968 memorandum requesting a "full written history" of the Johnson administration from government agencies and Senator John J. Williams' reaction are quoted in *The New York Times,* July 13, 1968, pp. 1, 19. Stuart H. Loory reported in the *Washington Post,* July 19, 1968, p. A10, that Arthur B. Krim was acting as Johnson's literary agent and seeking $1,000,000 for the President's memoirs. Aaron Asher wrote to me on February 25, 1972, in reply to a letter I had sent to him asking a number of questions about the Johnson memoir. The details about the HEC Public Affairs Foundation are from the files of the Internal Revenue Service regional office in Philadelphia; these foundation reports are public records and were made available to my research assistant by IRS in Washington. Johnson's financial assets as reported during the 1964 campaign are from David Wise, "The Twilight of a President," *The New York Times Magazine,* November 3, 1968, pp. 130–31. The fact that Holt, Rinehart and Winston had invited editors to read the galleys of Johnson's book *before* the *Times* published the Pentagon Papers was confirmed in Aaron Asher's letter to me (*idem*). It is clear from the sequence of events that Johnson was "locked in" and could not have made major changes in his book without the knowledge of the invited editors, who, according to Asher, began arriving at Holt's offices in Manhattan on Monday, June 14, and were present every day thereafter for two weeks.

In all, I interviewed seventeen persons, nine of them officials of the federal government, about President Johnson's declassification request and about the background to his book. Of the officials, all but General Schulz and two others asked not to be identified by name. In the first telephone conversation with Schulz, cited above, I asked whether Johnson had requested that material be declassified for use in his book. It was then that Schulz replied that Johnson had "wanted to use certain material out of certain files." Schulz's later assertion that Johnson wanted documents declassified and released "to the public" is from his letter to me (*idem*), p. 1. Schulz's letter added, in part: "Because the total amount of material involved was voluminous, it was decided to conduct a survey of one 'test sampling' to determine the feasibility of reviewing all the material for possible declassification. Several subject areas were proposed for this survey, from which former President Johnson and his staff selected the topic, 'Dominican Republic, 1965–1966.' " Schulz confirmed in his letter that the team of five officials—he declined to give their names or agencies—had reviewed the documents in Austin for three weeks. According to the letter, "it was the conclusion of the survey team that only a small percentage of the classified material would be releasable for several years to come." The team considered "sanitization" of the documents but decided, Schulz wrote, that this would "produce documents of little value to researchers and suspect in the eyes of historians. Of the small percentage of material that was releasable in its present form, it was concluded that its release would be of only marginal value, and hence a partial release of the documents would do little in clarifying the government's actions and the policy decisions made during the subject period. A copy of this survey team's report was provided to former President Johnson and his staff in Austin, and no additional requests for further action or review by the survey team were received."

William M. Franklin's comments, including the quotation that forms the title of this chapter, are from my interview with him (*idem*: notes to Chapter 4). As Franklin noted, FDR was the first President to give his papers to the government. According to the Office of the Presidential Libraries of the National Archives, Roosevelt did so by making arrangements in his lifetime that all his papers and objects be given to the government. President Johnson's declassification of a document on television is from CBS News Special, "LBJ: The Decision to Halt the Bombing," broadcast February 6, 1970, Transcript, pp. 17–19. Johnson's request to delete his remarks about the assassination of President Kennedy from the May 2, 1970, CBS broadcast was reported in the *Washington Post*, April 28, 1970, p. 1. The Kennedy-Khrushchev conversations at Vienna are in Arthur M. Schlesinger, Jr., *A Thousand Days* (*idem*: notes to Chapter 3), pp. 358–65. The Khrushchev letter quoted in Robert Kennedy's book was the first of two letters sent by the Soviet leader to President Kennedy on October 26, 1962. Only the second letter was made public. The first, long and emotional, is quoted in part in Robert F. Kennedy, *Thirteen Days* (Norton: New York, 1969), pp. 86–90. Sherman Adams tells of the Suez meeting in his *First Hand Report* (New York: Harper, 1961), pp. 262 ff. George Christian describes the secret peace negotiations in his *The President Steps Down* (*idem*: notes to Chapter 2), pp. 47–138.

G. Marvin Gentile was interviewed at his office in the State Department on December 28, 1971. The Roger Hilsman quote is from my interview with him at Columbia University on October 11, 1971. The incident involving Foy D. Kohler is from the *Washington Post*, December 7, 8, 10, 1952, and *The New York Times*, December 9, 1952, and January 4, 1953. Section 3301 of the Federal Records Act of 1950, as amended, exempts "extra copies of documents."

The government first obtained a temporary restraining order against Victor L. Marchetti on April 18, 1972. On May 19 U.S. District Court Judge Albert V. Bryan in Alexandria, Virginia, issued a permanent injunction, ordering Marchetti to submit in advance to the CIA any writing, "factual, fictional or otherwise" relating to CIA, and forbidding the publication of such material without approval of the director of CIA. A federal appeals court upheld the government in September. With the help of the American Civil Liberties Union, Marchetti sought to appeal his case to the U.S. Supreme Court. But on December 11 the Supreme Court declined to hear his appeal, thus allowing the lower-court decisions to stand. Marchetti left CIA in 1969 after fourteen years, during which he rose to the position of special assistant to Admiral Rufus L. Taylor, then deputy director of CIA. Robert P.B. Lohmann, a CIA agent assigned to New York City, obtained an outline of Marchetti's proposed book about the intelligence agency from an unidentified source—presumably in the publishing industry—"who has provided reliable information in the past," in the language of an affidavit filed by Lohmann on April 17, 1972, in the federal court in Alexandria.

William Franklin explained the Old Boy rule in the interview with him (*idem*). My unsuccessful efforts to locate the State Department's public reading room with the aid of the receptionists took place on December 27 and 28, 1971. Donald J. Simon was kind enough to take me there, and to show me the inner recesses of the Old Boy reading room, when I interviewed him at the State Department on December 28, 1971.

Robert J. Donovan was interviewed in Washington on December 1, 1971. Max Frankel's affidavit in the Pentagon Papers case is from *The New York Times Company v. United States: A Documentary History* (New York: Arno Press, 1971), Volume I, pp. 396–413. The account of the walking backgrounder with President Johnson on May 3, 1965, is from the typed transcript of the notes I took on that occasion.

James C. Hagerty described Eisenhower's annoyance with Top Secret stamps in testimony to the House Foreign Operations and Government Information Subcommittee, *Hearings*, Part 4, March 6, 1972, p. 1011. Melvin R. Laird's warning that the Soviet Union was deploying multiple warheads is from *The New York Times*, March 7, 1972, p. 5. The statistics on the number of persons in four major federal government departments with power to classify documents are from a study released August 3, 1972, by the Interagency Classification Review Committee and published in *Hearings*, House Foreign Operations and Government Subcommittee, Part 7, May, 1972, pp. 2826–27. William G. Florence's testimony to the subcommittee is *ibid.*, Part 1, June 24, 1971, p. 98. A useful analysis prepared by the subcommittee staff, comparing the Nixon classification order to its predecessor Executive Order, appears in Part 7 (*idem*), pp. 2851 ff. Florence's estimate of twenty million classified documents in Pentagon files is from Part 1 (*idem*), p. 97.

The State Department estimate that it had 151,000,000 documents in 1971, of which 25 percent were classified, and the percent in each category is from figures compiled in July, 1971, by Donald J. Simon, chief of the department's Records Services Division. Data on the volume of classified paper in the National Archives is from "Declassification of World War II Documents in the National Archives and Records Service," a report published by the Archives in July, 1971, pp. 7–8. Details of the Pentagon's 1966 review of 1,000,000 classified documents is from *Hearings,* Part 2 (*idem*), June 29, 1971, p. 664. The subcommittee's estimate that the Defense Department's classified documents would equal eighteen Washington monuments is *ibid.,* p. 685. The William G. Florence "born classified" quote is from his testimony, Part 1 (*idem*), p. 98; he was also the witness who estimated that the cost of unnecessary classification is $50,000,000 a year, *ibid.,* p. 105. The GAO study of classification and related security expenditures is from *Hearings,* Part 7 (*idem*), p. 2286. The Pentagon's figures on the cost of declassifying and transmitting classified documents appear at Part 2 (*idem*), p. 690.

Congressional Quarterly's estimate that secret funds comprise 10 percent of the federal budget is from the CQ *Weekly Report,* August 21, 1971, p. 1786. The debate between Senators John C. Stennis and Stuart Symington is from *Congressional Record—Senate,* November 23, 1971, pp. S19528–29, and the *Washington Post,* November 24, 1971, p. 2. Senator J. William Fulbright's colloquy with Senator Allen J. Ellender is from the *Congressional Record— Senate* (*idem*) p. S19527. Jack Anderson made copies of the ITT-Chile papers available to the news media on March 22, 1972; their contents are described in his column in the *Washington Post,* March 21, 1972, p. B13, and *The New York Times,* March 24, 1972, pp. 1, 6, 7.

The disappearance of Dr. Jesus Maria de Galindez, and the investigation conducted by Morris L. Ernst and Sydney S. Baron are briefly described in David Wise and Thomas B. Ross, *The Espionage Establishment* (New York: Random House, 1967), pp. 238–39. Baron was interviewed in his office in Manhattan March 10, 1966. Ernst was interviewed in his law office in Manhattan on November 2, 1966. Ernst and Alan U. Schwartz transferred their papers to the National Archives in a letter signed by both, dated December 28, 1964, and addressed to Dr. Wayne C. Grover, then archivist of the United States. Their letter suggested that the papers be restricted for ten years and screened for security by the CIA. On April 19, 1965, Lawrence R. Houston of the CIA wrote to Grover requesting that the papers be restricted for twenty years. Acting archivist Walter Robertson, Jr., agreed to this in a reply to Houston dated April 22, 1965.

President Nixon's condemnation of the classification system as having failed to "meet the standards of an open and democratic society" is from the statement he made March 8, 1972, when issuing his new Executive Order on classification. The full text of his statement is published in *Hearings,* Part 7 (*idem*), pp. 2308 ff. Senator Fulbright's view of secrecy was expressed during the Senate debate of November 23, 1971 (*idem*), p. S19527.

6. The President Leaks a Document

Soon after the *Chicago Sun-Times* published the full text of Roger Hilsman's memo on June 23, 1971, I was able to obtain a Xerox copy of the actual memo, dated August 30, 1963, and typed on State Department stationery, with the Top Secret classification crossed out. Typed on the bottom of the first page were the words "Declassified by authority of the President, 2/14/68," followed by the handwritten initials, "JPR." I learned that the memo had been circulated among a few members of the press in Washington in February, 1968. But how had a Top Secret memo come to be declassified and leaked in 1968? Who had done it and why? I was aware that John P. Roche had quoted from the memo in "The Jigsaw Puzzle of History," in *The New York Times Magazine,* January 24, 1971, pp. 14 ff. But it was not clear how Roche had obtained the memo. Moreover, the *Sun-Times* had identified a peace group, the Citizens' Commission of Inquiry on U.S. War Crimes in Vietnam, as *its* source for the memo. So a subsidiary question developed: how had the commission obtained a copy? If, as seemed likely, Roche was the source, had he knowingly provided it to the peace group? Or had it been obtained by clandestine means? Jeremy Rifkin and Robert B. Johnson, of the Citizens' Commission, discussed the memo in interviews but declined absolutely to say how they had obtained it. I learned independently, however, that Robert Johnson was close to Tran Van Zung, whose father, Professor Tran Van Dinh, had served as the number-two official in the South Vietnamese embassy in Washington. In an interview, John Roche recalled that he had sent copies of the memos to a Vietnamese scholar who had written to him asking for them; his name, Roche thought, was Dinh. Tran Van Dinh readily confirmed that he had obtained the memos from Roche in this manner and had released them to the *Sun-Times.* So one part of the mystery was solved. On the larger question of how the memo came to be declassified in 1968, Roche provided a detailed account in a lengthy interview in Washington, and in subsequent correspondence. Other valuable details were gathered in personal and telephone interviews with Roger Hilsman, through a telephone interview, and in later correspondence, with former Secretary of State Dean Rusk, and through interviews with several other officials, former officials and other individuals.

All quotations from the August 30, 1963, Hilsman memo are taken from a Xerox copy of the original document. The text was published in the *Chicago Sun-Times,* June 23, 1971, pp. 1, 6. President Kennedy's 1961 Vietnam decisions are from PPNYT (*idem*: notes to Chapter 3), pp. 79–91, 124, 127. Kennedy's remark about State Department officials who smile excessively was made to reporter Hugh Sidey of *Time* and is quoted in Arthur M. Schlesinger, Jr., *A Thousand Days* (*idem*: notes to Chapter 3), p. 406.

Henry Cabot Lodge's cable of August 23, 1963, Hilsman's reply of August 24, the details of the secret maneuvering against President Ngo Dinh Diem, and the United States role in his overthrow are chiefly from PPNYT (*idem*), pp. 158–233; Roger Hilsman, *To Move a Nation* (New York: Doubleday, 1967), pp. 483–523, and *The Pentagon Papers, The Defense Department History of United States Decisionmaking on Vietnam, Volume Two* (PPG, II) (*idem*: notes to Chapter 3), pp. 211, 235, 734–35. Dean Rusk was interviewed by telephone at his office at the School of Law, University of Georgia, at Athens, Georgia, on January 18, 1972. The Rusk quote in the footnote is from this interview. His statement that he did not recall seeing a draft of the controversial cable was made in a letter to me dated March 16, 1972, which reads in part: "I don't recall seeing any early draft of the August 24 cable at the U.N. Mission in New York. My recollection is that I first heard about it when George Ball called me on the telephone and discussed it in very guarded terms." Hilsman's contention that Rusk had seen an early draft is from *To Move a Nation* (*idem*), p. 488. The cable reporting Lodge's decision that "American official hand should not show," is from PPG, II (*idem*), p. 735. It was sent on August 26, 1963, to John A. McCone, the director of CIA, by John Richardson, the CIA station chief in Saigon. Roger Hilsman's explanation of the origins of his August 30, 1963, memo and his comments are from the Hilsman interview (*idem*: notes to Chapter 5). Dean Rusk's critical remarks about Hilsman were reported by Rowland Evans and Robert Novak in the *Washington Post,* October 11, 1967; Hilsman's reply is from the *Washington Post,* October 14, 1967. I interviewed three persons who had been at the William S. White dinner party, but none agreed about who said what to whom. Hilsman's testimony to the Senate subcommittee on refugees is from the *Washington Daily News,* September 30, 1965. His recollection of his telephone conversation with McGeorge Bundy is from the Hilsman interview (*idem*).

George Christian's comments on John P. Roche are from Christian's *The President Steps Down* (*idem*: notes to Chapter 2), p. 11. The quotes from Roche, and his account of how the Hilsman memo came to be declassified, are from my interview with him in Washington on October 29, 1971, and subsequent correspondence. Lyndon Johnson's comparison of Diem to Winston Churchill is from Eric F. Goldman, *The Tragedy of Lyndon Johnson* (*idem*: notes to Chapter 2), p. 387. Johnson's suggestion that the U.S. "stop playing cops and robbers" in Saigon is from PPG, II (*idem*), p. 743; his criticism of the August 24 cable and the coup against Diem is from *The Vantage Point* (*idem*: notes to Chapter 3), p. 61.

The background to Robert F. Kennedy's decision to seek the Democratic Presidential nomination in 1968 is from Theodore H. White, *The Making of the President 1968* (New York: Atheneum, 1969), p. 160. For Johnson's chronology of his "intention" to retire, see *The Vantage Point* (*idem*), pp. 366, 427–28. According to one account, typical of those leaked after the President disclosed his decision on March 31, Johnson meant to announce in his State of the Union address in January, 1968, that he would not run again, gave his notes to Lady Bird, who went to the beauty parlor, after which the notes ended up in the White House bedroom by the telephone. This version appears in Drew Pearson, "The Ghosts That Haunted LBJ," *Look*, July 23, 1968, pp. 27–28. For evidence that Johnson, after withdrawing, may have had lingering hopes of being nominated in 1968, see *The Making of the President 1968* (*idem*), p. 279n., and David Wise, "The Twilight of a President" (*idem*: notes to Chapter 5), p. 122.

The *Newsweek* account of Roche's speech in Boston appears in the issue of January 18, 1971, p. 20. Victor Navasky was interviewed by telephone at his office in New York City on January 17, 1972. Hilsman's letter and Roche's reply were published in *The New York Times Magazine*, February 21, 1971, pp. 59, 62.

Roche found Tran Van Dinh's letter of February 21, 1971, and sent it to me. Dinh and Tran Van Zung were interviewed at their home in Washington on November 12, 1971. Dinh provided me with a copy of Roche's reply to him. Jeremy Rifkin was interviewed at the offices in Washington of the Citizens' Commission of Inquiry on U.S. War Crimes in Vietnam on September 28, 1971. Robert B. Johnson was interviewed by telephone on September 29, 1971. Hilsman's press conference charge that the memos were leaked to damage Robert Kennedy was carried on the *Chicago Daily News* wire on June 23, 1971.

7. Secrecy, National Security, and the Press

The existence of the United States Office of Censorship, the background to its creation, and its functions are discussed in *Hearing,* House Foreign Operations and Government Information Subcommittee, June 5, 1963. Under its new name, WISP, the censorship office was explored more recently by the same subcommittee in *Hearings,* Part 8, May 12, 1972, pp. 2939–94. The location of WISP's headquarters at Western Maryland College in Westminster is not published in any hearings or available government documents, but was established to the author's satisfaction through interviews. That the change to the name WISP occurred since 1969, during the Nixon administration, is from a telephone interview with John W. Nocita, of the Office of Emergency Preparedness (OEP), July 10, 1972. Eugene J. Quindlen, assistant director of OEP, and the principal official in charge of WISP, was interviewed at his office in Washington by my research assistant, Stephen Collins, on January 26, 1972. Quindlen's discussion of circumstances in which censorship would be activated is from *Hearings,* Part 8, May 12, 1972 (*idem*), pp. 2941 ff. Drafts of the stand-by Executive Order and the stand-by censorship legislation are *ibid.,* pp. 2957–59. The *Office of Censorship Basic Plan* and the acknowledgment that censorship might be imposed in a "brushfire" war is *ibid.,* pp. 2943, 2950.

James W. McCord, Jr.'s role in the censorship apparatus, the existence of SAD, and the comments by Representative William S. Moorhead are from a press release issued by Moorhead on October 23, 1972. Byron Price's memorandum on peacetime censorship planning, and his letter to President Truman are from *Hearing,* June 5, 1963 (*idem*), p. 207; the quote from the memorandum is at p. 209.

Theodore F. Koop described his meeting with Pierre Salinger and Theodore Sorensen after the Bay of Pigs in an interview in Washington on June 29, 1972. Salinger discussed President Kennedy's meeting with newspaper executives in his book *With Kennedy* (*idem*: notes to Chapter 3), p. 158. The "Standby Voluntary Censorship Code" as last revised in September, 1963, is published in *Hearings,* May 12, 1972 (*idem*), pp. 2953–56. Samuel J. Archibald was interviewed at his office at the Freedom of Information Center in Washington on January 14, 1972, and generously made available to me copies of his correspondence with OEP and much other data. Koop was identified as the chief stand-by censor in the *Washington Star,* October 25, 1970, p. 6.

"We are under a Constitution, but the Constitution is what the judges say it is." Charles Evans Hughes made this celebrated remark in 1907 as governor of New York; it is quoted in Alpheus T. Mason,

The Supreme Court, Palladium of Freedom (Ann Arbor: University of Michigan Press, 1962), p. 143. Senator Albert B. Cummins' misgivings about the Espionage Act are from *The Congressional Record,* 1917, Volume 54, p. 3606.

The case of Mikhail Gorin is described in David J. Dallin, *Soviet Espionage* (New Haven: Yale University Press, 1955), p. 421, and in Allen W. Dulles, *The Craft of Intelligence* (New York: Harper, 1963), p. 202. The quotes, from the Supreme Court's decision of January 13, 1941, are in *Gorin v. United States,* 312 U.S. 19, 28, 32. The quote from *United States v. Drummond* is in *The New York Times Company v. United States: A Documentary History* (*idem*: notes to Chapter 5), Volume II, p. 804. The *Chicago Tribune* and the Japanese code are discussed in David Kahn, *The Codebreakers* (New York: Macmillan, 1967), p. 603. Attorney General Francis Biddle's announcement that a federal grand jury would investigate the *Tribune's* dispatch about the Battle of Midway for possible violations of the espionage laws is from *The New York Times,* August 8, 1942, p. 4. The reference to the *Amerasia* case is from *Soviet Espionage* (*idem*), pp. 445 ff., and *Congressional Record—House,* May 22, 1950, pp. 7428–29. The discussion of prior restraint, the history of British censorship, and the quote from Blackstone are from Thomas I. Emerson, *The System of Freedom of Expression* (New York: Random House, 1970), p. 504. The *Near* case is quoted from *Near v. Minnesota,* 283 U.S. 697 (1931); the famous "exceptions" appear at p. 716. The government's claim that the publication of the Pentagon Papers would cause "irreparable injury to the United States" and Erwin N. Griswold's comment are from *The New York Times Company v. United States: A Documentary History* (*idem*), Volume I, p. 11, and Volume II, p. 1233. For the Supreme Court's decision in the Pentagon Papers case, *see New York Times Company v. United States,* 403 U.S. 713 (1971).

Kevin T. Maroney's warning to newspaper editors about publishing classified information is from *Hearings,* House Foreign Operations and Government Information Subcommittee, Part 7, May 11, 1972, p. 2694. Paul A. Freund's comment on prior restraint is from his *The Supreme Court of the United States* (Cleveland: World, 1961), p. 63. The quotes from the brief filed by Thomas I. Emerson and Representative Bob Eckhardt are from *The New York Times Company v. United States: A Documentary History* (*idem*), Volume II, pp. 1057, 58. Professor Emerson's remarks to the Senate Subcommittee on Constitutional Rights are from the text of his prepared statement, October 13, 1971. The *New York Times rule* and the quote are from *New York Times v. Sullivan,* 376 U.S. 254 (1964). The backgrounder held by Herb Klein is reported in *The New York Times,* June 19,

1971, p. 1. For my discussion of the intricacies of Section 793(e) of the Espionage Act, I am indebted to a number of sources. These include the footnotes in Justice White's decision in the Pentagon Papers case, the *amicus* brief filed by the American Civil Liberties Union in the Supreme Court during the Pentagon Papers case, written by Norman Dorsen, *et al.*, and published in *Hearings*, House Foreign Operations and Government Information Subcommittee, Part 3, pp. 818 ff., as well as several interviews. On this and related legal points, former Senator Charles Goodell, a defense attorney for Daniel Ellsberg, was interviewed in Washington on March 17, 1972; Walter Slocombe, who assisted in the Ellsberg defense, was interviewed in Washington on May 15, 1972; Mitchell Rogovin was interviewed in Washington on November 22, 1971, and May 16, 1972; and Norman Dorsen was interviewed in New York City on March 30, 1972.

Dean Acheson's call for an Official Secrets Act is from *The New York Times* Op Ed page, July 7, 1971. Whitehall's lack of cooperation with Anthony Howard is from Jonathan Aitken, *Officially Secret* (London: Weidenfeld and Nicholson, 1971), p. 36; Aitken's characterization of the Official Secrets Act is *ibid.*, p. 27. My discussion of the *Sunday Telegraph* case is from *Officially Secret, ibid.;* the transcript of Mr. Justice Caulfield's summing up in *Regina v. Douglas Jeffrey Cairns, et al.;* the *Daily Telegraph*, February 4, 1971, p. 1; and Alan Watkins, "Official Secrets," *New Statesman*, February 5, 1971, p. 170. In addition, Jonathan Aitken answered several questions in a letter to me dated May 31, 1972. My discussion of the Official Secrets Act and the workings of the D-notice system is based on Halsbury's *Statutes of England*, 3d Edition, Volume 8, pp. 250 ff.; my own research in London in 1966; and David Wise and Thomas B. Ross, *The Espionage Establishment* (*idem*: notes to Chapter 5), pp. 122–29. See also, David Williams, *Not in the Public Interest*, (London: Hutchinson, 1965). The recommendations of Lord Franks' committee are from *The Times* of London, September 30, 1972, pp. 1, 3. The full Franks report, in four volumes, is entitled *Departmental Committee on Section 2 of the Official Secrets Act* (London: Her Majesty's Stationery Office, 1972).

Alexander M. Bickel's dialogue with Justice Potter Stewart is from *The New York Times Company v. United States: A Documentary History* (*idem*), Volume II, p. 1226. Judge Murray I. Gurfein's concern over compromising codes is *ibid.*, Volume I, p. 466, 469. Robert F. Kennedy's comment on secrecy is quoted in William McGaffin and Erwin Knoll, *Anything but the Truth* (*idem*: notes to Chapter 3), p. 78. Gurfein's conclusion that security lies "not at the ramparts alone" is from *The New York Times*, June 20, 1971, p. 26.

8. The Case of the Colorado Tibetans

The fact that the Central Intelligence Agency established a secret base in the Rocky Mountains where it trained Tibetan guerrillas to fight against Communist China was pieced together from various data, in part as follows:

Sometime ago I heard a bizarre tale from a confidential source. Somewhere in the United States in the early 1960's a commercial airliner had crashed or made a forced landing on what appeared to be a military installation. Armed U.S. troops had roughed up the civilian passengers, some of whom had glimpsed what appeared to be Chinese or other Oriental soldiers on the base. A few of the passengers had complained of their treatment, but the incident received little attention in the press. Somehow, Tibetans may have been involved.

A detailed search of *The New York Times Index, Facts on File,* and similar conventional sources failed to uncover any crash landing or aviation mishap in which the facts even remotely matched the story I had heard. The Associated Press, the United Press International, and NBC television news checked their central files in New York at my request but were unable to find any such incident. The records of the National Transportation Safety Board of the United States Department of Transportation reflect forced landings and aviation crashes, but are categorized only by state and date. Since I did not have the location or date, it appeared that my search was useless; the enormous haystack of daily news events would not yield up this particular needle—and perhaps it had never happened.

I decided, however, to approach the problem from another direction. Instead of attempting to find the event from masses of records, I would try to pinpoint the location. Where would *I* train Tibetans if I were going to train them? The answer suggested itself immediately, and my next telephone call was to the City Desk of the *Denver Post.* I was switched to the library, where it was my great good fortune to get Mrs. Rosie Frank, the newspaper's librarian, who not only listened to my tale without expressing the skepticism to which I had, by now, become accustomed, but who promised to try, when she had a few moments of spare time, to discover a story such as the one I described. Six days later she sent me a clipping from the *Denver Post* of December 7, 1961, reporting the mistreatment of civilians at Peterson Field. As Mrs. Frank pointed out in an accompanying letter, the "other details don't quite match . . ." She was right, of course. There was no civilian airliner involved, no forced landing, and above all, no mention of Oriental troops. Nevertheless, it seemed at least possible that this was the incident. I asked Stephen Collins, then my research assistant, to go the Library of Congress and start reading microfilms of every Colorado paper for December, 1961. He came across several news stories about the incident at Peterson Field, but none contained what we were looking for. Then he read the story in the *Colorado Springs Gazette Telegraph* of December 8, 1961. Halfway down into the story, he found these words: "The report that Oriental soldiers dressed in battle fatigues were seen entering the plane [was] confirmed today by student pilot Lynn Boese . . ." Collins ran out of the microfilm room to the nearest pay phone and called me. The search was over.

Henry M. Wood was traced to New Orleans, and interviewed by telephone there on November 18, 1971. My account of the events at Peterson Field on the morning of December 7, 1961, is based on this and other interviews with eyewitnesses, as well as news stories in the *Denver Post,* December 7 and 8, 1961, pp. 11, 3; the *Colorado Springs Gazette Telegraph (idem);* and the *Rocky Mountain News,* December 8, 1961, p. 5. Lynn Boese was interviewed by telephone in Colorado Springs on November 5, 1971. J. R. Smith, another eyewitness, was interviewed by telephone in Denver on November 16, 1971. Harold Ravnsborg, interviewed by telephone in Denver on November 22, 1971, confirmed that he had burned his film after the officer from Fort Carson had pledged everyone to secrecy and had warned that it was "a federal offense" to discuss what they had seen.

The procedure for discovering the reincarnation of the Dalai Lama and the account of the series of tests given to the present Dalai Lama are from the Dalai Lama of Tibet, *My Land and My People* (New York: McGraw-Hill, 1962), pp. 5–43. Some of the history of Leadville is from Harry Hansen, ed., *Colorado; a Guide to the Highest State* (New York: Hastings House, 1970), pp. 168–78. The fighting in Tibet in March of 1959 is from *The New York Times,* March 21, 1959, p. 1, and successive issues; the Dalai Lama describes his escape in *My Land and My People (idem),* pp. 164–216. Eisenhower's conference on Tibet with CIA director Allen Dulles is reported in *The New York Times,* April 12, 1959, p. 79.

For background to the Bay of Pigs invasion, see *The Invisible Government (idem:* notes to Chapter 3), pp. 8–90. Clifton Daniel's detailed account of how *The New York Times* handled the news about the Cuban invasion was made in his speech to the World Press Institute in St. Paul, Minnesota, on June 1, 1966. The text appears in *Anything But the Truth (idem:* notes to Chapter 3). President Kennedy's April 27, 1961, plea to the newspaper publishers is from John F. Kennedy, *Public Papers of the Presidents,* 1961 (Washington: U.S. Government Printing Office, 1962), p. 337. Kennedy's remark to Turner Catledge is from Clifton Daniel's speech in *Anything But the*

Truth (*idem*), p. 205. The reference to the Dalai Lama's life in exile and continued Tibetan guerrilla activity is from Colin MacAndrews, "Tibetans in Exile: Youth Gap Threatens Their Culture," in the *Washington Post*, November 14, 1971, p. B3.

9. The Selling of the Government

Oran K. Henderson's explanation that My Lai was briefed "as one of our successful operations" is from his testimony at his court-martial in Fort Meade, Maryland, as reported in *The New York Times*, November 24, 1971, p. 4. The Army's estimate of 347 civilian dead at My Lai is from Seymour M. Hersh, *Cover-Up* (New York: Random House, 1972), p. 7. William L. Calley, Jr.'s conviction of the premeditated murder of twenty-two persons is from *The New York Times*, March 30, 1971, p. 1.

Data on the Defense Information School and Robert Musil's comment are from *The New York Times*, June 12, 1971, and from *Congressional Record—House*, July 6, 1970, p. H6367. McGeorge Bundy's marginal note on Pierre Salinger's draft communiqué is from *The New York Times*, August 2, 1971, pp. 1, 6. The second story, reporting that Bundy had written "feed," not "fool," was published by the *Times* on August 12, 1971. Henry Raymont was interviewed by telephone at *The New York Times* on October 13, 1971, and May 22, 1972. Bundy's cable to Henry Cabot Lodge is from PPNYT (*idem*: notes to Chapter 3), p. 231.

Details of the false-alert broadcast from Cheyenne Mountain are from *The New York Times*, February 21, 1971, p. 1, "We interrupt this program . . ." The text is from Emergency Action Notification Message No. 1, which was made available to the author by the Federal Communications Commission. Chuck Kelley and the news director of WEVA are quoted in the *Washington Post*, February 21, 1971, p. A12. The Red Envelope is described in the official FCC regulations governing emergency broadcasts as published in the *Federal Register*, April 14, 1972, Paragraph 73.911. Data on the number of stations that complied with emergency regulations are from an FCC summary made public on April 6, 1971. The text of the tape prepared for use in Dade County is from an article by Verne O. Williams in the *Miami News*, February 23, 1971.

Melvin Laird's defense of his candor and his refusal to discuss the number of sorties flown in Vietnam are from "Informal meeting with Secretary of Defense Melvin R. Laird and newsmen at the Pentagon, Wednesday, September 2, 1970—11:00 A.M.," Transcript, pp. 12–13.

The description of the FM radio device that could be turned on by the government at will is from the *Washington Post,* November 1, 1972, p. A2; a press release by Congressman William S. Moorhead dated November 1, 1972; and "Communication for Social Needs," the 300-page report prepared for the White House by an interagency study group. This language appears on page v-11 of the report: "No wake-up capability—existing warning systems have no capability of alerting those not tuned in." On the same page, the study notes that the proposed system would have "full coverage—virtually 100 percent of the population of the affected area must be warned, even those who may be asleep."

General Bruce K. Holloway made his proposal for a government-controlled news program in testimony at a closed session of the House subcommittee on defense appropriations, March 23, 1971; later, the proceedings were published, and his testimony appears in the printed hearings at p. 285. Nixon's exchange with Barbara Walters is from "An Interview with the President of the United States," NBC Transcript, pp. 23–25. The interview was filmed for the *Today* show on March 11, 1971, and aired on March 15. Nixon's interview with Howard K. Smith was broadcast live on March 22, 1971, at 9:30 P.M. EST. Nixon's interview with a group of women reporters (*idem*: notes to Chapter 3) took place on the afternoon of March 11, 1971, and was embargoed for release on March 13. Biographical background on Harry Robbins Haldeman and Ronald L. Ziegler is from Karl Fleming, "Nixon and the Boys from J. Walter Thompson," *West* magazine, the *Los Angeles Times,* January 19, 1969, pp. 12–15; Dom Bonafede, "Men behind Nixon," *National Journal,* March 6, 1971, pp. 513–22; and James M. Naughton, "How the 2d Best-Informed Man in the White House Briefs the 2d Worst-Informed Group in Washington," *The New York Times Magazine,* May 30, 1971, pp. 9–30. Ziegler's spiel as a tour guide at Disneyland is *ibid.,* p. 25. The reference to Nixon's employment at the Slippery Gulch Rodeo is from Earl Mazo, *Nixon* (New York: Harper & Brothers, 1959), p. 15. The comparison of Ziegler to Pinocchio is from the James M. Naughton article (*idem*), p. 24.

"There will be no Sherman Adams . . ." This Haldeman quote is from *The New York Times,* November 14, 1968, p. 34. Klein's prediction that the Nixon administration would eliminate the credibility gap is from the November 25, 1968, Transcript (*idem*: notes to Chapter 1). "I have the President and the White House." The Ziegler quote is reported in the *National Journal,* December 6, 1969, p. 260. My account of the friction between Klein and Ziegler over Allen Drury's book is based on Allen Drury and Fred Maroon, *Courage and Hesitation* (New York: Doubleday, 1971), pp. 16, 165; an informal conversation with Fred Maroon in Washington on April 14, 1972; a telephone interview with Evelyn Metzger in Washington on June 1, 1972; and an interview with Ronald Ziegler in his White House office on June 14, 1972. The phrase "this commercial project" is attributed to Ziegler by Drury in *Courage and Hesitation* (*idem*), p. 165. When I questioned Ziegler about the matter, he replied: "It was a commercial project. Drury wrote a lousy book, and you can quote me. It was a horrible book." Ziegler declined to explain the basis of his displeasure. The biographical background on Herbert Klein is from David Wise, "Herb Klein: Image-Maker in the Middle," *West* magazine, the *Los Angeles Times*, January 18, 1970. Klein's warning that unless the press reexamined its handling of the news, "you do invite the government to come in," is from "Face the Nation," CBS Transcript, November 16, 1969, p. 14. Klein extolled the ABM in a speech in De Kalb, Illinois, reported in the *Chicago Sun-Times*, April 13, 1969; his prediction that Clement F. Haynsworth would make a "great" Supreme Court justice was carried in a UPI dispatch from Riverside, California, on October 13, 1969; his attack on George McGovern and his warning that children might eat potato chips bought with food stamps is from the De Kalb, Illinois, speech in the *Chicago Sun-Times* (*idem*).

Allen Drury's revealing discussion of the work of the "Plans Committee" is from *Courage and Hesitation* (*idem*), pp. 210–14. The biographical data on Charles W. Colson is from several sources, including Dom Bonafede, "Men Behind Nixon," the *National Journal*, August 8, 1970, pp. 1689 ff., and John Pierson, "Nixon Hatchet Man: Call it What you Will, Chuck Colson Handles President's Dirty Work," the *Wall Street Journal*, October 15, 1971, p. 1. Colson declined my request for an interview in a letter signed by an assistant, W. Richard Howard, and dated June 12, 1972. The bloody battle between construction workers and students in New York City, the subsequent rally at which Mayor John V. Lindsay was burned in effigy, and Nixon's meeting with Peter J. Brennan are reported in the *Washington Post*, issues of May 10, 21, and 27, 1970. Nixon appointed Brennan Secretary of Labor on November 29, 1972. Robert B. Semple, Jr., was interviewed in Washington on November 24, 1971. The explanation that E. Howard Hunt, Jr., met Charles Colson at the Brown University alumni club in Washington was offered by Ken W. Clawson, White House deputy director of communications, as reported in the *Washington Post* on June 20, 1972, p. A4. Hunt pleaded guilty in the Watergate bugging case on January 11, 1973. On January 15 four other defendants, all from Miami, also pleaded guilty—Bernard L. Barker, Eugenio R. Martinez, Virgilio R. Gonzalez, and Frank A. Sturgis. On January 30 a federal jury convicted the two remaining defendants: G. Gordon Liddy, former assistant to

President Nixon and counsel to the finance committee of the Committee for the Re-election of the President, and James W. McCord, Jr., security director of the President's campaign. Nixon's speechwriting staff is described in detail by Dom Bonafede in the *National Journal*, February 19, 1972, pp. 311 ff.

Data on the number of federal employees in the "Information and the Arts" categories and their salaries are from *Occupations of Federal White-Collar Workers* (Washington: U.S. Government Printing Office, 1968), pp. 154, 161. Nixon's memo to Haldeman is quoted by Don Oberdorfer in the *Washington Post*, May 1, 1971, p. A8. Nixon's "Memorandum to the Heads of Executive Departments and Agencies" ordering cuts in public relations activities is dated November 6, 1970; the quotes are from the text released by the White House. Data on size and cost of the government public relations structure as compiled by the Office of Management and Budget is from Dom Bonafede, "White House Report," the *National Journal*, July 24, 1971, pp. 1551 ff., and OMB press release of April 2, 1971. The AP estimates are from a story carried on its wires March 18, 1967. George Strauss was interviewed by telephone at his office at OMB on December 13, 1971.

Harry Treleaven was interviewed by telephone on December 30, 1971. The details of his employment as a consultant by the Interior Department are from the *Washington Star*, March 10, 1971, p. 1. For further background on Treleaven and his key media role in the 1968 Presidential campaign, see Joe McGinniss, *The Selling of the President 1968* (New York: Trident, 1969); Treleaven's relationships with James N. Allison, Jr., and George Bush are at *ibid.*, pp. 43–45. The Treleaven report was made available to me on a confidential basis and the quoted portions were copied by my research assistant, Susan M. Soper. Mitchell Melich, the Solicitor of the Interior Department, declined my request for a copy of the report. Treleaven's proposal for a mine-safety media campaign was assailed by Congressman Ken Hechler of West Virginia in a series of speeches on the House floor; see *Congressional Record—House*, June 14, 1971, pp. H5089 ff.; June 28, 1971, p. H5968, and June 29, 1971, pp. H6047 ff. Robert A. Kelly was interviewed at his office in the Interior Department on January 11, 1972.

The background to the 1913 law prohibiting the government from hiring publicity men is from Joseph S. Rosapepe, "Neither Pinkertons Nor Publicity Men," *Public Relations Journal*, October, 1971, pp. 12 ff. Mel White was interviewed in Washington on October 21, 1971. Jack Rosenthal's typology of government public relations men was offered in an interview in Washington on December 29, 1971, during which he also related the story of the telephone call from

President Kennedy. Supersonic Pussycat purrs in *Teacher's Guide for SST* (Washington: Department of Transportation, 1969), pp. 23–25. Maxwell the Mouse is quoted on pp. 19–21. Senator William Proxmire's estimate of the booklet's cost is from the *Chicago Sun-Times,* June 25, 1971, p. 2. The NASA, HEW, and Pentagon public relations budget figures are from OMB data published in the *National Journal,* July 24, 1971 (*idem*), p. 1555, and data furnished by the Defense Department office of public affairs. Congressman Jonathan B. Bingham's comment on hidden Pentagon public relations costs and the text of the GAO report are from *Congressional Record —Extensions of Remarks,* September 27, 1971, pp. E10118–23. The Pentagon's monitoring of news broadcasts is from the *New York Post,* June 11, 1971. Senator J.W. Fulbright's comment is from *Congressional Record—Senate,* December 8, 1970, p. S19650. "The Selling of the Pentagon" was broadcast by CBS-TV on February 23, 1971, and again on March 23, 1971. The second telecast included a "Postscript," in which Vice-President Agnew and other critics of the program were interviewed. CBS President Frank Stanton was cited for contempt by the House Commerce Committee on July 1, 1971; the House killed the citation on July 13, and both votes are reported on page one of *The New York Times* of July 2 and July 14. Jay Roberts' dispatch is discussed in Seymour M. Hersh, *My Lai 4* (New York: Random House, 1970), pp. 77–78. Ronald L. Haeberle's comment is from *The New York Times,* August 25, 1971, p. 10.

10. Nixon vs. the Press

Nixon's comment to Prime Minister Harold Wilson that he might give "contaminated" moon rocks to the press was reported by United Press International on August 12, 1969, in a dispatch from San Clemente, California. J. Roy Goodearle's remark at the Waldorf-Astoria is reported in Joseph Albright, *What Makes Spiro Run* (New York: Dodd, Mead, 1972), pp. 231–32, and in Jules Witcover, *The Resurrection of Richard Nixon* (New York: Putnam's, 1970), p. 456n. In addition, Joseph Albright was interviewed in Washington by telephone on June 23, 1972, and Victor Gold was interviewed in Washington by telephone on the same date. *Newsday's* series on Charles G. (Bebe) Rebozo was published October 6–13, 1971. Pages cited below are from a *Newsday* reprint of the series. Rebozo's dealings with the Small Business Administration, pp. 12–15; the Fisher's Island investment and Nixon's sale of stock for $371,782, pp. 14, 15, 42, 43; "Mr. Sturgeon," pp. 17, 20; the editorial, p. 43. Martin Schram was interviewed at length by telephone at his office in Washington on March 23, 1972; the interview was tape-recorded with his permission. The description of the hibiscus hedge at Key Biscayne, the shark net, and related details are from the *Newsday* reprint, pp. 38–39. Robert W. Greene was interviewed by telephone at *Newsday*'s offices in Garden City, Long Island, on March 31, 1972. David Laventhol was interviewed by telephone at *Newsday* on April 1, 1972, and again on June 19, 1972. William Attwood was interviewed at *Newsday* by telephone on June 19, 1972. Peter Ritner was interviewed by telephone at his office in New York on the same date.

Details of the "Nixon Fund" and the Checkers speech are from Richard M. Nixon, *Six Crises* (New York: Doubleday, 1962), pp. 73–129. The quotes are from pp. 91, 102, 103, and 115. The Theodore H. White quote is from his *The Making of the President 1960* (New York: Atheneum, 1961), p. 336. Nixon's reference in Chester, Pennsylvania, to his mother's lemon and cherry pies is from the *New York Herald Tribune*, October 23, 1960. The references to hamburger, the wind-up train, and the pony are from *Final Report of the Committee on Commerce, United States Senate, Part II, The Speeches of Vice-President Richard M. Nixon, Presidential Campaign of 1960* (Washington: U.S. Government Printing Office, 1961), pp. 701, 825, 835, and 849.

My account of the Casper landing is from the *New York Herald Tribune*, November 5, 1960, pp. 1, 3, and personal observation. "Screw them." The quote is from *The Resurrection of Richard Nixon (idem)*, pp. 13, 14. Nixon's 1962 press conference remarks are from Gladwin Hill, *Dancing Bear* (New York: World, 1968), Appendix Three. Nixon's private remarks to cabinet appointees and their wives is from James Keogh, *President Nixon and the Press* (New York: Funk & Wagnalls, 1972), pp. 2–3. After the 1972 Presidential election, Nixon named Keogh director of the United States Information Agency. The ACLU report is a useful summary of pressures on the news media during the first two years of the Nixon administration; see Fred Powledge, *The Nixon Administration and the Press: The Engineering of Restraint* (New York: American Civil Liberties Union, 1971). The quote is *ibid*, p. 5. For background to Spiro T. Agnew's speeches in 1969, including his attack on "network commentators," see Jules Witcover, *White Knight, The Rise of Spiro Agnew* (New York: Random House, 1972), pp. 304 ff. Ronald Ziegler's admission that Patrick J. Buchanan "may have, and I think did have, some thoughts" about Agnew's Des Moines speech is *ibid.*, at p. 316. Herbert G. Klein's comments paralleling those of Vice-President Agnew are from "The President's Men," broadcast over the National Educational Television Network, November 13, 1969, Transcript, p. 14. Dean Burch's praise for the Agnew speech is from *The New York*

Times, November 15, 1969, p. 20. Robert Dole's comments are from the *New York Post,* March 20, 1971; H.R. Haldeman's remarks, made to *Look* magazine, are reported in the *Washington Post,* August 10, 1971. Richard Kleindienst is quoted in the *National Journal,* October 2, 1971, p. 2007. Patrick J. Buchanan's suggestion that news bias might bring government anti-trust action was made during an interview with Elizabeth Drew over the educational television network, as reported in *The New York Times,* May 6, 1972, pp. 1, 52. L. Patrick Gray's remarks were delivered at the Orange County Law Day Banquet, Santa Ana, California, April 28, 1972; the quotes are from the text made public by the Justice Department. Kenneth W. Clawson's complaints are from *The New York Times,* May 20, 1972, p. 8. Nixon's comments to Allen Drury are from *Courage and Hesitation (idem:* notes to Chapter 9), p. 395. Nixon's statements over ABC television are from the Howard K. Smith interview *(idem:* notes to Chapter 9), Transcript, pp. 7-8. His comments on Daniel Schorr are from the interview with women reporters *(idem:* notes to Chapter 3), Transcript, p. 14; pie-baking reappears *ibid.,* at p. 2.

The description of the White House press rooms, old and new, are from personal observation plus *The New York Times,* April 3, 1970, p. 20, and the *Washington Post,* April 3, 1970. Hugh Sidey was interviewed in Washington on December 3, 1971. Edward T. Folliard was interviewed by telephone in Washington about June 12, 1972. Robert B. Semple's comments are from the interview with him *(idem:* notes to Chapter 9). The White House "China News Summary 24: Friday PM nets and Tuesday coverage from around the nation" was published in the March 31, 1972, monthly report of the Washington News Committee of the Associated Press Managing Editors Association and made available to me through the courtesy of Courtney R. Sheldon, committee chairman and Washington bureau chief of the *Christian Science Monitor.* Patrick Buchanan's letter to the *Post* is dated November 20, 1970. Stuart H. Loory was interviewed in Washington on May 26, 1972. His article reporting Nixon's cool reception at the Vatican appeared in the *Los Angeles Times,* September 29, 1970, pp. 1, 10. The Nicholas P. Thimmesch column about H. R. Haldeman was distributed on February 16, 1972.

The search of the Defense Department press room by agents of the Pentagon Counterintelligence Force was reported in a dispatch by Robert A. Dobkin of the Associated Press on November 18, 1971. David O. Cooke's memo to Daniel Henkin was made available by Henkin's office. The peculiar incident of the wife of a Pentagon newsman who overheard a conversation in the press room on her home telephone was reported by Fred Farrar in the *Chicago Tribune,* November 19, 1971, p. 1; Farrar was interviewed by telephone in Washington on December 23, 1971. Data on the Earl Caldwell case and the issue of newsmen's privilege is from Johnny H. Killian, "A Constitutional Newsman's Privilege" (Washington: Congressional Research Service, Library of Congress, 1970); the Supreme Court decision in *United States v. Caldwell* 408 U.S. 665 (1972), and *The New York Times,* June 30, 1972, p. 1. The statistics on network subpoenas are reported in *Congressional Quarterly Weekly Report,* January 1, 1972, p. 5. The imprisonment of Peter J. Bridge is from *The New York Times,* October 25, 1972, p. 51. William T. Farr, a Los Angeles newspaper reporter, was jailed in November, 1972, for refusing to disclose a news source, and on December 19, 1972, John F. Lawrence, Washington bureau chief of the *Los Angeles Times* was briefly jailed when he refused to furnish a federal district court tapes relating to the Watergate bugging case.

Stuart H. Loory made his comment about "losing pools" when interviewed in Washington on January 21, 1972. James H. McCartney agreed to a tape-recorded telephone interview, held in Washington on March 4, 1972. Ronald L. Ziegler's comments are from my interview with him (*idem*: notes to Chapter 9). On the subject of *Newsday* and Martin Schram, Ziegler said: "I was cool to Marty after the Rebozo series. It was a bad, lousy series . . . a rehash of a lot of things that had been written, full of innuendo. They spent a lot of time and money on it. My attitude was one of disgust. I don't deny I was cool to Marty Schram."

The figures on press conferences held by President Nixon were furnished by the White House press office. Data on the number of press conferences held by previous Presidents were provided by *Congressional Quarterly.* The Robert Semple and Hugh Sidey quotes are from interviews with them (*idem*). Tom Wicker's comments are from my interview with him (*idem*: notes to Chapter 1).

11. Television

Frank Stanton was interviewed at CBS headquarters in New York on November 8, 1971. Most of his comments during the two-hour conversation were on the record. Dean Rusk's remarks to the Democratic platform hearing are from the State Department text of his statement, as delivered, pp. 5–6. The description of how the wire copy reporting the invasion of Czechoslovakia was handed to Rusk, and his reaction, are from *The New York Times,* August 21, 1968, pp. 1, 33. Rusk's comments to me are from the telephone interview (*idem*: notes to Chapter 6). The account of the conversation between Senator John F. Kennedy and Frank Stanton after the Wisconsin primary and the related material are from my interview with Stanton (*idem*). Blair Clark was interviewed by telephone in New York on April 4, 1972. Newton Minow was interviewed by telephone at his law office in Chicago on November 17, 1971.

John Chancellor was interviewed at length in New York on October 12, 1971, in Washington on November 23, 1971, and also by telephone in New York in June and July of 1972. President Johnson's confrontation with John Chancellor took place during the walking backgrounder on the White House lawn described in Chapter 5.

Nixon's comment to Cyrus L. Sulzberger is from *The New York Times*, March 10, 1971, pp. 1, 14. The celebrated Roger Ailes quote is from *The Selling of the President 1968* (*idem*: notes to Chapter 9), p. 103. Ailes' advice to Nixon on the hazards of the UN podium and the other Ailes quotes are from *The New York Times*, September 21, 1969, p. 84. The Walter Cronkite quote is from the CBS text of his speech to the International Radio and Television Society, May 18, 1971. Dean Burch's request for transcripts of network commentaries on Nixon's speech is reported in *The New York Times*, November 15, 1969, p. 1.

My account of John Ehrlichman's breakfast at the Plaza, his complaints about Dan Rather, and subsequent events, is based on interviews with Dan Rather in Washington on November 1 and 3, 1971, with Richard S. Salant at CBS News in New York on October 11, 1971, and with John Hart in Washington on June 11, 1971. I wrote to John Ehrlichman on May 18, 1972, requesting an interview to obtain his general views on the subject of government and the news media as well as any specific comment he might have "concerning your remarks to CBS executives about Dan Rather." The request was declined in a letter dated May 26, 1972, and signed by Tod R. Hullin, Ehrlichman's executive assistant.

My account of the FBI investigation of Daniel Schorr is based on a series of interviews: with Richard S. Salant (*idem*); with Daniel Schorr at CBS News headquarters in Washington, on November 3, 1971, and by telephone in Washington on November 16, 1971, and June 30, 1972; with Ellen McCloy in New York on October 11, 1971; and with Matthew B. Coffey by telephone in Washington on July 25, 1972. There were several other sources; these include the transcript of Ronald L. Ziegler's press briefing of November 11, 1971, at 12:05 P.M., and the *Washington Post*, November 11, 1971, p. 1, and February 1, 1972, p. 1. Frederic V. Malek's vague explanation of how "something went wrong" is from Dom Bonafede, "White House Report," the *National Journal*, November 12, 1971, p. 2444. Dan Schorr's statement to the Ervin committee is from the prepared text of his remarks, February 1, 1972.

Richard Salant's account of Mrs. Agnew's objections to *60 Minutes,* as reported by Herbert G. Klein, is from the Salant interview (*idem*). The Agnew segment was broadcast February 2, 1971, and the quotes are from the CBS transcript of that date. Herb Klein's belief that television stations "seemed pleased" when he telephoned to ask about their editorial treatment of the President was expressed at a luncheon meeting of the International Radio and Television Society in New York, and is reported in *The New York Times,* November 20, 1969, p. 26. Wallace Westfeldt described Ronald Ziegler's telephone call to the NBC control room in an interview in his office at NBC News in New York on October 12, 1971.

Reuven Frank told of his two telephone calls from Klein in an interview in his office at NBC News in New York on November 9, 1971. Richard C. Wald was interviewed in New York on October 12, 1971. My discussion of the Supreme Court's interpretation of the extent to which the First Amendment protects broadcasters is based on the text of the decisions in *Red Lion Broadcasting Co., Inc. v. Federal Communications Commission,* 395 U.S. 367 (1969) and *Rosenbloom v. Metromedia, Inc.,* 403 U.S. 29 (1971). Julian Goodman was interviewed at his office at NBC in New York on November 8, 1971, and he elaborated on his remarks in a letter and a six-page memorandum dated January 5, 1972. The application for the license of Channel 10, Miami, by a group that included friends of President Nixon, was reported in *The New York Times,* January 7, 1970. Larry Israel was interviewed by telephone in Washington on November 13, 1972. Clay T. Whitehead's astonishing threat was voiced at a luncheon of the Indianapolis chapter of Sigma Delta Chi, the professional journalism fraternity, on December 18, 1972. The quote is from *The New York Times,* December 19, 1972, pp. 1, 51. Whitehead coupled his speech with two incentives designed to appeal to local broadcasting stations; he said the administration was preparing legislation to extend licenses to five years instead of three, and to make it much more difficult for competing applicants to win licenses held by existing stations.

Nixon's veto of the bill providing increased funds for the Corporation for Public Broadcasting and his praise of *Sesame Street* are from *The New York Times,* July 1, 1972, pp. 1, 9. Walter Cronkite was interviewed at length in his office at CBS News in New York on November 9, 1971.

12. The Government and the Press: Leaks and Techniques

Albert R. Hunt was interviewed in Washington on December 17, 1971. For the article that resulted from the White House leak, see

Richard F. Janssen and Albert R. Hunt, "War of Nerves Quickens: White House Hints It Plans Attack on Reserve Board's Independence," the *Wall Street Journal*, July 29, 1971, p. 26. DeVan L. Shumway was interviewed at his office in Washington on December 23, 1971. He declined to discuss the incident on the record. Norman Kempster was interviewed by telephone in Washington on December 24, 1971. Shumway's comments on the Watergate affair may be found in the *Washington Post*, June 20, 1972, p. 4. The White House announced that Charles W. Colson was unaware of the Watergate bugging; on June 19, 1972, Ken W. Clawson, Herb Klein's deputy, said: "I've looked into the matter very thoroughly and I am convinced that neither Mr. Colson nor anyone else at the White House had any knowledge of, or participation in, this deplorable incident at the Democratic National Committee." The statement is published in the *Washington Post, ibid.*

The leak to the *Pennsylvania Herald* during the Constitutional Convention of 1787 and Alexander Hamilton's proposal for a lifetime President are from Carl Van Doren, *The Great Rehearsal* (New York: Compass Books, The Viking Press, 1961), pp. 93, 145.

Townsend Hoopes was interviewed in Washington on September 15, 1971. Edwin L. Dale, Jr., was interviewed by telephone in Washington on July 19, 1972. The story of the leak of the request for 206,000 troops is told in detail in Don Oberdorfer, *TET!* (New York: Doubleday, 1971), pp. 264–67, 285–91. President Johnson's comment on the leak appears in *The Vantage Point* (*idem*: notes to Chapter 3), p. 402. Philip Potter's article appeared in the *Baltimore Sun* on February 10, 1971. Townsend Hoopes discusses the troop request and related events in *The Limits of Intervention* (*idem*: notes to Chapter 2), pp. 159–240.

The findings of the Coolidge committee, "Report to the Secretary of Defense by the Committee on Classified Information," are published in *Hearings*, House Special Subcommittee on Government Information, Part 8, March 11 and 12, 1957, pp. 2133 ff. The background to the formation of the Coolidge committee and the Anthony Leviero story are described in "Availability of Information from Federal Departments and Agencies," House *Report 1884* (*idem*: notes to Chapter 4), pp. 20 ff.

Jack Rosenthal's comments on the art of leaking are from the interview with him (*idem*: notes to Chapter 9). There is no published source for the fact that the CIA administered the lie-detector tests given to State Department employees in 1971, but it was confirmed to me by a high-level official source. *The New York Times* stories on the investigation of news leaks at the State Department appeared on September 3, 1971, p. 1, 9, and September 4, 1971, p. 2. J. Edgar Hoover's letter to the *Washington Post* was published October 1,

1971, p. A27. The letter called the newspaper's reports that "the FBI used polygraphs" in the investigation "totally and completely untrue." Daniel P. Moynihan's article, "The Presidency & the Press" ran in the March, 1971, issue of *Commentary,* pp. 41–52. Thomas B. Ross' reply is from his article "Is the press undermining the President?" in *The Bulletin,* American Society of Newspaper Editors, July/August, 1971, pp. 1, 12, 14. In a conversation with the author in Washington on December 18, 1972, and a telephone interview on January 9, 1973, Ernest K. Lindley said "the Lindley rule" came into use about 1948; but he said that backgrounders were being held in Washington in the 1930's by the Overseas Writers. Since President Coolidge and earlier Chief Executives sometimes talked to a few newsmen on background, it is difficult to say with precision when the practice began; but as an institution in widespread, almost everyday, use, the backgrounder is a post-World War II phenomenon. Admiral Ernest J. King's background sessions with reporters are described in Douglass Cater, *The Fourth Branch of Government* (Boston: Houghton Mifflin Company, 1959), p. 131.

Robert Roth was interviewed in Washington by Susan M. Soper on December 14, 1971. Robert L. Riggs was interviewed by telephone in Washington on December 23, 1971. Anthony Leviero's *New York Times* story resulting from the background dinner with Admiral Robert B. Carney led the paper on March 26, 1955. James C. Hagerty's counter dinner is reported in Robert L. Riggs, "What Political Reporters Are Told Off the Record," *New Republic,* April 11, 1955. Robert Roth's story based on Riggs' stenographic transcript was published in the *Philadelphia Bulletin,* April 6, 1955, pp. 1, 14.

Walt W. Rostow's suggestion to Senator John F. Kennedy that "the missile gap can be used as the Charles Van Doren of the Republican administration" and Rostow's reference to "Tricky Dick" are from an eight-page memo to Kennedy, entitled "A Democratic Strategy for 1960." As Rostow's memo analyzed the situation: "Nixon is already torn between presenting himself as the man who will simply carry forward the Eisenhower formulae or presenting himself as a young man of independence and vigor. If the Democrats can, from the present forward, weaken the effectiveness of peace and prosperity as a workable slogan, Nixon may be mightily tempted to break ranks; and his shift could then emerge not only as the ultimate rag of Tricky Dick—letting down the boss who made him—but also as fundamental confirmation of the phoniness of the peace and prosperity slogan.

"Whether or not Nixon cracks . . . the fact is that every responsible politician . . . and virtually every responsible journalist knows the facts to be much as I have assumed them here; they were waiting eagerly for Rockefeller to get the mush out of his mouth and say it, which he never did . . ."

Robert S. McNamara's backgrounder on the missile gap is reported in the *New York Herald Tribune*, February 8, 1961, pp. 1, 25, and February 12, Section 2, p. 4.

Several background meetings or conversations with President Johnson are quoted in this chapter; in the case of those I attended, the quotations are from the typed transcripts of my notes. I was not at the backgrounder at the LBJ ranch which took place on January 3 and 4, 1964. Henry Dearborn, U.S. consul in the Dominican Republic at the time of the assassination of General Rafael L. Trujillo, was interviewed at length in Washington on September 25, 1972; I am grateful for his help and his detailed answers to my questions. Johnson likened his position in Vietnam to standing on a copy of a newspaper during a conversation in the Oval Office of the White House on December 3, 1964, which began at 6 P.M. and ended at 9 P.M. The quotes are from the seven-page transcript of my notes. His comments on the overthrow of Nikita S. Khrushchev, on Charles de Gaulle, J. Edgar Hoover and Dr. Martin Luther King, Jr., Dean Rusk, Frank Stanton, and the White House lights are from the same conversation.

"Looks to me like he doesn't have any style or class." Johnson's remark was made at a background session with newsmen in the White House on December 16, 1964. Johnson described Senator Harry Byrd's legislative advantage in chatting with reporters at the White House on July 25, 1964. The reference to the bologna sausage was made during a five-lap walking backgrounder on the south lawn of the White House on March 26, 1965. Johnson's remarks about the Dominican intervention, Admiral William F. Raborn, and General William F. McKee were made during the walking backgrounder of May 3, 1965, also on the south lawn.

President Nixon's backgrounder with editors of the *Chicago Sun-Times* is described in detail in Richard Harwood, "The Anatomy of a 'Backgrounder' with the President," the *Washington Post*, September 20, 1970, p. B6. David Murray's article was published on page one of the *Sun-Times*, September 18, 1970. Clayton Kirkpatrick was interviewed by telephone in Chicago on September 19, 1972.

Spiro T. Agnew's comments at Williamsburg are described by Jules Witcover in *White Knight, The Rise of Spiro Agnew* (*idem*: notes to Chapter 10), pp. 414–18. Henry Kissinger's background warning about Soviet naval activity and construction in Cuba appears at p. 12 of the White House transcript of September 25, 1970. The subsequent story indicating that the submarine base had become a tennis court for Soviet sailors appeared in *The New York Times,* October 13, 1970, pp. 1, 4.

The exchange of letters between Kissinger and Clifford P. Case is from the texts as released by Senator Case on November 24, 1970. Kissinger's background briefing on India and Pakistan of December 7, 1971, appears in the *Congressional Record—Senate,* December 9, 1971, pp. S21012 ff. The transcript of the meeting of the Washington Special Action Group of the National Security Council at which Kissinger revealed the Pakistan "tilt" was released by columnist Jack Anderson and published in the *Washington Post,* January 5, 1972, p. A8. David Kraslow was interviewed on December 23, 1971. His remarks about the *Washington Post* are from the *Washington Post,* December 16, 1971, p. A3. A.M. Rosenthal and Benjamin Bradlee are quoted in the *Washington Post,* December 17, 1971, p. A3. Ronald Ziegler is quoted in the *Washington Post,* December 18, 1971, p. A22. Richard Harwood and Bernard Gwertzman were interviewed by telephone in Washington on July 25, 1972; Robert H. Phelps was interviewed by telephone in Washington on July 26, 1972. The House subcommittee study on backgrounders was written by Samuel J. Archibald: *see Government News from Anonymous Sources* (Washington: U.S. Government Printing Office, 1964). William L. Rivers data on the political party preferences of Washington correspondents is from his book *The Opinion Makers* (Boston: Beacon Press, 1965), p. 178. Data on editorial support for Republican and Democratic Presidential candidates is from *Editorial Research Reports,* September 2, 1964, p. 659, and *Editor & Publisher,* October 31, 1964, and November 2, 1968. Jerry W. Friedheim's comments are from the *Washington Post,* November 3, 1970, p. 1. Admiral Harry D. Felt's remark to Malcolm Browne, then of the Associated Press, is from James Aronson, *The Press and the Cold War* (New York: Bobbs-Merrill, 1970), p. 195. Felt's comment has sometimes erroneously been reported as having been directed at Neil Sheehan. Dean Rusk's "I'm on our side" comment is reported by William McGaffin and Erwin Knoll in *Anything But the Truth* (*idem*: notes to Chapter 3).

13. The President and the Press

"I like to get a good press." The quotation and Nixon's comments on Presidential press conferences are from his news conference of June 29, 1972. Data on the number of press conferences held by Nixon during his first term were provided by the White House press office.

George Washington's complaint about the press is from a letter of June 26, 1796 to Alexander Hamilton; quoted in James E. Pollard, *The Presidents and the Press* (New York: Macmillan, 1947), p. 19. The John Adams quotation is from his letter of June 30, 1813, to Thomas Jefferson, *ibid.*, p. 47. Jefferson's comment is from a February 19, 1803, letter to Thomas McKean, *ibid.*, p. 75. The 1884 headline from the *Buffalo Telegraph* publicizing Grover Cleveland's alleged illegitimate son is from Rexford G. Tugwell, *Grover Cleveland* (New York: Macmillan, 1968), p. 91. Cleveland immediately wired his friends in Buffalo: "Above all, tell the truth." And the truth, he said, was that he was not certain he was the father of the son born ten years earlier to Mrs. Maria Crofts Halpin, a young, attractive widow, but had assumed full responsibility for the child's support. Theodore Roosevelt's libel action against Joseph Pulitzer is from W.A. Swanberg, *Pulitzer* (New York: Scribner's, 1967), pp. 359–86. William Howard Taft is quoted in Pollard, *op. cit.*, p. 608. Woodrow Wilson expressed his lack of belief in what he read in the newspapers in a March 28, 1914, letter to Senator W. J. Stone, of Missouri, *ibid.*, p. 640. Wilson discussed the idea of a federal publicity bureau in a letter of June 1, 1914, to Harvard President Charles W. Eliot, *ibid.* Franklin D. Roosevelt's relations with the press are described in William McGaffin and Erwin Knoll, *Anything But the Truth* (*idem*: notes to Chapter 3), p. 51. Harry S. Truman's comment about Paul Hume is reported in James E. Pollard, *The Presidents and the Press, Truman to Johnson* (Washington: Public Affairs Press, 1964), p. 37. Dwight D. Eisenhower's irritation when questioned about Senator Joseph McCarthy is *ibid.*, pp. 71–72. " . . . reading more and enjoying it less." John F. Kennedy made this comment at a news conference May 9, 1962. For additional details of President Johnson's mercurial relations with the press, *see* James Deakin, *Lyndon Johnson's Credibility Gap* (Washington: Public Affairs Press, 1968), and Bruce Ladd, *Crisis in Credibility* (New York: New American Library, 1968), pp. 41 ff.

The data on William McKinley and Theodore Roosevelt are from Pollard's 1947 volume (*idem*), pp. 558, 574. Background on the growth of the Presidential press conference under Wilson, Warren G. Harding, Calvin Coolidge, Herbert Hoover and FDR is from Pollard, *ibid.*, pp. 637, 705, 716–19, 740–41, and 773 ff. Truman's celebrated exchange with newsmen concerning the atomic bomb is from Pollard's 1964 volume, p. 21, and Harry S. Truman, *Memoirs, Years of Trial and Hope 1946–1952* (New York: Doubleday, 1956), Volume Two, p. 395. The dates of Eisenhower's first taped and first filmed news conferences are from Pollard's 1964 volume, pp. 61, 69. Herbert G. Klein's article on Presidential news conferences was published in *The New York Times*, December 29, 1970, p. 29. John

Ehrlichman's reference to "dumb and flabby questions" is from the June 30, 1972, monthly report of the Washington News Committee of the Associated Press Managing Editors Association, p. 5. Nixon's comment on Ehrlichman's statement was made at the President's news conference of June 22, 1972. The general discussion of Presidential press conferences and their advantages and disadvantages is drawn from my experience in attending them under Eisenhower, Kennedy, and Johnson.

The comparison of the President to a matador is from Douglass Cater, *The Fourth Branch of Government* (*idem*: notes to Chapter 12), p. 28. President Nixon's comment on the hard work required to prepare for press conferences is from his news conference of June 29, 1972. The description of President Kennedy's preparation for his press conference of March 15, 1961, and Pierre Salinger's comment afterward is from the *New York Herald Tribune*, March 26, 1961, Section 2, p. 1. Bill D. Moyers' acknowledgment that he had planted questions as press secretary was made in an interview broadcast over the National Educational Television network, January 11, 1966, and reported in the *New York Herald Tribune* of that date. Herbert Klein's comments on this subject are from his television interview of November 13, 1969 (*idem*: notes to Chapter 10). Garnett D. Horner was interviewed by telephone in Washington on November 14, 1972. His question and Nixon's reply are from the President's news conference at Los Angeles on the evening of July 30, 1970. George Reedy discusses Presidential relations, including Johnson's, in *The Twilight of the Presidency* (New York: World, 1970), pp. 99–118. His observation that a President's "press problems" are really political problems reflected in the press is at pp. 104–5.

The cancellation of Marvin Watson's "Berlin Wall" was reported by Douglas Kiker in the *New York Herald Tribune* on January 12, 1966. Pierre Salinger describes the RB-47 story and the *Herald Tribune*'s role in his book, *With Kennedy* (*idem*: notes to Chapter 3). On page 140 Salinger wrote: "Olmstead and McKone might still be in Lubiynka Prison if it hadn't been for the *Herald Tribune*'s willingness to kill the story in the national interest." The White House telegram to John Hay Whitney was published in the *New York Herald Tribune*, January 26, 1961, pp. 1, 7. Fendall Yerxa was kind enough to set down his memory of the early-morning hours of January 25, 1961, in a letter he sent to me in September, 1972. Robert J. Donovan likewise recalled the sequence of events that night in a telephone interview in Washington on September 25, 1972.

For details of Kennedy's cancellation of the *Herald Tribune*, see my story in the *New York Herald Tribune*, June 1, 1962. In explaining the cancellation, Pierre Salinger said the newspaper's handling of a story of the Senate stockpile investigation on May 22, 1962, was "the

culmination of it." On that date, a Senate subcommittee headed by
Senator James Symington of Missouri heard testimony that the Calu-
met & Hecla company gained a windfall of more than $6,000,000
from the copper stockpile during the Eisenhower administration. As
Salinger noted, the story was carried on page one of *The New York
Times* of May 23, 1962. The story appeared only in the late city
edition of the *Herald Tribune* of May 23; it was mentioned in the
page-one news digest, and carried under a three-column headline on
page 32, in the financial section. Eisenhower's biblical defense of
George Humphrey and the criticism by the *Pilot* is from *The New
York Times Index*, 1962, p. 1014.

Richard Dougherty was interviewed in New York on October
11, 1971, about his experience with Lyndon Johnson and the quadriad. Douglas Kiker was interviewed in Washington on November
25, 1971. Robert B. Semple, Jr., plumbed his memory of events at the
Driskill on the evening of November 30, 1965, during my interview
with him (*idem*: notes to Chapter 9). The David R. Jones story was
published in *The New York Times*, December 1, 1965, p. 1. The
Times editorial of December 2, 1965, is at p. 40. The *Wall Street
Journal's* analysis of the drop in the Dow-Jones industrial average is
from "Abreast of the Market," December 2, 1965. The Federal Reserve Board's action raising the discount rate is from the *New York
Herald Tribune*, December 6, 1965, p. 1. The comments by President Johnson and William McChesney Martin, Jr., after their meeting at the LBJ ranch, and the reaction of the savings banks, the
Federal Deposit Insurance Corporation, and the Bank of Canada are
from the *New York Herald Tribune*, December 7, 1965, pp. 1, 32.
Wright Patman's investigation is from the *New York Herald Tribune*,
December 8, 1965, pp. 1, 37.

Harry Truman's comments on the importance of Presidential
news conferences were made at his last press conference as Chief
Executive on January 15, 1953.

14. Summing Up

The Knight newspapers' report on skepticism about the moon
landing was written by James K. Batten and Clarence Jones of the
Washington Bureau. The quotations are from the article as published
in the *Miami Herald*, June 14, 1970, pp. 1, 32A. On February 10,
1971, NBC news carried a similar report from New Orleans of doubt
over the moon landings; of 1,100 students polled at Walter Cohen
High School, NBC said, 56 percent reported that they did not believe
the astronauts had really gone to the moon and back.

Frank Mankiewicz's comment is from the *National Journal*, August 19, 1972, p. 1334. The Max Frankel quote is from his reply to Daniel P. Moynihan in *Commentary,* July, 1971, p. 16. The data on the number of planes and men under the command of General John D. Lavelle are from *Newsweek,* June 26, 1972, p. 17. Lavelle's testimony is from *The New York Times,* June 13, 1972, pp. 1, 6. His claim that his superiors tacitly encouraged his actions is from *The New York Times,* October 7, 1972, p. 6. General John D. Ryan's testimony that he was prevented from telling the truth by Melvin Laird is from the *Washington Post,* September 26, 1972, p. 1.

President Johnson's NSAM 328 of April 6, 1965, is cited in the notes to Chapter 3. The Hannah Arendt quote is from her book *Crises of the Republic* (New York: Harcourt Brace Jovanovich, Inc., 1972), p. 39. Leslie H. Gelb's comment is from his article in *Life,* September 17, 1971, p. 35.

The Walter Lippmann quote is from his book *The Public Philosophy* (New York: New American Library, 1955), p. 99. Congressman Paul N. McCloskey, Jr.'s comment is from *Hearings,* House Foreign Operations and Government Information Subcommittee, Part 1, June 23, 1971, pp. 79–81. The Anthony Lake quote is from his excellent article "Lying Around Washington," *Foreign Policy,* Spring 1971, p. 113.

The Seitz report is officially entitled *Task Force on Secrecy,* Report of the Defense Science Board, Department of Defense, July 1, 1970. The quotations are from pp. iv, 1, 3–11. Ironically, this report was stamped For Official Use Only. When I obtained a copy from the Office of Defense Research and Engineering, it arrived with this administrative classification crossed out in black crayon, and the following notation written in ink, alongside it: "Unclassified per E. Rechtin, ODDR&E 1/21/72."

Dr. Jerome B. Wiesner, now president of the Massachusetts Institute of Technology, confirmed the details of the U.S. Air Force flights to test Soviet radar defenses, and his action in alerting President Kennedy, in correspondence with me dated May 17, 1972.

"The President's medium." Ben H. Bagdikian's apt phrase is from his book *The Effete Conspiracy* (New York: Harper & Row, 1972), p. 95. The late Justice Hugo Black's eloquent comment on the role of a free press in a democracy is from *New York Times Company v. United States* 403 U.S. 713 (1971). The V.O. Key, Jr., quote is from his book *Public Opinion and American Democracy* (New York: Knopf, 1961), p. 7. Representative Sam Gibbons' testimony is from *Hearings,* House Foreign Operations and Government Information Subcommittee, June 24, 1971, Part 1, p. 205. No one could answer his question.

Index

About the Author

DAVID WISE is a political writer based in Washington. He is co-author of *The Invisible Government*, the book about the Central Intelligence Agency which became the nation's number-one best seller and was widely credited with bringing about a reappraisal of the role of the CIA in a democratic society. He is former chief of the Washington Bureau of the *New York Herald Tribune*. A native New Yorker and graduate of Columbia College, he joined the *Herald Tribune* in 1951, served as the newspaper's White House correspondent during the Kennedy administration and as chief of the Washington Bureau from 1963 to 1966. During 1970–71 he was a Fellow of the Woodrow Wilson International Center for Scholars in Washington, D.C. With Thomas B. Ross, he is co-author of *The U-2 Affair* (Random House, 1962), *The Invisible Government* (Random House, 1964), and *The Espionage Establishment* (Random House, 1967). He has also contributed articles on government and politics to *The New York Times Magazine*, the *New Republic*, *Esquire*, and other national magazines. In 1969 he received the Page One Award of the Newspaper Guild of New York for best magazine writing. He is married and has two children.